EDUCATION
& the Great Depression

Alan R. Sadovnik and Susan F. Semel
General Editors

Vol. 46

PETER LANG
New York • Washington, D.C./Baltimore • Bern
Frankfurt am Main • Berlin • Brussels • Vienna • Oxford

EDUCATION
& the Great Depression

Lessons from a Global History

E. Thomas Ewing & David Hicks, Editors

PETER LANG
New York • Washington, D.C. / Baltimore • Bern
Frankfurt am Main • Berlin • Brussels • Vienna • Oxford

Library of Congress Cataloging-in-Publication Data

Education and the Great Depression: lessons from a global history /
edited by E. Thomas Ewing, David Hicks.
p. cm. – (History of schools and schooling; v. 46)
Includes bibliographical references.
1. Education–History–20th century. 2. Depressions–1929.
I. Ewing, E. Thomas. II. Hicks, David. III. Series.
LA128.E38   370.973'09043–dc22   2006008943
ISBN 0-8204-7143-7
ISSN 1089-0678

Bibliographic information published by **Die Deutsche Bibliothek**.
Die Deutsche Bibliothek lists this publication in the "Deutsche
Nationalbibliografie"; detailed bibliographic data is available
on the Internet at http://dnb.ddb.de/.

Cover illustration: from *School Life* (1933), published by the United States Office of Education
Cover design by Lisa Barfield

The paper in this book meets the guidelines for permanence and durability
of the Committee on Production Guidelines for Book Longevity
of the Council of Library Resources.

© 2006 Peter Lang Publishing, Inc., New York
29 Broadway, New York, NY 10006
www.peterlang.com

Printed in the United States of America

Table of Contents

Editors' Preface

We first conceived of this project in the summer of 2002, at a time when an expanding global war coincided with evidence of a looming economic crisis. As educators, we were concerned about the impact of these convergences on contemporary schooling; as historians, we were thinking about the ways that similar kinds of critical situations have affected teachers, pupils, and parents in recent American and world history. Approaching the Great Depression as a moment of crisis that called into question the practices and ideals of education thus appeared as a way to explore a research topic that had received relatively little attention in the scholarly literature, yet offered numerous potential lessons for thinking about ways to respond to national and international crises. While avoiding simplistic arguments about the historical repetition, we believe that the chapters in this volume offer powerful and subtle insights that remain relevant in the present and the future at local, national, and global levels.

We wish to thank the contributors to this volume for their patience with the editing process. Representing in approximately equal numbers the disciplines of history and education, the authors, like the editors, have demonstrated the fruitful dialogue that can result from this kind of inter-disciplinary approach to educational history. We hope that they will find their contributions have provided some valuable lessons along these same lines.

Amy Johnson, the author of the final chapter, died tragically in December 2004. She was a dedicated and accomplished scholar, and we are honored by her family's permission to publish her chapter. It is in her memory that we have dedicated this volume.

At Peter Lang Publishing, we wish to thank Alan Sadovnik and Susan Semel, editors of the History of Schools and Schooling Series, for their support. We are also grateful to Christopher Myers, Bernadette Shade, Sophie Appel, and Set Sokol for their assistance.

Finally, the editors thank their families (Amy and Claire, and Megan, Connor, Sophie, and Evan) for their encouragement, support, and good humor. As usual, we had no idea what would be involved in this project, and we appreciate their willingness to put up with us, once again.

Introduction

Education in the Great Depression

E. Thomas Ewing and David Hicks

In an article published in September 1931, Philip C. Lovejoy, formerly superintendent of schools in Hamtramck, Michigan, asked: "Can we expect the schools of the world to aid materially in the solution of the economic problems with which we are now faced?" Lovejoy's answer was, not surprisingly for an educator, affirmative:

> If the schools of the world cannot develop solutions for these problems, then all the money being spent in them will be to no avail, for the world will not have been made a better place in which to live. . . The public schools of the world should constitute the foremost line of defense against social and economic ills.

Asking what the public schools could do "to solve the problems now facing the entire world," Lovejoy recommended that schools find ways to teach "the three Rs" more efficiently so that the extra time could be allocated to teaching the urgent need for disarmament, which he declared to be the only way to counter the spread of "intangible bureaucracies of fear and illusion that are extremely costly."[1]

Yet history teaches a different lesson about the years that followed. The Depression continued to worsen in the United States, in Europe, and to a great extent the rest of the world.[2] Governments responded slowly and inadequately. President F. D. Roosevelt's New Deal was still two years away, and even this ambitious effort did not fully overcome the effects of the Depression. In Western Europe, the Depression forced political opponents to build coalitions as a means of survival, while implementing measures that moderated but did not eliminate the critical economic situation. Only in Germany, where the Depression played an important role in bringing Adolf Hitler to power, did a European government undertake the extensive public works and rearmament projects that finally eliminated unemployment, the most visible sign of difficult times. Throughout Asia, Africa, and Latin America, the deterioration in world trade weakened economies dependent on exporting primary materials to industrial nations. In these countries, governments could impose austerity measures that shifted the burden of the Depression upon the least affluent populations, but could do little else from their position of economic dependency. The only regions not directly affected by the Depression were those completely isolated from the world economy, such as the communist Soviet Union, while even the least developed regions of the world felt the indirect effects of declining trade, market instability, currency fluctuations, and political crisis.

Rather than constituting "the foremost line of defence against social and economic ills," as Lovejoy asserted, public schools became victims of the crisis. In 1932, educator George Strayer described the impact of the Depression on American schools:

> It is in this situation that in cities and in rural areas schools have been closed, terms have been shortened, teachers' salaries have been reduced, classes have been increased in size, some of the more significant offerings have been eliminated from the curriculum, adequate educational supplies and books have been denied, health service and physical education have been dropped, the attendance service has been crippled, proposals have been made for the lowering of the standards for entrance into the profession, building programs which were to provide adequate housing have been abandoned, night and continuation schools have been closed—in short, the whole program of education is being curtailed, if not indeed placed in jeopardy.

Yet such a response to economic crisis, according to Strayer, failed to recognize the crucial contribution that education made to democracy by teaching "common knowledge, ideals, and beliefs" to a generation that would be committed to "the well-being of the whole group."[3] Making a similar warning, the National Education Association urged American citizens "to choose carefully the public enterprises which they support during the crisis with a view to averting the sacrifice of children," while the Committee on the Emergency in Education formed by the Progressive Education Association proclaimed that continued retrenchments would mean that schools in many states "would continue in their downward plunge to educational disaster."[4]

Similar processes occurred in other countries, as the economic crisis forced governments to make significant cuts in educational budgets. In London, the *Times Educational Supplement* discussed national education in terms of "anxieties and setbacks," the "more and more threatening" state of the financial situation, the need for "retrenchment," and an "atmosphere of gloom."[5] A survey of "education throughout the world" conducted by the United States Office of Education stated that 1933 had been "the most difficult and leanest of three successive years of severe trial and testing."[6] Educators across the world described the same processes outlined by Strayer: delaying construction or repair of buildings, reducing supplies, restricting course offerings, shortening the school day or curtailing the school year, and especially reducing the money spent on employing teachers. In a 1934 article, Austrian educator Paul L. Dengler declared that the "economic situation of school teachers all over the world is more pitiable than words can explain."[7] Salary cuts, hiring bans, dismissals, and requiring teachers to work without pay all made sense economically, as teachers' salaries made up the largest single item in most school budgets, but these short-term solutions threatened to have long-term consequences in terms of both student learning and teachers' professional development.[8]

The link between economic crisis, the young generation, and world peace in particular failed to materialize in the ways expected by Lovejoy and many other educators. Many of the boys enrolled in schools in the 1930s in the United States, across Europe, and in East Asia would become the soldiers who went to war. Rather than learning the lessons of peace, this generation experienced the most bitter conflicts between nations that consumed millions of lives, both military and civilian. Ironically, it was the demand for weapons and other materials necessary to wage total war that finally brought an end to the Depression in the United States, Europe, and the rest of the world.[9]

And yet it was precisely the optimistic, progressive, and constructive role that Lovejoy and others assigned to schools in the midst of crisis that makes the relationship between the Depression and education historically significant. How could educators, facing the realities of this economic crisis, assign such great expectations to their schools, to the ideas and practices of pedagogy, and to the future of this young generation? It is easy from a later vantage point to dismiss these views as naïve, politically opportunistic, or simply misguided, yet at the time, these views represented a broad current in both American and world educational perspectives that assigned a constructive role to the ideals and the institutions of schools. It is this combination of economic conditions, educational ideals, government policies, and institutional practices that make the chapters in this collection significant as both historical interpretations and statements about the possibilities of schools even in times of economic and political crisis.

The Great Depression as World History

Understanding the Great Depression as world history requires an appreciation of both global processes and specific circumstances.[10] The Wall Street Crash of October 1929 became the catalyst that transformed a combination of economic situations into a critical situation. As argued by Dietmar Rothermund, all the countries of the world except the United States imported the Depression, although in each case their indigenous conditions exacerbated the international situation.[11] The main economic preconditions that made the world vulnerable to the Depression were agricultural overproduction, unstable currency values, war debts and reparations, growing unemployment, speculative investment, rising government expenditures, a weak banking system, and protectionist policies. The worsening financial crisis in the United States following the Wall Street Crash spread first to Europe and then to the rest of the world. A wave of bank failures in the early 1930s eliminated savings, caused currency devaluation, and spread fear and uncertainty especially among the middle-classes, while mass unemployment made the suffering of the working class visible to all of society. Policies adopted to deal with specific symptoms of the crisis actually worsened the world situation by shifting the burden of the crisis to more dependent states. By reducing demand for imported goods through protectionist measures, by requiring other nations to meet their debt obligations, and by devaluing currencies in order to maintain control of capital reserves, the American and European governments pursued domestic recovery with little concern for the implications of these policies on the world economy.

The Depression provides a powerful example of how common responses by different governments facing similar conditions produced undesirable outcomes that exacerbated the economic crisis.[12] Modernizing states, such as Egypt, Turkey, Brazil, and Mexico, were especially affected by the Depression, as their dependence on the export of primary materials in a time of decreasing demand, falling prices, and rising protectionist barriers prevented the acquisition of capital needed to invest in further development. While unemployment was limited to the small industrial working class in these countries, the middle classes suffered from the financial uncertainty of lost savings and cutbacks in state employment, while the agricultural sector was most critically affected by declining exports and increased taxation. Among the peasantry, which constituted the vast majority of the world's population at this time, the loss of earnings from farming was accompanied by more aggressive tax collection, tighter credit, and greater indebtedness. In this context, the relative absence of unemployment, which in the developed world constituted one of the main measures of the impact of the Depression, tended to conceal the deeper damage done by the world economic crisis. Because agricultural producers could not adjust easily to market changes, a downward cycle of falling prices, overproduction, decreased income, and deprivation deepened the crisis in agricultural regions. While some agricultural production could be shifted to domestic consumption (such as rice), the increasing penetration of the global market ensured that large sectors (such as cotton, coffee and rubber) could not easily adapt. While the Depression did reinforce trends toward self-determination, including import substitution industries, autonomous systems of banking and currency valuation, and political independence, the immediate impact was far more destructive and pervasive. From the vantage point of most Americans and Europeans, however, pre-occupations with domestic crisis ensured that these broader effects were barely noticed. By exploring both specific cases and broader processes, however, a global perspective illustrates the great significance of the Depression in shaping twentieth century world history.

New Perspectives on Schools in Crisis

The chapters in this collection examine the history of schools in terms of pedagogies, curricula, policies, and practices at the point of intersection with world wide patterns of economic crisis, political instability, and social transformation. These issues are considered in a number of different regional and national contexts, drawing upon the disciplinary perspectives of both historians and educational researchers, and thus address the broader implications of this earlier period of crisis in schools and society. By approaching the Great Depression in this historical context, this collection broadens understanding of the scope of this crisis while also locating the more familiar American examples in a global framework.

The first chapters explore the political contexts of schools by asking how the economic crisis provoked educators to engage in a diverse range of responses. In "Regional Variations in Union Activism of American Public Schoolteachers," John F. Lyons argues that regional comparisons can illuminate the central question of why some American teachers responded to economic crisis by pushing an activist agenda through unions, while others pursued "individual" solutions that distinguished this profession from the organizational surge evident in other sectors. Challenging the prevailing view in the historiography about the apparent reluctance of American teachers to engage in confrontational union politics, Lyons shows that increased militancy, especially in the spring of 1933 when tens of thousands of Chicago teachers demonstrated publicly, coexisted with other patterns and practices that promoted more moderate responses to the Depression. While even the supporters of militant union activism, for example, proclaimed their determination to keep on teaching so as not to harm the interests of the children entrusted to their care, activist teachers and union organizers in other districts faced opposition, discrimination, and retaliation from school boards, government administrators, and community elites, which certainly shaped the extent and character of teachers' responses to the Depression. Through this discussion of teacher militancy, therefore, this chapter explores the underlying structures and personal interests that shaped the ways that educators responded to the Depression.

Shifting the focus of analysis in a more comparative direction, E. Thomas Ewing's chapter, "The 'Virtues of Planning': American Educators Look at Soviet Schools," asks how desperate economic conditions reinforced the perception that real reform of schools and society depended on wholesale changes in values and structures. Many progressive educators, and George Counts in particular, saw the onset of the Depression as confirmation that a materialist, competitive, and market-driven society corrupted the values and practices of schools. At the same time that American education was showing the full effects of the Depression, an alternative vision of the relationship between politics, society, and education was developing in the world's first communist state, where the value assigned to education by state planning agencies appeared in direct contrast to the seemingly fragmented, stagnant, and outdated structures of American schools. As argued in this chapter, however, these visions of Soviet education reveal more about the ways American educators responded to the Depression than they do about the actual processes and practices of Soviet education. By exploring these perceptions, this chapter demonstrates both the powerful impact of the Depression and the ways that thinking comparatively about schools can expand understanding of educational possibilities.

Broadening the scope of inquiry in a chapter entitled "Civilization: Its Rise and Fall in New Deal School Murals," Michele Cohen examines the ways in which public art programs promoted a particular view of historical narrative and social engagement consistent with progressive pedagogical projects. The public schools murals were a direct result of the Depression, as the Federal Arts Project emerged as a New Deal initiative to use public funds to employ artists as both a relief effort and an educational program. When artists chose to make the history of civilization into a central theme of their works, Cohen argues, they drew upon the ideological belief, associated most strongly with Charles Beard and Harold Rugg, that a new society could be founded on rational principles, committed to egalitarian ideals, appreciative of other cultures, and dedicated to improving opportunities for all citizens. By describing in detail the artistic qualities, pedagogical purpose, and political significance of one mural, James Michael Newell's *Evolution of Western Civilization,* this chapter illustrates how the Depression-era school seemed to prepare the way for a new society by drawing on the positive experience of the past while advancing to a more promising future.

The intersection of educational conditions and political authority in Germany is the focus of Charles Lansing's chapter, "The Great Depression, German Teachers, and Nazi Revolution in the Schools." While the Depression has long been recognized by historians as an important factor in bringing Hitler and the National Socialists to power in 1933, this chapter uses a case study of teachers in one city to provide a different perspective on the relationship between economic crisis, state power, and the experiences of Germans. In particular, Lansing argues, the severe measures taken by the Weimar government in response to the Depression, including salary reductions and mass dismissals, actually made the teaching profession *less vulnerable* to repressive measures implemented by the Nazi government. The acute shortage of qualified teachers that developed following these cutbacks meant that teachers were better able to resist Nazi efforts to "cleanse" the teaching profession of politically suspect teachers. While describing a similar dynamic of economic crisis, reduced public expenditure, and educational curtailment, Lansing demonstrates that the long-term impact of the Depression on German teachers resulted, however ironically and inadvertently, in a strengthening of their position professionally and politically.

Later chapters focus more explicitly on how the crisis in funding shaped the attitudes and practices of pupils, teachers, and administrators. In her chapter, "Reading, Writing, and Racial Uplift: Education and Reform in Cleveland, Ohio," Regennia N. Williams traces the growing engagement of African-American parents, educators, and community leaders around issues of resource allocation, educational attainment, and political representation. Focusing in particular on Mary B. Martin, an African-American woman elected to the Cleveland Board of Education in 1929, Williams demonstrates how deteriorating conditions produced a commitment to make equality in education a long term civil rights goal. The Depression exacerbated the inequality of educational conditions, as overcrowding, delayed maintenance, salary reductions, layoffs, and selective dismissal of married women teachers all imposed a disproportionate burden on African American pupils and teachers. As the National Association for the Advancement of Colored Peoples became increasingly assertive in protesting educational inequality, the position of Martin became increasingly difficult, as the expectations upon her as the sole African-American member of the School Board grew even as the resources available to the public schools decreased. For Martin, the pressure to eliminate institutionalized racism had to be balanced against the immediate task of keeping the schools open in the face of extreme economic crisis. This chapter thus illustrates how the Depression exacerbated pre-existing conditions and conflicts, while also stimulating new approaches and strategies in response to changing conditions.

"'Caught in a Tangled Skein': The Great Depression in South Carolina's Schools," by Edward Janak, uses one American state as a case study of decreased state funding, rising unemployment, and lack of social services, situated in a broader context of regional economic dependency and uneven development. In contrast to both existing historiography and popular perceptions, Janak argues that this crisis actually produced a new attitude toward education as well as substantive improvements in public schools in South Carolina. In particular, New Deal projects aimed at providing immediate relief and reducing unemployment, in combination with funding from the General Education Board intended to support vocational education for African-Americans, promoted greater acceptance of federal assistance to and intervention in public education. Infrastructure developments, managed and funded in part through New Deal relief efforts, provide evidence of the historical significance of education in the Depression.

In her study of New Zealand education, Carol Mutch uses the image of men on relief wearing clothes made of food sacks—so-called "sugar bags"—to illustrate both the lived experience and the collective memory of these difficult years. The Depression became a defining moment as New Zealand made the transition from a British colony through independence to a liberal-progressive state that enacted a wide-ranging welfare system, including guaranteed public education. Focusing on key individuals who led this transition, including a political leader, Peter Fraser, and a leading educator, Clarence Beeby, this chapter examines how responses to the Great Depression were transformed into opportunities to engage in wide-ranging social reforms. The importance of political leadership is clearly evident in this chapter, as leaders used the circumstances of economic crisis to invest in public services intended in part to prevent the recurrence of these devastating conditions.

A more gradual, yet equally significant, process of educational change in the midst of social transformation is illustrated in "One-Room and Country Schools Depicted in Farm Security Administration Photographs," by Eugene F. Provenzo, Jr. One of the major propaganda initiatives of Roosevelt's New Deal was the effort to photograph rural American life. According to Provenzo, the thousands of photographs of schools taken under the auspices of the F.S.A. provide not just a documentary record, but were themselves a commentary on education during the Depression. In particular, this chapter argues, photographs of one-room schoolhouses in effect served the double function of reminding the viewer of the continued presence of the one-room in rural America even as images of impoverished facilities, isolated teachers, and desperate children be-

came a visual testimony to the need for change. By presenting and
analyzing these images, this chapter demonstrates how the Depression and the government response contributed to broader patterns
of social and educational changes by justifying the need for reform
through documenting problems associated with existing schools.

The final chapters ask how the conditions of the Depression and
the ideas of educators prompted innovative pedagogical approaches. Barak Salmoni's chapter, "The Pedagogy of Work and
Thrift: Economic Intentionality as Turkish Educational Priority," describes how leaders of an avowedly modernizing state made educational reforms into a primary response to the worsening global
economic crisis. Because the Turkish government had been actively
involved in promoting economic development throughout the
1920s, the onset of the Depression reinforced and extended, rather
than dramatically changed, the relationship between educational
policy and economic conditions. By demonstrating how the primary
and secondary curriculum was permeated by these ideals of productive labor, economic self-determination, and national identity, the
Turkish example demonstrates how educators and politicians came
to see the Depression as an opportunity to advance pedagogical and
political agendas in ways that shaped the evolution of schools on a
broad scale.

Asking "'Shall the Youngest Suffer Most'? U.S. Kindergartens in
the Depression," Kristen D. Nawrotzki examines how the economic
crisis forced advocates of early childhood education to find new institutions, justifications, and alliances to sustain their campaigns for
reform. By the late 1920s, kindergarten advocates believed they had
finally secured the support of the educational establishment for
these programs. Yet when the full effects of the Depression were felt
by school administrators, the kindergartens were among the first
programs to be curtailed or eliminated completely. Whereas previously kindergarten advocates had emphasized the advantages of
providing a varied and enriching experience for pre-school children,
the conditions of the Great Depression forced proponents to argue
that social stress and family disruption increased the need for institutional early childhood education. Closing or restricting kindergartens, by contrast, were condemned as the worst form of economy, as
short-term savings would impose long-term costs on children, families, and society as a whole. The era of the Depression thus marked
only a temporary decrease in the long-term expansion of kindergar-

ten enrollment, as renewed support from early childhood educational professionals, local and state administrators, and concerned parents made up for the reluctance of the federal government to make a permanent commitment to providing this expensive and still-controversial form of schooling to all children.

In their chapter, "Progressive Schools for a Democratic Society: Reforming Education in Rio de Janeiro," Alberto Gawryszewski and Michael L. Conniff describe how the Depression affected schools in Brazil, where the economy depended heavily on exporting primary products such as coffee, rubber, cocoa, and sugar. As both demand and prices decreased, causing unemployment, revenue shortfalls, and cutbacks in public expenditures, the domestic political situation became increasingly polarized. Bitterly contested elections followed by military intervention resulted in the formation of a revolutionary government led by Getulio Vargas. The new municipal authorities in Rio de Janeiro, including the progressive educator Anisio Teixeira, who had studied with John Dewey and William Heard Kilpatrick in the United States, undertook a series of social reforms that included a massive expansion in public education. Teixeira embraced a vision of the school as constantly changing in response to the present and future needs of society, with a curriculum based on real life experiences rather than fixed traditions, and where the student, not the teacher, was situated at the center of the learning process. Within a few years, however, educational reforms were defeated by traditional elements who used the crisis situation of the Depression to obstruct the implementation of radical pedagogical reforms.

In "'A Magnificent Adventure': Negotiating and Structuring Curricular Change in Virginia," David Hicks and Stephanie Van Hover examine how economic crisis served as a catalyst through which an emerging social and cultural reconstructionist agenda was implemented and brought to fruition within the curriculum laboratory that was the Commonwealth of Virginia between 1931 and 1934. Initiated by the new Superintendent for Instruction, Sidney B. Hall, the Virginia Curriculum Revision Program was designed to improve instruction by moving away from locally organized, discipline-oriented curriculum toward a State-wide Core Curriculum that focused on a sequence of specific student-based centers of interest and merged them with major functions of social life in order to prepare young citizens for life in the modern world. Hall and his curriculum advisor, Hollis Caswell, stressed that the success of the Curriculum Revision Program lay with the cooperation and participation of Virginia teachers. This chapter contends, however, that the reportedly successful implementation of the Virginia Program had more to do with the processes by which a network of influential educational leaders and curriculum designers conceptualized and managed the structure of curriculum reform while skillfully employing the rhetoric of teacher involvement and cooperation, than with the ongoing and thorough participation of Virginia teachers. While for many the Depression fostered uncertainty, fear, and trepidation, for "frontier" educational thinkers, such as Hall and his associates, this same era provided an opportunity to play in the emerging field of curriculum design.

Finally, in "Encouraging Education, Increasing Income: The al-Manayil Village and Rural Education in Egypt," Amy J. Johnson examines a country that had nominal political independence but remained economically dependent on European markets. As the crisis in international trade, especially in cotton, worsened, one result was to strengthen tendencies within Egypt toward self-sufficiency, including both the campaigns for independence led by the nationalist Wafd Party and the efforts of educators to promote indigenous models suitable for the Egyptian population. Both political activists and educational reforms identified Egypt's rural population (fellahin) as a potential source of political and economic strength, but only after the problems of their environment and daily life—summed up in the phrase "poverty, ignorance, and disease"—could be transformed through government-sponsored reform programs. By focusing on the model of the al-Manayil school, which combined academic instruction, religious teaching, and practical skills, this chapter provides another example of how the difficult conditions of the Depression led to innovative pedagogical approaches. In Egypt, as in other situations discussed in this collection, educators argued that these innovations would not only help resolve the immediate problems of the Depression, but would over the long-term prevent the recurrence of similar kinds of economic crisis by addressing structural conditions, such as rural poverty, social inequality, and barriers to opportunity. Interviews conducted by Johnson with residents of al-Manayil village suggest that these connections between chronic poverty, the establishment of the school in the 1930s, and the current possibilities for improvement are remembered in popular memory and thus remain part of daily life into the present.

The Significance of Schooling during the Depression

This volume makes a unique contribution to scholarship on the history of education in the global twentieth century. Education is generally a neglected topic in histories of the Depression in the United States, Europe, and the world. Schools are sometimes included as examples of government projects that suffered reductions, the decision of whether to attend school is described as an example of how families were affected by the broader economic crisis, teachers are mentioned for their surprising lack of militancy in the face of salary reductions and decreasing unemployment, and the experience of attending school in a time of deprivation emerges as one of the defining memories for the "Depression generation."[13] As the chapters in this collection indicate, schools provide an excellent way to evaluate the impact, the experience, and the significance of the Depression. Far more than "filling in" an existing gap in the historiography of the Depression, these chapters demonstrate how central the history of education is to understanding a complex process of change on local, regional, and global scales.

This collection also moves beyond the available scholarship on education during the Great Depression. Certainly the most thorough examination of these issues in an American context is *Public Schools in Hard Times. The Great Depression and Recent Years,* by David Tyack, Robert Lowe, and Elizabeth Hansot.[14] This book is an excellent example of how the history of education can provide lessons for contemporary educators and policy-makers, but the book is limited to American schools, thus leaving out the global perspective presented in these chapters. A more recent study by Dominic W. Moreo, *Schools in the Great Depression,* uses a series of case-studies to explore the ways that educators responded to the impact of the Depression. Moreo's attention to the conflicts between progressive educators, school administrators, teachers, and parents is an important contribution to understanding changes in education in this period. Moreo also focuses exclusively on the United States, while his overall thesis that the Depression represented a "lost opportunity" imposes a certain teleology that determines that materials, interpretations, and conclusions of the book.[15]

Most histories of education in other parts of the world during 1930s tend to overlook the specific relationship between economic crisis and schooling in order to deal with broader processes, such as the failures of progressive educators to implement their visions of schooling, the rise of interventionist states in Europe and Latin America, and challenges to colonial authority in Asia and Africa.[16] In one of the few accounts to recognize the central tension outlined above, W. F. Connell described the period of the Depression as "education's golden years," as the economic crisis forced educators around the world to reconsider the fundamental objectives of schooling, to devise new curricula, and to persuade the public of the significance of education. Yet while this survey of twentieth century world education covers a number of countries during the 1930s, it focuses primarily on educational theorists and devotes little attention to the relationship between economic crisis and educational transformation that is the subject of this collection.[17]

This collection, by contrast, places economic globalization, political instability, and curricular experimentation at the center of analysis. This book responds to the call made by historian Roy Rosenzweig for an approach to history that is "somehow simultaneously more local and intimate and more global and cosmopolitan, more shaped by local concerns and enriched by insights based on systematic and detailed study of the past."[18] By exploring the local impact of the economic crisis as well as its global effects, by demonstrating the power of individual responses as well as the limits imposed by structural forces, and by recognizing the opportunities pursued by educators as well as the constraints that weakened the schools, these chapters illustrate the complex actions and subtle processes of history. As will be explored in more detail in the "Afterword," this history remains significant in the contemporary world, as new processes of globalization and old structures of power, opportunity, and access continue to shape the meaning and experience of schooling nationally and internationally.

Notes

1. Philip C. Lovejoy, "The Public Schools as Important Factors in World Economics," *The Nation's Schools* Vol. 8 (September 1931) pp. 84, 86, 88.
2. This survey draws primarily on Dietmar Rothermund, *The Global Impact of the Great Depression, 1929–1939* (London: Routledge, 1996); Patricia Clavin, *The Great Depression in Europe, 1929–1939* (New York: St. Martin's Press, 2000); T. H. Watkins, *The Hungry Years. A Narrative History of the Great Depression in America* (New York: Henry Holt and Company, 1999).
3. George Drayton Strayer, "Adequate Support of Education the Condition of an Effective Service," *School and Society* Vol. 35 (March 19, 1932) pp. 374–375.
4. "The Economic Situation and the Schools," *School and Society* Vol. 34, No. 887 (December 26, 1931) pp. 876–877; Paul R. Mort, "National Support for our Public Schools," *Progressive Education* Vol. 10, No. 8 (December 1933) p. 442–443. For a contemporary explanation of the link between economic crisis and the school crisis, see Avis D. Carlson, "Deflating the Schools," *Harper's Magazine* Vol. 167 (November 1933) pp. 705–714.
5. "Dangers of Economy," *Times Educational Supplement* No. 866 (December 5, 1931) p. 461; "Education in 1931," *Times Educational Supplement* No. 869 (December 26, 1931) p. 487; "Economies," *Times Educational Supplement* No. 870 (January 2, 1932) p. 5; "Marking Time," *Times Educational Supplement* No. 886 (April 23, 1932) p. 143; "The Cost of Education," *Times Educational Supplement* No. 907 (September 17, 1932) p. 357; "A Year of Anxiety and Hope," *Times Educational Supplement* No. 922 (December 31, 1932) p. 477.
6. James F. Abel, "Education Throughout the World," *Nation's Schools* Vol. 19 (June 1933) p. 188.
7. Paul L. Dengler, "The Crisis of Education in Austria," *Journal of Educational Sociology* Vol. 7, No. 5 (January 1934) pp. 291–298.
8. For contemporary reports on education, see "Bolivian Strike Halts Mail and Wire Service," *The New York Times* April 14, 1931, p. 8; "Saving and Spending," *Times Educational Supplement* No. 849 (August 8, 1931) p. 313; "Dangers of Economy," *Times Educational Supplement* No. 866 (December 5, 1931) p. 461; "Reich to Force Cuts in Food Cost to Idle. Prussian Government Dismisses 3,500 Teachers to Reduce Budget for Year," *The New York Times* September 15, 1931, p. 5; "Teachers Protest Cuts," *The New York Times* September 19, 1931, p. 8; "Mexican Teachers on Hunger Strike," *The New York Times* October 24, 1931 p. 8; "80 Unpaid Teachers Are Jailed in Mexico," *The New York Times* November 25, 1931, p. 11; "Economies," *Times Educational Supplement* No. 870 (January 2, 1932) p. 5; "Education under the London County Council," *School and Society* Vol. 35, No. 909 (May 28, 1932) pp. 733–732; "Saving on London Education," *School and Society* Vol. 35, No. 897 (March 5, 1932) p. 310; James F. Abel, "Schools Abroad. How They Fare in the Depression," *School Life* Vol. 18 (January 1933) pp. 93–94. For discussion of education and the Depression in specific contexts, see David Tyack, Robert Lowe, and Elizabeth Hansot, *Public*

Schools in Hard Times. The Great Depression and Recent Years (Cambridge: Harvard University Press, 1984); Dominic W. Moreo, *Schools in the Great Depression* (New York: Garland Publishing, Inc., 1996); W. F. Connell, *A History of Education in the Twentieth Century World* (New York: Teachers College Press, 1980) pp. 153, 271–272, 288–292, 312; Rolland G. Paulston, *Educational Change in Sweden: Planning and Accepting the Comprehensive School Reforms* (New York: Teachers College Press, 1968) pp. 60–64; Joseph S. Szyliowicz, *Education and Modernization in the Middle East* (Ithaca: Cornell University Press, 1973) pp. 214–215; J. W. Selleck, *English Primary Education and the Progressives, 1914–1939* (London: Routledge and Kegan Paul, 1972) pp. 132–133; S. J. Curtis, *Education in Britain since 1900* (Westport: Greenwood Press, 1952) pp. 96–97, 105–106; John E. Talbott, *The Politics of Educational Reform in France, 1918–1940* (Princeton: Princeton University Press, 1969) pp. 169, 205–206, 230; Carol Summers, *Colonial Lessons. Africans' Education in Southern Rhodesia, 1918–1940* (Cape Town: David Philip Publishers, 2002) pp. 11, 164; C. K. Graham, *The History of Education in Ghana. From the Earliest Times to the Declaration of Independence* (London: Frank Cass, 1971) pp. 160–161; Judith Arbus, "Grateful to be Working: Women Teachers during the Great Depression," in Frieda Forman, et al., eds., *Feminism and Education: A Canadian Perspective* (Toronto: University of Toronto Press, 1990) pp. 169–190.

9.   Rothermund, *Global Impact of the Great Depression*, pp. 150–155; Robert S. McElvaine, *The Great Depression. America, 1929–1941* (New York: Three Rivers Press, 1984) pp. 320–322.

10. For discussion of the Great Depression in world history, see Rothermund, *Global Impact of the Great Depression*; David Reynolds, "American Globalism: Mass, Motion, and the Multiplier Effect," in A. G. Hopkins, ed., *Globalization in World History* (New York: W. W. Norton, 2002) pp. 252–254; C. V. Findley and J. A. M. Rothney, *Twentieth Century World* (Boston: Houghton Mifflin Company, 2002) pp. 105–111; Clavin, *The Great Depression in Europe*; John A. Garraty, "The New Deal, National Socialism, and the Great Depression," *The American Historical Review* Vol. 78, No. 4 (October 1973) pp. 907–944.

11. Rothermund, *Global Impact of the Great Depression*, pp. 10–12.

12. See discussion of a comparative approach to the Depression in Garraty, "The New Deal, National Socialism, and the Great Depression," pp. 907–908; Rothermund, *Global Impact of the Great Depression*.

13. Rothermund, *Global Impact of the Great Depression*, p. 80; McElvaine, *Great Depression*, pp. 184–185; Watkins, *The Hungry Years*, p. 62; William E. Leuchtenburg, *Franklin D. Roosevelt and the New Deal, 1932–1940* (New York: Harper, 1963) p. 21; Robert Cohen, ed., *Dear Mrs. Roosevelt. Letters from Children of the Great Depression* (Chapel Hill: University of North Carolina Press, 2002) pp. 91–145.

14. Tyack, Lowe, and Hansot, *Public Schools in Hard Times*.

15. Moreo, *Schools in the Great Depression*. See also Diane Ravitch, *Left Back. A Century of Battles over School Reform* (New York: Touchstone Books, 2000)

pp. 202–321; C. A. Bowers, *The Progressive Educator and the Depression* (New York: Random House, 1969).

16. Paulston, *Educational Change in Sweden,* pp. 60–64; Szyliowicz, *Education and Modernization in the Middle East,* pp. 214–215; Selleck, *English Primary Education and the Progressives,* pp. 132–133; Curtis, *Education in Britain since 1900,* pp. 96–97, 105–106; Talbott, *The Politics of Educational Reform in France,* pp. 169, 205–206, 230; Summers, *Colonial Lessons,* pp. 11, 164; Graham, *History of Education in Ghana,* pp. 160–161.

17. Connell, *History of Education,* pp. 153, 271–272, 288–292, 312.

18. Roy Rosenzweig, "How Americans Use and Think about the Past: Implications from a National Survey for the Teaching of History," in Peter N. Stearns, Peter Seixas, and Sam Wineburg, eds., *Knowing, Teaching, and Learning History* (New York: New York University Press, 2000) p. 280.

Chapter One

Regional Variations in Union Activism of American Public Schoolteachers

John F. Lyons

On April 5, 1933, thousands of students from Chicago's public schools walked out in protest at a six month delay in the issuing of teachers' pay. A number of schoolteachers staged a one-day strike by reporting themselves "sick," and some who turned up for work joined the students' protest. On the following day there was, according to the *Chicago Daily News*, "an endemic series of strikes, demonstrations and disorder in protest to the delay in the payment of teachers' salaries."[1] Within weeks, up to 20,000 teachers, pupils and parents regularly marched through the downtown area, demanding payment of back salaries to the schoolteachers, and on more than one occasion over 3,000 teachers battled with police as they rioted in the city's banks.[2] By 1937, these same teachers had formed the Chicago Teachers' Union (CTU) and, with more than two-thirds of the teachers joining the new organization, the CTU became the largest teachers' union in the country.

The events in Chicago illustrate the effect of the Great Depression on public schoolteachers and the desperate response of some to improve their plight. Under-funded public school systems across the nation ran out of money, and teachers faced delays in payment of salaries, unemployment, and deteriorating working conditions. The teacher union activism that took place in Chicago, however, proved unusual during the Depression. While many industrial workers engaged in strikes and sit-down stoppages in the 1930s and union membership rose from 3.6 million in 1930 to 9 million in 1940, more than a third of non-agricultural workers, with few exceptions schoolteachers remained at their posts and membership of the American Federation of Teachers (AFT) stayed below four percent of the national workforce throughout the decade.[3]

With relatively few teachers engaging in union activism, educational historians have focused their attention on explaining the failure of American teachers to strike or unionize during the Great Depression. Many researchers have noted that most teachers came from middle class and rural backgrounds which were more inclined towards conservatism than the urban working-class. Teachers' individual responsibility for their work, either in the classroom or preparing and grading at home, meant that they had little contact with their fellow workers which hindered collectivity. The constant need to maintain order and establish themselves as authority figures in the classroom, according to this interpretation, left teachers cautious and preferring stability to change. Other scholars suggested that public schoolteachers adhered to an ideology of professionalism. Teachers believed that their professional status made them middle class, this argument contends, prompting them to identify with their employers rather than the working class and to reject labor unions and militant industrial action. Teachers seemed more concerned with maintaining an ideal of service and the tenets of a noble profession than with seeking economic remuneration or taking part in undignified behavior.[4]

Little attention has been given to those teachers in Chicago and elsewhere who, even in the face of enormous opposition, joined unions, walked off the job, and engaged in demonstrations. These examples of regional militancy, though few, raise important questions about teacher union activism during the Great Depression. What was the effect of an increasingly powerful and militant private sector workers' movement on teachers' unions? Why was there such regional variation in teacher union activism? How did the different conditions of teachers' employment—ranging from the bureaucratic political machines of some large cities to the paternalistic communities of small towns—shape decisions about union activism? Why did most teachers not respond more militantly to the difficult conditions of the Depression? By comparing events in Chicago to those elsewhere, we can see how the existence of a strong private sector labor movement, a tradition of teacher unionism, the acceptance of labor by political elites and school administrators, and the paternalistic nature of small school systems help explain why teacher unionism flourished in some places during the Depression but not in others.

Teacher Unionism in United States History

The organization of US public schoolteachers dates back as far as 1857 with the formation of the National Education Association (NEA). The NEA served primarily as an organization of male educational administrators that disseminated ideas on public policy. The Association moved its headquarters to Washington, D.C. in 1917 and concentrated its energies on lobbying Congress on education matters and calling for the establishment of a federal Department of Education. The NEA promoted the professionalization of schoolteachers but refused to actively campaign for improvements in teachers' wages or working conditions. Although schoolteachers joined the organization in the early decades of the twentieth century, the NEA leadership denied them any policy-making roles.[5]

In reaction to the inactivity of the NEA on teachers' welfare, some public schoolteachers turned to the labor movement to pursue their demands. In September 1902 teachers in San Antonio, Texas, became the first group of schoolteachers to join organized labor when they directly affiliated with the American Federation of Labor (AFL). A few weeks later, the 4,000 member Chicago Teachers' Federation (CTF) joined the Chicago Federation of Labor (CFL), the municipal affiliate of the AFL, becoming the first group of teachers to affiliate with a local labor federation. Subsequently, teacher unions began to appear in other school districts across the country. Reflecting disparities in pay and working conditions, the teachers in each community were organized into separate men and women's locals and high school and elementary school unions.[6]

In April 1916, after the Chicago teachers' unions issued a call for a national organization of teachers, eight locals formed the American Federation of Teachers (AFT). Chicago became the first headquarters of the AFT, and Charles Stillman of the Chicago Federation of Men Teachers became the first president of the organization. To appease opposition, and recognizing teachers' strong commitment to public education, the federation adopted a no-strike policy. Appealing to public opinion, lobbying local politicians, and depending on the strength of organized labor, locals of the organization demanded higher teachers' salaries, job security through pensions and tenure, and a greater say in classroom management and school policy. The AFT differentiated itself from the NEA by its affiliation with organized labor and its insistence on excluding school administrators from membership. With wartime conditions favoring labor organization, membership of the AFT reached 11,000 in approximately 100 locals in 1919, 1.5% of the teaching force.[7]

From their formation, AFT locals faced enormous opposition from employers, politicians, and local government officials who condemned labor unions in general, but public sector unions in particular. In a representative democracy, presidents, governors, mayors and judges argued, the will of the people was vested in elected officials who acted in the "public interest," and answered to the electorate. For public officials to recognize public sector unions, to bargain over conditions with them, or to allow them to strike, would require the public employer to share its decision-making authority with unelected people and violate the sovereignty of the government and the democratic will of the people.[8]

During and immediately after World War I, some politicians and Boards of Education attempted to destroy the fledgling teacher unions. The onslaught started in Cleveland in 1914 when the Board of Education announced that it would not rehire teachers in the fall who remained members of a labor union. Inspired by the events in Cleveland, authorities in St. Louis, New York and Washington D.C. forced teachers to give up union affiliation.[9] In June 1916, the Chicago Board of Education refused to re-employ 68 teachers, the majority of whom were CTF members. Board of Education president Jacob M. Loeb stated that the CTF, run by elementary teacher Margaret Haley, "is a curse to the school system. In a large municipality as this there is no need for lady labor sluggers."[10] In return for the re-instatement of the teachers, in May 1917 the CFT disaffiliated from the AFT, thus breaking all formal links with organized labor.

By the mid 1920s, the Chicago Board of Education once again accepted teacher unions but the picture was different elsewhere. During the postwar Red Scare and in reaction to the Boston Police strike of 1919, the St. Louis Board of Education and the San Francisco authorities told their teachers to withdraw from unions or else they would lose their jobs.[11] In the anti-union Open Shop climate of the 1920s, school superintendents encouraged and often cajoled their employees to leave the AFT and join the NEA. By 1930, the AFT encompassed only 7,000 schoolteachers while the NEA comprised 172,000 members.[12] While the resistance to union organization by administrators continued to hinder unionization in most regions during the 1930s, in certain areas, notably Chicago, teachers showed a renewed enthusiasm for union activism as a response to the Depression.

The Great Depression

Economic problems and the policies of local governments made it difficult for communities to collect taxes and finance the public school systems during the Great Depression. From 1929 to 1933 the U.S. gross national product fell from $103 billion to $56 billion and unemployment rose from 3% of the workforce to 25%.[13] As the economic crisis deepened in the early 1930s and despite increasing school enrollments, a host of local and national organizations formed to promote the curtailment of public expenditure in general and spending on public schooling in particular. Prominent amongst them were the National Economic League, formed in the spring of 1932 and organized in 35 states with former presidents Herbert Hoover and Calvin Coolidge on its advisory council, and the U.S. Chamber of Commerce which coordinated with local chambers of commerce to cut expenditures.[14] Under pressure from these and other local business groups, communities across the nation cut educational expenditures. Some school districts reduced school supplies and curtailed so-called "fads and frills" courses such as arts and physical education while others closed their doors completely. In March 1933 over 300,000 students stayed at home as districts shut their schools due to lack of income. Because of local control of the economy, the effects of educational cuts varied widely. Rural areas and southern states which often had poorer facilities to begin with suffered the most. Georgia, for example, closed 1,318 of its schools which affected over 170,000 of its children.[15]

The cuts in the Chicago public school system were particularly severe. The Board of Education, under the control of Chicago politicians, had long overspent as it practiced widespread patronage in the granting of contracts for school construction and equipment. Approximately 90% of the funding for the Chicago public schools came from an unequally distributed property tax. Due to declining revenue brought on by the Depression, an investigation of the tax system that delayed tax collection, and pressure from sections of the business community to cut taxes, the Chicago Board of Education curtailed public education expenditures in the early 1930s. Beginning in 1932 the Chicago Board of Education shortened the school year by one month and in July 1933 the Chicago school board slashed the number of kindergartens by half, abolished the junior high school system, discontinued the city's junior college, and dropped or curtailed several other services.[16]

As school districts reduced expenditures, public schoolteachers saw their economic position worsen. Some school boards laid off teachers, particularly married women teachers, while others stopped paying employees and cut teachers' salaries. In Iowa, for example, the state mandated a flat salary of $40 a month to its teachers.[17] In New York City teachers faced a 10% pay cut and the Board of Education hired lower paid substitute teachers.[18] Between January 1931 and May 1933, 14,000 Chicago public school teachers received their monthly salary on time on only three occasions. Pay usually arrived weeks or months late. The Chicago Board of Education paid the teachers in "scrip" or in tax-anticipation warrants, which teachers then had to sell to merchants or banks often at less than the face value.[19] In the eighteen largest cities in the nation, Cincinnati, Jersey City and Chicago endured the largest curtailments in teachers' salaries while Portland and Chicago suffered the largest cuts in their school term.[20] At the beginning of 1937, Cleveland teachers still sustained a pay cut of 4%, St. Louis teachers of 6%, and Los Angeles teachers of 10%, but Chicago teachers continued to endure a pay reduction of 23.5%.[21]

The sufferings of the Great Depression changed the political views of many public schoolteachers. Comparing an earlier study on teachers' views that he published in 1927 with a study published in 1937, M. H. Harper suggested that the Depression "has given [teachers] strong social concern, revealed to them vital information, and stimulated social reflection."[22] A survey of the beliefs of 814 Californian secondary school teachers taken in 1940 found that 80% of the questions received liberal responses. Compared to a study taken in 1922, teachers "seem to be slowly moving from a somewhat conservative position to a middle-of-the-road position with some liberal ideas on certain issues," concluded the author of the study. For example, 69.5% agreed with government ownership and 82.2% believed that controversial political issues should be taught in the classroom.[23] A random sample of the electoral returns of schoolteachers in the 1932 presidential election confirmed this view. The sample revealed that 42% of teachers voted for Democrat Franklin Roosevelt, 40% for Republican Herbert Hoover and only 0.064% for socialist Norman Thomas. In contrast, 47% of a random sample intended to vote Democrat in 1936, 33% Republican, and 6% socialist.[24]

While the AFT generally relied on relieving the distress of their members, educating public opinion about the crisis, and pressuring elected officials to obtain teachers' pay, some teachers struck to protest their situation. The anthracite coalmining areas of Pennsylvania had been severely hit by recession before other parts of the country and had less income from taxes to pay teachers. In October 1929, public schoolteachers in Luzerne County, Pennsylvania, walked off the job to obtain three months back pay. The Board of Education claimed that they had no money to pay the teachers but the teachers received their pay after a week's strike. In the fall of 1933 and through 1934, as the situation worsened during the Depression and teachers' pay was delayed for months, a series of teacher strikes, often backed by parents and students, swept through mining areas in Pennsylvania and later into Alabama.[25]

Teachers in Chicago turned to other militant methods to improve their situation and to new unofficial leaders who emerged from their ranks. Owed some six months pay in 1933, teachers expressed anger at the banks and the business community for refusing to pay their property taxes or financially support the cash-strapped schools. Teachers were further disillusioned by corrupt politicians led by Democrat Mayor Edward Kelly who used the schools for patronage and financial gain. Due to the weakness of old feuding union leaders hopelessly split between men and women and high school and elementary school unions, Chicago teachers built organizations outside the unions which sought to unite the workforce. A group of teachers constituting themselves as the Volunteer Emergency Committee (VEC) formed in March 1933 to demand six months back pay owed to them and obtain regular payment of their salaries. For the next four months, thousands of angry teachers regularly stormed Board of Education and city council meetings, paraded with parents and students in downtown Chicago, and marched on city banks demanding that they buy tax warrants from the Board of Education.[26]

The leader of the VEC was John M. Fewkes, a 32-year-old high school teacher. Fewkes became a physical education teacher in 1925 in the south side of the city, and then joined the Chicago Men Teachers' Union (MTU) in 1928. Holding no union office and originally unknown outside a small circle of activists, Fewkes had become the most powerful and widely known teachers' leader by the spring of 1933. *Time* magazine called Fewkes "the John L. Lewis of the teaching profession." Yet Fewkes and the VEC were no political radicals. Physical education teachers marshaled the demonstrations to keep away communists and radicals. Fewkes was a virulent anticommunist who later led the expulsion of the communist leaning local in New York from the AFT.[27]

Stopping short of calling for an all out strike, the VEC organized a number of sensational events to publicize the plight of the teachers and to obtain their pay. On April 8, teachers delayed the flag raising ceremony at the Century of Progress Exposition held in Chicago to celebrate the city's hundredth birthday. The VEC organized boycotts of businesses that remained tax delinquent and personally called on tax strikers to pressure them into paying their taxes. In response to plans for a huge downtown demonstration on April 15, the Chicago Board of Education rushed checks for seven days' salary to the schools, and directed teachers to pick them up the day of the demonstration. The pay did not halt the protest march, as most principals brought the checks to the parading teachers. Approximately 20,000 teachers, parents, and pupils, led by Fewkes marched down Michigan Avenue, the main city thoroughfare, demanding payment of the rest of the teachers' back salaries.[28]

The teachers' protests reached a violent climax in April. On April 24, the first day of spring vacation, 5,000 teachers gathered in Grant Park in downtown Chicago. The crowd divided into five columns and marched to the large banks that had refused to buy tax warrants. Inside the banks, teachers chucked ink on the walls, overturned desks, and broke windows. The bank executives finally had to call for the police to remove the teachers. On the following Wednesday more than 3,000 teachers invaded the Chicago Title and Trust Company, and ransacked the building. Mounted police clubbed the teachers, as they threw books at the police and their horses. On Saturday, May 13, as 15,000 teachers assembled in Grant Park ready to raid the banks once more, Fewkes told those present that the teachers would receive nearly four months' pay in cash. The teachers did not receive all their back pay until August 1934, however, and their salary remained cut until the beginning of 1943.[29]

Many of those who took part in the demonstrations had to overcome their own aversion, and that of the public, to direct action on the part of teachers. The public expected teachers, and particularly women teachers, to maintain a dignified demeanor and refrain from drawing attention to themselves. One Chicago teacher was reluctant to parade because she did not want "to make a spectacle of myself. Nevertheless I am trampling down my pride...and I too perhaps shall soon join the more radical elements of the teaching force." With no pay forthcoming, on April 14 she wrote in her diary: "Tomorrow I shall parade. I've come to it at last. I loathe the idea, but the public must be awakened. I feel a little like Joan of Arc."[30] Another teacher, Mary Winifred Carey, believed that teachers should join her and "cast aside the cloak of super sensitiveness and mock modesty, and march forward in the army of the mistreated, shoulder to shoulder with her colleagues. It was only the weak sisters who shrank from marching."[31] Ultimately, the teachers "threw off their cloak of dignity and answered the call for a mass parade through the streets of the loop to awaken public attention to their plight," insisted Chicago schoolteacher Bessie Slutsky.[32]

The events in Chicago had long term consequences for teacher unionism in Chicago and the nation. In May 1937, John Fewkes became president of the Chicago Men Teachers' Union on a platform calling for amalgamation of all teachers' unions in Chicago. The four existing AFT affiliates, the Men Teachers' Union, the Federation of Women High School Teachers, the Elementary Teachers' Union and the Playground Teachers' Union began to work together. Subsequently, in October 1937, the four Chicago teachers' unions merged to form the Chicago Teachers' Union with Fewkes as first president and with over 5,000 members. In September 1938, the CTU with 8,500 members proclaimed itself not only the largest teachers' union in the country, but "the largest teachers' union in the world." Approximately two-thirds of Chicago public schoolteachers joined the CTU and not until 1960 did another teachers' union in a large city secure a majority of those eligible for membership. Reflecting the influence of Chicago, Fewkes became the president of the AFT during World War II, and Chicago remained the dominant force in the national union until the 1960s.[33]

Regional Variation in Teacher Unions

Teacher unionism grew dramatically in other cities and industrialized states. Even though some of the union leadership and hundreds of teachers left the New York Teachers Union in 1935 to form the Teachers' Guild in protest at the union's increasingly left-wing orientation, the New York Teachers Union increased its membership from 2,000 in 1935 to 6,500 in 1939, out of a workforce of 36,000 teachers.[34] Teachers in Indiana formed the Gary Teachers' Union in 1914 but the organiza-

tion remained dormant until its revival in the mid 1930s when it embraced a majority of the teaching force and became one of the most
influential locals in the AFT.[35] Membership in the Philadelphia teachers' local expanded over 2,000% between 1933 and 1934.[36] State Federation of Teachers were formed, beginning in Ohio in 1934. By 1939
the AFT had twelve state federations. Teachers forged new AFT locals
across the country and AFT membership rose from 7,000 in 1930 to
30,000 in 1940.[37]

Surveys of public schoolteachers undertaken during the Depression further showed that many supported teacher unions and unions
in general. A study of students in teacher training colleges in five
states completed in 1930 found that only 12% of the prospective
teachers reacted "unfavorably" to labor unions.[38] A national survey of
schoolteachers undertaken in 1936 showed that 37% of respondents
thought teachers should affiliate with a labor organization, 86% disagreed with the statement that "Trade unions do more harm than
good to our industrial progress," and 52% did not believe that the
Chamber of Commerce had been "more helpful to the cause of public
education" than the American Federation of Labor (AFL).[39] A researcher asked the same question to freshmen women who entered
Illinois State Normal University in September 1938 and found rather
similar results. Some 29% thought teachers should affiliate with a labor organization, 74% disagreed with the statement that "Trade unions do more harm than good to our industrial progress," and 33%
did not think that the Chamber of Commerce had been "more helpful
to the cause of public education" than the AFL.[40]

Although many teachers expressed sympathy with the labor
movement and joined unions in unprecedented numbers, the vast
majority of them remained unorganized and growth was confined to
a few larger cities. Despite the fact that public school teachers across
the country faced pay cuts and payless paydays, it was evident
throughout the 1930s that most public school teachers seemed unwill-
ing to strike, engage in militant forms of protest, or join a union to obtain their pay. Both the AFT and the NEA rejected strike action and
cautioned their members against militant action. With little public
funds available, and a large supply of unemployed teachers, striking
was not necessarily an effective way to obtain back pay. Teachers
thus had few other options but to carry on working in the hope of obtaining pay. Also they recognized the despair and poverty around
them and were reluctant to sacrifice their students' education or to

add more misery to the children's plight. "We [were] determined on one thing," commented one Chicago teacher, "we were not going to hurt the children. We went on teaching, whether we were paid or not." Indeed, teachers proved willing to relinquish at least some of their pay to help their students. To alleviate the ravages of the Depression, teachers collected money and clothing for the poorer students and served breakfast to hungry children. In 1931 New York City teachers gave food to 11,000 hungry children and Chicago teachers contributed more than $112,000 for food and clothing for their students.[41]

Clearly, as a number of educational historians argue, many public schoolteachers in the U.S. came from lower middle-class and socially conservative backgrounds, and some adhered to an ideology of professionalism which restrained them from striking or unionizing during the Great Depression. The noted educationalist John Dewey argued that "in the main the most docile among the young are the ones who become teachers when they are adults. Consequently, they still listen docilely to the voice of authority."[42] Chicago teacher William McCoy claimed that "Teachers are too conservative in all matters which concern their financial interests. They are slow to present their own cause to the public."[43] As some Chicago teachers forged a union, other teachers formed the Association of Chicago Teachers (ACT) to campaign against "unprofessional" teachers' unions. The ACT declared:

> We respect labor groups and admit the necessity of their existence for the industrial and commercial worker. HOWEVER, we believe that, just as in the past, teaching as a PROFESSION, independent of affiliation with LABOR groups has attained its present comparatively high level...Do not be misled—REMAIN a professional.

The ACT claimed about 600 members by the summer of 1939.[44]

Another impediment to teacher militancy was that government and public antagonism against public sector unions remained strong. In 1935 the National Labor Relations Act, or Wagner Act, gave private sector workers the right to bargain with employers but public sector workers were excluded from its provisions. A poll published in August 1937 found that 76% of respondents favored labor unions and only 24% disapproved. Another poll undertaken in the same month, however, found that only 26% of those asked believed that government employees should be able to join labor unions while 74% did not.[45] The prevailing prejudice against public sector unions, and especially industrial action by government workers, was expressed in 1937 by President Franklin Roosevelt when he wrote to Luther C. Steward, president of the National Federation of Federal Employees:

> Since their own services have to do with the functioning of the government, a strike of public employees manifests nothing less than an attempt on their part to prevent or obstruct the operations of government until their demands are satisfied. Such action, looking toward the paralysis of government by those who have sworn to support it, is unthinkable and intolerable.[46]

Despite these barriers to teacher unionism, why did teachers in Chicago and some other regions of the country engage in union activism while others did not? Undoubtedly, teachers joined unions in those cities that had a strong tradition of private sector labor activism. Chicago, for example, was a union town and schoolteachers were historically very much part of that union movement. At the beginning of the century, Chicago had the largest and the most militant labor movement in the nation. Margaret Haley's CTF was the first teachers' union to affiliate with a local labor federation. Since the formation of the AFT in 1916, the national organization had maintained their headquarters in Chicago. Even before the Depression, union membership in Chicago was about 15% of the teaching force.[47] In the 1930s the Congress of Industrial Organizations (CIO) campaigned to unionize the steel and meatpacking industries. Chicago Federation of Labor (CFL) membership comprised about 293,000 members in 1929; by the end of the 1930s, the combined CFL and CIO membership in Chicago stood at about 393,000, or over a quarter of the work force.[48] It seemed that everyone could, and was, joining a union in Chicago. As one schoolteacher, Elsa Ponselle, recalled: "Everybody was heart and soul in the unions those days. Somebody said, 'Why not a teachers' union?' And why not?"[49]

Other centers of teacher unionism in the 1930s had similar labor traditions and a militant union movement. New York City, the home of the Labor Day holiday and the center of socialist and communist party activity, became one of the centers of the CIO organization in the Depression. Historian Joshua Freeman suggests that when the Depression ended, "the labor movement had achieved a size, robustness, legal standing, and degree of influence previously outside its grasp. Nowhere was that more true than in New York." He believes that more than a quarter of the city's workforce was unionized after World War II.[50] Organizing efforts among steel workers and the CIO helped schoolteachers in the steel town of Gary, Indiana to unionize.[51] Even those few communities that saw teacher strikes were in the highly unionized militant mining regions of Pennsylvania and Alabama. The United Mine Workers of America and other unions supported the strikers, and unemployed miners and other citizens joined teachers on picket lines.[52]

Just as important for teacher unionism in these cities, teachers who wanted to join the union faced relatively little opposition from politicians and the Board of Education and enjoyed the protection of tenure. After the Illinois Otis Law strengthened teacher tenure in 1917 and the Chicago Board of Education rescinded the Loeb rule in the early 1920s, authorities tolerated teachers' unions in the city. Edward J. Kelly, Democratic mayor of Chicago from 1933 to 1947, sought the support of the CFL and did not want to oppose a CFL affiliated union.[53] The Board allowed the CTU to operate in the schools, gave Fewkes leave of absence for his time as union president, and allowed union delegates time off to attend conferences.[54] Similarly, only after the AFL affiliated New York City Trades Council expelled the New York Teachers' Union in 1938 for participation in CIO activities, and the AFT barred the Union for communist infiltration in 1940, did the Teachers' Union face real opposition from state and city politicians.[55] To gain members, the teachers' union in Gary, Indiana claimed that "the Union has the friendly support of the Mayor and the School Board."[56] In his study of Gary schools, historian Ronald D. Cohen argued that: "Within a few short years the union had become a significant force in school politics due to teacher militancy, a pro-union climate, local political support from a revived Democratic party, a weakened school administration...and, perhaps most important, a cooperative school board."[57]

Elsewhere, many school boards dismissed or would not hire members of teachers' unions who lacked the protection of tenure or sympathetic politicians. In 1938, only 17 states had teacher tenure laws and the number of teachers covered by tenure was merely 37.4% of the national workforce. Boards of education saw unions as unprofessional and expressed an unwillingness to share power with them. From May 1928, the Seattle, Washington, Board of Education had a policy that required schoolteachers to sign a contract denying union membership. The St. Louis, Missouri, Board of Education had a similar policy in operation as far back as 1919. The Detroit Federation of Teachers (DFT), formed in February 1931, came under attack from local newspapers, the Employers' Association of Detroit, and the Board of Education, and was forced to lead an underground existence. Only in the late 1930s did the Detroit Board of Education let up its campaign against the Federation and by 1940 the DFT still had only 300 members. In June 1938 two teachers were dismissed for union activity in Monongalia, West Virginia, and school administrators were "riding around the country-side, calling teachers out of the classrooms and asking them whether they belonged to the Teachers Union."[58] In early 1936, the Memphis Board of Education declared that it would not renew the contracts of those teachers who remained in the Memphis Teachers Union.[59] In the fall of 1936, the Wisconsin Rapids Board of Education dismissed thirteen teachers for belonging to a newly formed teachers union. In Walker County, Alabama, the Board of Education refused to allow unions in the schools, and Superintendent A. S. Scott, who sacked three teachers active in the local union, vowed "to keep the schools out of the union muddle."[60] As a result, these direct, interventionist, and systemic mechanisms prevented teachers from becoming activists in the Depression era.

Some smaller school districts made a concerted effort to recruit more submissive teachers and forge a paternalistic relationship in the schools. Educational historian Richard A. Quantz, who interviewed women teachers who had remained aloof from unionization in the 1930s in Hamilton, Ohio, found that school administrators recruited middle-class unmarried women teachers who lived at home whom they believed would be compliant and accepting of authority. Moreover, the subordination of teachers to principals and administrators replicated the patriarchal relations that the teachers had grown up with and further produced docility and deferment on the part of the women. According to Quantz, teachers identified with the school and felt part of a family rather than an alienated worker.[61] In Chicago and other large cities, however, fewer teachers were of middle-class origin, and they worked in a larger bureaucratic and anonymous school system which militated against paternalist relations and facilitated unionization. With the establishment of teacher tenure, the superintendent of the Chicago schools had less power to recruit compliant teachers.[62]

The codes of behavior and community control over teachers was much stronger in rural areas than in urban ones, which further constrained rural teachers' behavior and made them less likely to take an active part in political or labor organizations. In rural areas teachers faced close supervision by politicians, school boards and religious groups who sought to restrict the teachers' behavior. In 1929, a Kansas board of education dismissed eleven high school teachers for attending a dance at a local country club.[63] In one North Carolina town teachers had to sign a contract which stated that "I promise to abstain from all dancing, immodest dressing, and any other conduct unbecoming a teacher and a lady...I promise not to fall in love...I promise to sleep at least eight hours each night."[64] One teacher, who obtained a job in a high school near Pittsburgh, remembered that when she started teaching administrators called the teachers together and gave them a lecture on their social activities. "We were told that they expected us to spend our weekends in town—at least three out of four—and it was 'suggested' we go to church." She also remembered that "We didn't dare smoke out in the open, even in our apartment! It would have meant instant dismissal, if caught."[65]

The desire for stability and the shortage of positions relative to the supply of teachers meant that teachers, and particularly women teachers, were more vulnerable to these informal systems of control during the Depression than they were before. Many school districts traditionally prohibited married women from teaching in the schools, but the deprivations of the Depression made many more school systems prioritize male over female employment. An NEA survey of 1,500 towns in 1928 found that 39% of the school districts employed married women as new teachers, and 49% retained women who married. A similar survey undertaken by the NEA in the depths of the Depression of 1931 found that only 23% of school districts hired married women as new teachers and only 37% retained women teachers if they married.[66]

The physical space of the big city, on the other hand, allowed a teacher more freedom than in rural schools. Carl Megel, who taught in a small town before coming to Chicago in the mid 1930s, explained the difference:

> I had a different feeling about teaching, I had freedom for the use of my material, freedom of expression, freedom to teach the truth as I knew it without being concerned about losing my job, or somebody raise hell about it, it was a great feeling of—of release.[67]

Moreover, particularly in an urban setting, teaching allowed women a degree of social freedom. In rural areas, women often lived with local families and found it difficult to escape the watchful eye of moral guardians. In the city, however, teachers were more likely to live in their own apartments. Frances Donovan, a teacher in both Chicago and rural schools, declared that "Smaller communities are critical and demand a 'lady-type' of teacher. The rural teacher, moreover, is in closer touch with the community and more influenced by its attitudes." In contrast, in cities the teacher "will be left in a world of her own...she may live her private life in comparative isolation from various community groups."[68] Similarly, Fleta Childs Petrie, a Chicago public schoolteacher from 1932 to 1961, remembered that when she taught in a small town in Missouri before coming to Chicago, "the townsfolk, well some of them, could tell you all about where you'd go and with whom; what you'd wear, do, and say—even before you knew about it yourself."[69] Little wonder that teachers in big cities felt more confident to join unions while those in rural communities mostly continued to shun all forms of collective action in the 1930s.

Conclusion

During the Great Depression, the public school system and its workforce faced severe economic problems, but only a small proportion of teachers joined unions and an even smaller number engaged in any kind of direct action. While most historians argue that conservatism and an ideology of professionalism explain this lack of activism, the regional variation in the actions of teachers explored in this chapter suggests that the phenomenon was more complex. The majority of teachers did not strike, demonstrate or join unions, but teacher union activism was an important development in certain major cities. Some teachers, notably in Chicago, became radicalized by the Depression, which led to a series of direct actions to improve conditions, in the immediate term, and increased union membership over the course of the 1930s. The existence of a strong private sector labor movement, a tradition of teacher unionism, the acceptance of labor organizations by political elites and school administrators, and the greater social freedom of the large school systems each contribute to an explanation of why teacher militancy and unionism flourished in some places during the difficult conditions of the Depression but not in others. It was only after collective bargaining between employers and labor unions gained greater acceptance in the U.S. during the 1960s that the AFT was able to substantially increase its membership. By the late 1950s, opinion polls showed for the first time that a majority of Americans supported unions for public school teachers.[70] Finally, with President John F. Kennedy's Executive Order in 1962 granting federal employees the right to organize and bargain collectively, all public sector unions gained legitimacy and a new era in teacher unions began.[71]

Notes

1.   *Chicago Daily News,* April 5, 1933, pp. 1, 3; April 6, 1933, p. 1; *Time,* April 17, 1933, p. 24.

2.   *Chicago Daily News,* April 15, 1933, pp. 1, 4; "The Chicago Riots," *American Teacher,* June 1933, pp. 18–19.

3.   Figures for union membership from U.S. Bureau of the Census, *Historical Statistics of the US* (Washington D.C.: U.S. Government Printing Office, 1975) p. 178. AFT figures from William J. Moore and Ray Marshall, "Growth of Teachers' Organizations: A Conceptual Framework," *Journal of Collective Negotiations* Vol. 2 (Summer 1973) p. 274.

4.   Richard A. Quantz, "The Complex Vision of Female Teachers and the Failure of Unionization in the 1930s: An Oral History" *History of Education Quarterly* Vol. 25 (Winter 1985) pp. 439–458; Willard Waller, *The Sociology of Teaching* (New York: John Wiley, 1965, originally published in 1932); Dan C. Lortie, *School Teacher: A Sociological Study* (Chicago: University of Chicago, 1975); Wayne Urban and Jennings Waggoner, Jr. *American Education: A History* (New York: McGraw-Hill, 1996) pp. 261–265; Marjorie Murphy, *Blackboard Unions: The AFT and the NEA, 1900–1980* (Ithaca: Cornell University Press, 1990); Marvin Lazerson, "If All the World Were Chicago," *History of Education Quarterly* Vol. 24 (Summer 1984) pp. 165–179; Marvin Lazerson, "Teachers Organize: What Margaret Haley Lost," *History of Education Quarterly* 24 (Summer 1984) p. 264; and David Hogan, *Class and Reform: School and Society in Chicago, 1880–1930* (Philadelphia: University of Pennsylvania Press, 1985) p. 225.

5.   Wayne J. Urban, *Why Teachers Organized* (Detroit: Wayne State University Press, 1982) chapter 5; idem, *Gender, Race, and the National Education Association: Professionalism and Its Limitations* (New York and London: Routledge-Falmer, 2000); and Edgar B. Wesley, *The National Education Association: The First Hundred Years* (New York: Harper, 1957).

6.   Marshall O. Donley, Jr., *Power to the Teacher: How America's Educators Became Militant* (Bloomington and London: Indiana University Press, 1976) p. 17. Figures from Marjorie Murphy, "From Artisan to Semi-Professional: White Collar Unionism Among Chicago Public School Teachers, 1870–1930" (Ph.D. diss., University of California, Davis, 1981) p. 225.

7.   AFT figures from William J. Moore and Ray Marshall, "Growth of Teachers' Organizations: A Conceptual Framework," *Journal of Collective Negotiations* Vol. 2 (Summer 1973) p. 274.

8.   Sterling D. Spero, *Government as Employer* (New York: Remsen Press, 1948) pp. 1–15; Morton R. Godine, *The Labor Problem in the Public Service* (Cambridge, Mass.: Harvard University Press, 1951); Joseph E. Slater, *Public Works: Government Employee Unions, the Law, and the State, 1900–1962* (Ithaca and London: Cornell University Press, 2004).

9.   Spero, *Government as Employer.*

10.   Quoted in Murphy, "From Artisan to Semi Professional," p. 72.

11. Murphy, *Blackboard Unions*, p. 83; James Earl Clarke, "The American Federation of Teachers: Origins and History from 1870 to 1952" (Ph.D. diss., Cornell University, 1966) p. 93; Robert L. Reid, "The Professionalization of Public School Teachers: The Chicago Experience, 1895–1920" (Ph.D. diss., Northwestern University, 1963) pp. 168–184; Russell C. Oakes, "Public and Professional Reactions to Teachers' Strikes, 1918–1954" (Ph.D. diss., New York University, 1958) pp. 86–87; Spero, *Government as Employer*, pp. 4, 29.

12. Murphy, *Blackboard Unions*, pp. 90–95.

13. U.S. Bureau of the Census, *Historical Statistics of the United States*, pp. 1, 224.

14. S. Alexander Rippa, "Retrenchment in a Period of Defensive Opposition to the New Deal: The Business Community and the Public Schools, 1932–1934," *History of Education Quarterly* 2 (June 1962); David B. Tyack, Robert Lowe, and Elizabeth Hansot, *Public Schools in Hard Times: The Great Depression and Recent Years* (Cambridge, Mass.: Harvard University Press, 1984).

15. William Edward Eaton, *The American Federation of Teachers, 1916–1961* (Carbondale and Edwardsville: Southern Illinois University Press, 1975) p. 42.

16. *Teacher News and Views*, February 15, 1936, pp. 1, 3; "The Assault on the Schoolhouse," *The Nation*, August 16, 1933, p. 173; "Defrilled Chicago," *Time*, July 24, 1933, p. 31.

17. Tyack, Lowe, and Hansot, *Public Schools in Hard Times*, p. 32.

18. Eaton, *American Federation of Teachers*, p. 91.

19. David B. Tyack, *The One Best System: A History of American Urban Education* (Cambridge, Mass.: Harvard University Press, 1974); Tyack, Lowe, and Hansot, *Public Schools in Hard Times*.

20. *Teacher News and Views*, February 15, 1936, pp. 1, 3.

21. *Chicago's Schools*, March 1937, pp. 1–2; Mary J. Herrick, *The Chicago Schools: A Social and Political History* (Beverly Hills and London: Sage, 1971) p. 228; *CTU Weekly News Bulletin*, November 26, 1937, p. 1.

22. Manly H. Harper, "Social Attitude of Educators," *Social Frontier* Vol. 3 (February 1937) p. 147.

23. *Social Frontier/Frontiers of Democracy* May 15, 1940, pp. 247–249.

24. William H. Kilpatrick, ed., *The Teacher and Society. The First Yearbook of the John Dewey Society* (New York: D. Appleton Century, 1937) p. 222.

25. Oakes, "Public and Professional Reactions to Teachers' Strikes," pp. 94–171, 177–185.

26. For more on the events of spring 1933 in Chicago, see John F. Lyons "The Limits of Professionalism: The Response of Chicago Schoolteachers to Cuts in Education Expenditures, 1929–1933," *Journal of Illinois History* 1 (Autumn 1998) pp. 4–22.

27. For more on Fewkes, see *Time*, May 8, 1933, p. 34; November 8, 1937, p. 34; John Fewkes interview by Renee Epstein, Transcript, July 30 and 31, 1986, 4, AFT Oral History Project, Archives of Labor and Urban Affairs, Walter Reuther Library, Wayne State University, Detroit, Michigan.

28. Lyons "Limits of Professionalism," pp. 4–22.

29. Ibid., pp. 4–22.

30.   "Spasmodic Diary of a Chicago School Teacher," *The Atlantic Monthly* (November 1933) pp. 517–520.

31.   *Commerce* (October 1933) pp. 3–4.

32.   Bessie Slutsky, "The Chicago Teachers' Union and Its Background," (MA Thesis, Northwestern University, 1945) p. 18.

33.   The CTU claimed that Paris, with 7,000 members, ranked second. For more on the CTU, see John F. Lyons, "The Chicago Teachers' Union, Politics and the City's Schools, 1937–1970," (Ph.D. thesis, University of Illinois at Chicago, 2001).

34.   Eaton, *American Federation of Teachers*, p. 105.

35.   Ronald D. Cohen, *Children of the Mill: Schooling and Society in Gary, Indiana, 1906–1960* (New York and London: Routledge Falmer, 2002) p. 145.

36.   *AFT Proceedings* 1934, p. 14.

37.   Clarke, "American Federation of Teachers," p. 225; *Illinois Union Teacher,* May 1944, p. 4.

38.   Margaret Kiely, *Comparisons of Students of Teachers Colleges and Students of Liberal-Arts Colleges* (New York: Columbia University Press, 1931) pp. 94–97.

39.   Kilpatrick, ed., *Teacher and Society,* pp. 180–189.

40.   Marie Finger, "A Study of Freshmen Women in a Teachers College," (Ph.D. thesis, Northwestern University , 1940) pp. 79–90.

41.   *Chicago Tribune,* September 6, 1931, p. 4; Studs Terkel, *Hard Times: An Oral History of the Great Depression* (New York: Pantheon, 1970) p. 442; *American Teacher* (February 1931) p. 5; *New York Times,* June 19, 1931, p. 14; *Chicago Schools Journal,* March 1931, p. 348; April 1931, p. 399; Special Report issued by the Joint Board of Teachers Unions, June 22, 1931, CTU Collection, Box 1, Chicago Historical Society; Eaton, *American Federation of Teachers,* p. 42.

42.   John Dewey, "Education as Engineering," *New Republic* (September 20, 1922) p. 91.

43.   *American Teacher* (April 1920) p. 77.

44.   "Why Teachers Do Not Want Their Calling Unionized," Association of Chicago Teachers (ACT) flyer, September 27, 1937; Letter from John Myers to J. Edward Huber, May 16, 1939, CTU Collection, Box 18, Folder 2, Chicago Historical Society; ACT flyers, n.d., CTU Collection, Box 18, Folder 3, Chicago Historical Society; *Chicago Tribune,* May 22, 1939.

45.   George H. Gallup, ed., *The Gallup Poll: Public Opinion, 1935–1971*, Vol. 1 (New York: Random House, 1972) pp. 66–67.

46.   Charles S. Ryan, *Labor Unions and Municipal Employee Law* (Washington, D.C.: National Institute of Municipal Law Officers, 1946) p. 436. The legal status of teachers is covered in *NEA Research Bulletin* (April 1947) pp. 25–72.

47.   Cannella, *171 Years of Teaching in Chicago,* p. 26.

48.   Barbara Warne Newell, *Chicago and the Labor Movement: Metropolitan Unionism in the 1930s* (Urbana: University of Illinois Press, 1961) pp. 198–205.

49.   Terkel, *Hard Times,* p. 442.

50.   Joshua B. Freeman, *Working-Class New York: Life and Labor Since World War II* (New York: New Press, 2000) pp. 31–32.

51.   Cohen, *Children of the Mill,* p. 143.

52. Oakes, "Public and Professional Reactions to Teachers' Strikes," pp. 123–125.

53. John Fewkes to John Fitzpatrick, December 6, 1938; John Fewkes to William Johnson, March 25, 1939, CTU Collection, Box 19, Folder 2, Chicago Historical Society.

54. John Fewkes to James McCahey, October 17, 1938, and August 5, 1938, CTU Collection, Box 19, Folder 1, Chicago Historical Society.

55. Murphy, *Blackboard Unions*, p. 164.

56. Cohen, *Children of the Mill*, p. 143.

57. Ibid., p. 145.

58. Willard S. Elsbree, *The American Teacher: Evolution of a Profession in a Democracy* (New York: American Book Company, 1939) p. 478; Joseph Slater, "Down By Law: Public Sector Unions and the State in America, World War I to World War II" (Ph.D. diss., Georgetown University, 1998) pp. 133–201, 172; Eaton, *American Federation of Teachers*, p. 35; Jeffrey Mirel, *The Rise and Fall of an Urban School System: Detroit 1907–1980* (Ann Arbor: University of Michigan Press, 1993) pp. 111–124; Ruth Markowitz, *My Daughter the Teacher, Jewish Teachers in the New York City Schools* (New Brunswick: Rutgers University Press, 1993) pp. 159–160; *American Teacher* (May-June 1938) p. 10; Illinois State Federation of Labor *Proceedings*, 1939, pp. 193–195.

59. *American Teacher* (May-June 1936) p. 5.

60. *Social Frontier* (October 1936) p. 4; *Social Frontier* (November 1936) p. 36.

61. Quantz, "Complex Vision of Female Teachers," pp. 439–458.

62. See William J. Moore and Ray Marshall, "Growth of Teachers' Organizations: A Conceptual Framework," *Journal of Collective Negotiations* Vol. 2 (Summer 1973) p. 285; Donley Jr., *Power to the Teacher*, pp. 195–197, for more on big city bureaucratic school systems.

63. Elsbree, *American Teacher*, p. 536.

64. *Social Frontier* (February 1936) p. 158.

65. Jeane Westin, *Making Do: How Women Survived the 30s* (Chicago: Follett, 1976) p. 213.

66. *NEA Research Bulletin* Vol. 10 (January 1932) p. 20.

67. Carl Megel interview by DG, October 25, 1984, Tape Carl 9 C, pages 2–3, Carl Megel Collection Box 23 folder 19, Archives of Labor and Urban Affairs, Walter Reuther Library, Wayne State University, Detroit, MI.

68. Frances R. Donovan, *The Schoolma'am* (New York: Frederick A. Stokes, 1938) pp. 22, 215–216.

69. *Chicago Union Teacher* (November 1961) p. 4.

70. Gallup, ed., *Gallup Poll*, p. 1970.

71. Donley, *Power to the Teacher*, pp. 197–202.

Chapter Two

The "Virtues of Planning": American Educators Look at Soviet Schools

E. Thomas Ewing

In 1931, American educator George S. Counts began his book, *The Soviet Challenge to America*, with the striking image of two societies moving in seemingly opposite directions. American society was marked by unemployment, misery, hunger, and "profound physical insecurity," all due to the economic paralysis and dissipation brought on by the Depression. Soviet society, by contrast, was marked by bold ideals, confidence, enthusiasm, and passion, all due to a determined effort to establish rational control over economic resources.[1] Describing an "experiment" that was "so bold indeed in its ideals and its program that few can contemplate it without emotion," Counts argued that "the Soviet challenge to America" came not from the Communist International or the Red Army, but "through her State Planning Commission and her system of public education":

> The Russian experiment challenges the American educational tradition at many points; but it is the principle of social planning more than anything else that gives to Soviet education its unique character and distinguishes it most fundamentally from education in the United States. Scarcely a single phase or practice or theory has escaped the impress of this principle: it has left its stamp on the purpose, the organization, and the support of education; it has affected the content of the curriculum, the methods of instruction, and the position of the teacher; it has raised in acute form a number of basic considerations regarding the question of indoctrination, the nature of freedom, and the integration of culture.[2]

Directly contrasting the Soviet Union under the Five Year Plan and the capitalist world in the grips of the Depression, Counts described how the "virtues of planning" allowed Communist leaders to construct a system that did not have any of the "great wastes of capitalism":

> Natural riches will be exploited in the light of the abiding interests of all, and not for the purpose of enriching the few by hurried and wasteful methods of production. The discovery of knowledge in the field of industry will proceed according to a general plan designed to benefit the whole of society, and not in response to the competitive efforts of separate firms, each bent on guarding as precious trade secrets whatever it may learn. There will be no suppression

of inventions which purposes to guard private profits at the expense of the general welfare; no industrial crises which periodically shake the economic order and throw millions of workers out of employment; no costly advertising which increases the number of unproductive occupations and stimulates vast numbers of people to live beyond their means; no idle capital which is a useless burden for society to carry and which is the product of general economic incoordination; no technological unemployment which places the costs of progress on the shoulders of men and women least fit to bear them; no speculation on the stock exchange which consumes credit, takes men out of production, generates a get-rich-quick psychology among the people, and contributes to the development of the tradition that "only saps work"; no struggles for world markets which turn nation against nation, breed economic rivalries and military conflicts, and threaten to destroy civilization in the holocaust of war.[3]

By examining "the relationship between education and social planning," Counts challenged Americans to re-evaluate their own schools and the future of their society:

> The idea of building a new society along the lines developed by the Communists should provide a genuine stimulus to the mind and liberate the energies of millions. It is certainly no worse than the drive toward individual success which permeates not only the schools but every department of culture in the United States. If one were to compare the disciplined effort of the Soviets to industrialize the country, to socialize agriculture, to abolish poverty, to banish disease, to liquidate unemployment, to disseminate knowledge, and generally to raise the material and spiritual level of the masses, with the selfish scramble for wealth and privilege, the cruel disregard of the less sensational forms of human suffering, the relative absence of a sense of social responsibility, the reluctance to come honestly to grips with the major problems of the time, and the apparent decay of the political, ethical, and religious life in America, one would find small grounds for complacency. Whatever may be said on the other side concerning the regimentation of opinion and the restriction of individual freedom, there exist in Soviet Russia today an idealism and a driving passion for human betterment which contrast strangely with the widespread cynicism of the United States.[4]

For Counts, Soviet schools became not just a location for pedagogical experimentation, but more broadly a symbol of the "principle of social planning" on a comparative and even global scale.[5]

The significance of Counts' argument lay in the coincidence of two distinct—and to a great extent unrelated—historical phenomena: first, the launching of the Soviet Five Year Plan in October 1928, and second, the Great Depression which began in October 1929 in the United States and quickly spread to the rest of the world. As these quotes suggest,

Counts thought in terms of the opposite trajectories of a polarized world. The United States economic crisis was presented as a set of known negatives against which the Soviet "experiment" could easily be contrasted. The language used to describe America in the Great Depression emphasized society's loss of control to destructive political, economic, and social forces, while descriptions of Soviet planning expressed the great possibilities of a deliberate effort to build a new society.

This chapter draws on publications by Counts and other American observers to ask how the conditions of the Depression encouraged educators to look elsewhere for ideas and inspiration, and how the apparent achievements of Soviet schools were perceived as such a model by advocates of social planning. Why did American educators identify planning as the crucial factor in explaining the apparent success of Soviet educational expansion? How did American perceptions compare to the actual practices of Soviet education? Finally, what do the lessons that American educators learned from Soviet education reveal about the broader implications of thinking about schooling in a global context?

By 1929, when the crisis of the Depression coincided with the expansion of Soviet mass education, American educators had spent more than a decade in fascinated, and often partisan, contemplation of communist schooling. Immediately after the 1917 revolution, Soviet educators attracted international interest by openly proclaiming their desire to adopt progressive methods, such as encouraging pupils to see the teacher as a peer rather than an authority, fostering pupil self-government, rejecting traditional methods of instruction, and eliminating boundaries between classrooms and society by sending pupils to factories and building workshops in schools. Communist schools fascinated leading progressive educators in the United States, and led to visits to Soviet Russia by Counts, Jerome Davis, Thomas Woody, John Dewey, and others.[6] While scholars have previously explored American educators' interest in—and some would argue seduction by—the progressive experiments of Soviet education, relatively little attention has been paid to their consideration of planning.[7] Yet in a 1930 article, Counts declared that it was precisely "the system of planning organs and the relationship of that system to the institutions of public education" that made up "the most distinctive features of the new society which is evolving beyond the Vistula today."[8] A year later, Counts wrote that "perhaps the most profound effect of the plan upon the school is the way in which it has given content, purpose, and even in-spiration to the program of instruction," which meant that "the most challenging aspect of the whole Soviet experiment [is] the intimate un-ion of education and social planning."[9]

This chapter argues that what American educators called "social planning" should be understood more fully as a state directed process of mobilization. While Soviet educational expansion of the early 1930s was a remarkable achievement fully deserving of this global attention, the dynamic of change was shaped more by forceful intervention than by rational principles. Responding to an increasingly disturbing crisis in an American educational system that sanctioned individualist, ma-terialist, and traditional values, educators adopted the Soviet rhetoric of planning in ways that legitimized an alternative vision of schooling that privileged their collectivist, progressive, and transformative ide-als. Asking how American educators viewed Soviet schools is thus ul-timately more revealing of the visions articulated by the former than of the actual virtues (and vices) of planning in the Soviet Union. As this chapter will conclude, however, these perceptions were extremely sig-nificant on their own, both as illustrations of a certain response to the Depression and as examples of a distinctively global framework for understanding schools in times of economic disruption, ideological contests, and political transformations.

"An Instrument of Extraordinary Power"

In the summer of 1930, at the very moment that American educators were coming to realize the full implications of the Depression for public schools, the Communist Party of the Soviet Union announced plans for the universal education of all children aged eight to eleven years by the fall of 1931. In just one year, from 1929/1930 to 1930/1931, elementary and secondary enrollment grew from 14 to 17 million, an increase of nearly one quarter. By the spring of 1933, at a time when many American schools were ending the year early, firing teachers, and cutting services because of a lack of funds, Soviet enrollment reached 21 million. By 1939, as more pupils attended school for longer periods, as the campaign for universal education extended to the secondary level, and as state schooling penetrated even so-called "backward" national regions, Soviet enrollment exceeded 31 million pupils, more than doubling the number from a decade earlier.[10]

Soviet educational expansion caught the attention of Western observers, who praised the "distinct stride forward," "energetic measures," and "remarkable progress" of Soviet education, which "felt the driving, quickening influence of the five-year plan" on the way to "stupendous" achievements.[11] American newspaper correspondent Walter Duranty declared that mass education illustrated both the promise and shortcomings of the new Russian regime:

> Of the whole system, from kindergartens to universities, one may say the same thing—the demand outruns the supply, which is true of nearly everything in Russia. In this country education is a fever of duty, pride and achievement eagerly desired by the tens and tens of millions to whom it was formerly denied.[12]

In 1932, Thomas Woody observed that it was "no exaggeration to say that the whole Union is at school," while a year later, Harry C. Krowl echoed this observation with his statement that "the whole nation is at school."[13]

Even as they conceded that the reality of Soviet schools did not always match the rhetoric, American observers believed and repeated Soviet claims of substantial achievements. In 1935, Counts acknowledged that statistics on Soviet education "may be subject to considerable discount," that many teachers and students might be poorly trained, that the quality of instruction might be inferior, and that "the entire cultural apparatus has undoubtedly been pervaded by a shallow form of propaganda of the moment." Even with these qualifications, however, Counts offered a remarkable assessment of Soviet education since the 1917 revolution:

> Yet when all the necessary qualifications have been made, the fact remains that at least on the quantitative side the development of education in the Soviet Union during the past seventeen years is without parallel in history. A psychological ferment has been started that already has profoundly disturbed and transformed the mentality of a population of one hundred and sixty millions. People have been taught to read; men and women have been told to hope; ideas have been disseminated on an unprecedented scale. Forces have been released that can never be controlled.[14]

This statement was especially striking in the way that the "quantitative side" was defined not so much by the number of schools or pupils as by the dimensions of the changes in behavior, abilities, and attitudes that were associated with "the development of education."

American observers attributed the remarkable expansion of Soviet schools to a broader effort to transform society according to comprehensive social planning. In 1931, Counts declared that "the relationship between education and social planning" was one of "the greatest assets of the Soviet regime in its attempt to achieve the Five-Year Plan":

> Scarcely a single phase or practice or theory has escaped the impress of this principle: it has left its stamp on the purpose, the organization, and the support of education; it has affected the content of the curriculum, the methods of instruction, and the position of the teacher; it has raised in acute form a number of basic considerations regarding the question of indoctrination, the nature of freedom, and the integration of culture.[15]

According to Counts, "the principle of social planning" meant that Communist leaders had "fashioned an instrument of extraordinary power for the achievement of the goals of the revolution."[16]

While the rapid expansion in enrollment caught the attention of American educators, Soviet schools more generally seemed to embody the possibilities of a truly integrated "nation-wide system of education."[17] In *The Soviet Challenge to America,* Counts declared that planned education was based on the assumption that "social phenomena are capable of being controlled and that the development of society can be made subject to the human will."[18] On a more emotional level, Counts evoked "the new spirit" that the Five Year Plan brought into the school:

> On the walls of the classroom and the halls may be found the placards, diagrams, and maps of the Plan. The children have brought socialistic competition into the school and have organized their own shock brigades. But there is a yet more significant effect. The most characteristic and the most challenging feature of Soviet educational theory and practice is the emphasis on socially useful labor. The work of the classroom is supposed to revolve about activities which are useful to the surrounding community and which thus make the school a genuine part of the life. The launching of the Five-Year Plan has added in striking fashion to both the content and the significance of this socially useful work. By establishing intimate and reciprocal relations between school and factory and between school and village, children are made conscious participants in the vast program of construction.[19]

Most fundamentally, Counts argued, throughout Soviet education "a systematic effort is made to change the very character of the people inhabiting the Union."[20] The Five Year Plan provided Soviet education with "a concrete and comprehensive formulation of purposes":

> The "program of great works" has banished this sense of bewilderment, put genuine content into Soviet ideals, and given precise direction to the tasks of the education. It has defined the building of socialism in terms so clear and unequivocal that even the most simple-minded can understand.[21]

As a result, Counts asserted, education has become "a necessary and serious function of the community," assuming "the major responsibility for the promotion of the common welfare," and "at once a central concern of society and a matter of vital importance to practical men."[22]

Evaluating the Soviet Five Year Plan was thus significant not only in terms of the development of communism in Russia, but also as a test for social planning. The "extraordinary power" attributed to this "instrument" reflected this combination of dramatic changes in quantity with equally impressive, if less easily measurable, changes in attitudes, beliefs, and expectations. Arguing that the outcome of the Five Year Plan would determine the success or failure of revolutionary movements around the world, Counts declared that Soviet planning "should be followed therefore with both interest and concern by sober-minded citizens throughout the world."[23] After the next section examines in greater depth these efforts to "control" education through planning, the final section takes up the broader claims that Counts and others associated with this "instrument of extraordinary power."

Soviet Educational Planning in Theory and in Practice

How did Soviet educational expansion *in practice* compare to the *perceptions* of American observers? In education, as in industry and agriculture, the Five Year Plan meant not only significant acceleration of the pace of change, but pursuit of maximum goals in the shortest possible time. Whereas objectives outlined by the Soviet Commissariat of Education in 1923 and reaffirmed in 1927 called for the achievement of universal education no sooner than 1933, plans adopted in the summer of 1930 called for enrolling nearly every child aged eight to eleven years no later than the fall of 1931. In a characteristically Stalinist pattern of decision making, the goal (enrolling the most

children in the shortest possible time) was defined by political leaders
without consideration of whether sufficient resources were available to
achieve these objectives. Stalin's declaration in 1930 that "we now have
everything necessary" to make primary schooling universal and
compulsory was a statement of determination, rather than an
assessment of actual levels of preparation. As the goals of universal
education went through several revisions, always in an upward
direction, it became clear that, in education as in other campaigns,
initial successes quickly convinced Party leaders that even more
accelerated tempos were possible.[24] Soviet educational expansion was
"planned," to the extent that political authorities defined goals and
mobilized resources to meet these goals, but at the decision-making
level, Soviet practice diverged considerably from the kind of "rational"
control perceived by American observers.

Soviet education during the First Five Year Plan supports recent
historical interpretations of the complex relationship between
structure, agency, and intention that defined Stalinism. According to
Gail Warshofsky Lapidus, Soviet educational expansion was a clear
example of how long-term planning was abandoned in favor of crash
programs intended to mobilize all resources to meet immediate goals.
Rather than a blueprint for any kind of coordinated or directed change,
"planning" became an instrumental concept that concealed and thus
denied significant conflicts between the central control demanded by
political authorities and the local actions that actually determined
outputs.[25] Crash programs were both justified and required, according
to historian Moshe Lewin, by Stalin's approach that presented "plans"
as accomplished facts—and then demanded that Party and
government organizations get in line with the situation as it allegedly
existed elsewhere.[26] Stephen Kotkin describes Stalinist planning as "a
sustained, albeit improvised, crash mobilization," with elements
characteristic of wartime engagement, but with internal as well as
external real and imagined opponents.[27] The widespread use of the
phrase "the battle for the plan," as argued recently by Paul Gregory,
illustrated the extent to which conflict and struggle, rather than
rationality and control, shaped resource allocation, production output,
and managerial decisions.[28] While the plan both affirmed a broadly
shared goal and defined the markers of progress toward the goal, the
practices of Soviet education in these years were shaped primarily by
the mobilization strategies of the regime, the constraints of resource
distribution, the relentless pressure to expand state power, and the

elimination of any space for oppositional, dissenting, or non-conforming positions.[29]

On the ground, the Soviet campaign for universal education seemed less like a rationally planned effort and more like a "front" of the Stalinist "revolution from above."[30] Quantitative indices, such as building schools, enrolling children, and employing teachers, were assigned more priority than the content of the curriculum, the capacities of pupils, or the qualifications of educators. Yet American observers who commented on these "shortcomings" seemed to assume that these were temporary conditions that would disappear with the full achievement of the plan—rather than results of the mobilization strategies themselves.[31] The rhetoric used by Counts and others who spoke of the release of "forces...that can never be controlled" obscured the ways that the loss of control due to the disruptive effects of rapid transformation provoked political authorities to enact ever more repressive mechanisms in order to reclaim this control over individuals and institutions.

American observers of Soviet education, like those assessing other aspects of Stalinist modernization, thus underestimated the extent and nature of coercion involved in these campaigns.[32] Any suspected opposition to mass education, whether from policy-makers who questioned the tempo of change or parents who resisted the hegemony of state schooling, was denounced as treason, wrecking, or anti-Soviet activities. The campaign for universal education coincided with new forms of political repression, including the collectivization of the countryside and anti-religious campaigns, which implicated the spread of schools in expanding and deepening cycles of state violence.[33] Most importantly, the ends of planning—maximum enrollment—not only justified any means, but in fact became the means, so that education meant being in school, rather than the content of what was being taught and learned in the school. Observers looked for and found deliberate efforts to plan the entire life of the country, but the experience of the Soviet people and the actions of government and Party organizations were far more disrupted and disruptive than rationalized and rational.

These complexities of the Stalinist transformations rarely appeared in the enthusiastic accounts of American educators. As argued by Lewis Feuer, American observers of the Soviet Union "saw the official surface; they did not experience the inner tensions."[34] While Counts devoted a whole chapter to explaining the structure and procedures of the State Planning Commission, he overestimated the extent to which the planning process actually resulted in what he referred to as "the general pooling of knowledge and...the focusing of experience on the surmounting of any obstacle."[35] Counts also underestimated the extent to which political leaders, through their intervention and manipulation, disrupted the very processes they were claiming to "plan" and thus contributed to the spread of conflict, intimidation, and repression throughout society. Yet Counts did acknowledge, however inadvertently, a key dynamic of Stalinism in his explanation of the term, *fstretchny promfinplan* [accelerated industrial-financial plan] as "a process which proceeds from the bottom upward, from the point of production through the successive levels of management, and establishes indices for the year on the basis of the actual accomplishments of the better workmen."[36]

In practice, however, quantitative goals were subject to revision—always in an upward direction—depending on the actual output of those involved in processes of production. The higher the productivity, the higher the goals. In education, the more students enrolled, the higher the target percentages could be raised—regardless of whether teachers, classrooms, or textbooks were available or whether the quality of instruction met minimum requirements. The expansion of Stalinist education did follow a direction of change from "bottom" to "top," but with implications far different from those assumed by Counts, whose enthusiasm for planning led to a misunderstanding of practices at the point of implementation. Rather than promoting democratic and participatory decision-making, this pattern of exhorting, coercing, and then rewarding the most aggressive local officials—and then reconfiguring "plans" to match or exceed their results—actually contributed to the increasingly repressive character of the Stalinist system.[37]

American accounts of Soviet education did at times discuss the more repressive aspects of schooling in a single-party dictatorship, although this recognition was often grudging, usually limited, and always conditional. In his 1930 article, for example, Duranty conceded "the stress laid on Marxist doctrine," but then proclaimed that Soviet education's "prime purpose, whether the Bolsheviki admit it or not, is to make free and self-respecting citizens of a nation of former slaves."[38] In *The Soviet Challenge to America*, Counts declared that the "dictatorship of the proletariat rules in the realms of education, science, and art no less than in the spheres of economics and politics."[39] In 1935, Counts stated that Soviet education has "one all-pervasive and dominant aim—that of serving the revolutionary forces and of building a socialist state along the lines laid down by the Party."[40] While recognizing the tension between promises and practices involved in the Soviet repudiation of academic freedom, however, Counts saw the system of planning as an integrated whole, with no tension between the goals proclaimed by authorities and the implications for the schools.[41] Yet this tension exerted a direct effect on the schools, with consequences ranging from over-crowded classrooms, insufficient supplies, and teacher shortages to the increased penetration of coercive state power at the level of communities, families, and individuals. The "revolution from above" that brought violent repression, forced expropriation, and widespread famine to the countryside and abysmal living conditions, draconian labor laws, and expanding police operations to the cities exerted a similar, although less immediately destructive, effect on schools and the associated communities of pupils, teachers, and parents.

Communist Lessons: Soviet Schools and American Visions

These evaluations of Soviet education need to be understood as part of a broader discourse on social planning in the early 1930s. For many American intellectuals, the onset of the Great Depression in 1929 only served to confirm their reservations about and objections to individualist, competitive, and materialist capitalist culture.[42] Proposing a "Five Year Plan for America," the historian Charles Beard argued that while the immediate crisis of the Depression made the need for planning seem immediate and obvious, it was the long-term waste of human and material resources through overproduction, unemployment, and "the untrammeled acquisitive instinct" that needed to be brought under "rational" control in ways that would restore "confidence in the will and the power of the nation."[43] By 1937, the question had become, in the words of Lewis Mumford, "not *if* we shall plan, but *how* we shall plan, for the reason that planning itself is inherent in the whole program of living and thinking that sustains modern men."[44]

The growing appeal of planning as a response to the Depression transformed American thinking about the Soviet Union. In 1932, Georges Soule made this observation: "It is curious how the idea of economic planning has come to dominate all others in foreign views of the Russian revolution."[45] Introducing a translation of an official Soviet statement on planning, Findlay MacKenzie defined the Five Year Plan as "a map of policy and a guide to action . . a program, an objective…a philosophy of statesmanship and a goal towards which organization, technology, and legislation are constantly directed."[46] *The New York Times* correspondent Duranty clearly believed that the Depression was changing American attitudes toward the Soviet Union, as "the growth of distress and unemployment, the public anxiety and the inability of statesmen to solve problems each day more pressing and ominous" in the capitalist world had reinforced the belief that "the Russian system of planned economy is superior to the undirected methods which are obtained elsewhere."[47] The growing interest in the communist alternative was acknowledged, far more bitterly, in President Herbert Hoover's reference to "the 'plan' idea" as "an infection" generated by the Soviets.[48] Most remarkably, Stuart Chase ended his book, *A New Deal*, which argued for planning as a "third way" between capitalism and revolution, by asking: "Why should Russians have all the fun of remaking the world?"[49]

American educators clearly hoped that the growing appeal of planning would lead to a dramatic transformation in the organization, ideals, and purposes of schooling. This interest in educational planning tends to confirm Feuer's argument about the ways that American attitudes toward the communist system responded to the crisis of the Depression: "the American need shaped the perception of Soviet reality; the experiment became the practicable alternative."[50] In a similar way, Engerman argues that American intellectuals in the 1930s were captivated by the "romance of economic development," as their "enthusiasm for social transformation" tended to "ignore its human costs."[51] In 1936, educator Francis Brown attributed the growing interest in social planning in education to two converging "objective facts": "maladjustment growing out of the depression and the increasing body of literature on the European systems of planned education."[52] After describing how the Soviet system of education was "systematically and comprehensively planned to impress upon the mind of pupils the significance and value of the Communist order," Brown appealed to Americans to redefine the purposes of education in terms of social welfare rather than individual rights:

> Having accepted such a basic tenet, the school must conceive itself in its true function—the agency of the state developed for the welfare of all—and teachers as servants of the state, must develop a social intelligence based not on

critical evaluation and individual judgment but on consistent indoctrination of the philosophy of the common good.[53]

Thus Brown saw the "maladjustment" of the Depression as the result of a more fundamental conflict between individual values and the common good that could only be reconciled in favor of the latter through educational planning.

Counts also promoted the Soviet model as an alternative to the American approach to schooling.[54] At times, Counts assumed a cautious tone that allowed for a range of possible outcomes and implications, as in this 1930 statement:

> While it is altogether too early to pass judgment on the work of the planning organs, we cannot continue to ignore that great body of experience which the Soviet economists are gaining. If the five-year plan is successful and if it is followed, as it no doubt will be, by other plans of a yet more grandiose character, the power which social planning may give to a society can then be gauged with some degree of accuracy. Possibly we shall find that our present practice of placing our confidence in the uncoordinated efforts of separate enterprises represents the last word in human efficiency; possibly we shall find that the society which endeavors to plan its future has a tremendous advantage over the society which entrusts its future to the fates. Whatever the outcome, the experiment now under way in Soviet Russia should be watched by the most intelligent observers that our country can provide.[55]

Just a year later, however, as the deepening crisis of the Depression coincided with dramatic progress on the Five Year Plan, Counts offered a remarkable contrast between the values embedded in American and Soviet schooling:

> The idea of building a new society along the lines developed by the Communists should provide a genuine stimulus to the mind and liberate the energies of millions. It is certainly no worse than the drive toward individual success which permeates not only the schools but every department of culture in the United States. If one were to compare the disciplined effort of the Soviets to industrialize the country, to socialize agriculture, to abolish poverty, to banish disease, to liquidate unemployment, to disseminate knowledge, and generally to raise the material and spiritual level of the masses, with the selfish scramble for wealth and privilege, the cruel disregard of the less sensational forms of human suffering, the relative absence of a sense of social responsibility, the reluctance to come honestly to grips with the major problems of the time, and the apparent decay of the political, ethical, and religious life in America, one would find small grounds for complacency. Whatever may be said on the other side concerning the regimentation of opinion and the restriction of individual freedom, there exist in Soviet Russia today an idealism and a driving

passion for human betterment which contrast strangely with the widespread cynicism of the United States. It is only natural that this idealism and this passion should sweep through the schools as well as through the rest of the social order...We in America may not care to adopt the philosophy and program of the Communists, but unless we face the basic problems of human living with equal honesty and courage we shall do well to suspend judgment and learn what we can from the Soviet experiment.[56]

In an article published in *The New York Times* in July 1931, Counts drew a similar comparison between education in America, which "fosters the egoistic impulses, serves the interest of a political democracy reared on capitalistic foundations, and in so far as it is effective, helps the individual to succeed in the struggle for wealth and social position," and education in the Soviet Union, which "stimulates the growth of the social tendencies, engages actively in the building of a socialistic State and prepares the individual to serve the group."[57] In both cases, the juxtaposition of terms was most revealing, as the language of building, liberation, collectivism, idealism, and disciplined effort used to describe the Soviet Union stood in striking contrast to the language of selfishness, decay, disregard, egoism, and cynicism that described America.

Asserting that "society as a whole must accept sooner or later the responsibility for satisfying the basic economic needs of the population and for establishing a condition of general material security for all," Counts presented planning as the only solution to the crisis of the Depression:

> In a world where great masses of people live in dire poverty and the grim specters of sickness, unemployment, and old age perpetually hover in the background, there can be no genuine freedom. These evils can be laid to rest in industrial society only through organization and by placing definite limitations on the exercise of certain forms of freedom characteristic of historic capitalism...Industrial society in its present form is a monster possessing neither soul nor inner significance. It has succeeded in destroying the simpler cultures of the past but has failed to create a culture of its own worthy of the name...Whether this state of moral chaos is the temporary maladjustment of a transition epoch or the inevitable product of a society organized for private gain is one of the most crucial questions of our time. Unless industrial capitalism can go beyond the production of material things and meet the spiritual needs of men, it cannot and should not endure...Although the Communists realize that they are living in an exceedingly dynamic world, they by no means surrender themselves to the onward sweep of the machine age and the general drift of civilization. On the contrary, they believe that the evolution of

human institutions, even in the modern era, is subject to some measure of control and that within limits society may be molded to their desire.[58]

Counts ended *The Soviet Challenge to America* with an explicit call to Americans not only to know more about the Soviet Union, but to use this knowledge to pursue purposeful change in their own society:

> This cultural revolution possesses a single mighty integrating principle—the building of a new society in which there will be neither rich nor poor, in which the mainspring of all industry will be social need rather than private profit, in which no man will be permitted to exploit another by reason of wealth or social position, in which the curse of Eden will be lifted forever from the soul of woman, in which a condition of essential equality will unite all races and nations into one brotherhood. Although the cultural applications of this principle often assume crude and exaggerated forms, as in the case of Proletcult and the censorship of art, it is nevertheless authentic and vital. There is consequently in the Soviet Union today a sensitiveness to the more fundamental human wrongs and a passion for social justice that simply cannot be matched in any other quarter of the globe. A devotion to the common good and a deep interest in the oppressed of all lands penetrate and color every aspect of the cultural life of the country. That the pursuit of the goal may often be blind and unintelligent during the current period of stress and experimentation is only to be expected. The school, the press, the theater, the cinema, and life generally in Russia are full of excesses and of imbecilities and of sound conceptions poorly executed. But back of it all, even the excesses and imbecilities, there stands a great and challenging ideal which the rest of the world cannot continue to ignore and which may in time serve to bring art, science, and philosophy into essential harmony. In the meantime, the leaders in American industry, politics, and thought, instead of dissipating their energies in the futile attempt to erect barriers against the spread of Communist doctrines, would do well to fashion an alternative program of equal boldness and honesty to discipline the energies and humanize the spirit of industrial civilization.[59]

This remarkable endorsement of Soviet education makes sense more as a response—an emotional and to some extent visceral response—to the crisis of Depression-era American schools than as an effort to investigate, understand, or explain the Five Year Plan. Soviet achievements were praised and exaggerated while shortcomings were excused or minimized in ways that allowed for specific commentaries on the current crisis in American schools and society. Counts was a devoted and informed student of Soviet schooling, yet he was an even more passionate advocate for the transformative potential of American schooling. The Depression confirmed his criticism of the limits of the traditional organization, materialist values, and individualist practices of American education at precisely the same time the Five Year Plan seemed to embody the collectivist ideals, rational structure, and transformative potential that Counts saw as the great unfulfilled promise of schooling.

The views of American observers of Soviet education in the 1930s have been dismissed as naive, idealist, or misguided.[60] As argued recently by David Engerman, however, this dismissal of intellectuals' fascination with Stalinist modernization ignores the underlying continuities in American views of Russia as well as the complexity of meaning embedded in these perceptions.[61] While these criticisms call necessary attention to both the extent of political partisanship and the limits of foreigners' perspective on the Soviet Union, a more interesting analytical question is to ask how the circumstances of economic crisis led American educators to look elsewhere for alternative visions of the purposes of education. The Depression caused many Americans to rethink schooling; Soviet planning seemed to offer a promising alternative that could address both the immediate crisis within classrooms and the broader relationship between school and society. The reality of Soviet educational expansion and the rhetoric of the Five Year Plan convinced many American educators that planning offered the potential for both quantitative and qualitative transformations of schooling. A closer look at the tensions involved in Soviet education suggests that the key issue was not the rationality of the plan but rather the process of mobilization. American educators embraced the discourse of planning, but they were really fascinated by the purpose, value, and significance assigned to education in the Soviet context. At a time when American schools seemed most stagnant, disengaged, and adrift, Soviet schools appeared especially dynamic, integrated, and purposeful. The "virtues of planning" were in fact the virtues of schools that would, in Counts' most famous expression from this era, dare to build a new social order.

In the decade after 1929, Counts and the other observers were initially disappointed by the narrow and utilitarian response of American schools to the Depression, but they were increasingly critical of the repressive character of Stalinist schools and society.[62] Yet the significance of the American view of Soviet educational planning remains the way that a crisis situation provoked an entirely new way of thinking that was openly and even enthusiastically comparative in approach.[63] While recognizing that American educators failed to see the real problems and limitations in Soviet education in the early 1930s, they deserve credit for recognizing how the promise of a new and better future was energizing the people of the Soviet Union and how this energy was manifested in the schools. By asking about the absence or suppression of such a commitment in American schools, these educators contributed to a broader shift in political culture that integrated aspects of social planning into strategies for dealing with the Great Depression. At a critical moment in the histories of two different systems, the ways that American observers looked at the Soviet Union provide a model of how a global perspective can broaden understanding of the problems and the promise of schooling in modern society.

Notes

1. George S. Counts, *The Soviet Challenge to America* (New York: John Day Company, 1931) pp. ix–x, 11–12.
2. Ibid, p. 304.
3. Ibid, pp. 298–299.
4. Ibid, pp. 329–330.
5. In his 1932 publication, *Dare the School Build a New Social Order*, Counts made an even more emphatic case for "a new vision of American destiny." In this text, however, Counts explicitly confined his text to the situation in the United States, relegating his views on international education to a footnote "because of the limitations of space." George S. Counts, *Dare the School Build a New Social Order?* (New York: Arno Press, 1969, Reprint of 1932 First Printing). For a discussion of how the "lessons" Counts derived from Soviet schooling were supposed to be applied by American educators, see David C. Engerman, *Modernization from the Other Shore. American Intellectuals and the Romance of Russian Development* (Cambridge: Harvard University Press, 2003) pp. 184–185.
6. Because this chapter focuses on the American responses to the Depression, it leaves out the influential studies by Scott Nearing, Lucy Wilson, Samuel Harper, John Dewey, and others published in the 1920s which focused primarily on pedagogical approaches. See discussion in Larry E. Holmes, "Western Perceptions of Soviet Education: 1918–1931," *The Educational Forum* Vol. 39 (November 1974) pp. 27–29. The extensive interest in the Soviet experiment shown by foreigners other than Americans, including both Europeans and their colonial subjects, lies beyond the scope of this chapter.
7. In an earlier article Larry Holmes discusses American educators' interest in Soviet schooling prior to the Depression, while his most recent study looks more specifically at Counts' observations of Soviet schools, with particular attention to his assessment of teaching styles and pupils' engagement. Holmes, "Western Perceptions of Soviet Education," pp. 27–32; idem, *Stalin's School. Moscow's Model School No. 25, 1931–1937* (Pittsburgh: University of Pittsburgh Press, 1999). Diane Ravitch looks in more detail at Counts and other progressives in the 1930s, although her focus is more on politics than planning. Diane Ravitch, *Left Back. A Century of Battles over School Reform* (New York: Touchstone, 2000) pp. 205–214, 234–236. In his article on how American perceptions of the Soviet Union shaped the pragmatism of New Deal policies, Lewis Feuer offers a brief discussion of educational planning. Lewis Feuer, "American Travelers to the Soviet Union 1917–32: The Formation of a Component of New Deal Ideology," *American Quarterly* Vol. 14, No. 2 (Summer 1962) pp. 119–149. David Engerman has recently published the most thorough and suggestive study of the American interest in Soviet industrialization. Engerman, *Modernization from the Other Shore.*
8. George S. Counts, "Education and the Five Year Plan of Soviet Russia," *Journal of Educational Sociology* Vol. 4, No. 1 (September 1930) p. 20.
9. George S. Counts, "Russians Educate through Activities," *The New York Times* July 19, 1931, III, p. 7. For a perceptive analysis of how Dewey's pragmatist

philosophy influenced the view of Stalinism as a "worthwhile and perhaps even essential" experiment in planned social transformation, see Engerman, *Modernization from the Other Shore*, pp. 182–184.

10. *Kul'turnoe stroitel'stvo SSSR* (Moscow: Gosizdat, 1940) pp. 38–39; E. Thomas Ewing, *The Teachers of Stalinism. Policy, Practice, and Power in Soviet Schools of the 1930s* (New York: Peter Lang Publishing, 2002) pp. 60–61.

11. Counts, *Soviet Challenge*, pp. 236, 281; Jerome Davis, "Education under Communism Contrasted with That under Capitalism," *Journal of Educational Sociology* Vol. 9, No. 3 (November 1935) p. 159.

12. Walter Duranty, "Soviet Introduces Compulsory Study," *The New York Times* November 9, 1930, p. 3.

13. Thomas Woody, *New Minds: New Men? The Emergence of the Soviet Citizen* (New York: The Macmillan Company, 1932) p. 475; Harry C. Krowl, "A Nation at School," in Jerome Davis, ed., *The New Russia between the First and Second Five Year Plans* (Freeport: Books for Libraries Press, 1933) p. 163.

14. George S. Counts, "Education in the U.S.S.R.," *The New Republic* (February 13, 1935) p. 9.

15. Counts, *Soviet Challenge*, pp. 303–304.

16. Ibid, pp. 64–65.

17. Krowl, "Nation at School," pp. 170–171.

18. Counts, *Soviet Challenge*, pp. 13–14.

19. Ibid, pp. 179–180.

20. Ibid, pp. 304–305.

21. Ibid, pp. 305–306.

22. Ibid, p. 306.

23. Ibid, p. 83.

24. Ewing, *Teachers of Stalinism*, pp. 58–59.

25. Gail Warshofsky Lapidus, "Educational Strategies and Cultural Revolution: The Politics of Soviet Development," in Sheila Fitzpatrick, ed., *Cultural Revolution in Russia* (Bloomington: Indiana University Press, 1978) pp. 92–93, 97.

26. Moshe Lewin, *Russian Peasants and Soviet Power. A Study of Collectivization* (New York: Norton, 1968) p. 457.

27. Stephen Kotkin, *Magnetic Mountain. Stalinism as a Civilization* (Berkeley: University of California Press, 1995) pp. 31–32.

28. Paul R. Gregory, *The Political Economy of Stalinism. Evidence from the Soviet Secret Archives* (Cambridge: Cambridge University Press, 2004) pp. 168–169.

29. Holland Hunter, "The New Tasks of Soviet Planning in the Thirties," in Padma Desai, ed., *Marxism, Central Planning, and the Soviet Economy* (Cambridge: MIT Press, 1983) pp. 173–197.

30. Robert C. Tucker, *Stalin in Power. Revolution from Above, 1929–1941* (New York: Norton, 1990).

31. Walter Duranty, "Gains in Education Recorded in Soviet," *The New York Times* August 15, 1931, p. 6.

32. Engerman, *Modernization from the Other Shore*.

33. Ewing, *Teachers of Stalinism*, pp. 17–52.

34. Lewis Feuer, "American Travelers to the Soviet Union," p. 143.

35. Counts, *Soviet Challenge*, p. 58.

36.   Ibid, p. 62; Engerman, *Modernization from the Other Shore*, pp. 182–183.
37.   R. W. Davies, *The Soviet Economy in Turmoil, 1929–1930* (Cambridge: Cambridge University Press, 1989) pp. 139, 177, 208–214.
38.   Duranty, "Gains in Education Recorded in Soviet," p. 3.
39.   Counts, *Soviet Challenge*, p. 318.
40.   Counts, "Education in the U.S.S.R.," p. 9.
41.   The broader question of American perceptions of indoctrination, ideology, and repression in Soviet education—which also involved a strong comparative element—remains beyond the scope of this chapter. These questions are discussed briefly in Holmes, "Western Perceptions of Soviet Education," pp. 27–32; idem, *Stalin's School*, pp. 169–170; Ravitch, *Left Back*, pp. 212–214. See also the perceptive discussion of why American intellectuals' assumptions about Russian national character led them to discount the possibility that Soviet modernization could ever be democratic in Engerman, *Modernization from the Other Shore*, pp. 157–158, 163–166, 177–178.
42.   Feuer, "American Travelers to the Soviet Union," p. 121; Ravitch, *Left Back* pp. 202–204; Holmes, "Western Perceptions of Soviet Education," pp. 121, 136, 144; Engerman, *Modernization from the Other Shore*, pp. 4–6, 154–193.
43.   Charles A. Beard, "A 'Five Year Plan' for America," in idem, ed., *America Faces the Future* (Boston: Houghton Mifflin Company, 1932) pp. 119–120.
44.   Lewis Mumford, "Foreword," in Findlay MacKenzie, ed., *Planned Society. Yesterday, Today, Tomorrow* (New York: Prentice Hall, 1937) pp. vi–vii.
45.   Feuer, "American Travelers to the Soviet Union," p. 144.
46.   Findlay MacKenzie, "Preface," in idem, ed., *Planned Society. Yesterday, Today, Tomorrow* (New York: Prentice Hall, 1937) p. 877.
47.   Walter Duranty, "Bolshevik Policy Winning Respect," *The New York Times* January 31, 1932, p. 4.
48.   John A. Garraty, *The Great Depression* (New York: Harcourt Brace Jovanovich, 1986) pp. 144–145.
49.   Stuart Chase, *A New Deal* (New York: The Macmillan Company, 1932) p. 252. Chase's remark is cited in Engerman, *Modernization from the Other Shore*, p. 165.
50.   Feuer, "American Travelers to the Soviet Union," p. 136.
51.   Engerman, *Modernization from the Other Shore*, pp. 1–5, 154.
52.   Francis J. Brown, "Social Planning Through Education," *American Sociological Review* Vol. 1, No. 6 (December 1936) p. 934.
53.   Ibid, pp. 941–942.
54.   Engerman, *Modernization from the Other Shore*, pp. 177–183.
55.   Counts, "Education and the Five Year Plan of Soviet Russia," p. 29.
56.   Counts, *Soviet Challenge*, pp. 329–332.
57.   Counts, "Russians Educate through Activities," p. 7.
58.   Counts, *Soviet Challenge*, pp. 332–335.
59.   Ibid, pp. 338–339.
60.   William. C. Bagley, "The Soviets Proceed to the Liquidation of American Educational Theory," *School and Society* Vol. 37, No. 942 (January 14, 1933) pp. 62–63; Dmitri von Mohrenschildt, "American Intelligentsia and Russia of the

N.E.P," *Russian Review* vol. 6, no. 2 (Spring 1947) p. 66; Ravitch, *Left Back*, pp. 211–215, 234.

61. Engerman, *Modernization from the Other Shore*, pp. 158, 192.
62. Ibid, pp. 185–186; Ravitch, *Left Back*, pp. 235–237; Feuer, "American Travelers to the Soviet Union," pp. 148–149.
63. This shift also reflected the growing influence of "universalist" interpretation of Soviet modernization, which rejected earlier assumptions of cultural difference in favor of assumptions about common paths to a rational, industrial, and cosmopolitan future society. For this interpretation, see Engerman, *Modernization from the Other Shore*.

Chapter Three

Civilization: Its Rise and Fall in New Deal School Murals

Michele Cohen

In 1938, James Michael Newell completed the *Evolution of Western Civilization* for the library of Evander Childs High School, the same year this noted Bronx school celebrated its twenty-fifth anniversary. Although not an educator himself, Newell grasped the core of Evander's educational mission, creating a mural that promoted the same democratic, progressive values informing Evander's curriculum. The *Evolution of Western Civilization* suggests that society's advancement as a whole depends on the labor and social cooperation of individuals. It is a pictorial counterpart to the principal's belief "that education in a free democracy demands the highest possible development of each individual for happy and efficient collaboration in a progressively changing society."[1] In his grand epic, Newell's voice meshed seamlessly with the principal's own call to teachers and students.

Significantly, Newell was one of many New Deal artists to examine the idea of civilization for New York City public school murals.[2] Approximately fourteen of the fifty murals commissioned for the public schools during the 1930s reveal a preoccupation with change, progress and civilization.[3] Other examples include *Spirit of Modern Civilization*, *World Progress in Written and Printed Arts*, *Evolution of Music*, and *Major Influences in Civilization*. All of these wall paintings can be found in high schools, which were larger buildings with ample lobbies, auditoriums, and libraries where artists had greater liberty to paint more ambitious subjects and extensive cycles. The group as a whole can be divided into two primary subject areas: murals about the history of civilization for academic high schools and murals chronicling the industrial process of specific industries for vocational high schools, a dichotomy which reflected the educational divisions inherent in the public school system of the 1930s.[4]

These "History of Civilization" murals came and went with the Great Depression. They mark a unique moment when it was permissible for artists to tackle enormous questions in an effort to make sense of the uncertainty of the 1930s and to provide students with a hopeful outlook for the future. Naturally, the question emerges why this theme was so prevalent at this time and why artists chose it for educational murals? Several reasons are plausible: "civilization" was an ideological construct preoccupying historians, scientists, and educators as evidenced in numerous publications and innovative curricula issued in the 1920s and 1930s; the rise of fascism in Germany, Italy, and Japan were making it increasingly evident that America would have to become a world player; and lastly, by recognizing and celebrating the art, music, and culture of other nations, "civilization," artists were also validating a more inclusive viewpoint, termed "pluralism" in the 1930s and "multiculturalism" today.

This chapter will provide an overview of these murals in New York City schools and a close reading of Newell's fresco. It will also contextualize them in the intellectual climate of their time, linking them to the writings of the "new historians," notably Charles and Mary Beard, and developments in the social studies curriculum of the 1930s. As a group, the murals present a complex world view, arguing for the interdependence of historical epochs and peoples across the globe, but at the same time, the murals situate America at the apex of civilization. They prompt students to consider how their actions will affect not just the future of America, but the world.

Murals to Educate

In contrast to the transient nature of audiences for post office or hospital murals, the audience for school murals was relatively constant. Artists and New Deal program administrators understood that murals commissioned for schools would become part of a child's education for several years and that students would see murals with an increasing awareness as they, themselves, matured. There was great potential for children to be affected on many levels.

In shifting their gaze from post office walls to school walls, muralists adapted aspects of the American Scene, which characterized so many Works Project Administration (WPA) murals, to a school context. Like murals in other public places, school murals also portray the dignified worker, the common person engaged in ordinary activities, which in school images frequently included children, and recognizable landmarks, traits that mark history of civilization murals as well. Since murals commissioned for schools were intended to be didactic, the lack of totally abstract images is not surprising.

In view of the broader democratic aims of the WPA/Federal Arts Project (FAP) and the desire to use murals as an educational tool, program administrators involved principals and other Board of Education personnel in the process of commissioning murals for schools. WPA/FAP officials were careful not to foist art on an unknowing public: they wanted to cultivate an audience and clientele for mural projects. By having institutions initiate requests and pay for materials, the WPA/FAP hoped they would become invested in the program.[5] Furthering that goal, artists developed subjects in consultation with principals and teachers. The Board of Education even issued a circular to principals encouraging them to solicit ideas from students, but there is no real evidence that student opinions were taken into account. Superintendent of Schools William O'Shea wrote:

> This Committee suggests as a valuable educational activity the cooperation of the pupils in the selection of themes for the preliminary studies. Such participation should awaken interest in local history and geography as well as in art appreciation, and a spirit of community and school pride. It is, therefore, requested that principals of schools that may be selected for such works, endeavor through the medium of appropriate lessons, exercises or contests, to secure pupil cooperation in suggesting the motifs or themes for the proposed paintings.[6]

Principals, however, did exercise substantial control. Mural supervisor Burgoyne Diller recollected that there was "quite a bit of consultation between the artist and the principal before it [the design] started out on that long siege of approvals." In most cases the principals were cooperative, seeking input from teachers and going to "great lengths to aid in the research because in some subjects it was rather difficult."[7] This was especially true of Maxwell Starr's mural for Brooklyn Technical High School, where the artist portrayed famous scientists and their contributions. Starr's theme reflected the school's specialized curriculum and appealed to a particular student body, underscoring the commitment of New Deal artists to connect with their public.

Artists also reached beyond the school community for inspiration. For those painters engaged in weaving vast panoramas about the birth and development of civilization, the pictures themselves suggest that WPA/FAP muralists were attuned to the theoretical concerns of the day. In light of the Depression and the threat of world war on the horizon, it is not surprising that Americans of the 1930s struggled to comprehend from whence they came and whither they were going. It was as if America had come of age and was destined to take her place among the great nations of the world, and an investigation of civilization legitimized America's position at the summit of this grand evolution. At the very least, with the spread of totalitarianism in Europe, America felt justified in her self-appointed role as the guardian of Western civilization.

In the 1920s and 1930s American scholars fixated on the notion of civilization as a key to understanding American culture. Historians Charles and Mary Beard asserted: "The view of the world, of life and its surrounding universe, called the idea of civilization, was unmistakably a center of interest in America as the middle of the 20th century drew near."[8] In *Century of Progress*, a collection of essays published in 1933 in conjunction with the Century of Progress exposition in Chicago, Beard wrote:

> [the] concept of progress is one of the most profound and germinal ideas at work in the modern age....Briefly defined, it implies that mankind, by making use of science and invention can progressively emancipate itself from plagues, famines, and social disasters, and subjugate the materials and forces of the earth to the purposes of the good life—here and now.[9]

Beard's idea of progress was predicated on the belief that there will be continued improvement for all humankind and he idealized the potential of technology. He identified three factors as essential to the idea of progress: "respect for industry and labor, a preoccupation with secular enterprise, and a spirit of experimentation and invention."[10] These keys to progress are the hallmarks of New Deal school murals portraying the history of civilization.

Espousing beliefs similar to Beard's, a group of New York City engineers gathered to evaluate the impact of technology on civilization. This interchange fueled the publication edited by Beard entitled *Toward Civilization*,[11] perhaps the conceptual blueprint for Maxwell Starr's mural, *The History of Mankind In Terms of Mental and Physical Labor* at Brooklyn Technical High School. In this anthology, professionals in industry, architecture and the arts contributed papers with such titles as "The New Age and the New Man, Science Lights the Torch, The Spirit of Invention in an Industrial Civilization, Power, Transportation, Communication, Education and the New Age, Machine Industry and Idealism, and Spirit and Culture under the Machine." With striking parallels to the subjects examined in *Toward*

Civilization, Starr's initial plan for this new Brooklyn high school proposed to explore themes of power, communication, and transportation in three mural cycles. Eventually he settled on "The History of Mankind in Terms of Mental and Physical Labor" for the primary mural in the main lobby.[12]

In his completed mural, Starr acknowledges the educational mission of the school and presents history through the lens of invention and the evolution of scientific developments. Starr explained he began with primitive man working his way "up the line to Steinmetz[13] with panels for the Egyptians, the Greeks, Italians and physicists, chemists and biologists of all nations."[14] The mural is an illustrated encyclopedia of scientific luminaries coupled with the application of their concepts. [Figure 1] The story begins in the central image of "the Thinker," branches left and right, and culminates in the opposite wall with the Riveraesque clenched hands, symbolizing the union of mind and body. Starr underscores his artistic intentions by running this inscription, reminiscent of Beard's clarion call, along the lower edge:

THUS BY THE UNION OF MIND & MATTER MAN LEARNS TO HARNESS THE NATURAL FORCES/BECOMES MASTER OF THE MACHINE AND WITH FREEDOM HE HOLDS WITHIN HIS HANDS POWER OVER HIS DESTINY/THE PROGRESS OF MAN'S CREATIVE MIND IS A RECORD OF EVOLUTIONARY CHANGE BY MEANS OF OBSERVATION ANALYSIS & SYNTHESIS TOWARDS A MORE ENLIGHTENED CIVILIZATION TRIUMPHANT OVER IGNORANCE & SUPERSTITION.

Just as Starr equated civilization with science and technology, other artists qualified civilization in terms of art or music. For Jean Charlot, civilization meant the sum of artistic achievement as seen in his *The Art Contribution to Civilization of All Nations and Countries*, completed in 1936 for what was then Straubenmuller Textile High School, now Bayard Rustin High School for the Humanities. The mural covers the same time period as Starr's, but branches out into the art of Asia, Persia, and India as well as documenting major periods of Western art.

For Lucienne Bloch, another muralist of this era, music was the common thread that linked people across continents and centuries. Painted in rich earth tones, her fresco for George Washington High School conveys Bloch's vision of music as a unifying force. Panels represent African, Asian, European, and American musical forms and art, each a mélange of instruments, patterns and figures engaged in music and dance. Carefully researched, the mural contains many recognizable details such as Persian miniatures, Turkish rugs, even a shofar, constituting what Bloch describes as a "sort of a travelogue."[15] Wedged between Balinese cymbals and a medieval harp, stands the Modern Chorus, a multi-racial ensemble with voices uplifted in song, positively affirming ethnic diversity and racial harmony. [Figure 2]

For the grand auditorium at Brooklyn's Tilden High School, Abraham Lishinsky created forty-two panels illustrating *Major Influences in Civilization* (begun 1937) encompassing such diverse subjects as agriculture, science, art, political philosophy, and technology. Using all available wall space, Lishinsky placed panels in opposition to one another to emphasize dichotomies, for example, contrasting democracy with theocracy on either side of the auditorium stage.

Not only did the work of the "new historians" affect the thinking of artists, scientists, and specialists, their publications had tremendous impact on the work of progressive educators. Ideas about the fluidity of history and the importance of a global interdisciplinary approach permeated the comprehensive K–12 social studies curriculum developed by Harold Rugg, who began formulating his ideas in the 1920s. By the 1930s, he had produced a series of textbooks that were in widespread use in American classrooms.[16]

Two central viewpoints shaped Rugg's work: he sought to integrate history, civics, and geography into a unified study, and he argued that the material should be presented as a way to solve a pressing social problem, not just as factual information. Rugg aimed "to bring forth on this continent—in some form of co-operative commonwealth—the civilization of abundance, democratic behaviour, and integrity of expression and of appreciation, which is not potentially available."[17] In designing murals which stressed continuity across epochs and oceans and emphasized progress through social cooperation and technological advancement, artists like Starr, Charlot and Bloch articulated in paint what historians and educators formulated in writing. The murals posit an optimistic world view despite the realities of Depression-era hardships and uncertainty. By celebrating the accomplishments of the human race they encourage students to work hard toward an inevitably better future.

Newell's *Evolution of Western Civilization*

Of all the murals on the history of civilization in the New York City public schools, James Michael Newell's *Evolution of Western Civilization* at Evander Childs High School in the Bronx is the best example of a visual equivalent to Beard's writings and Rugg's innovations in the social studies curriculum. With this ambitious fresco, Newell joined the national discourse on the meaning of civilization, celebrating technology and America's role as inheritor and protector of Western culture. When Newell began the project in 1935, largely at the urging of Evander's art teacher, Anne Bebarfald, the principal had requested a mural portraying the history of the Bronx. This theme was more in keeping with the themes previously outlined by Schools Superintendents. Newell complied, but he also developed sketches for this broader historical epic and ultimately convinced school authorities that this was a better subject.[18]

Interestingly enough, the mural would grace the walls of a library that housed the very books that helped inspire it. According to the high school's student newspaper, Evander acquired Beard's *Whither Mankind: A Panorama of Modern Civilization,* in 1934 along with *America Faces the Future,* also by Beard. Other books on similar themes in Evander's library at the time were *A New Deal* by Stuart Chase, *Epic of America* by J. T. Adams, and *Rise of the Common Man* by C. R. Fish.[19] In designing his mural, Newell seems to have taken his cue from Beard's 1928 anthology, *Whither Mankind,* a compendium of writings based on an international symposium that included contributions from American, Chinese, German, and British writers and touched on Eastern and Western philosophies, all historical periods, and all areas of human endeavor.

Newell initially estimated one year to paint the mural, which was proposed as a true fresco. Considering he created designs to cover 1,400 square feet, basically all available wall space in the main room of the library, it is not surprising that it actually took three and one half years to complete.[20] Among Newell's numerous assistants on the project were Otto Botto, Jacob Van Aalte, Gerhard Duhmert, and Mardy Allen. They helped with research, preparation of the plaster wall, transfer of the cartoon, and execution of the mural.

The process of making a fresco was labor intensive. Newell's mural is one of thirteen frescoes out of 200 WPA murals painted in New York City.[21] In creating the work, Newell had to remove the finish layer of the painted wall and replace it with a layer of rough plaster before he could outline the major areas in sinopia, the red under drawing of the mural. When he began painting, an assistant had to prepare a small area with a thin finish coat of plaster, which Newell then covered in a single session before it dried. Although fresco painting was arduous, it suited two aims of WPA administrators: it was labor intensive, providing employment for more people, and it had an educational potential. In fact, the WPA made a film about fresco painting, using Newell's mural as the case study. And Newell himself exploited the medium's educational qualities by talking to students about the process as he painted and creating an exhibition on the history and technique of fresco for the library at Evander.

Newell was among the minority of WPA artists who had training in fresco and prior experience painting murals. He was born in Pittsburgh, Pennsylvania in 1900. After serving in World War I, he studied in New York at the National Academy of Design and the Art Student's League, followed in 1927 by a trip to Paris, where he attended the Académie Julian and École des Beaux Arts. In 1928, Newell won the Fountainbleau Prize, enabling him to travel to Italy where he studied frescoes in Rome, Naples and Florence. Shortly before his commission at Evander Childs, he completed a mural cycle for the Potomac Electric Power Company in Washington, D.C. During the period of Roosevelt's administration he was a favorite artist and several of his paintings decorated the White House.[22]

Given Newell's knowledge of the grand tradition of European frescoes and his long-term preoccupation with the subject of civilization,[23] he wanted to move beyond the creation of textbook illustrations of various epochs. His approach was more like Rugg's, searching for the underlying principles, the broad generalizations—the big picture. In an artist's statement published in 1938, Newell offered this explanation of his intentions: "I have tried to interpret in pictorial symbols the important historical forces that determined the evolution of western civilization." In his mural, in keeping with Beard's interpretation of civilization, rational science replaces superstition and technology is the key to a better way of life. In developing his historical panorama, Newell took liberties, conflating places, cultures, and time periods. He also quoted various artistic sources, particularly Giotto and Diego Rivera, and synthesized a style indebted to these masters of fresco art.

Newell wanted to capture in a visual language the forces that have shaped western civilization: humankind's basic need of sustenance and shelter, human curiosity, and the desire for communal life resulting in the formulation of a common set of laws. Summing up this approach, Newell later provided this description of the *Evolution of Civilization*:

> the murals…show primitive man building his society, youth migrating from it to new lands, the meeting and mingling of tribes, the clashing of eastern culture and scientific knowledge with western force, building knowledge and ideas of law and democracy.

The dark ages of plague are shown next, with the church alone perpetuating knowledge. Then come the beginnings of scientific experiment and the awakening of the people to nature, the force of which destroys their bondage and leads to the great flowering of the Renaissance. The exploration which follows founded a new country to which all nations and all time have contributed, and which has developed into a varied, dynamic, and powerful civilization.[24]

Throughout the cycle, Newell repeats the motifs of migrating figures, the act of writing and by association the dissemination of knowledge, and cultivation of the earth. The progression follows the natural architectural divisions of the walls and the composition of the panels grows in complexity, particularly when Newell reaches modern America. In this extensive panel which bridges several doors, Newell fractures the space and shows various but concurrent activities, approximating the complexity of modern, industrial life.

In an unconventional fashion, the cycle reads from right to left, perhaps because Newell wanted to devote several panels to America and could only accomplish that by ordering them in this way. He begins by reinventing Prometheus seen in the seminal figure on the far right, who seizes a bolt of lightning in one hand while cradling fire in the other. Stone Age tools above the doors frame the central panel, featuring a primitive, nameless, agricultural society, whether Babylonian, Egyptian or Peruvian. Figures are harvesting wheat and corn, historically an impossible combination, which suggests the synthesis of the new and old worlds. Newell also shows the building of protective shelters and the codification of laws, represented by the figure chiseling a tablet next to another figure pointing skyward, perhaps an allusion to the Babylonian code of Hammaurabi. (Figure 3) The repetition of figures in similar poses, their facial characteristics and generalized anatomy, and the very subject of an agrarian society, recall

Rivera's depictions of Mexico's Aztec past in such murals as the *History of Mexico* (1929) in the National Palace in Mexico City. Out of this basic social order, civilization evolves, moving to the next phase through the migration of its youth.

The next panel combines elements from several different periods and locales. Directing the viewer's eye toward the center is the figure of Galileo pointing toward the rings of Saturn and an astronomical sphere. Also in this panel is a group of hooded warriors with spears, perhaps representing the western movement of nomadic tribes from the east; an artist chiseling a sculpture; a figure bent over a map showing outlines of the silk trade, juxtaposed with two sheaves of wheat, a link to the first panel and a reference to the exchange of goods. A scribe refines written language, moving from the pictographs of the previous panel to a more recognizable, although generalized alphabet. The message of the panel is that the growth of science, trade, and art pushed civilization forward.

Next comes the panel partially inspired by Giotto's *Lamentation*. (Figure 4) A sick man replaces the body of the dead Christ. Prostrate figures praying for his health shield him from the aggressive specter of death.[25] Other figures have already succumbed to the ravages of the plague. The panel's composition and articulation of the figures with their elongated bodies and small heads bear a striking resemblance to Giotto's figurative style. Like Giotto's figures, Newell's make dramatic gestures but they lack the psychological intensity of the proto-Renaissance master.

Although Newell described the next panel as the "awakening of the people to nature," suggesting a strong secular orientation, the image of the head with flowing hair against a brilliant sun evokes Christ; however the Riveraesque torch and fist give it a militant nuance. In the following panel, reason destroys superstition, portrayed as a devilish monster filled with a spring, and the printing press disseminates knowledge. This image, together with the preceding panel, suggests that exploration of the natural world, the basis of scientific inquiry, supports the destruction of superstition. Newell painted this panel last, and added this inscription: "In the years 1937 and 1938 these murals were designed and executed by James Michael Newell...under the Federal Art Project sponsored by the United States government."[26]

Jumping several centuries and across the Atlantic, the next panel shows European explorers—Norsemen, Spaniards, the Dutch and the

English—arriving in the New World, leading to the pioneer migration westward and the vanquishing of the Native American, represented as a defeated Indian brave modeled on the classical sculpture of the *Dying Gaul* (ca. 240 B.C.E.) to the lower left. One explorer holds the Masonic tablets encoded with numbers 1–10. His fingers point to 3 and 8, suggesting the mural's completion date and/or the 8th commandment "Thou Shall Not Steal," Newell's veiled commentary on the white man's arrival in the New World.

Following the discovery of the New World, *The Evolution of Western Civilization* culminates in a panorama of 1930s America showing three primary geographic areas: the west—represented by cattle ranchers and the railroad; the south—represented by miners and black sharecroppers picking cotton [Figure 5]; and the northeast—represented by an electrical generator, steel workers, surgeons, and a chemist. Also depicted is American justice in the form of a contemporary jury and the new one hundred-inch Mount Palomar telescope, another symbol of cutting edge technology. Here Newell celebrates humankind's mastery of nature, industrial growth, and scientific progress.

The extensive use of a pictorial language based on real life activities drew upon the new standard vocabulary of New Deal murals. The murals represented the new symbols of the 1930s: construction workers with pneumatic drills, steel workers riveting, surgeons gathered around a patient on the operating table, a chemist, pioneers, Indians bundling sheaves of wheat and corn, and the superstition of the Middle Ages vanquished by modern science.[27] These images are in stark contrast to the allegorical figures and portraits of famous Americans employed in earlier murals. In New Deal murals, where history is often synonymous with social history, the everyday actions of ordinary people take on special significance.

Newell's mural culminates with the last two lines from Walt Whitman's "With Antecedents" from *Leaves of Grass* (1891):

> And that where I am or you are this present day, there is the center of all days, all races. And there is the meaning to us of all that has ever come of races and days, or ever will come.[28]

The quote implies that history is fluid and that peoples across the globe are interrelated. It is also Newell's way of dating the mural, of recognizing that his mural is an interpretation of history in the year

1938. Whitman's words pictured against an open book resting in dark-skinned hands broken free of shackles suggests freedom and knowledge for all. This element, coupled with the imagery of the mural, conveys an optimistic view of civilization's progress and America's role in its evolution.

Newell was being fashionable in quoting Whitman, viewed as the quintessential American poet for the working man and symbol of democracy at a time when fascism was on the rise in Europe. Whitman appears in several murals of the 1930s, including Ben Shahn's *America at Work* (1939) at the Bronx post office and the *History of the Needlecraft Industries* by Ernest Fiene at the High School of Fashion Industries in Manhattan.[29] Thus Whitman's poem in its entirety can also be seen as a philosophical treatise for Newell's mural. Whitman makes references to "Egypt, India, Phenicia *(sic)*, Greece and Rome," to a range of human endeavors such as "maritime ventures, laws, artisanship, wars and journeys," to the "crusader" and the "monk." He evokes the solar system and former kingdoms. Whitman writes, "I respect Assyria, China, Teutonia, and the Hebrews, I adopt each theory, myth, god, and demi-god..." Whitman speaks of the contradictory forces of "materialism" and "spiritualism" and how America is the inheritor of all those things, and at the center stands the individual.

One would think, given Newell's progressive stance and effort to be inclusive, the mural would be well received. It was in its time. It won top honors in the Architectural League's fiftieth Annual exhibition in 1936. It was included in the Museum of Modern Art's New Horizons show featuring art commissioned under the Federal Art Project. Two films were made about it: *The Making of a Fresco*, previously mentioned, and a short clip made by Paramount News documenting WPA art projects throughout the country. Critics praised it. Edith Halpert, an assistant to Diller, offered this evaluation:

> [T]he Newell mural is really extraordinary. After careful consideration I sincerely think that it is superior to any of the American murals I have seen... As a young person he has the advantage of a fresh vision, but added to that Newell understands and handles the medium with real maturity. This fresco should raise the standard of mural painting in America to a high degree.

First Lady Eleanor Roosevelt herself and Mayor Fiorello LaGuardia were invited to its unveiling on November 9, 1938, thus providing further evidence of its contemporary significance.[30]

However, by the late 1960s, the mural became a target of student unrest and parts of it were severely defaced. Sensitized by the civil rights movement, African-American students did not view the black sharecroppers picking cotton as emblematic of the south, but as a stereotype, a negative image of African-Americans reminiscent of slavery. Viewers did not perceive the men on horses as western cowboys but as overseers of the black workers picking cotton. Although Newell had intended this panel to be a panorama of America, within three decades after the mural was completed, it struck a discordant chord. By showing people of color and quoting Whitman, Newell had wanted to be inclusive. Ironically, in the context of the civil rights movement, these references took on other meanings and students objected to the very images Newell had included to broaden the mural's appeal. The school ended the dispute by erecting a curtain in front of the panel depicting the cotton pickers. The curtain has since been removed and the intact mural is on view, having been conserved in 1998.[31]

Conclusion

In evaluating school murals, critics of the 1930s were quick to judge artworks according to their educational potential. Of the pictorial maps being painted at Julia Richmond High School under the supervision of Ben Knotts and Guy Maccoy, *New York Times* critic Edward Alden Jewell noted, "The educational value of these handsome panels ought to prove considerable, and the work is being accomplished with painstaking and distinguished artistry." Jewell also praised Eric Mose and Burgoyne Diller for their mural, *Abstraction of the Machine Age*, at Samuel Gompers High School:

> ...these murals dramatize energy, as harnessed and transmitted into power by the genius of man. The well integrated design is intelligently, imaginatively and never egregiously abstract in its use of symbols. Here is a mural that, besides serving the purpose of decoration, may be called quite as "functional" as a class-room blackboard.[32]

Art Commission painter member, the muralist Ernest Peixotto, also remarked upon the educational value of WPA/FAP school murals as did Brooklyn Technical principal, Albert L. Colston, who de-

clared that Starr's encyclopedic history of science was "a great educational factor with our student body."[33]

From all accounts, students and faculty also embraced Newell's
mural at the time it was painted. On several occasions during the
course of its creation, students interviewed Newell and provided
lengthy descriptions of the project in the student newspaper. There
was a concerted effort to understand the mural's imagery, and students aptly made the connection between Newell's mural, Whitman's
poem and the advancement of civilization as a metaphor for the advancement of education.[34] The school's celebration of the completed
mural coincided with the twenty-fifth anniversary of Evander's
founding and the mural was featured in the jubilee anniversary edition of *The Bridge*. The school also marked that occasion with a choral
presentation dedicating the future to youth, declaring that youth
"must now uproot the powers of evil" and continue the "interrupted
march to a higher civilization," articulating in words what Newell
communicated in paint.

The New Deal art programs gave rise to the most ambitious mural
cycles ever painted in American public schools. Labor was cheap, resulting in far more painted square footage than could be commissioned today. Paralleling the trend for physical expansiveness, artists
tackled sweeping epic histories, encompassing centuries and all parts
of the globe. New Deal school murals chronicling the history of civilization added a new chapter to suitable subjects for school murals and
marked a pervasive cultural phenomenon. Like their counterparts in
the social sciences and education, muralists promoted a global approach to understanding history and contemporary society. The collection of murals in the New York City public schools put a face on
the dialogue taking place in print, presenting students with ideas and
viewpoints as they were taking hold in intellectual circles and the
curriculum itself.

Figure 1: *The History of Mankind in Terms of Mental and Physical Labor*, Maxwell Starr, artist, located at Brooklyn Technical High School (1934–41). All images courtesy of New York City Department of Education.

Figure 2: *Evolution of Music.* Lucienne Bloch, artist, located at George Washington High School, Manhattan (1936).

Figure 3: *Evolution of Western Civilization*, James Michael Newell, artist, located at Evander Childs High School, Bronx (1935–38).

Figure 4: *Evolution of Western Civilization*, James Michael Newell, artist, located at Evander Childs High School, Bronx (1935–38).

Figure 5: *Evolution of Western Civilization,* James Michael Newell, artist, located at Evander Childs High School, Bronx (1935–38).

80 Cohen

Notes

1. Foreword by Hymen Alpern, in "The First 25 Years," 1913–1938 Silver Anniversary edition of *The Bridge,* Evander Childs High School, p. 5.
2. Described by the Federal Art Project as representing "epic themes of the rise of civilization," these murals are more common in New York City than in any other region of New York State. See "WPA Muralists Paint for the Public Schools," press release, February 9, 1939, RG 69, box 75, p. 1, quoted in Marlene Park and Gerald E. Markowitz, *New Deal for Art; The Government Art Projects of the 1930s with Examples from New York City & State.* (Hamilton, N.Y.: Gallery Association of New York State, 1977) p. 46.
3. Of the fifty or so murals painted for all school types, about fourteen portray the development of civilization, nine depict industrial production, six focus on an aspect of local history, five portray juvenile activities, three illustrate literature, and five are on miscellaneous themes.
4. For a discussion of this aspect of school murals, see Park and Markowitz, *New Deal for Art,* p. 46. For an analysis of subject differences between New York City and New York State murals, see Marlene Park, "City and Country in the 1930s: A Study of New Deal Murals in New York," *Art Journal* Vol. 39 (Fall 1979) pp. 37–47. Park convincingly shows that murals painted for city schools and other types of municipal institutions explored dynamic themes of national and international import while murals for state sites focused on local history and industry.
5. "The cost of the materials which the sponsoring institution paid was usually about $1–2 per square foot for WPA/FAP murals." See Park and Markowitz, *New Deal for Art,* p. 34. For example, James Michael Newell's 1,200 square-foot *Evolution of Western Civilization* at Evander Childs High School cost the school a mere $100.00 for materials. See Exhibition File 1543, Art Commission of the City of New York.
6. Special Circular No. 21, 1933–1934, IV A.I.C., Circular Special 1933–1934, Box #31, Municipal Archives, City of New York.
7. Interview with Burgoyne Diller conducted by Harlan Phillips, October 2, 1964, Burgoyne Diller Papers, transcript, p. 24, Archives of American Art.
8. Charles A. Beard and Mary R. Beard, *The American Spirit: A Study of the Idea of Civilization in the United States* (New York: Collier Books, 1942) p. 21. For an excellent discussion of how civilization monopolized the interest of intellectuals, politicians, and the general public, see Chapter 2, "Civilization-Center of Interest," pp. 19–62. *The American Spirit: A Study of the Idea of Civilization in the United States* is the fourth volume in the series. The other volumes are *The Agricultural Era, The Industrial Era,* and *America in Midpassage.* These constitute *The Rise of American Civilization.*
9. Charles A. Beard, ed., *A Century of Progress* (New York and London: Harper & Brothers, 1933) p. 3.
10. Ibid., p. 11.
11. Charles A. Beard, ed., *Toward Civilization* (New York: Longmans, 1930).

12.   Gregory William Frux, "The History of Mankind in Terms of Mental and Physical Labor," website for Brooklyn Technical High School Alumni Association, www.bthsalum.org/mural.htm, accessed March 2004.

13.   Charles Proteus Steinmetz (1865–1923) was an electrical engineer who developed theories on alternating current.

14.   "History of Science to be Shown in Huge High School Murals," *News* December 23, 1934, Scrapbooks, vol. VI, 204, Art Commission of the City of New York.

15.   Interview with Lucienne Bloch, August 11, 1964, conducted by Mary McChesney, Archives of American Art, 63.

16.   See Elmer A. Winters, "Man and His Changing Society: The Textbooks of Harold Rugg," *History of Education Quarterly* Vol. 7, No. 4 (Winter 1967) pp. 493–514.

17.   Harold Rugg, "Curriculum-Design in the Social Sciences: What I Believe," in James A. Michener, ed., *The Future of Social Studies: Proposals for an Experimental Social-Studies Curriculum* (Cambridge: The National Council for the Social Studies, 1939) p. 141.

18.   Several articles in Evander's school newspaper provide details about Newell and this commission not found elsewhere. See "Colorful Murals in Library Portray Panorama of Occidental Civilization," *Evander News*, September 25, 1935, 2; "New Mural Shows the Rise of Man," *Evander News*, October 7, 1936, 1. For the best account by the artist, see James Michael Newell, "The Evolution of Western Civilization," in Francis V. O'Connor, ed., *Art for the Millions* (Greenwich: New York Graphic Society, 1973) pp. 60–62.

19.   See *The Evander News*, April 18, 1934, p. 1.

20.   The Art Commission gave the mural preliminary approval on July 9, 1935 and final approval, three and half years later on December 13, 1938. The school hosted the dedication of the mural on November 9, 1938.

21.   See Greta Berman, *The Lost Years: Mural Painting in New York City Under the WPA Federal Art Project, 1935–1943.* (New York and London: Garland Publishing, Inc., 1978) p. 45. In the New York City public schools, true frescoes (meaning painted on wet plaster) are Monty Lewis' *History of the Cotton Industry* at Sarah J. Hale High School. and Lucienne Bloch's *Evolution of Music* at George Washington High School.

22.   Several new websites include biographical information on Newell. See Bronx Public Art at bronxart.lehman.cuny.edu/pa/biography.htm, and http://newdeal.feri.org/echs/. Both sites were accessed January 2006.

23.   "Colorful Murals," p. 2.

24.   Newell, "The Evolution of Western Civilization," p. 62.

25.   Ernest Fiene employs a similar figure to portray Greed in his 1938 mural entitled *History of the Needlecraft Industry* at High School of Fashion Industries, Manhattan.

26.   In a photo of the mural in an Evander Yearbook for 1937, this is the only wall that is blank.

27.   See Berman, who notes that similar subjects are depicted in murals by Laning, Refregier, Guston, Brooks, Mose, Crimi, Palmer, Alston, and Penney. Berman, *The Lost Years*, p. 132.

28.   Quoted here from Walt Whitman, *Leaves of Grass* (New York: Penguin Put-
        nam Inc., 2000; a Signet Classic reprint of the 1892 edition) pp. 205–207.

29.   Coupled with these pictorial venerations, several studies on Whitman were
        published during the 1930s, including *Whitman* by Edgar Lee Masters, *Walt
        Whitman and the Springs of Courage* by Haniel Long, *Walt Whitman's Pose* by
        Esther Shephard, and *Whitman* by Newton Arvin. See discussion in Alfred
        Haworth Jones, "The Search for a Usable American Past in the New Deal
        Era," *American Quarterly*, Vol. 23 (December 1971) p. 723.

30.   See Holger Cahill, *New Horizons in American Art*, exhibition at the Museum
        of Modern Art, September 14–October 12, 1936; "Paramount News Cam-
        eramen Take Reels of Prize Winning Murals in Library; James Newell Inter-
        viewed," *Evander News*, December 23, 1936, Vol. 29, No. 8, p. 1; "High School
        to Get WPA Mural Today," *New York Times* November 9, 1938, Scrapbooks,
        X, p. 138; Art Commission; Edith G. Halpert to Thomas Parker, n.d. copy in
        collateral file Evander Childs High School, Art Commission.

31.   In 1998, the Board of Education received funding from the Open Society In-
        stitute to undertake conservation of the mural in conjunction with creation
        of a new mural in dialogue with it and the creation of a project web site. See
        web site newdeal.feri.org/echs/ for additional information about the con-
        troversy and the recent project. At the time Newell was painting his mural,
        another project in New York prompted controversy. A mural at the County
        Courthouse depicting the history of law included one panel about America
        focused on the emancipation of the slaves. The panel showed African-
        Americans eating watermelon. Black New Yorkers objected to this cliché
        image and argued it was demeaning. As a result of their protest, the artist
        substituted the figure of Frederick Douglass. See "Court Art Altered on Ne-
        gro Protest," *New York Times* December 1, 1936, Scrapbook 1936, p. 176, Art
        Commission.

32.   Edward Alden Jewell, "Diverse Mural Projects," *New York Times* May 19,
        1935, Scrapbooks (1935) vol. VIII, 111, Art Commission.

33.   "Peixotto Calls W.P.A. Murals Good Teachers," *Tribune*, June 7, 1936, Scrap-
        books, vol. VIII, 93, Art Commission.

34.   "Colorful Murals," p. 2.

Chapter Four

The Great Depression, German Teachers, and Nazi Revolution in the Schools

Charles Lansing

In the spring of 1933, the Personnel Committee for the Cleansing of the Civil Service operating in the city of Brandenburg an der Havel advised Prussian education authorities to terminate secondary school teacher Dr. Heinrich M. for his political convictions.[1] As a local rightist newspaper had publicized in March, Dr. Heinrich M. was a long-standing member of the Social Democratic Party as well as an alleged atheist. Moreover, he was closely identified with the hated Weimar Republic: the Republic's education officials had hired him to teach at the Von Saldern Secondary School, and he had successfully held on to his position through the Great Depression. He was, therefore, exactly the kind of individual the nascent Nazi government intended to purge from the civil service by means of the broad and powerful Law for the Restoration of the Professional Civil Service. Yet Dr. Heinrich M. was not dismissed from the city's teaching staff. School principal Ferdinand G. defended him, claiming that his military service in the First World War, in which he lost an eye, established his nationalist credentials. Unable to cover up the teacher's affiliation with Germany's Social Democratic party, the principal nonetheless denied the teacher's alleged "godlessness," stating that Dr. Heinrich M. was not only an excellent pedagogue but also a Christian. Ferdinand G. also forwarded to regional education officials pupils' testimonies in support of the secondary school teacher. Such entreaties bore fruit. In November, the Prussian Minister of Education overrode the Committee's recommendations and formally permitted Dr. Heinrich M. to remain teaching, which he did through the Second World War and into the postwar era.[2]

Exceptional only in its particulars, the story of Dr. Heinrich M. raises important questions about the relationship between German state responses to the Great Depression and later National Socialist efforts to transform one important element of the German school system, its teaching staff.[3] In an effort to combat the worsening economic situation with a radical deflationary program, Heinrich Brüning's government in the early 1930s implemented a broad series of measures that reduced teachers' wages and benefits, worsened their working conditions, and adversely impacted their professional and social standing in Germany society. This chapter will investigate how the effects of these measures continued well beyond Brüning's chancellorship and had a significant impact on Nazi efforts to purge racial and political "undesirables" from the classroom.

The chapter begins with a brief overview of the conditions in Germany and in the city of Brandenburg an der Havel on the eve of the Depression. The main body of the work consists of an examination of two major efforts by the Nazi state and party to identify and punish teachers who did not fit National Socialist political and racial criteria. The chapter evaluates the implementation and the efficacy of the Restoration for the Professional Service Law and the anti-Masonic decrees of the early Third Reich. By means of this approach, the chapter will seek to answer the following questions: to what extent were teachers with suspect political histories or organizational affiliations fired, demoted, or transferred? How extensive and consistent were Nazis efforts to purify the teacher corps? Historians have long established the important role played by the Depression in the rise of the Nazi Party and the collapse of Germany's parliamentary democratic system in the period 1929–1932; the question remains whether the Depression and the state's responses to it weakened the collective political, economic, and social standing of German teachers, thereby allowing the Nazi state beginning in 1933 to transform more easily the teaching staff along National Socialist lines? Or, as this chapter will argue, did the response of the Brüning government to the Depression inadvertently strengthen the position of teachers relative to Nazi measures to transform the state?

This chapter will show that despite the Nazi state's broad, sustained attack on the traditional German teaching community, very few teachers were dismissed in a representative city like Brandenburg an der Havel. Examining the professional history of one community of pedagogues reveals that earlier state measures to combat the Great Depression played a significant role in shaping the implementation of Nazi policies regarding teachers in the early Third Reich. This analysis of teachers from the Depression through the Nazi period suggests a rethinking of previous assumptions about both the degree to which 1933 marked a caesura in German history and the structural constraints on the exercise of Nazi power in the schools.

The Great Depression and Brandenburg an der Havel

The Great Depression overwhelmed Germany's first democratic state, the Weimar Republic. Having been established after the First World War, the Republic experienced revolutions, hyperinflation, and foreign occupation in its first six years. The stability of the second half of the 1920s was extremely fragile and short-lived. The onset of the Depression in late 1929 profoundly destabilized the Republic politically and economically, as the explosion in the number of unemployed Germans and bankrupt firms contributed to the collapse of Germany's democratic political system. Beginning with Brüning, Germany was governed by a succession of chancellors who did not have parliament's support, requiring them to rule by emergency powers authorized in the Republic's constitution. The appointment of Adolf Hitler to chancellor in January 1933 marked the de facto end of the Weimar Republic, as the National Socialists over the course of the year erected the Nazi dictatorship.[4]

Many of the same problems facing the national government afflicted communities throughout Germany, including the men and women of the city of Brandenburg an der Havel. Fifty kilometers west of Berlin, straddling the Havel River, Brandenburg was a highly industrialized mid-sized city whose population in the period 1930–1933 experienced both the economic devastation of the Depression and the corresponding radicalization of politics. An important element of this population was the city's teaching staff. Brandenburg employed at this time more than two hundred pedagogues at eighteen institutions, ranging from selective secondary schools to public elementary schools, to teach its more than six thousand pupils.[5] Who were these pedagogues? A large number of them began their careers not in the democratic Weimar Republic but in its predecessor, the authoritarian Second Empire.[6] Moreover, men dominated the teaching profession in Brandenburg. They filled more than 66% of the positions, and the gender imbalance was especially pronounced in the male-dominated middle and high schools. The overwhelming majority of the teachers were Protestant, though a small number were Catholic and at least one was Jewish.[7]

Brandenburg's teaching staff was also fragmented politically and organizationally. Here extant sources offer only partial insight into the situation, identifying individuals' party affiliations in a small number of cases representing approximately 15% of the teaching staff.

There was strong support by teachers for liberal-bourgeois parties, in particular the German Democratic Party and the German People's Party, though a not insignificant number had joined the socialist Social Democratic Party and the conservative German National People's Party (DNVP). Although the Communist Party had established its political strength in industrial centers like Brandenburg in the early 1930s, it found little support among the city's teachers. Teachers' membership in the Nazi Party was also quite low; no more than ten teachers—less than five percent of the total—were, as of January 30, 1933, NSDAP members, a percentage that corresponded to membership data for all German teachers.[8]

Similarly, the city's teaching staff lacked a unified professional voice, as the existence of a multitude of organizations—from German Philogist Association to the Intermediate School Teachers' Association to the Prussian Teachers' Union—exemplified and reinforced significant and long-standing social, professional, and religious divisions among the country's pedagogues. For example, secondary school philologists ensconced themselves in the German Philogist Association in order to promote the study of Greek and Latin, thereby defending their social and professional elitism. Many middle school instructors joined an organization that emphasized their particular needs, the Intermediate School Teachers' Association. Just as various issues, especially those touching upon status, prevented serious cooperation between the philologists and the intermediate school teachers, similar forces created chasms of understanding and attitude between the middle and elementary school teachers.

Shunned by their socially and professionally acknowledged superiors, elementary school instructors nursed their collective feelings of inferiority in the Prussian Teachers' Union. Even German middle and elementary school principals had their own organization, the Principals' Association, and at least some of Brandenburg's principals were members. Finally, most German female teachers belonged to their own organization, the All-German Female Teachers' Association. Nominally an umbrella institution that served female teachers' needs, this organization was in reality a collection of largely autonomous sub-associations, such as the German Female Philologist Union, which promoted their members' specific professional needs and desires. City records indicate that some female teachers, working at various types of schools, were members of this organization. As a professional group, Brandenburg's teaching staff was in January 1933 highly fragmented organizationally.[9]

With a highly-developed industrial sector driving the economy and a political landscape marked by bitter class struggle, Brandenburg was devastated by the economic crisis that overtook Germany in the late Weimar Republic. A very large part of the city's production consisted of luxury goods like bicycles and toys that were among the first items to suffer from the dramatic shrinkage of consumer demand.[10] A subsequent wave of bankruptcies idled businesses and factories, resulting in massive layoffs that grew the city's unemployment numbers. Market shares secured in the mid-1920s by record production levels failed to save the internationally-renowned Brennabor Works from bankruptcy in 1931.[11] The closing of the Elisabeth Works iron foundry and the collapse of the Brandenburg Bank Association revealed that the city's economic troubles extended far beyond those industries involved in the production of luxury goods.[12] Consequently, an unprecedented number of Brandenburgers—approximately 50% of the population—were by January 1932 living partially or exclusively on some form of state welfare.[13]

In order to respond to the problems afflicting Brandenburg and most other German communities, Chancellor Brüning initiated a broad deflationary program that for reasons of politics, expediency and ideology disproportionately affected the civil service.[14] Between September 1930 and December 1931, for example, the national government cut the wages of teachers and other civil servants five times, reducing their gross income by more than 20%. The Prussian regional government also instituted its own set of economy measures consisting of wage reductions, the abolishment of certain bonuses and increases in teaching loads and responsibilities. By the end of 1932, teachers' income had decreased by more than 30%, and in some cases even 40%.[15]

More ominously, the Prussian government in September 1931 ordered the cutting of more than 7,000 positions in the school system, to be carried out by means of mandatory early retirements and dismissals of young teachers with non-permanent appointments. Aware of the inevitable increase in the number of unemployed pedagogues as a result of their measures, authorities also encouraged large numbers of unemployed young pedagogues to leave the profession. Similarly, the Prussian government in February 1932 closed more than half of the region's teacher training academies. A subsequent governmental order calling for a complete ban on admitting new students beginning in 1933 was eventually revised so that a nominal number, 350 for the entire state of Prussia, could study.[16]

The measures represented not only a halt to but even a rolling back of the significant professional, social, and economic advancements made by German teachers since 1918. The academies had fulfilled a long-held desire of elementary school teachers to have their teacher training more closely resemble that of their social superiors, the secondary school teachers who studied at universities; the academies' closings in 1932 seemed to many to threaten this. Similarly, the pay cuts largely erased the economic progress made in the previous wage reform of 1927, as teachers' real wages were now reduced to those of 1913.[17] As a result, German teachers were increasingly politicized, and many directed their anger and resentment squarely at the state. Teachers used public rallies, their professional organizations, and the media to protest the government's demand that they sacrifice more than those in private employment.

The radicalization was evident to political observers. Aware that many civil servants blamed the Weimar Republic's parliamentary system for their sufferings, Nazi Party leaders targeted them for recruitment and mobilization in the election campaigns of 1932.[18] The national and Prussian governments had not intended to mobilize teachers against the state. Cutting teachers' wages, increasing their workloads, curtailing the number of individuals training to become teachers, and actively seeking to push younger pedagogues out of the profession were measures to combat the effects of the Depression. By implementing these measures, officials also unknowingly created conditions—including a future labor shortage—that would impact the political program of its successor, the National Socialist state.

Purging Teachers

After President Paul von Hindenburg appointed Hitler chancellor in January 1933, Nazi leaders began planning a purge of the German civil service as a means of increasing their control over the German state. On April 7, 1933, the Minister of the Interior, Wilhelm Frick, issued the Law for the Restoration of the Professional Civil Service, a far-reaching measure aimed at legally purging Germany's civil servants—including primary and secondary school teachers—according to National Socialist racial and political criteria.[19] Minister Frick, echoing the sentiments of Hitler, intended to use the measure to create an ethnically pure, ideologically homogenous, and politically conformist civil servant corps. By doing so, Nazi leaders hoped to strengthen the bonds of loyalty between the civil servants (*Beamte*) and the state and to efface what they regarded as the pernicious legacy of the Weimar Republic regarding the state bureaucracy. Senior career bureaucrats hoped to use the law to restore order to the "wild," decentralized wave of firings and purges within the bureaucracy carried out by local and regional Nazi Party leaders since January 30, 1933. Ostensibly a measure to identify and purge unqualified civil servants hired during the Weimar Republic, the Restoration Law gave the Nazi state unprecedented control over the lives of *Beamte* by providing it with the legal mechanism to remove those they regarded as unfit for civil service.[20]

Article One of the Restoration Law both symbolized the measure's extra-judicial nature and defined its scope. Rather than initiate a lengthier process of formally revising or repealing current statutes, Nazi leaders drafted an extraordinary law empowering them to punish *Beamte* "even when the necessary conditions under the relevant law do not exist."[21] Article Two targeted civil servants hired after November 9, 1918, if, in the Nazi state's eyes, they lacked the "requisite or usual training or other qualifications." Such individuals were to be dismissed and denied traditional rights such as receiving a pension.[22] Article Three ordered the blanket dismissal of Jewish civil servants regardless of qualifications or training.[23] Article Four again targeted the regime's political opponents. Officials "who because of their previous political activity do not offer security that they will act at all times and without reservation in the interests of the national state" could now be dismissed from government employment. Implementation decrees both instructed authorities to scrutinize state employees' "total political engagement" (*gesamte politische Betätigung*) in order to determine their suitability and also shifted the Article's emphasis from proscribing past political activity to prescribing current and future political engagement.[24] The Law's final two articles made it much easier for the state to transfer, demote or prematurely retire civil servants.[25]

Exactly which *Beamte* were to be examined and possibly punished? Who qualified as Jewish? How should local and regional authorities define "previous political activity" when applying Article

Four? In order to provide answers to these important questions, throughout the spring and summer of 1933 Nazi officials were repeatedly forced to issue implementation decrees that sought to clarify particular points. In some cases, the authorities succeeded. One decree established that public school teachers were civil servants and were thus to be evaluated.[26] Other cases proved less clear-cut, and the implementation orders did little to clarify the situation for the Personnel Committees examining individual teachers. At the insistence of Reich President Hindenburg, for example, Nazi officials decided that not all Jewish civil servants were to be dismissed; permitted to continue teaching were those who had fought in World War One for the Central Powers or after 1918 against the "enemies of the national revolution" in the Baltics, Upper Silesia, and elsewhere. Officials modified this further, deciding in the late spring that simply serving in World War One no longer sufficed; now one had to have seen combat and also remained a civil servant with a distinguished record without interruption since the war's end.[27]

Overall, the implementation decrees failed to resolve completely the Restoration Law's essential vagueness, which added to its potential impact. Free from stringent limitations, the Nazi state could judge the past political actions of its teachers by standards of its own and decide who had acted and was acting in support of a "national" Germany and who was not. Or, as this chapter will show, the Law's essential vagueness and the ad hoc nature surrounding its implementation enabled local officials to retain pedagogues who otherwise qualified for purging according to the Law.

In the Potsdam Governmental District, which included Brandenburg an der Havel, regional authorities quickly moved to implement the Restoration Law in the city's schools. The first step was requiring the district's almost four thousand teachers to complete a "Questionnaire for the Implementation of the Law for the Restoration of the Professional Civil Service" that focused on one's previous political activities and racial background. There were questions regarding the teachers' official rank and title, their professional training, and whether their promotion to full civil servant status (*Beamtentum*) took place before August 1, 1914. More ominous, however, were the questions regarding political activity and racial background. Teachers were asked whether they had belonged to Weimar political parties or activist organizations that included the Social Democratic Reichsbanner and the League for Human Rights. In order to classify teachers according to racial criteria, the Nazi state required all pedagogues to provide detailed information regarding not only their own "Aryan" origins but also that of their parents and grandparents.[28]

The questionnaires, along with the teaching staff's personnel records, were evaluated beginning in late April 1933 by a special three-man Personnel Committee for the Cleansing of the Civil Service, created at the request of Prussian Education Minister Bernhard Rust. Local chapters of the Nazi Party and National Socialist Teachers' League provided the Personnel Committee with additional information regarding individual teachers' political background and behavior. Throughout the summer and into the early fall, cases were considered, and evaluation reports were drafted and then sent to the Education Ministry, where the final decision was made regarding possible suspension, retirement, transfer or dismissal. Only in late September, months after the originally anticipated conclusion date, did Potsdam's *Regierungspräsident*, Dr. Ernst Fromm, inform the Education Ministry that the Personnel Committee for the Cleansing of the Civil Service for the Potsdam District had completed its task.[29] In late November, Minister Rust formally thanked the Personnel Committees for their work. As the result of their efforts, Rust claimed that:

> based on reports currently in my possession, all teachers who are openly resisting or secretly working against the successful construction of the National Socialist state have been removed from the school or will soon be. A secure foundation for a healthy renewal of the education system in Prussia has thus been created.[30]

The dissolution of the Personnel Committees represented a milestone in an exceptional period of change in German history, one that began with Hitler's appointment to chancellor in January 1933. Rust's statement notwithstanding, however, the Nazification of the schools remained unfinished. Over the course of the next three years, Nazi officials continued to search for politically unsuitable individuals to purge, targeting in 1935 and 1936 current and former Freemasons.

The Nazi State's Campaign Against Freemasons

Beginning in July 1935 and lasting for more than a year, the persecution of Freemasons represented another important step in the National Socialist plan to establish a politically homogenous and ideologically loyal teachers corps. Nazi opposition to Freemasonry resulted not from a realistic understanding of its principles and activities, but grew instead out of a worldview that linked international Freemasonry with "World Jewry's" supposed drive for global domination. Although the Prussian Freemasons were overwhelmingly nationalistic, Protestant, and politically conservative, Nazi ideologues like Alfred Rosenberg believed that their institutions and values were fundamentally antithetical to National Socialism. The attacks on Freemasonry were part of the Third Reich's broader rejection of the Republican liberal order. To rid the country of this "un-German" spirit, the Nazi state targeted both the Masonic lodges and those members who were active in politics, state administration, the arts, and the economy.[31]

In 1935 Nazi persecution of Freemasons entered a new and more serious phase as state ministries replaced the uncoordinated, piecemeal harassments, arrests, and confiscations with a comprehensive, centrally-directed program aimed at destroying German Freemasonry once and for all. Nazi officials pressured many lodges and "lodge-like" organizations to dissolve themselves voluntarily; those that failed to do so were forcibly closed down by the Interior Ministry in August 1935.[32] State leaders like Frick and Rust also sought to identify Freemasons among Germany's civil servants and to curtail their possible influence in state and society. In a published decree dated July 10, 1935, the Interior Ministry required that all civil servants, including teachers, declare formally and in writing all previous or current ties to Freemasonry. Teachers' statements regarding possible affiliation with Freemasonry were to be placed in their personnel files, thereby joining incriminating material regarding political activities and racial background as potential justifications for future punitive action. Although authorities maintained publicly that no one would be punished for the information provided, Frick ordered in a confidential memo accompanying the July decree that no former Freemason be hired for, or promoted to, a leadership position in the civil service.[33] Regional and local authorities quickly acted upon Frick's directives. The Brandenburg Province *Oberpräsident* and the Potsdam *Regierungspräsident* collected the declarations, drafted reports that listed the names of former Freemasons and their membership dates, and then sent the materials to the Education Ministry.[34]

At the same time, state ministries worked to strengthen the anti-Masonic measures. In September and October, the Education Ministry sent out hiring and advancement guidelines for teachers who had been members. Moreover, Rust instructed authorities to include in their evaluations of former Masons the important criterion of the date the individual had resigned from the lodge. Men who quit only after January 30, 1933 were to be subject to the full range of discriminatory measures, including in certain cases transfer to another position according to Article Five of the Restoration Law. Finally, the areas of prohibited work were expanded beyond "leadership" positions to include any post involving personnel administration.[35] Like the Restoration Law, the anti-Masonic decrees provided the Nazi state with a broad and powerful legal framework with which to identify and purge targeted individuals, in this case Freemasons. Unclear at this time, however, was to what extent regional and local education authorities would use these measures to dismiss or punish German teachers.

The Effects on Brandenburg's Teaching Staff

The Restoration Law and the anti-Masonic decrees were part of a panoply of measures intended to create, as expressed by Nazi educational theorist Dr. Wilhelm Hartnacke, "a new generation of teachers who can put educational values in their correct order of worth."[36] These teachers, argued Hartnacke, "must learn that they are agents of the State and, if they do not conform, must take the consequences."[37] In order to attain and then preserve this desired conformity, Nazi leaders used available legal and political mechanisms. On Minister Frick's orders, for example, Potsdam officials in the spring of 1933 suspended, replaced, or dismissed Brandenburg an der Havel's chief of police, mayor, assistant mayor and numerous city councilmen. To take another example, authorities announced in early February 1933 their intention to close all progressive Secular Schools and soon afterward suspended the principal of Brandenburg's Secular School, Otto W., who had been affiliated with the Social Democratic Party.[38] According to historian Laurenz Demps, the Potsdam Governmental District ranked fourth nation-wide in the number of arrests made during a two-week period in March 1933.[39]

How did the Restoration Law affect the composition of the city's teaching staff? Despite the fate of the Secular School and many of its instructors, Nazi state and party leaders failed to change substantially

the composition of Brandenburg's teaching staff. The vast majority of
pedagogues who were teaching in 1933 in Brandenburg continued to
do so as of 1938. At the Augusta Intermediate School, for example, no
more than a couple of teachers—out of a teaching staff of approximately sixteen—left the school in this period. To take another example, in 1938 at least 85% of the Franz Ziegler School's teaching staff
had been teaching since before Hitler's ascension to power. Moreover,
some of these changes did not result from punitive state actions but
rather from illnesses, voluntary transfers, and changes of careers.
Maria S., for instance, quit her job at the Catholic Community School
because of health problems. Men such as *Ritterakademie* philologists
Kurt B. and Ernst G. joined the military, sometimes serving as instructors in military schools. Others such as Von Saldern Secondary
School's Adolf S., Augusta School's Ernst G. and Rochow School's
August E. left the city's service having reached the mandatory retirement age. Ardent Nazi and *Ritterakademie* principal, Dr. Ludwig Z.,
quit the school administration to enter the nascent Nazi city government.[40]

   The Restoration Law, arguably the Nazis' most powerful weapon
against political, ideological, and racial enemies, did not result in a
large-scale purge of the city's teachers. Extant records indicate that
only a small group of teachers were terminated. The Potsdam
Regierungspräsident informed the Education Ministry that 47 of the
Potsdam District's more than 3,700 teachers had been fired in accordance with Article Four. Of the city's more than 200 pedagogues, only
two, elementary school principals Otto H. and Otto W., were dismissed under these terms. Furthermore, both men belonged to a
group of five city teachers who had been suspended pending the
Education Minister's final decision. Two of the other three individuals, also principals, were simply demoted.[41]

   The city's vocational schools were the scene of an especially bitter
campaign to purge "Marxist" and other "unworthy" pedagogues,
though its final results were not that different from the process underway in the elementary schools. The primary driving force behind
this attempted purge was the efforts of two vocational school teachers
who sought to use the current political climate to settle old scores. Although the rightist newspaper *Die Brandenburger Warte* had publicly
denounced a small group of teachers for their previous political actions, state and NSDAP investigations commenced only after Friedrich R. and Walter R. in the summer of 1933 enlisted the district Nazi

Teachers' League to pressure the city government to punish ten vocational teachers. In a report titled "The Bossified Conditions at the Brandenburg Municipal Trade Institute," Walter R. accused his principal and two colleagues of unpatriotic activities. Principal Wilhelm K., he argued, was guilty of favoritism towards Social Democratic teachers and men like Alfred H. were unfit for public service as a consequence of their memberships in and actions on behalf of liberal, pro-Weimar Republic professional organizations such as the Republican Teachers' Association.[42] Friedrich R. authored a report titled "The Bossified Conditions at the Brandenburg Trade Vocational School," in which he accused seven of his colleagues of an array of alleged political and ideological misdeeds. Such actions had resulted, he claimed, in the Marxist contamination (*marxistische Verseuchung*) of the pupils and the teaching staff.[43]

Having decided to transfer two of the teachers and to fire the rest, Brandenburg's city government forwarded its decisions and the necessary documentation to Potsdam for review and execution. The *Regierungspräsident* concluded, however, that there was sufficient cause for dismissal or transfer of only two of the ten individuals. Moreover, the officials reported to their Berlin superiors that the entire case was an elaborate act of revenge by Friedrich R. and Walter R. and their accomplice, vocational school principal Otto H. Their grievances extended back as far as the late 1920s and centered on alleged hindrances to their professional advancement at the hands of the "Marxist" teachers running and staffing the schools.[44]

Potsdam officials nonetheless decided to act on some of the teachers' complaints and to punish two pedagogues. Despite recognizing his good teaching performance and his minimal involvement in "Marxist" activities, state authorities retired Deputy Principal Karl L. as a consequence of his membership in the Republican Teachers' Association and the Republican Club and his "unpolitical" articles published in the local Social Democratic newspaper, the *Brandenburger Zeitung*.[45] Similarly, officials demoted and transferred Deputy Principal Alfred H. because they believed he did "not offer security that he will act at all times and without reservation in the interests of the national state," even though they conceded that he was a talented teacher, that there was no proof of his alleged "Marxist" agitation in the classroom, and that they were not certain he was even supportive of "Marxism."[46] This very small purge of the vocational schools not only illustrates the role individuals, the press, Nazi organs and different state agencies played in implementing the Restoration Law, but also highlights the paradox that despite the potentially low standards necessary for punishment, very few teachers were purged.

The Restoration Law had even less of an impact on the city's university-educated pedagogues. At the *Ritterakademie*, for instance, the initial wave of evaluations and punitive measures did not result in the permanent dismissal of a single teacher.[47] Denounced first by a local paper for alleged anti-nationalist statements and actions and then fired officially for his Social Democratic affiliations, Von Saldern pedagogue Julius S. appealed his termination. Director Ferdinand G. wrote to Prussian education authorities and successfully argued for his subordinate's reinstatement, citing Julius S.'s professionalism. Despite the very public nature of his case, Julius S. weathered the Restoration Law's implementation and continued to teach at the Von Saldern secondary school.[48] On the other hand, the Prussian Education Ministry used the law to demote and transfer the Upper Lyceum's Elisabeth W. to an elementary school. Although her case seems to exemplify the law's successful application, later developments belie its efficacy. Elisabeth W. resumed teaching at the selective girls' secondary school soon after the war's outbreak and continued to do so into the post-war era.[49] Although Minister Rust hoped to use the Restoration Law as a means to apply "stricter" standards "to teachers and educators of youth than to other officials," the law's implementation did not transform significantly the city's teaching staff.[50]

The campaign against Brandenburg teachers who were Freemasons fared no better. On August 27, 1935, for instance, *Oberpräsident* Kube informed the Education Ministry that five of the Von Saldern's teachers were former Freemasons and that four of them had been long-standing members.[51] Nevertheless, the authorities took no disciplinary action against any of them. In a report sent in late September to the Education Ministry, *Regierungspräsident* Fromm identified a total of 92 additional Freemasons teaching in the Potsdam District. Eight of these men worked in Brandenburg. Included in this small group were two principals and one vice principal; the rest were elementary or intermediate school teachers. Whereas principal Karl P. had resigned from his lodge before January 30, 1933, the rest had maintained their memberships well into the Nazi period.[52] All eight men continued to teach, regardless of Masonic membership tenure or school leadership position. If former Freemasons were proscribed from training junior civil servants, one would think that state and party leaders would have prevented such individuals from training the next generation of National Socialists, Germany's pupils. Nevertheless, the statistics for Brandenburg lend credence to historian Thomas Neuberger's claims that despite police harassment, the vast majority of former Freemasons "led a fully normal life professionally and socially, undisturbed by the state and Party, and, loyal to the fundamentals of Freemasonry, strove to be loyal citizens of the state, even now of the Third Reich."[53]

Conclusion

The Nazi state failed to use measures such as the Restoration Law to transform Brandenburg's teaching staff as the result of personal, political, and economic factors, many of which were deeply influenced by the Depression and the state's reaction to it. The absence of a comprehensive plan for the transformation of Germany's teaching staff is one explanation why the Nazis failed to take advantage of legal and administrative purge mechanisms. Provided by the regime with only platitudes and vague notions about the ideal Nazi pedagogue, state and party authorities were forced to conceive and implement measures in an ad-hoc fashion, and this absence of systematic clarity and foresight limited their efficacy. The string of qualifications in the form of decrees that characterized the Restoration Law's implementation contributed to the confusion and delay in identifying, evaluating and disciplining Brandenburg's pedagogues. Similarly, the campaign against Freemasonry and its former members was hampered by state-party and center-periphery disagreements over the policy's intent and scope.[54]

Known Freemasons or Social Democrats were also not punished to the law's full extent as a result of local school authorities intervening on their behalf with state and party officials. Some directors or school administrators, more familiar with the individuals in question and more aware of their past actions and current capabilities than regional or national state and party leaders, petitioned for exemptions from punitive or discriminatory measures. For example, *Ritterakademie* principal Dr. Ludwig Z. wrote in July 1933 to the Prussian school authorities in an attempt to convince them that his teachers need not fill out the Restoration Law's questionnaire. Although the

principal included his own questionnaire and a list of the teachers, he
nevertheless argued that he:

> was convinced that [applying the political [criteria] of the Restoration Law
> C.L.] or something similar was invalid for these teachers,…thus it is unnec-
> essary for them to fill out the questionnaires. I would like to note that the
> *Ritterakademie*'s character requires that only such teachers and *Beamte* be
> hired about whose nationalist reliability there can be no doubt.[55]

To take another example, the *Oberlyzeum*'s principal Gustav S. wrote
to Brandenburg Province's *Oberpräsident* to make the case that four
teachers, presumably previously targeted by the state in connection
with the Restoration Law's implementation, were in fact not guilty of
"deleterious" previous political activity. Regarding the Nazi campaign against Freemasons, historian Neuberger writes that such intervention was very common. By informing the responsible ministry
that an incriminated *Beamte* was neither in a leadership position nor
in charge of personnel matters, immediate superiors often successfully removed individuals from the state's scrutiny.[56]

School principals were able to protect many of their teachers from
the state's purges because Germany by the mid-1930s was suffering a
shortage of teachers. Originating in the late Weimar Republic and
continuing into the early Third Reich, hiring freezes and restrictions
on access to higher education resulted in a "drastic instructor deficit."
The closing of more than half of the Prussian pedagogical academies
in 1931, for example, sharply limited the state's capacity to train new
teachers. Searching for ways to cut state expenses, the Prussian education ministry in 1932 went so far as to admit not a single new student for teacher training for the following year, although the
remaining seven academies were eventually compelled to admit a total of 350 students in 1933.[57]

Such policies left cities like Brandenburg struggling by the mid-
1930s to ensure that enough teachers stood in front of the classrooms.
In response, Reich education authorities in April 1935 lifted the permanent hiring freeze for teachers and soon afterwards resumed normal hiring activities. The Prussian academies were renamed colleges
for teacher training (*Hochschulen für Lehrerbildung*) and in some cases
moved out of cities and into the countryside. Such reforms, however,
did little to solve the immediate problem. Only one new college was
opened in Prussia during the prewar years.[58] Moreover, since the
length of study at a college remained two years, newly minted teach-

ers would enter the classroom in 1936 at the earliest.[59] As a result of these limited measures, the situation failed to improve. In 1936, officials were unable to fill more than 1,300 vacant elementary school positions in Germany. Moreover, the dearth of teachers increased during the second half of the 1930s. By 1938, the teacher training colleges were graduating a total of 2,500 pedagogues per year, but German schools needed to fill 8,000 positions.[60] The failure to expand the teacher training institutes in the early 1930s meant that by the time the Nazi state had reversed its hiring policies, there were still too few formally trained men and women to begin teaching.

In Brandenburg, such problems were exacerbated by a population explosion that consisted not only of new workers for the growing industrial sector but also additional children for the schools.[61] By 1936, more than 1,000 new pupils had enrolled in the city's vocational schools.[62] In the period 1933–1938, more than 20,000 people moved to Brandenburg; this population increase of 33% seriously worsened the city's shortage of teachers. In 1938, the Von Saldern Secondary School, for instance, exceeded its usual capacity by more than 600 pupils. Turning to regional authorities, city officials urgently sought permission to solve this problem by opening an additional school, one that would require a new teaching staff.[63]

Low wages for pedagogues and feelings of embitterment among them, another legacy of earlier efforts to combat the Great Depression in Germany, also contributed to the increasingly serious labor shortage in the classrooms. Despite recent salary increases, teachers' wages in the second half of the 1930s were still below late imperial or Weimar levels. Moreover, ridicule of teachers in the press and popular culture, as well as occasionally in prominent Party leaders' public statements, convinced some that they and their contributions to transforming Germany were not sufficiently appreciated. Many of these pedagogues chose to escape the low pay and "the continual defaming of the profession and the work" by changing careers. Others chose simply never to become teachers.[64]

Faced with the imperative of providing classes with teachers, some principals and school administrators took into account the crisis in gaining new and retaining current pedagogues when deciding how to implement punitive measures such as the Restoration Law and the anti-Masonic decrees. Moreover, they were aided in doing so by the laws' very vagueness. In addition to enhancing officials' power, the measures also contained an inherent sense of maneuverability that could be exploited when school administrators applied them. When pressured by Teachers' League and Party leaders in June 1937 to punish a small group of former Freemasons, Potsdam's *Regierungspräsident* and former DNVP supporter Count Gottfried von Bismarck-Schönhausen used this flexibility to spare several teachers from serious consequences. In reporting his discussion with the Party leaders, Bismarck-Schönhausen noted that:

> They mentioned first, that it is the Party District Leadership's wish that these principals and senior teachers be dismissed according to the Restoration Law. In the course of the discussion agreement was reached that the list would be first checked by the School Department for its completeness and then requests would be made according to Article Five of the Restoration Law—due to the great teacher shortage—regarding the principals and the senior teachers.[65]

Since Article Five stipulated transfer, not termination, the teachers' shortage played here an important role in shielding these pedagogues from outright dismissal. Although transfers certainly qualified as a form of punishment, one that probably adversely affected the teacher, it clearly belied the Nazi goal of removing "unsuitable elements" from the classroom. Teachers thus shielded could now move to a new locale and, by the standards of the Nazi state, there potentially corrupt the minds of a different set of young Germans.[66] More than four years after the Nazi seizure of power, the legacy of German efforts to combat the Great Depression continued to thwart the creation of a National Socialist school system.

Notes

1. In accordance with German federal and Brandenburg state law, I have anonymized the names of Brandenburg's teachers.

2. Letters from Ferdinand G. to Provinzialschulkollegium, Berlin, March 15 and 29, 1933, "Rote Pädagogen," *Die Brandenburger Warte*, March 11, 1933, and letter from the Province Brandenburg *Oberpräsident* to the Minister of Education, November 13, 1933, all in Brandenburgisches Landeshauptarchiv (BLHA) Pr. Br. Rep. 34 Provinzialschulkollegium, Nr. 5261. Regarding his professional biography, see the Von Saldern Secondary School annual reports in BLHA, Pr. Br. Rep. 34 Provinzialschulkollegium, Nr. 5264, and the city's teachers' registry, Stadtarchiv Brandenburg an der Havel (StadtA Brandenburg) 2.0.12.25/249.

3. For a more complete discussion of German teachers in the Third Reich, see the author's dissertation, "Brandenburg an der Havel's Teachers, 1933–1953: German *Lehrer* under Two Dictatorships" (Ph.D. diss, Yale University, 2004).

4. For an excellent account of this period, see Gordon Craig, *Germany 1866– 1945* (New York: Oxford, 1978) pp. 396–468, 534–601.

5. Included in the eighteen schools are all of Brandenburg's primary, middle and secondary schools. See Lehrer-Verband der Provinz Brandenburg (ed.) *Lehrer-Verzeichnis für die Provinz Brandenburg*, (13. Jahrgang, Berlin, 1928) pp. 29–35; *Die Erzieher der Kurmark 1936, Verzeichnis der Parteidienststellen, Schulbehörden, Lehranstalten und Lehrkräfte*, (Berlin: Verlag 'Nationalsozialistische Erziehung' GmbH, 1936) pp. 107–112; Franz Breskow, *Brandenburger Schulen von 1300–1990*, unpublished manuscript, Stadtarchiv Brandenburg an der Havel, p. 115.

6. Statistical information regarding the teaching staff's characteristics was compiled from a diverse group of sources: the city's teachers' registry, StadtA Brandenburg, 2.0.12.25/249, the NSLB's membership card catalogue (*Mitgliedskartei*) for the Gau Kurmark, Bundesarchiv Berlin (BAB) NS 12 Band II 82–88, and individual files from the BLHA's *Provinzialschulkollegium* record group and from the Domstiftarchiv (DStA) Brandenburg an der Havel.

7. This statistic was drawn from a comparison of tables of 'instruction hours' (*Unterrichtsstunden*) for the *Ritterakademie* for the period 1931–1934, DStA, BR 328/488, as well as from information found in *Lehrer-Verzeichnis für die Provinz Brandenburg*, pp. 29–35, *Die Erzieher der Kurmark 1936*, 107–112, and the registry of teachers, StadtA Brandenburg, 2.0.12.25/249. In contrast, only 48% of the city's population in June 1933 was male; *Statistisches Jahrbuch für Preussen*, (ed.) Preussischen Statistischen Landesamt, 30. Band, (Berlin: Verlag des Preussischen Statistischen Landesamts, 1934) pp. 258–259. Regarding the city's Jewish teacher, see Report, BLHA, Pr. Br. Rep. 2A Regierung Potsdam II Spezifica Nr. 152. The dismissal of the very small number of Jewish or "jüdisch versippt" teachers as a result of the 1935 Nuremberg racial laws had only a minimal impact on the teaching staff's com-

102   Lansing

position. For a more complete analysis, see Lansing, "Brandenburg an der Havel's Teachers, 1933–1953," pp. 46–51, 59–60.

8.   The registry of teachers, StadtA Brandenburg, 2.0.12.25/249; *Lehrer-Verzeichnis für die Provinz Brandenburg*, pp. 29–35; *Die Erzieher der Kurmark 1936*, pp. 107–112. For general information on the political topography of Brandenburg, see Laurenz Demps, "Die Provinz Brandenburg in der NS-Zeit (1933–1945)," in Ingo Materna and Wolfgang Ribbe, eds., *Brandenburgische Geschichte* (Berlin: Akademie Verlag, 1995) p. 620. The extant information, while sufficient to enable historians to establish a broad overview of city's pedagogues' political affiliation with non-Nazi parties, does not permit accurate determinations of the teacher type and political party correlations discussed in Bölling, *Sozialgeschichte*, pp. 131–132; Konrad Jarausch, *The Unfree Professions. German Lawyers, Teachers, and Engineers, 1900–1950* (New York: Oxford University Press, 1990) pp. 70–71; idem and Gerhard Arminger, "The German Teaching Profession and Nazi Party Membership: A Demographic Logit Model," *Journal of Interdisciplinary History*, Vol. 2, No. 2 (1989) pp. 197–225.

9.   The registry of teachers, StadtA Brandenburg, 2.0.12.25/249; *Lehrer-Verzeichnis für die Provinz Brandenburg*, pp. 29–35; *Die Erzieher der Kurmark 1936*, pp. 107–112. For a description of the various teachers' professional organizations, see Sebastian Müller-Rolli, "Lehrer," in Dieter Langewiesche and Heinz-Elmar Tenorth, eds., *Handbuch der deutschen Bildungsgeschichte. Die Weimarer Republik und die nationalsozialistische Diktatur. Band V 1918–1945* (München: C. H. Beck, 1989) pp. 240–256; Johannes Erger, "Lehrer und Nationalsozialismus. Von den traditionellen Lehrerverbänden zum Nationalsozialistischen Lehrerbund (NSLB)," in Manfred Heinemann, ed., *Erziehung und Schulung im Dritten Reich Teil II: Hochschule, Erwachsenbildung* (Stuttgart: Klett Cotta, 1980) pp. 206–228; Bölling, *Sozialgeschichte*, pp. 98–101; Jarausch, *Unfree Professions*, pp. 31–66.

10.   Klaus Hess, *Brandenburg so wie es war* (Düsseldorf: Droste Verlag, 1992) p. 71.

11.   Ibid.

12.   Otto Tschirch, *Geschichte der Chur- und Hauptstadt Brandenburg an der Havel* (Brandenburg (Havel): J. Wiesike, 1936) p. 255.

13.   Ibid.; Hess, *Brandenburg*, p. 71.

14.   For a discussion of Brüning's reasons for targeting the civil service, see Hans Mommsen, "Die Stellung der Beamtenschaft in Reich, Ländern und Gemeinden in der Ära Brüning," *Vierteljahrshefte für Zeitgeschichte*, Vol. 21, No. 2 (1973) pp. 151–165.

15.   Johannes Erger, "Lehrer und Schulpolitik in der Finanz- und Staatskrise der Weimarer Republik 1929–1933," in Ulrich Engelhardt, Volker Sellin, and Horst Stuke, eds., *Soziale Bewegung und politische Verfassung. Beiträge zur Geschichte der modernen Welt* (Stuttgart: Ernst Klett Verlag, 1976) pp. 239–240; Bölling, *Sozialgeschichte*, p. 122.

16.   Erger, "Lehrer und Schulpolitik," pp. 240–247; Bölling, *Sozialgeschichte*, pp. 113–114, 121–125.

17.   Erger, "Lehrer und Schulpolitik," pp. 238–240.

18. Ibid., pp. 246–247; Marjorie Lamberti, "German Schoolteachers, National Socialism, and the Politics of Culture at the End of the Weimar Republic," *Central European History* Vol. 34, No. 1 (2001) p. 57; Jarausch, *Unfree Professions*, p. 107.

19. Hans Mommsen, *Beamtentum im Dritten Reich*, (Stuttgart: Deutsche Verlags-Anstalt, 1966) pp. 39–46.

20. Mommsen, pp. 31, 39; J. Noakes and G. Pridham, eds., *Nazism 1919–1945 Volume 2: State, Economy and Society 1933–1939. A Documentary Reader* (Exeter: University of Exeter Press, 2000) p. 29. The Restoration Law was the Nazi's first "universally applicable statute," superseding individual states' laws and applying to all civil servants throughout Germany. Jane Caplan, "The Politics of Administration: The Reich Interior Ministry and the German Civil Service, 1933–1943," *Historical Journal*, Vol. 20, No. 3 (1977) pp. 720–721.

21. Reichsgesetz zur Wiederherstellung des Berufsbeamtentums, vom 7. April 1933, RGBl I, 175, reprinted in G. A. Grotesend and Dr. C. Cretschmar, *Das gesamte deutsche und preussische Gesetzgebungsmaterial*, Jahrgang 1933, Band I, pp. 326–27, 432.

22. Ibid., pp. 326–327, 344, 432–433. As a consequence of the politicization of the concept of "unsuitability" in the implementation decrees, individuals who, according to the very vague formulation, had been previously active "in a communist sense," could now be punished according to Article Two.

23. *Gesetzgebungsmaterial*, pp. 326–327.

24. Ibid., pp. 344, 435–436. According to Mommsen, Article Four constituted the Restoration Law's "politically decisive core" that provided the state with its full power of attorney (*Generalvollmacht*) *Beamtentum*, p. 49.

25. *Gesetzgebungsmaterial*, pp. 327, 436. Jane Caplan notes that these two provisions formed the heart of Frick's administrative reconstruction of the German civil service. Caplan, "Politics of Administration," pp. 720–721.

26. Third Implementation Decree of May 6, 1933, reprinted in *Gesetzgebungsmaterial*, pp. 432–435.

27. Noakes, *Nazism*, p. 30; Mommsen, *Beamtentum*, p. 48; *Gesetzgebungsmaterial*, p. 435. Expanding and intensifying after the Nuremberg racial laws of 1935, the Nazi campaign against Jewish teachers continued until late 1937, by which time all Jewish and "jüdisch versippt" pedagogues in Germany had been dismissed. Delia and Gerd Nixdorf, "Politisierung und Neutralisierung der Schule in der NS-Zeit," in Hans Mommsen and Susanne Willems, eds., *Herrschaftsalltag im Dritten Reich. Studien und Texte* (Duesseldorf: Schwann im Patmos Verlag, 1988) p. 256; Jarausch, *Unfree Professions*, pp. 145–146. At least three Brandenburg teachers ultimately lost their teaching jobs. See report, BLHA, Pr. Br. Rep. 2A Regierung Potsdam II Spezifica Nr. 152; handwritten report "über jüdisch versippte Lehrpersonnen, die gemäss # 6 BBG in den Ruhestand versetzt worden," draft letter from *Regierungspräsident* Potsdam to Minister of Education, August 23, 1937, the circular from the Education Ministry, August 13, 1937, all in BLHA, Pr. Br. Rep 2a Regierung Potsdam II Gen. Nr. 733; and copy of a letter from Prussian Minister for Economics and Labor to Frans S., June 29, 1937, BAB, R4901/7849. Such ac-

tions demonstrate that regarding an issue as important as the racial purity of the teaching corps, the Nazi state achieved its objective regardless of labor shortages and other potential obstacles.

28.   Included in the Decree of the Prussian Education Ministry, June 14, 1933, BLHA, Pr. Br. Rep 2a Regierung Potsdam II Gen. Nr. 733.

29.   Report from the *Regierungspräsident* Potsdam to Prussian Ministry of Education, Ibid., October 7, 1933.

30.   Circular of the Prussian Ministry of Education, Ibid., November 28, 1933.

31.   Harassment of and discrimination against Freemasons by Nazi activists had existed since the Third Reich's creation. In the spring of 1933 there were widespread attacks against Masonic lodge members by SA and NSDAP thugs, and state police placed their activities under surveillance. Helmut Neuberger, *Freimaurerei und Nationalsozialismus. Die Verfolgung der deutschen Freimaurerei durch völkische Bewegung und Nationalsozialismus*, Volume I (Hamburg: Bauhütten Verlag, 1980) pp. 158–160, 168–169; Volume II (Hamburg: Bauhütten Verlag, 1980) pp. 118–119.

32.   Ibid., pp. 133, 136–139, 150; Neuberger, *Freimaurerei*, Volume II, pp. 104–106.

33.   Decree from the *Oberpräsident* of Brandenburg Province, August 13, 1935, and Internal letter from the *Oberpräsident* of Brandenburg Province to the Head of the Secondary Schools Department, July 10, 1935, BLHA, Pr. Br. Rep. 34 Provinzialschulkollegium Nr. 3786, pp. 28, 32–34; Neuberger, *Freimaurerei*, Volume II, p. 124.

34.   Report from the *Oberpräsident*, August 27, 1935, BLHA, Pr. Br. Rep. 34 Provinzialschulkollegium Nr. 3786, pp. 39–55; Report from the *Regierungspräsident* to the Education Ministry, September 30, 1935, BLHA, Pr. Br. Rep 2a Regierung Potsdam II Gen. Nr. p. 733.

35.   Letter from the Education Ministry, October 3, 1936 and February 18, 1937, BLHA, Pr. Br. Rep. 34 Provinzialschulkollegium Nr. 3786, pp. 76, 86.

36.   Quoted in I. L. Kandel, *The Making of Nazis* (originally published 1935) (Westport, Connecticut: Greenwood Press, 1970) p. 42.

37.   Ibid.

38.   Letter from Brandenburg Magistrat to the Potsdam Government, April 12, 1933, BLHA, Pr. Br. Rep. 2A Regierung Potsdam II Brd, Nr. 124, and letter, with attachment, from Reich Education Ministry to *Regierungspräsident* Potsdam, April 13, 1934, BLHA, Pr. Br. Rep 2a Regierung Potsdam II Gen., Nr. 733.

39.   Regarding the purge of local leaders and senior municipal officials, see the *Brandenburger Anzeiger*, March 20, 1933, special edition; "Für Brandenburg," *Brandenburger Anzeiger*, March 2, 1933; charges against the city's Secular School can be found in "Die weltlichen Schulen werden abgebaut," *Brandenburger Anzeiger*, February 23, 1933; "Für Brandenburg," *Brandenburger Anzeiger*, March 23, 1933; Laurenz Demps, "Die Provinz Brandenburg in der NS-Zeit (1933 bis 1945)," in Materna and Ribbe, *Brandenburgische Geschichte*, p. 630.

40.   The registry of teachers, StadtA Brandenburg, 2.0.12.25/249; *Lehrer-Verzeichnis für die Provinz Brandenburg*, pp. 29–35; *Die Erzieher der Kurmark*

1936, pp. 107–112; "Für Brandenburg," *Brandenburger Anzeiger*, March 31, 1933 and March 28, 1934; Report, BLHA, Pr Br Rep 2A Regierung Potsdam I, Nr. 5260. For information about Dr. Ludwig Z.'s diverse political involvement starting in spring 1933, see the transcript of his denazification hearing in BLHA, Rep 203 Ministerium des Innern Entnazifizierung, Nr. 791.

41.   Report "Nachweisung über beurlaubte Lehrer," an undated report from the Potsdam *Regierungspräsident*, and Report of the Personnel Committee for the Cleansing of the Civil Service for the Potsdam District, May 24, 1933, all in BLHA, Pr Br Rep 2A Regierung Potsdam II Gen, Nr. 733. The fate of the fifth individual cannot be determined from the records.

42.   Attachments, *Die Brandenburger Warte* article titled "Aus der Mitgliederliste des 'Republikanischen Clubs Brandenburg,'," June 4, 1933, and report "Die bonzokratischen Verhältnisse an der Handelslehranstalt Brandenburg-Ha.," to correspondence from the Potsdam *Regierungspräsident* to Education Minister, August 31, 1933, BAB, R4901/7849.

43.   Attachment, report "Die bonzokratischen Verhältnisse an der gewerblichen Berufsschule Brandenburg-Ha, " Ibid.

44.   Report from Potsdam *Regierungspräsident* to Prussian Economics and Labor Minister, August 31, 1933, BAB, R4901/7849.

45.   Letter from Potsdam *Regierungspräsident* to Prussian Economics and Labor Minister, August 31, 1933, and draft letter from Prussian Economics and Labor Minister to Karl L., January 18, 1934, BAB, R4901/7849.

46.   Letter from Potsdam *Regierungspräsident* to Prussian Economics and Labor Minister, August 31, 1933, and draft transfer notice from Prussian Economics and Labor Minister to Alfred H., February 4, 1934, Ibid.

47.   The registry of teachers, Stadtarchiv Brandenburg an der Havel, 2.0.12.25/249; *Lehrer-Verzeichnis für die Provinz Brandenburg*, pp. 29–35; *Die Erzieher der Kurmark 1936*, pp. 107–112; Table, DStA, BR106/272.

48.   Letter from Director Ferdinand G. to the Provinzialschulkollegium, Pr. Br. Rep 34 Provinzialschulkollegium, Nr. 5261.

49.   Report, BLHA, Pr. Br. Rep. 34 Provinzialschulkollegium, Nr. 5313; the registry of teachers, Stadtarchiv Brandenburg an der Havel, 2.0.12.25/249.

50.   Quoted in Jarausch, *Unfree Professions*, p. 130.

51.   Report from the *Oberpräsident* of the Province of Brandenburg, August 27, 1935, BLHA, Pr. Br. Rep. 34 Provinzialschulkollegium Nr. 3786.

52.   Draft report, "Nachweisung über die Zugehörigkeit von Beamten zu Freimaurerlogen, anderen Logen oder logenähnlichen Organisationen und deren Ersatzorganisationen," from the Potsdam *Regierungspräsident* to the Education Ministry, September 30, 1935, BLHA, Pr. Br. Rep 2A Regierung Potsdam II Gen. Nr. 733.

53.   Neuberger, *Freimaurerei*, Volume II, pp. 118, 144.

54.   Michael H. Kater, "Hitlerjugend und Schule im Dritten Reich," *Historische Zeitschrift* No. 228 (1979) pp. 579, 581, 593; Bernd Zymek, "Schulen, Hochschulen, Lehrer," Dieter Langeweische and Heinz-Elmar Tenorth, "Bildung, Formierung, Destruktion," and Heinz-Elmar Tenorth, "Pädagogisches Denken," ibid., p. 139, all in Langeweische and Tenorth,

eds., *Handbuch der deutschen Bildungsgeschicht* pp. 20, 139, 190–193; Jarausch, *Unfree Professions*, p. 120; Bölling, *Sozialgeschichte*, pp. 136–142; Delia and Gerd Nixdorf, "Politisierung und Neutralisierung," p. 229.

55.　Letter from Dr. Ludwig Z. to the Provinzialschulkollegium, July 8, 1933, BLHA, Pr. Br. Rep 34 P.S.K. Nr. 5294.

56.　Letter from Gustav S. to *Oberpräsident* of the Brandenburg Province, BLHA, Pr. Br. Rep. 34 P.S.K., Nr. 5315; Neuberger, *Freimaurerei und Nationalsozialismus*, Volume II, p. 134; Nixdorf, "Politisierung und Neutralisierung," p. 228.

57.　Bölling, *Sozialgeschichte*, 113; Harald Scholtz and Elmar Stranz, "Nationalsozialistische Einflussnahmen auf die Lehrerbildung," in Manfred Heinemann, ed., *Erziehung und Schulung im Dritten Reich Teil II: Hochschule, Erwachsenbildung*, (Stuttgart: Klett Cotta, 1980) pp. 110–111.

58.　Ibid., pp. 116–117.

59.　Bölling, *Sozialgeschichte*, p. 148. In an effort to expand and accelerate the production of new teachers, Nazi officials in 1939 introduced special teacher training courses (*Aufbaulehrgänge*) for young men and women with only elementary or middle school qualifications. Scholtz and Stranz, "Nationalsozialistische," p. 116.

60.　Rolf Eilers, *Die nationalsozialistische Schulpolitik. Eine Studie zur Funktion der Erziehung im totalitären Staat* (Köln: Westdeutscher Verlag, 1963) p. 74.

61.　Wolfgang Kusior, *Die Stadt Brandenburg im Jahrhundertrückblick. Streiflichter durch eine bewegte Zeit* (Berlin: Verlag Bernd Neddermeyer, 2000) pp. 50–51.

62.　Tschirch, *Geschichte*, p. 254.

63.　Notes of Oberregierungsrat Heckel, November 14, 1938, BAB, R 4901/5144.

64.　Kater, "Hitlerjugend," pp. 596–597; Jarausch, *Unfree Professions*, pp. 132–133, 156–162; Bölling, *Sozialgeschichte*, pp. 116–125, 153–155.

65.　Vermerk of the Potsdam *Regierungspräsident*, June 24, 1937, and an attached draft letter of *Regierungspräsident* Count Gottfried Bismarck-Schönhausen to the Education Ministry, BLHA, Pr. Br. Rep 2a Regierung Potsdam II Gen. Nr. 733.

66.　Jarausch, *Unfree Professions*, pp. 158–161.

Chapter Five

Reading, Writing, and Racial Uplift: Education and Reform in Cleveland, Ohio

Regennia N. Williams

In northern Ohio there is the city of Cleveland. For fifty years the colored group in Cleveland has fought for municipal recognition and equality and it has accomplished a splendid work. Our great colored author, Charles W. Chesnutt, is a member of one of the leading literary and social clubs. A colored lawyer, Harry Davis, is a member of the Cleveland City Club and long has served in the Ohio legislature. We have colored councilmen. We have colored teachers in the public schools who teach without segregation or discrimination. There is not a single "Jim Crow" institution in the city, and this is because with fifty years fighting we have achieved real democracy in Cleveland.[1]

W.E.B. Du Bois, 1924

Mary Brown Martin made history on Monday, January 6, 1930. At the regular meeting of the Cleveland Board of Education, she took the oath of office and became the first African American member of the board. She was assigned to the Finance Committee and the Committee on Housing and Supplies.[2] Immediately, she was faced with the reality of the Great Depression's negative impact on school fortunes, dwindling school finances and a physical plant that could not supply adequate housing for the thousands of students in need of classroom space. That was just the tip of the iceberg.

The challenges facing Martin as the only African American member of the School Board were further complicated by the fact the African American community had its own special concerns about racism in public education. Members of the local branch of the National Association for the Advancement of Colored People (NAACP) had aggressively campaigned for Martin's election to the Board in 1929, believing that the presence of an African American member would result in the community's concerns being addressed. Needless to say, Martin had her work cut out for her.

This chapter will consider the history of the African American struggle for educational and social reform in Cleveland, Ohio just before the onset of and in the early stages of the Great Depression. I maintain that despite the scarcity of financial resources during this era, African American community activists and NAACP leaders were able to identify on-going problems associated with educating African American children, increase their level of protest against perceived racist activities, and alter institutionalized racism in the schools. Clevelanders elected an African American to the School Board, and other men and women of color attained prominent leadership positions in the 1920s and 1930s. An interracial coalition of organizations, including all-African American groups such as the Future Outlook League, worked with—and in some instances independently of—the legalistically-oriented NAACP from the earliest periods of their histories. Together, they made structural changes possible in Depression-era school programs and in the employment sector.

Freedom to Learn: The NAACP, the Race, and Public Schools

In 1910, the founding principles of the NAACP suggested that keeping the general public informed about the plight of African Americans and the need for social reform were high on the organization's list of priorities, since the primary means by which the NAACP would achieve its goals would be "education, organization, agitation, [and] publicity—the only force of an enlightened public opinion."[3] William Edward Burghardt Du Bois, historian, sociologist, and master of propaganda, used his position as editor of the NAACP's monthly magazine, *The Crisis*, to promote the belief that African Americans would never enjoy full citizenship rights until they were granted equal educational opportunities.[4] When the Cleveland Branch of the NAACP was organized on January 25, 1914, it openly embraced the philosophy of the parent body. The first annual report to the national office described a rather uneventful year and stated that "Cleveland [was], to a large degree, free from the baneful prejudice with which some of their brethren must contend."[5] However, a close examination of the treatment of African Americans in the city's public schools reveals that they faced many of the same problems that plagued other cities with sizable communities of color.

African American teachers, for example, were routinely subjected to discrimination, and that discrimination often escaped the attention of even the most vocal critics of racial injustice, including Du Bois. In a system where African Americans were approximately 2% of the student population in 1915, teacher assignments were only made in communities where large numbers of African American students lived and in those white communities where no objections were raised about the race of the teacher. Noted African American author and businessman Charles W. Chesnutt challenged the district's teacher assignment policy and insisted that classroom assignments be made without regard to the race of the teacher. The superintendent of schools was convinced, however, that the schools were best served by the existing policy, a point made clear in his response to Chesnutt's demand:

> I will not argue the matter with you on the basis of abstract principle. I will speak from the practical standpoint of my responsibility as superintendent of the Cleveland Schools…as I see it, it is my job to see that the schools operate as efficiently as possible. Efficiency demands harmony and co-operation, not only within school halls but among the people, especially the parents…However unjust and regrettable, it is a fact that in many sections of this city there is strong opposition to the employment of colored teachers…[6]

With this kind of policy in place, the apologetic members of the local NAACP affiliate would not have to wait long for conditions for African Americans to worsen, and by the 1920s the Cleveland branch of the NAACP was the primary vehicle through which African Americans would agitate for educational and social reforms.

Population Growth and Community Change

The efficiency desired by school leadership in 1915 became an urgent need in times of economic downturn. The Cleveland Public Schools experienced tremendous population growth during the post World War I years and enrollment increased from 110,000 students in 1920 to more than 144,000 by 1930. Many of the new students were the children of European immigrants and African American migrants from the deep South.[7]

A Chamber of Commerce committee chaired by Chesnutt reported that by 1923, a peak year for the Great Migration, approximately 9,000 of Cleveland's 137,000 public school students were African American. Most African Americans were concentrated in schools on the city's east side. Of the system's 142 schools, six had enrollments that were more than 40% African American, and one elementary school, Rutherford B. Hayes, was more than 82% African American. More than 10% of the African American students were in "retarded" / "overage for grade" classes. The Chamber of Commerce report cited the following as reasons: firstly, those migrating from the South were "disadvantaged because of the lack of educational opportunities; secondly, [there were] low moral standards among Southern-bred Negroes; and finally, [there was a] lack of incentive on the part of the Negro to improve himself."[8] The Chamber of Commerce was not alone in blaming the victims of miseducation for their plight, but most members of the Cleveland Branch of the NAACP usually sided with African American students and parents in working to improve educational opportunities.[9]

Like the overall student enrollment, the enrollment of African Americans in Cleveland's public schools increased steadily throughout the 1920s, and leaders of the Cleveland branch of the NAACP devised their own strategy for dealing with school administrators and this growing population of students. At the start of the decade there was some reluctance on the part of officers to announce an NAACP-led frontal assault on racism in the Cleveland Public Schools, but by the mid-1920s the dramatic increase in the number of African Americans in the schools emboldened members of the organization.[10] In 1927, branch President Charles White was keenly aware of "certain trends in the public school system that on the surface [were] not healthy signs."[11] During the first quarter of 1927, the NAACP received and acted on a report on ongoing problems with racial isolation and over-crowding in the Outhwaite, Rutherford B. Hayes and Sibley Schools.

By 1929, the year of the stock market crash, the 13,430 African American children enrolled in the system were 9% of the total student population. Most still attended majority African American schools, and the problem of racial isolation became more entrenched during the Depression. Enrollment reports suggest that 71.7% of African American students attended majority African American schools in the 1931–32 school year. By the end of the 1939–1940 school year the proportion of African American students in majority African American schools had increased to 77.4%.[12]

Concurrent with the African American population increases and the racial isolation of children in the schools was the growing popularity of the notion reflected in the editorials of the African American *Gazette* newspaper that African Americans should be "represented" in all aspects of public school programming.[13] In fact, the number of African American teachers also increased during this era, although not as rapidly as the number of African American students. Of the 84 African American teachers employed in the public schools, most (78) were employed in elementary schools serving the African American community.[14] Only one African American, Helen Chesnutt—daughter of Charles W. Chesnutt and a graduate of Smith College—taught at the high school level in the 1920s. She had been hired to teach Latin at Central High School in 1904. Her sister, Dorothy Chesnutt Slade, began teaching at Wilson Junior High School in 1919.[15]

The Great Migration also had a powerful impact on the Central High School and the community around it. In 1929, the superintendent of schools discussed the dramatic change and eventual decline of the community, insisting that the once stately mansions of Central had given way to tenements and rooming houses, junk in yards, and burning debris.[16] Likewise, the student body at the high school, while showing traces of the diversity celebrated by poet Langston Hughes in the description of his 1920 graduating class, was overwhelmingly African American and increasingly poor.[17] In "Racial Isolation in the Cleveland Schools: A Report of a Study Sponsored by the United States Commission on Civil Rights," author Willard Richan noted the severity of the racial isolation, stating that: "In the early 1930s, virtually all Negro high school students attended three schools, with the highest concentration at Central High. Its enrollment in 1931 was 614 Negroes and 21 whites."[18] As the neighborhood continued to decline and the poverty rate among the student body increased, African American parents and community leaders increased their calls for improvements in the curriculum and the physical plant at Central. At the end of the 1920s, school officials and others were still concerned about the growing numbers of "overage" students in the system and the need for additional classes to serve this population.[19] The NAACP expressed its opposition to the on-going random "dumping" of African Americans into institutions serving these students.

The challenges related to migration, racial segregation, and the school community in Cleveland were not uncommon in other urban areas, and school leaders in Detroit, Chicago, and Philadelphia expressed similar concerns. By the start of the Great Depression, none of the African American communities in these cities had been able to secure the appointment or election of a person of color to their local school boards, despite their expressed desire for such representation.[20]

In Cleveland, however, the evolving strategies of the NAACP high-lighted the need for school reform and helped create a climate for change in the city's public schools.

Mary B. Martin and the Cleveland School Board

When the Stock Market crash occurred in October 1929, the NAACP simply added the increasing economic woes to its already lengthy list of concerns. In November 1929, NAACP officers, trustees, and other members of the African American community were somewhat encouraged by Mary Brown Martin's election to the school board. Martin was comfortably situated in Cleveland's African American middle class at the time of her election to the Board of Education, but she had come from very humble beginnings. A native of Raleigh, North Carolina, Brown's family migrated to Cleveland in 1886. Martin and her younger siblings were educated in the public schools, and she graduated from Central High School in 1900.[21] She also attended the Cleveland Normal School of Western Reserve University and subsequently taught school in Alabama and Arkansas, before meeting and marrying attorney Alexander H. Martin in Cleveland.[22]

Martin often stated that her November 1929 victory in the school board race came as a surprise. As a candidate for the "member at large" position, she had conducted a citywide campaign and built strong support that crossed color and class lines in Cleveland. Republicans dominated Cleveland politics in the 1920s, and in 1929 Martin was one of several African American Republicans to receive the support of the "machine" while Maurice Maschke was the leader of the Cuyahoga County Republican Party.[23] Despite an impressive showing among whites, headlines in the African American *Gazette* newspaper proclaimed that Martin was "Our School-Board Member."[24]

Before the end of 1929, however, those who expected Martin to behave like a "race woman" reacted with more than a little surprise at what appeared to be her unwillingness to be seen as the "Negro member" of the board. In an article in the *Cleveland News*, Martin was quoted as saying, "For some reason the impression has gotten around that I am only representing the colored pupils...Nothing could be further from the truth. I was elected to my present post by persons of all classes, and I will do my best to represent all of them."[25]

Martin's remarks caught many race leaders off-guard. She certainly had never avoided racial issues. In fact, she appears to have gone out of her way to associate with other race leaders in the community, especially those working with the NAACP. While the race of all officers and board members in 1929 was not available, many had long been African American community activists, including Dr. W.H. Biggs, a dentist; Dr. Arman Evans, a physician; Clayborne George, an attorney and councilman; William R. Green, an attorney and member of the Executive Committee of the Cleveland Association of Colored Men; Rev. Wade H. McKinney, pastor of Antioch Baptist Church, the city's largest African American congregation; and L. Pearl Mitchell, a probation officer and member of Alpha Kappa Alpha, the nation's oldest service sorority for college educated African American women.[26]

As someone who wanted to "serve all the citizens," Martin had her hands full trying to address the concerns of NAACP members and a broad-based constituency that needed and demanded so much. The fact that her election occurred during the financially lean times of the Great Depression did not make her job any easier.[27] The growing economic crisis made conditions even worse for African Americans, and school board members, especially Martin, would be held accountable for the growing problems in the schools.

As the Depression deepened, an already serious problem with overcrowded, unsafe schools reached the crisis level in Cleveland. In some neighborhoods, the schools continued to employ relay plans that had become popular during World War I. By requiring students to attend half rather than full day sessions, schools designed to accommodate 700 students could enroll as many as 1,000. Even before the onset of the Depression, in the spring of 1929, the superintendent of schools had submitted a letter to the board stating that the system needed to adopt a new program of building cheaper schools to relieve these conditions. His immediate concern was the need for new schools in the city's West Park and Brooklyn neighborhoods and additional classrooms in Hough School, where "the children passed through narrow corridors filled with steam pipes, close to furnaces and part open wash rooms, which all in all, the board agreed, was an unhealthy condition." While he succinctly and accurately described the nature of the problems, he also knew that the cash-strapped board could ill-afford to address these matters.[28]

Economic woes also plagued the households of many students, since Cleveland, like many northern industrial cities, was especially hard-hit by the economic downturn of the Great Depression. In the year following the Stock Market crash, Cleveland's industrial workers experienced a 50% unemployment rate.[29] Needless to say, unemployed workers could ill-afford to pay taxes.

Race, Class, and the Politics of Public Education

The Depression forced the board to begin to tighten its belt, first by suspending salary increases and eliminating cumulative sick leave for teachers in 1931, and then by reducing salaries for teachers, principals, supervisors and assistant supervisors by 15% for the 1932–33 academic year.[30] Interestingly enough, the system continued to provide special programs for children who were blind, deaf, and those with speech impediments during the Depression era. There were also evening programs for adults, and course offerings in arts and music, which would come to be looked upon as luxuries in later decades. School leaders still considered the classes for the "mentally retarded," which included disproportionately high numbers of African Americans, an essential part of the curriculum, although they continued to be the objects of NAACP scorn.

If these programs were evidence of the schools' commitment to providing essential services even in economically lean times, evidence of Depression-era anxiety about work is found in the proposed board policy that discouraged the re-hiring of married teachers. Board member Alfred A. Benesch had submitted a resolution in the spring of 1931 which, if passed, would have prevented the schools from re-hiring "married women in any department of the School Board, except on special recommendation of either the superintendent or director of schools."[31] Benesch was convinced that discharging married women "would distribute employment among a much larger number of families."[32] This practice was vigorously protested by members of the Women's City Club and others and was eventually defeated, thereby saving the jobs of 350 married teachers and 500 married women who cleaned school buildings.[33] The decision left in place, however, a policy which allowed the board to dismiss a woman when she got married, with the understanding that she would be re-hired only if she was rated in the top 25% of the teaching staff for efficiency.[34] These actions demonstrate both the gravity of the crisis facing the schools and the willingness of Cleveland's public organizations to rally in defense of measures deemed too harmful to schools.

The evolving position of Martin reflected the intersection of the economic crisis in the schools with Cleveland's changing racial politics. In January 1931, Martin was one of two board members appointed to serve on the Joint Committee on Relief Measures with representatives from Cuyahoga County, the City of Cleveland, and the Community Fund.[35] In June 1932, she joined other colleagues on the board in adopting a policy that gave preference to Cleveland residents when filling vacancies in the schools.[36]

By 1932, however, the timidity that characterized earlier NAACP complaints was obviously of the past. The organization launched a formal protest against the discriminatory treatment of African American students in the schools in the summer of 1932. In a report submitted by the organization's Committee on Schools and Agencies, they called for the removal of the principal from Central High School because he "was out of touch with the community and community problems and the school had retrograded scholastically and otherwise during the seven years he [had] been principal."[37] In that same year, and again in 1933, the NAACP Committee on Education charged that African American high school students were being forced to attend Central High School, even though other schools, with a superior physical plant, were serving the same geographic area.[38] Moreover, the NAACP identified numerous problems in the curriculum, support services and co-curricular activities of African American students. Most troubling was the lack of variety in academic course offerings. There were, for example, no electives in many foreign languages and business courses offered in high schools outside of the Central community.[39]

Segregation of African Americans became even more entrenched in the 1930s, as the number of residents in the Central community increased dramatically. Racial isolation in the schools was a problem at all levels, but the tendency to isolate was greatest "at the elementary school level, where districts [were] smaller and therefore more likely to be racially homogeneous" because of residential segregation in the neighborhoods.[40] At the same time the deepening economic depression and the related banking crisis was the cause of widespread demoralization of students and employees throughout the schools. Most troubling was the fact that by 1933 the city was home to 4,500 unemployed teachers, many of them recent graduates from the Cleveland School of Education.[41]

A newspaper account of concerns expressed at the North Eastern Ohio Teachers Association's convention held in Cleveland 1933 suggests the gravity of the economic problems, even for those fortunate enough to have jobs: "Many employees, including teachers in the lower pay brackets and clerks, have had to walk miles to their work for lack of car fare. Married men teachers have been especially hard hit. Teachers are watching standards of their work fall through the heavy teaching loads being placed on them."[42] Cleveland voters did approve a 1-mill school levy in November 1933, but it simply continued the levy that had been approved in 1929. It did not make additional funds available, but it did help the schools avoid "financial collapse" as they struggled to meet the needs of the city's students. As one of the city's major dailies had editorialized in urging the passage of the levy: "The schools are hard hit by reductions in the tax duplicate and delinquent collections. Their income has been cut by millions. Their work has grown. School children can't wait for their education until the Depression is over."[43]

Martin was reelected to a second four-year term in November 1933. The number of votes cast for Martin exceeded by 20,000 the total African American population in the city, once again demonstrating Martin's ability to attract support from the wider community.[44] As board members braced themselves for the possibility of additional cuts in the next school year, President Franklin D. Roosevelt announced that an additional $400 million of public works funds would be made available for programs targeting the nation's unemployed. This announcement not only lifted the spirits of the approximately 250,000 Ohioans who would be the direct beneficiaries, it also boosted the image of the Democratic party in what had traditionally been a Republican stronghold in Cleveland.[45]

During the Depression, the Cleveland Board of Education also received some much-needed assistance from the federal government's Civil Works Administration (CWA) program. For example, in February of 1934, board records reported that CWA projects were completed at a cost of $1,250,000. These projects employed 4,000 men, who were responsible for making improvements to the interiors of 80 schools.[46] While information on the race of the employees is not included in the board's records, and NAACP records are silent on this matter, African Americans and other students certainly reaped bene-fits from the improved physical plant.

In addition to discussing the tangible evidence of work relief and "brick and mortar" improvements involving the schools, Board re-cords also document school leaders' on-going concerns about social segregation and race relations during the Depression. One of the most visible signs of progress in this area occurred in 1934 when Superin-tendent Charles H. Lake decided to cancel all Cleveland Public School picnics at Euclid Beach [Amusement] Park, because it routinely dis-criminated against African American students. Founded in 1895, the lakefront park was a popular attraction for local families and resi-dents and visitors to the city. Parents and students had long com-plained about the treatment of African Americans at the hands of park employees—including prohibitions against their use of the beach and the dance hall.[47]

As part of this broader campaign against segregation, African American members of the NAACP continued to file their formal complaints about racial discrimination in the schools. Jane Edna Hunter, an outstanding civic leader and nationally known African American club woman, continued her work with NAACP members, pressing for improved facilities for Central High School students, by submitting "a report of a study and findings of certain conditions af-fecting the Central High School" at the regular board meeting on April 9, 1934.[48] By the fall of 1935, Martin was serving on the Commit-tee on Housing and Supplies and chairing the Committee on Educa-tional Matters, which received Hunter's report. In her renewed call for board action, Hunter led a "committee of citizens residing in the school district served by Central High School" in asking that the board forgo plans to remodel the school and erect a new building in-stead.[49] Sensing a greater willingness on the part of the board to hire African American teachers for schools serving predominantly African American populations, less than two weeks later Dr. Joe Thomas "re-quested that the faculty of Central High School be composed of 50% Negroes."[50] Although this was also referred to Martin's committees, no action was taken on either matter. This inaction on Martin's part highlights the increasingly difficult course that she was forced to navigate. As the lone African American member of the Board, she could receive the complaints and she could encourage, but not force, the Board to act.

One notable example of her ability to achieve her aims occurred during her second term, when Martin encouraged the board to again revise its policy on school picnics at Euclid Beach Park. In 1935, the board modified the superintendent's earlier policy to allow picnics, if the "skating rink and dance hall [were] closed to all of the school children, both white and colored, attending said picnic." Later in 1936, in keeping with the language of a resolution submitted by Martin, the Superintendent approved a new policy that prohibited school picnics "at Euclid Beach Amusement Park or any other park until and unless full enjoyment of all of the privileges offered by said parks, including dance hall, skating rink and bathing beach, be accorded to all school children regardless of race or color."[51] Members of the Cleveland Branch of the NAACP had asked Martin to prepare and submit this resolution, and, on this rare occasion, Martin and the NAACP were, again, in agreement.

Debating the Goals and Tactics of Racial Integration

Like the Cleveland branch, the national office of the NAACP had continually challenged segregation in public facilities, including beaches and schools, since its inception. By the era of the Great Depression, however, one of the charter officers of the parent body, Du Bois, began to publicly express serious reservations about the wisdom of devoting so many of the organization's resources to placing African American students in desegregated settings. In "Does the Negro Need Separate Schools?" Du Bois stressed that "using a little child as a battering ram upon which the nastiness of race hatred can be thrust" was not the wisest course of action in desegregation programs:

> I have repeatedly seen wise and loving colored parents take infinite pains to force their little children into schools where the white children, white teachers, and white parents despised and resented the dark child, made mock of it, neglected or bullied it, and literally rendered its life a living hell.[52]

Instead of forcing white institutions to accept African Americans, Du Bois envisioned not just separate schools, but a new system of education controlled by the African American community, believing that "the control of the teaching force, the expenditure of money, the choice of textbooks, the discipline and other administrative matters of this sort ought, also, to come into our hands, and be incessantly demanded and guarded."[53]

Du Bois was of the opinion that African Americans needed to exercise more control over their own lives, and he was not alone. In fact, public schooling was one of several issues on the agendas of activist groups in the African American community in 1935. Even as the federal government's New Deal for American workers was launched with the WPA and Social Security, NAACP members stepped up their efforts to improve conditions for African American workers in local communities and living conditions for African people in the global community. When Italy invaded the sovereign African nation of Ethiopia, African Americans expressed public indignation, raised money for defense programs, and even volunteered to join the Ethiopians in fighting the Italian Fascists.[54] Nationally, Ella Baker exposed "slave-like" conditions for domestic workers in New York and worked with housewives to encourage collective purchasing during the Depression.[55] In Cleveland, the Future Outlook League, under the leadership of John O. Holly, led "Don't Buy Where You Can't Work" boycotts and demanded jobs for African Americans in white owned businesses operating in their communities.[56] Faced with this kind of activism, even reserved leaders like Cleveland's Martin were forced to respond.

Her opportunity came in the 1936/37 school year when the Board of Education received persistent complaints from the NAACP and local African American media outlets about the treatment of African American students in the city's schools, but especially those in the Central community. On April 12, 1937, another resolution requesting a new Central High School building was submitted by a subcommittee representing the Citizen's Committee of Central High School, a group formed in 1935 by the principal to address community concerns. Initially, these matters had been referred to the Board's Educational Committee, chaired by Martin, who was still the only African American board member. By May 1937, it appeared that many African Americans had, understandably, completely lost faith in Martin as a leader, and the negative criticism of her work came not just from former friends in the NAACP, but also, increasingly, from the African American press.

In a lengthy and scathing editorial, the *Call and Post* called Martin to task for what it perceived as her lack of respect for other members of her race. The editorial referred specifically to Martin "snubbing

and ridiculing" the disgruntled NAACP members, who challenged
the board's position in the Longwood/Outhwaite controversy regarding the segregation of overage students at those schools and her suggestion that the problems at Central High School had been
exaggerated. Before closing the editorial, the writer lamented, "As for
Mrs. Martin, we realize she is completely lost in the maze of education questions that surround her and can only move from one problem to another when she is led. Her trouble is she is being led by the
wrong people." That the writer took it upon himself to remind Martin
that, "[W]hatever happens to Negroes in Cleveland, Mrs. Martin must
share it," speaks volumes about the growing rift between Martin and
many African Americans who had supported her in her successful
bids for office in 1929 and 1933. Many NAACP members joined the
newspaper editors in calling for a change in leadership at the school
board.[57]

As Martin's second term drew to a close, the Depression continued, even as conditions improved in some areas. At the start of 1937,
there were 98,000 employable persons unemployed in Cuyahoga
County, a 50% decrease from the peak figure of 199,000 four years
earlier at the beginning of Martin's second term in office.[58] Employed
teachers also had some reason to be optimistic about recent changes
in board financial policies. In the spring of 1937, members of the
American Federation of Teachers and the Cleveland Teachers Federation thanked the Board of Education for voting to restore salaries to
96% of schedule.[59] Clearly keeping the school doors open during this
lengthy period of economic downturn was the top priority for school
board members, including Martin.

While Du Bois and Martin were miles apart geographically, they
were obviously in the same camp when it came to making difficult
choices about the allocation of scarce educational dollars in the 1930s.
It appears that both rejected narrow-minded integrationist programs
that worked only to ensure equal access to inferior education in
poorly equipped classrooms staffed by underpaid and, perhaps,
overworked and frustrated teachers.

The Racial Politics of Special Education

In 1937, the Cleveland Board of Education found itself at the center of
a heated controversy involving the NAACP, the Interdenominational

Ministerial Alliance and others protesting what they perceived to be unfair Board policy of routinely labeling African American students "mental deficients" and "slow learners." Articles in the *Call and Post* alleged "Too many students were enrolled at Longwood and Outhwaite schools...permanent dumping grounds for not only the average but also the mentally deficient and slow-learning students."[60] To the dismay of African American parents, both institutions were located in the expanding ghetto of the Central community. The official reason given for the existence of schools of this type was the obligation of the schools to provide for the individual differences in children. According to one superintendent's report, there were three primary aims of the Special Education program:

> Socially, they were intended to make handicapped children acceptable and useful members of the community in which they live and to train them to become law-abiding citizens. Vocationally, they were designed to lessen the probability of the students becoming public charges (dependent or criminal) and help them become self-sufficient. Finally, they were designed to develop self-respect and self-reliance to enable him to employ his leisure with as much pleasure and profit to himself as a normal individual might expect.[61]

The work at the Longwood School was ungraded and often non-academic.[62] Many African American parents were convinced that the Board was trying to make Longwood and Outhwaite vocational schools for African Americans, so that they could justify their reluctance to admit African American students to East Technical and Jane Addams vocational schools attended by white students. By the time news articles appeared in 1937, the battle with the school board had raged on for years.

Several explanations have been offered for requiring a disproportionately high number of Negro students to attend these two schools. African American historian and educator, Russell H. Davis, was convinced that the assignment of African American students to these schools had less to do with racism than the inability of these children of recent migrants to the city to succeed in "regular classes." According to Davis, the under-prepared migrant students from the South needed the remedial classes offered in these schools. Statistics from the Division of Reference and Research of the Cleveland Public Schools showed that the 9,000 African American pupils were 6.6% of the total enrollment but over one-third (37.4%) of the children in the "over age for grade" classes, and 15.5% of the pupils in the classes for mental defectives.[63] As a school administrator and former classroom teacher, Davis's research and experiences in the schools had convinced him that precious time and energy were being wasted trying to close these institutions, when these resources could have been devoted to strengthening programs designed to meet the needs of under-prepared African American students. Martin's actions in 1937 suggest that she agreed with Davis.

When Martin announced that she would not seek re-election in 1937, many media observers assumed, with good reason, that it was due to her disagreement with the NAACP in the Longwood/Outhwaite controversy. In the second week of June 1937, both major dailies reported that the NAACP was urging the defeat of Martin. Chester K. Gillespie, president of the Cleveland branch, stated on June 8 that "he would appoint a committee of 50 in the next few days to choose a colored candidate to oppose Mrs. Mary B. Martin at the next election for membership on the Cleveland Board of Education."[64] For her part, Martin did not seem disturbed by the opposition movement:

> They didn't support me four years ago if you remember, and they never have given me any support. The NAACP is not doing anything to help us advance…They say I haven't gone along with them…I haven't gone along with them because I do not agree with them. I think they are all wrong.[65]

The NAACP's School Committee confronted members of the Board of Education about its policies related to the assignment of large numbers of African Americans to "special activity" schools for the mentally retarded or "overage for grade" pupil. After a month of inaction by Martin's committee, board member Ray Miller stated at the next scheduled meeting he would "present a motion to remove the [Longwood/Outhwaite School] issue from the consideration of the committee, and bring the matter to a vote by the entire Board,"[66] knowing that only a majority vote—rather than the three-fourths vote required by the committee—would be required for a final decision on the matter.

To the dismay of proponents of the NAACP resolution, the proposal to close the two schools was defeated by a vote of four to three. One NAACP representative insisted from the floor of the meeting that the board had "utterly failed to disprove any of the allegations contained in the resolution that had been submitted for action," but his efforts were to no avail.[67] Neither the board records nor newspaper accounts offer explanations for the motives of board members, including Martin, who voted against it.[68]

As far as many NAACP members were concerned, Martin had betrayed the trust of both the organization that whole-heartedly supported her candidacy and the African American students in the schools. On the day following the Board's rejection of the NAACP's request to have the schools closed, Education Committee Chair L. Pearl Mitchell confided in an NAACP colleague that she was "pretty much upset over the school fight here." In describing the failed effort to close the two "'Jim Crow' dumping schools for our children," Mitchell stated that segregating students by race in this manner was "a dangerous, subtle plan in our most democratic cities; one we must fight equally as hard—to retain—as to gain where we have been denied." In closing, Mitchell noted her plan to write to Thurgood Marshall, with whom she had discussed the needs of the Cleveland branch. She also enclosed with her letter a clipping from the July 7, 1937 edition of *The Plain Dealer*, with the headline "SPECIAL ACTIVITY SCHOOLS GET O.K.—Board Balks on Change at Outhwaite and Longwood." Mitchell hoped the clipping would be passed on to Marshall or Charles Hamilton Houston. They were among the most prominent men in the NAACP's nascent struggle for equal opportunities in education. Houston led NAACP efforts to document the inequities in programs serving African American and white students in the Jim Crow schools of the South. With his young protégé Thurgood Marshall, Houston perfected a legal strategy that would eventually lead to the landmark 1954 Brown decision, in which the Supreme Court would finally declare "Jim Crow" schools unconstitutional.[69]

In 1937, however, this victory was not even on the horizon when the Cleveland branch of the NAACP had lost an important battle in their local struggle against segregation. The record of Martin's work from 1930–1937 suggests that she could not or would not address publicly any of the controversial issues related to pupil and teacher segregation within in the classroom, or in certain "special" schools, But the story did not begin and end with Martin. Mitchell's desperate effort to reach out to the activist attorneys leading the NAACP's struggle to equalize educational opportunities at the national level suggests that at least one of Cleveland's African American school reformers was not yet ready to admit defeat.

Conclusion

By 1937, Martin was obviously disappointed in the leadership of the civil rights organization that she had helped launch. Her eight years on the board, however, could not have erased the memory of the important role played by the NAACP and other African American organizations during her 1929 campaign. Martin did run again, however, and she was re-elected to the school board in November 1939. Unfortunately for her supporters, she was not able to take her place on the board. On November 19, 1939, just two weeks after the election, she succumbed to bronchial pneumonia and a cerebral hemorrhage at City Hospital. The news of her death was greeted with shock, confusion about who might take her place on the board, an outpouring of sympathy for the family, and praise for Martin's work with the schools. Even the *Call and Post*, which had been very critical of Martin's behavior in the last years of her life, paid tribute to her:

> Mrs. Martin exemplified Negro motherhood and typified the new awakening of our women to public service...While we disagreed much and often with Mrs. Martin on her policies, at no time did we ever question her sincerity. She was a woman of strong convictions and once taking a position, was immovable.[70]

The awakening described by the *Call and Post* editor is one that some observers say was energized by the economic exigencies of the Great Depression, during which African American communities engaged in numerous protest activities.[71]

In 1930, at the start of Martin's service on the board, Charles W. Chesnutt had pointed to her success in winning the post and the historically open method of providing education at the public's expense as one advantage of which Clevelanders could be proud. He wrote: "There has never been racial segregation in the public schools. A colored woman is a member of the Board of Education, elected thereto by popular vote, the majority of which was white."[72] The use of the term "never" is misleading, given Chesnutt's knowledge of deliberate segregation of students and teachers during the tenure of Superintendent Spaulding. Chesnutt and other longtime residents of the African American community could, however, look upon the greater number of African Americans in the schools as a mixed blessing, of sorts. It is true that the strength of sheer numbers, made possible by the Great Migration, helped to convince the Cleveland Board of Education of the need for more African American teachers and administrators. It is also true, however, that the 1930s saw a greater effort on the part of school officials to segregate African Americans at all levels within the system.

While desegregation was not on the board's list of priorities during the Great Depression, it was near the top of the NAACP's list, along with demands for improvements at the majority African American Central High School. Due in part, perhaps, to the NAACP members' persistence, the new—and still segregated—Central High School, built with funds made available by New Deal legislation, opened in 1940, and the number of African American teachers there increased slowly but steadily throughout the twentieth century. It is also difficult to say whether these things occurred because of Martin's leadership in the 1930s. It is noteworthy, however, that these issues were addressed at all, given the difficult financial times brought on by the Depression and then World War II.

While NAACP members and other African Americans in Cleveland were waging their local battles against segregation, James Weldon Johnson, who served as Executive Secretary for the national body for a decade, used the occasion of the NAACP's twenty-eighth annual conference to address the crisis in African American "leadership" and the dangers associated with expecting too much from one person. The speech was delivered in Detroit, Michigan on July 2, 1937. At that time, it clearly and succinctly identified the urgent needs of the African American people. Today, it offers an interesting postscript to discussion of the Depression-era struggles of Martin:

> There is an old idea of leadership to which most of us cling—the idea of a single leader who combines within himself all the elements of leadership necessary for our guidance and salvation, of a Moses who will surely deliver us out of the hands of the Egyptians. The day for that type of leadership is past. The present situation requires a diversified leadership. The situation requires leadership on all fronts of the single battle in which we are engaged. We must have leaders in the fight for civil equality, industrial equality, political equality, and too, for social equality.[73]

Martin's style suggests that like Johnson, she also understood the challenges associated with being an African American leader in the 1930s.

Notes

1. William Edward Burghardt Du Bois, "Diuturni Silenti," in Herbert Aptheker, ed., *The Education of Black People: Ten Critiques, 1906–1960* (New York: Monthly Review Press, 2001) p. 78.

2. Cleveland Board of Education, *Official Proceedings*, January 6, 1930.

3. These ideas are discussed in "Principles of the NAACP," a brochure printed by the national organization and obtained from the Cleveland branch office in 1999.

4. For a discussion of the importance that Du Bois placed on education, see Aptheker, ed., *Education of Black People.*

5. *Annual Report,* Cleveland Branch Files, NAACP, 1914.

6. Frank Spaulding, *School Superintendent in Action in Five Cities* (Rindge: R. R. Smith, 1955) pp. 618–619. Apparently, Cleveland's "Little Italy" was not one of the communities that objected to the presence of African American teachers. Bertha Blue, a member of a well-known African American family in Cleveland, was a teacher at the Murray Hill School (located in Little Italy) from 1903 to 1947. See manuscript collection at the Western Reserve Historical Society for more information.

7. Cleveland Board of Education, *Superintendent's Annual Report* (Cleveland: Bureau of Child Accounting, 1933, 1935, 1945).

8. Cleveland Chamber of Commerce, "Report of the Negro Migration and Its Effects," in *The Charles W. Chesnutt Papers,* Western Reserve Historical Society, n.d.

9. For a discussion of the African American experience in urban schools, see David Tyack, *The One Best System. A History of American Urban Education* (Cambridge: Harvard University Press, 1974).

10. Russell H. Davis, *Black Americans in Cleveland* (Washington, D.C.: Associated Publishers, 1985) p. 252. Russell H. Davis, an African American and a native Clevelander, worked as both and teacher and an administrator in the Cleveland public schools.

11. "Communication to Executive Committee from the Cleveland Branch of the NAACP," (Charles White, President) February 14, 1927. Papers of the NAACP, Selected Records of Midwest Branches.

12. Willard Richan, *Racial Isolation in the Cleveland Schools: A Report of a Study Sponsored by the United States Commission on Civil Rights* (Cleveland: Case Western Reserve University, 1967).

13. Alonzo Grace, "The Effects of the Great Black Migration on the Cleveland Public Schools," (Unpublished dissertation, Case Western Reserve University, 1942); Kenneth Kusmer, *A Ghetto Takes Shape: Black Cleveland, 1870–1930* (Urbana: University of Illinois Press, 1976) pp. 160–161; *Encyclopedia of Cleveland History,* "Cleveland Public Schools" entry.

14. Grace, "Effects of the Great Black Migration," p. 24. Grace, a longtime employee of the Cleveland City Schools, also served on the Board of Trustees for the Negro Welfare Association.

15.   Davis, *Black Americans in Cleveland*, pp. 180, 252; Grace, "Effects of the Great Black Migration," p. 24.

16.   Cleveland Board of Education, *Superintendent's Annual Report* (1929) p. 26.

17.   Ibid., pp. 24–27.

18.   Richan, "Racial Isolation in the Cleveland Schools," p. 33.

19.   Cleveland Board of Education, *Official Proceedings*, April 15, 1929.

20.   See Jeffrey Mirel, *The Rise and Fall of an Urban School System: Detroit, 1907–81* (Ann Arbor: The University of Michigan Press, 1993) pp. 186–187; Michael W. Homel, *Down from Equality: Black Chicagoans and the Public Schools, 1920–41* (Urbana: University of Illinois Press, 1984) p. x; Allan H. Spear, *Black Chicago: The Making of a Negro Ghetto, 1890–1920* (Chicago and London: The University of Chicago Press, 1967); Vincent P. Franklin, *The Education of Black Philadelphia: The Social and Educational History of a Minority Community, 1900–1950* (Philadelphia: University of Pennsylvania Press, 1970) pp. xix, 137–140.

21.   "Slavery Gave City New Board Member," *Plain Dealer*, November 7, 1929; "Says Victory in School Board Race Surprise," *Cleveland Press*, November 7, 1929; Biographical sketch of Mary B. Martin (1877–1939) written "To the Children of the Mary B. Martin Elementary School," (n.d.) by Lydia J. Martin, in Mary B. Martin, Papers, Western Reserve Historical Society.

22.   *Legacy of Pride: Distinguished African American Alumni Families of Case Western Reserve University* (Cleveland: Case Western Reserve University, 1990) pp. 30–31.

23.   See Davis, *Black Americans in Cleveland*, pp. 232–234; Kusmer, *A Ghetto Takes Shape*, pp. 245–246. The longtime African American leader in Republican machine politics was Thomas Fleming, the first African American member of Cleveland's city council and husband of Lethia Fleming, a Republican organizer in local, state, and national activities. Mrs. Fleming was also a close friend and sister clubwoman to Mary B. Martin. See *Plain Dealer*, September 29, 1929; March 10, 1930.

24.   *Gazette*, November 16, 1929.

25.   *The Cleveland News*, December 27, 1929.

26.   For more information on these individuals, see Davis, *Black Americans in Cleveland*.

27.   Cleveland Board of Education, *Official Proceedings*, Resolution No. 21098, "Board's Approval for Appeal to Governor for Relief Measures," January 18, 1932.

28.   "Asks for Cheaper School Buildings," *Cleveland Press*, June 25, 1929.

29.   George W. Knepper, *Ohio and Its People* (Kent: Kent State University Press, 1989) p. 368.

30.   "Lift Teachers' Sick Leave Ban," *Cleveland Press*, December 23, 1930. Initially, board members had proposed to eliminate sick leave beginning January 1, 1931, but later changed the effective date to July 1, 1931. Cleveland Board of Education, *Official Proceedings*, May 16, 1932.

31.   "Teachers Face Ban If Wedded," *Cleveland Press*, May 7, 1931.

32.   "A Just Decision," *Cleveland Press*, May 19, 1931.

33. Cleveland Board of Education, *Official Proceedings,* March 20, 1933; "Married Women Stay in Schools," *Cleveland Press,* May 1931.
34. "A Just Decision."
35. Cleveland Board of Education, *Official Proceedings,* January 1, 1932.
36. Cleveland Board of Education, *Official Proceedings,* June 6, 1932.
37. "Say Discrimination Hits Colored Pupils," *Plain Dealer,* August 3, 1932.
38. Ibid.; Richan, "Racial Isolation in the Cleveland Public Schools," p. 33.
39. "Confidential Report on the Work of the Special Committee Organized to Study the Educational Problems of the Central High School District," June, 1933, cited in Richan, "Racial Isolation in the Cleveland Public Schools," pp. 33–34.
40. Richan, "Racial Isolation, p. 3.
41. "School Board Hit as Demoralization Grips Employees," *Cleveland Press,* May 11, 1933.
42. Ibid.
43. "Save Schools and Relief," *Plain Dealer* November 8, 1933.
44. Mary B. Martin Scrapbook, Western Reserve Historical Society.
45. "The Better Way," *Plain Dealer,* November 10, 1933.
46. Cleveland Board of Education, *Official Proceedings,* February 12, 1934.
47. Davis, *Black Americans in Cleveland,* p. 274.
48. Cleveland Board of Education, *Official Proceedings,* April 9, 1934.
49. Cleveland Board of Education, *Official Proceedings,* October 2, 1935.
50. Cleveland Board of Education, *Official Proceedings,* October 14, 1935.
51. Cleveland Board of Education, *Official Proceedings,* February 28, 1936.
52. W.E.B. Du Bois, "Does the Negro Need Separate Schools," (1935) in Waldo E. Martin Jr., *Brown v. Board of Education: A Brief History with Documents* (Boston: Bedford/St. Martin's, 1998) p. 97.
53. Ibid., p. 99.
54. See Joseph E. Harris, *African-American Reactions to War in Ethiopia, 1936–1941* (Baton Rouge and London: Louisiana State University Press, 1994).
55. See chapter 2, "Reveling in New Ideas," in Joanne Grant, *Ella Baker: Freedom Bound* (New York: John Wiley & Sons, Inc., 1998); Joy James, "Ella Baker, Black Women's Work and Activist Intellectuals," *The Black Scholar* Vol. 24, No. 4 (Fall 1994) pp. 9–15.
56. See Regennia Simpson, "The League's Legacy" *Clubdate* (March 1998) pp. 22–24; Kimberley L. Phillips, *Alabama North: African-American Migrants, Community, and Working-Class Activism in Cleveland, 1915–1945* (Urbana and Chicago: University of Illinois Press, 1999).
57. *Call and Post,* May 13, 1937.
58. "City's Employable Jobless Now 98,000," *Cleveland Press,* January 7, 1937.
59. Cleveland Board of Education, *Official Proceedings.*
60. *Call and Post,* July 16, 1936; January 7, 1937.
61. Cleveland Board of Education, *Superintendent's Annual Report* (1930) p. 14.
62. Ibid., p. 88.
63. Davis, *Black Americans in Cleveland,* p. 253.

64. "Urge Defeat of Martin," *Cleveland Press*, June 8, 1937; "Oppose Re-Election of Mrs. Mary Martin," *Plain Dealer*, June 9, 1937.
65. "Oppose Re-Election of Mrs. Mary Martin."
66. *Call and Post*, May 27, 1937.
67. *Call and Post*, May 27, 1937, and July 8, 1937.
68. Cleveland Board of Education, *Official Proceedings*, July 6, 1937.
69. Letter from L. Pearl Mitchell to "Roy" at the NAACP national headquarters, July 8, 1937, in NAACP Papers.
70. *Call and Post*, November 23, 1939.
71. Grant, *Ella Baker*, pp. 42–43.
72. Chesnutt, "The Negro in Cleveland," p. 24.
73. *Call and Post*, July 15, 1937.

Chapter Six

"Caught in a Tangled Skein": The Great Depression in South Carolina's Schools

Edward Janak

T he federal government of the United States historically treated education as a delegated power, leaving it almost exclusively in the hands of the states, until the 1950s. In the almost two decades following World War I, the federal government rarely chose to get involved in educating the nation's youth. However, as the nation's economy suffered during the Great Depression, many schools were seriously impacted. Schools lost funding in the initial years after the crash, teachers were unemployed, and children were left to wander. Especially hurt were those students who were already being victimized by American schools—children from low socioeconomic classes and African-Americans, for example. As the federal government chose to aid the nation's economy in its series of New Deal programs, so too did these programs aid the nation's schools.

South Carolina mimicked the pattern of the federal government regarding education; initially, the state was content leaving most decisions and funding issues in the hands of local control. However, the advent of the Great Depression drastically altered this notion. In the words of a former state superintendent of education, South Carolina found itself "temporarily caught in the tangled skein of the widespread economic depression."[1] While the Biblical reference may seem a bit of an exaggeration, to those living in the state during this period the reference was apt. Relief had to come in many ways in order for the schools to survive.

This relief did come from a variety of sources in a variety of means. In general, New Deal programs "literally saved thousands of Carolinians from starvation."[2] The federal government provided $154 million in federal loans and an additional $258 million in grants and outright expenditures,[3] of which much went into improving the schools, such as school lunch programs. New Deal programs actually had tremendous benefit on South Carolina schools; these efforts at Roosevelt's three "R"'s provided more assistance to South Carolina's schools than the state had been willing or able to do in the preceding years. In addition to the federal and state relief efforts, private funding sources such as New York City's General Education Board provided a variety of monetary and personnel aid to help save the schools. This combination of private and public sources supported South Carolina's public day schools, construction of school facilities, and the development of the school curriculum in the midst of the Great Depression.

School historians agree that philosophically, schools did not make much progress during this period. As explained by Dominic Moreo:

> the events of the Depression outdistanced contemporary thought in education. There was neither a new conception of the role of the schools nor a new institutional mechanism for delivery of schooling...thus, bereft of ideas, vehicles, and leadership, the schools, singly and collectively, were left to drift.[4]

This philosophical stagnation notwithstanding and contrary to popular belief, this chapter seeks to prove that as a result of the financial efforts of the federal government and philanthropic foundations, the schools of South Carolina specifically, and across the United States generally, actually thrived during the years of the Depression.

South Carolina and the Great Depression

As the twentieth century dawned and progressed, much of the South was reinventing itself in the "New South." Encouraged by Henry Grady's editorials, portraits of Confederate dead were removed and industry was encouraged to relocate to the Southern side of the Mason-Dixon. Cities such as Atlanta and Charlotte were beginning to spring up where farmland punctuated by mills had previously existed. Southerners were trying to abandon their image of white suits and mint juleps in favor of a more cosmopolitan, urbane persona. Many Southern states were able to lay the groundwork of reinventing themselves in the 1920s.[5]

Prior to the Great Depression, however, South Carolina ran contrary to this New South rhetoric. Cotton was still king. The economy was predominantly linked to agricultural production and process, the farms and the mills. As noted by historian Jack Irby Hayes, South Carolina "was Dixie, the land of cotton." The majority of the state's land—one in every eleven total acres—was planted in cotton. Even those not working on or around the cotton farms still had their careers dictated by the crop. The majority of workers scraped by in a cotton mill and spent their leisure time in a cotton mill village. By the years of the Great Depression, 1 million of the 1.7 million South Carolinians were cotton farmers, mill workers, or their families.[6]

Although "Black Friday," October 29, 1929, marked the start of the Great Depression, South Carolina had been feeling the effects of a statewide depression since 1917 when the boll weevil was first detected in South Carolina. Across the state, the weevil would eat up to 93% of counties' cotton crops before Depression's beginning. Hardest hit were the Sea Islands, where 90% of the cotton crop was destroyed and commercial cotton was never raised again. Between 1910 and 1920, South Carolina averaged 1,365,000 bales of cotton produced; during the 1920s, it averaged just 801,000.[7] The agriculture crash led to vast outmigration of poor whites and African-Americans from the state and to the spread of diet-related diseases such as pellagra.

As went South Carolina's cotton crops, so too turned the fortunes of its mills. In the aftermath of the agricultural crash, the cotton mills had to make adjustments to remain profitable. Further complicating the scenario, many of the state's mills had been purchased on the heels of a very profitable World War I period for greatly inflated prices; as such, the owners were already trying to regain as much of the market as they could. Techniques such as the "speed up," in which workers were faced with minimum quotas in order to get paid and machines were set at faster speeds, and the "stretch out," in which workers were given a greater number of machines to tend, led to overall worker pay in the mills declining. Worse, in mill owner's desire to regain their investments, the mills began to overproduce—in spite of the declining cotton crops. By 1928, not only was the state in an agricultural crash, but the prices of its textiles were dropping to record lows—producing the beginning of an industrial depression long before Black Friday.

These agricultural and related textile crises placed the state in a financial crunch. Tourism provided one possible route to recovery. South Carolina cities such as Aiken, Camden, and Summerville had for years developed resorts catering to "well-to-do northerners enroute to and from Florida."[8] Coupled with these programs was the newly-emerging form known as highway tourism. Many highways were built or connected linking the North to the South; for example, in 1910, the Capital Highway opened connecting Washington, D.C. with Atlanta, Georgia by way of Columbia. Quickly, towns such as

Columbia along the route found their business booming as tourists came to them.[9]

By the 1920s, other cities developed means of attracting tourists: Columbia held Palmafesta, a celebration meant to imitate Mardi Gras; Spartanburg began an annual music festival; and Folly Beach began a beauty pageant. Charleston held the South Carolina Interstate and West Indian Exposition in 1901[10] and soon thereafter developed its annual Azalea Festival.[11] Charleston also boasts one of the nation's oldest natural tourist parks: Magnolia Gardens, which was the site of the nation's first importation of azaleas in 1843.[12]

Coastal development catering to tourism also flourished in the 1920s. The first resort in Myrtle Beach opened in 1926, and the city plan was established. Soon family resort communities would arise up and down the coast in Floral Beach, Atlantic Beach, Ocean Drive, and Cherry Grove.[13] This newly-emerging tourism industry was shunted aside with the onset of the Depression, as more Americans spent significantly less money on tourism. Tim Hollis explains that most histories of the tourism industry begin after 1936 because "the Great Depression did stunt the fledgling industry's growth..."[14] Most Americans were choosing to stay home or only travel locally, and tourism across the nation suffered.

With its decline, tourism was not enough to correct the economic damage created by the Great Depression. Farmers watched as the cash value of the state's crops dropped more than 50% between 1929 and 1931. Cotton that had sold for seventeen cents a pound in 1917 was selling for less than six cents a pound in 1931. For the cotton mill worker, the situation was no better. Mills only ran on the average 237 days per year by 1930 and average annual wages dropped from $719 in 1929 to $495 by 1932. Cotton prices dipped to their lowest level since 1894. The effect was felt on Wall Street as well; by 1933, the securities rate of the majority of mills was not even being reported.[15] One of the wealthiest South Carolinians, John Woodside, owned both cotton mills and resort developments. By 1932 he had lost not only all of his business property, selling them for a fraction of their worth, but his own home as well.[16]

Because most South Carolinians were engaged in agriculture, their loss of income equaled a loss of educational income. Throughout the twentieth century, the South Carolina Legislature had linked the majority of school funding bills to districts collecting local levies; by 1928, all of South Carolina's 45 counties, except Charleston, had districts levying taxes of at least 10 mills[17] for support of the schools, and Charleston averaged 8 mills. For example, Lodge School District, in Colleton County levied a 30-mill tax in support of the schools. In 1928, $7,895,183 of total receipts (46% of $16,988,189) came from local sources.[18]

Table 6.1: Local Revenue Sources Through the Depression[19]

Year	Poll Tax	Dog Tax	3-Mill Constitutional Tax	4-Mill Ad Valorem Tax*	Local Tax, Ordinary Use	Local Bond Interest
1928	$197,407	$62,078	$1,195,017	$1,583,831	$4,952,887	$903,964
1929	179,903	54,668	1,209,222	1,642,849	5,173,243	1,048,122
1930	181,199	49,226	1,188,628	1,591,301	5,196,106	1,002,202
1931	175,343	67,211	1,097,402	1,485,206	4,706,773	911,696
1932	132,153	30,873	1,059,871	1,432,541	4,354,108	1,054,523
1933	117,407	23,139	998,133	1,326,257	3,808,870	1,002,149
1934	146,921	30,570	1,152,365	302,409	4,529,566	1,048,672
1935	136,706	32,683	1,073,105	*	4,850,094	966,739
1936	143,391	38,137	1,084,195	*	4,583,817	989,896
1937	171,790	43,250	1,123,096	*	4,884,842	959,815
1938	151,937	35,178	1,068,702	*	4,758,647	934,232
1939	170,017	50,546	1,075,584	*	4,691,154	999,798

As delineated in Table 6.1, not only did school income fluctuate from county to county due to millage rates, but also from year to year by what people were able to pay. For example, the state was collecting less than half of its 1928 dog tax rate by 1933. This fluctuation of revenue troubled the State Department of Education for obvious reasons. By 1933, the year of the state's lowest collection of taxes, State Superintendent of Education James Hope explained that "[l]ocal units of taxation have about broken down." He further explained that if not "for the fact that our public schools are financed in part from taxes collected from indirect sources hundreds of schools in South Carolina this year would have closed their doors against the children who sought admission to their classrooms."[20]

Clearly the general loss of income resulted in a simultaneous loss of educational income. As much as the state board of education wanted to avoid it, the tax revenue to support schools had simply become nonexistent. By 1933 the loss of local education funds caused the closing of several hundred rural schools.[21] Hardest hit were the schools serving the poor communities and African-Americans that relied on state funding to remain open. Unfortunately for these groups, the problems caused by the Great Depression were both reflective of and symptomatic of inequities in long-term patterns of economic development in South Carolina. As such, the state could not remain self-sufficient; federal intervention was necessary. South Carolina was not unique in this regard; federal relief programs had to step in if the nation's schools were to reopen with any continuity.

A New Deal for South Carolina Education

As Regina Werum explains, there was some disconnect as to the purpose of education in helping to relieve the nation. The legislative branch of the federal government did not see education as a means of helping the nation, noting in the record of the House of Representatives, "education and training are not a guaranty against dependency and destitution." However, New Deal leaders and the relief agencies they spearheaded realized that education could provide two means of assistance to the nation: training local workers in whatever vocations were needed in their areas, and warehousing the unemployed.[22] As such, federal relief programs immediately began hiring teachers and re-opening schools.

Federal aid programs and their state and local divisions came to the rescue of South Carolina's schools. By April 1934, the Federal Emergency Relief Administration (FERA) had hired 800 teachers in South Carolina, paying their salaries out of federal funds. The state division of this program, the South Carolina Emergency Relief Administration (SCERA), took this action to another level and spent more than $750,000 to employ 3,350 additional teachers. When schools closed, the lines between grades, public, and adult education became blurred in the drive to keep educators working. Teachers implemented lessons any place they could: "teachers found themselves conducting classes in churches, private homes, and in one instance at the end of a row of cotton where a plowman stopped his mule to receive a lesson."[23]

Even as teachers were getting put back to work, though, the nation's banking crisis adversely impacted South Carolina's educational system.[24] By 1933, fully two-thirds of South Carolina's banks were closed.[25] While state revenues were kept in banks around the South Carolina, mostly in county seats, the State Department of Education held all of its accounts in the South Carolina National Bank (SCNB) in Columbia. When the SCNB failed—when it closed its doors and would no longer make any payouts—that failure meant the failure of the entire State Department to meet payroll, appropriations, and travel funds.

In an effort to alleviate the crisis, Superintendent of Education Hope met with Jackson Davis, a representative of the General Education Board (GEB) of New York City in March of 1933. Like the majority of states in the recently reconstructed south, South Carolina had become dependent upon GEB funds to provide money to African-American schools as well as fund positions within the State Department. Educational historian Charles Biebel describes the GEB as starting a full regional movement regarding African-American education in the south, trying to get the southern states to adopt the Hampton-Tuskeegee model of vocational education. As such, South Carolina's dependency upon GEB funds was arguably exactly what the Board desired in order to enforce its policies across the state. Members of the GEB described vocational education (with no academic preparation) as "the solution to the southern race problem."[26] South Carolina was no exemption; quite a few of its schools, and several positions within the state department, relied on GEB funds.

These funds, however, were on deposit in the failed bank. Worse, the State Department had to provide the GEB a detailed accounting of how funds were spent each year in order to be eligible to receive any more funding. The bank had promised the State Department 40% of its money back; however, there was no guarantee that any more would be replaced. As such, the State Department had to take two actions with the GEB. First, it provided a detailed accounting of the exact amount that was still on deposit in the bank, rather than having been spent in salaries or school construction; and second, it requested an additional $1,800 from the GEB until the bank came through.

In a letter to Davis, Hope detailed the specific needs of the State Department. Due to the bank's closure, the State Department had not been able to pay salaries of six State Department officials.[27] By the end of November, the GEB had sent $2,300 to cover their expenses and salaries, an advance on the following year's appropriations. By June of 1934, the State Department had received $1,434 of its money from the South Carolina National Bank; however, it was still owed $2,150. That same month the GEB provided an additional $1,268 to the State Department to cover travel expenses and salaries. The money woes and funding help from the GEB would continue for another four years. In 1937, the State Department began receiving its money back from the bank and began repaying the GEB. It took until February 1938, however, before the State Department could repay the GEB in full. Interest on the loans was paid in full by 1940.[28]

The bank closure and the subsequent delinquent payments from the South Carolina State Department of Education may have been contributing factors in the gradual withdrawal of GEB support in the state. In 1930, the GEB financed six positions within the State Department: the Supervisor of Negro Schools, the Acting Assistant Supervisor of Negro Schools, the Director of the Bureau of Information and Research, the Director of Schoolhouse Planning and Construction, a draftsman, and a stenographer to this office. By 1940, when the State Department finally paid all debts to the GEB, these had been reduced to partial payment of the salaries to two positions: the State Agent of Negro Schools and the Assistant State Agent of Negro Schools.[29] Thus, there was a concomitant increase in public money in the form of federal aid with a decrease in private money in the form of philanthropic aid that provided for, even in the face of bank failures and revenue shortfalls, the continuation of public education— even if this continuance placed some strain on the teachers and the individual schools.

Relief for Teachers and Schools

There was a marked contrast in educational funding patterns during these years: while teachers' salaries dropped, only to be partially replenished with federal aid, schools were expanding the services they would offer in order to become the centers of their respective communities. Before New Deal programs began relief efforts, government agencies were forced to reduce salaries of their employees, specifically school district employees. By 1933, the city governments of Columbia, Charleston, and Greenville paid school district employees in city scrip.[30] Even teachers who were not paid in scrip were greatly affected. In 1928, the average white teacher was paid $1,022 annual salary; by 1935, this salary had dropped to $751.[31] This salary trend in South Carolina was greater than the national decline. Nationally, teachers were paid an average of $1,420 in 1929; by 1934, this salary had dropped to $1,227.[32] African-American teachers were even harder hit. Already lower paid due to institutional racism, African-American teachers watched their salaries drop from the 1928 average of $302 to the 1935 average of $267.[33]

Hope noted that "teachers have not had fair treatment" by way of salary difficulties in his 1933 report. He reported that South Carolina knew that "under prevailing financial conditions of the past few years financial salaries and other school services had to be reasonably curtailed." However, Hope was quick to add that "teachers are being paid wages for expert services that are in comparison with ordinary unskilled labor unfair and unjust."[34]

The federal government relief programs alleviated some of this difficulty. One such act early into the New Deal was the National Recovery Administration (NRA). As described by historian Moreo, this act was created to protect workers who had managed to keep their jobs. Nationally, the codes were seen as a protective godsend and welcomed by union and nonunion workers alike. However, teacher unions in the U.S. balked, making the NRA codes "a lost opportunity for the teachers of the land" as many teachers and teacher unions did not understand or apply the codes to their profession.[35] In South Carolina, however, the NRA was somewhat more useful. Under the NRA, 1,300 teachers were employed for four months per school year and the NRA contributed $71,000 to their salaries.[36]

Even as there was a decline in tax revenue supporting the schools and an increase in various relief forms that lowered teacher's salaries, the schools assumed more prominent community roles during the Great Depression. As noted by Henry Perkinson, the public schools of the United States have always had a "messianic purpose"—have always been placed in the role of social savior.[37] Throughout their history, the public schools have been asked to solve a variety of social ills. This role of school as social problem-solver became even more clearly defined after the crash.

With the decline in the average citizen's income came a need for entertainment that was affordable, a place to gather with supportive community members, and even a place to seek work. Following the pattern of the nation, local schools more than ever moved to the forefront of South Carolina's social life in fulfilling these needs within the community. With the dearth of money, the schools became not only a place of education, but also "an opportunity to gain work" and a social center. Students remembered schools hosting turkey dinner contests, in which students cooked and the community ate. Athletes recalled community social events such as dances being scheduled at the schools immediately following athletic contests. Other students remembered community dances being held weekly at the school. Allendale High School featured May Day activities, such as maypole wrapping, for the community.[38]

With the various relief efforts taking place and the rising need for schools as community centers, schools became enhanced during this period, even if teacher salaries did not reflect this trend. Schools run by mill owners were just one example of this trend. In Greenville, South Carolina, the Parker School District operated for mill workers' children. Founded in 1924, Parker High School grew to become the "best equipped vocational school in the United States."[39] The district used the first school bus in South Carolina. In 1934, it opened a museum, victory gardens, and warehouse. Four years later, a new vocational building featured shops for welding, machine tool, power sewing, textile equipment, drafting, arts and crafts, and auto and fender repair; this building was also occupied by district offices. In 1939, the school opened its own clinic and a gymnasium, complete with two basketball courts.[40]

While Parker was an exceptional school, it was not the exception to school growth during this period. Opened in 1925, the Robert Smalls School of Beaufort served African-American students in grades 1–10 until 1932. That year, the school burned down. However, the community was able to raise funding not only to rebuild the school out of brick, but it expanded the school to include an 11th grade as well.[41]

Not all construction went as smoothly as with Parker or Smalls. The University of South Carolina broke ground on its Wardlaw College of Education in 1930 with the stipulation that a laboratory school be included. This laboratory school became the Peabody School. Opened in 1932, the Peabody School contained the most amenities of any modern high school: a gymnasium, principal's office (to be shared with the State High School Inspector), library, and cafeteria. Peabody even offered shop and mechanical drawing classes in the basement. However, building funds were exhausted, leaving the Peabody School without lockers, water fountains, intercom system, or lights. The school's Hi-Y Club held a fundraiser, and was able to raise enough money to put lighting in the school.[42]

The Progressivist Influence on Schools and Politics

The new, expanded curricular and extracurricular efforts taking place in South Carolina's schools reflected the national trend toward Progressivism in education. In general, Progressivism was a wide variety of changes affecting American political, social, and institutional behavior in response to societal worries about factors such as immigration, economic competition, rapid urbanization, farm outmigration, monopolies, political corruption, economic instability, class conflict, privilege, social unrest, and the plight of children. In education, Progressivism was defined by four objectives: first, to make schools more useful by adding programs such as health and vocational training; second, to turn schools into social centers via programs such as adult education and literacy clubs; third, to remove the schools from politics by abolishing ward systems, making school board members nonpartisan, and redefining districts so they did not match political zones; and fourth, making schools more scientific in terms of administration, curriculum, and pedagogy. Even though money was tight at all levels, the general public continued to demand that the schools receive as much funding as feasible. As such, they also demanded politicians that shared their beliefs of how tightly stretched budget dollars should be spent.

With this belief, the schools were not alone in this new spirit of progressivism; the New Deal made South Carolina's politics more progressive as well. Governor Ibra Blackwood's response to the economic difficulties was almost pure Herbert Hoover: a balanced budget, sales tax, and reduction to state aid to education. Blackwood's last year in office marked the lowest appropriations from the state legislature in eleven years that, in part, reduced teacher's salaries and decreased aid to education by 19%. His rhetoric almost guaranteed his loss in the election of 1934.[43]

The first New Deal governor was Olin D. Johnson, holding office from 1934 to 1938. He "presided over a mini-New Deal in South Carolina" getting many beneficial acts of legislation through the State House such as workmen's compensation, a forty-hour-work week, social security, reduced fees for license plates and a fifty-six-hour work week for non-textile workers. Truly becoming the "Education Governor," Johnson introduced for the first time statewide compulsory education for children between the ages of seven to sixteen (previously only a local option), established a statewide textbook rental agency, lengthened the school term from six to eight months, and raised teacher salaries.[44]

The passage of the 1937 Attendance Act, making education compulsory statewide, generated the need for relief programs outside the schools. As such, educators quickly began to cite the need for public funding outside the realm of education. Superintendent Hope commented in his 1937 report that passage of this act made it "necessary to supply clothing, books, shoes, medical attention, eye glasses, and other helpful services for children of indigent parents." Local, state, and federal relief efforts did help this problem. Locally, church groups, individuals, and merchants helped; statewide Federation of Women's Clubs and medical associations pitched in; national fraternal organizations such as the Masons contributed; and the Works Progress Administration (WPA) provided assistance. Collectively these groups generated "the most helpful programs of education" for students "in the history of public education in the State."[45]

The WPA assisted in efforts to feed South Carolina's schoolchildren in two manners. First, the WPA provided surplus foodstuffs secured from the federal government to the schools. This surplus food was used in a relief effort still in existence in today's schools: the free and reduced charge lunch program. Second, the WPA began a school garden program, providing both fresh produce to the schools and canning extra food for community use, a program that has unfortunately fallen out of vogue. By 1940, over 100,000 children had eaten a WPA-provided hot lunch.[46]

Programs such as these had a lasting impression on the public perception of the role of schools. No longer simply places to educate the children, as previously cited in this chapter, schools expanded their purpose to include helping solve social problems. While these examples are limited to curbing hunger, the precedent quickly expanded into a variety of other programs. Like many other times in American history, South Carolina used its schools to bring about Progressive ends. When a problem faced society, the schools became the answer to the problem.

Race and Education

Progressivism in South Carolina was not limited to the educational and political realms, however, as this new-found belief spread to social progressive movements as well. The New Deal is considered to be the birth of the civil rights period in the United States. Superintendent Hope realized that education was one means of recovery for all citizens of the state; the Great Depression had begun the process of shattering color lines in his mind. Superintendent Hope brought the race issue to the forefront of his 1931 *Annual Report.* On the first page, Hope wrote "[w]e have in our midst today a race of little children that challenges our responsibilities." He used patriotic rhetoric in issuing his call for African-American education, cautioning the state that "[w]hen the opportunity of education for all classes and races declines, this democracy of ours and the liberties we enjoy under it shall decline also."[47]

However much the State Department of Education wanted to begin taking down color lines, the federal government did not follow suit. It is an unfortunate fact that the majority of relief programs strictly benefited white South Carolinians. For example, 95% of Public Works Administration (PWA) appropriations before 1938 were devoted to white school construction.[48] The development of African-American schools was left almost primarily up to private means, including donations from local residents and national philanthropic groups.

Yet private philanthropic contributions to African-American schools declined during the Depression as well. In 1930, African-American schools received a total of $56,984. Of this, $10,039 came from the aforementioned GEB to continue its program of fostering vocational education. The Jeanes Foundation was a group of investors who trained African-American teachers who were then expected to train more teachers at the district level. This foundation supplied $9,250. The Rosenwald Fund was established by Sears-Roebuck magnate Julius Rosenwald. While different in source than the GEB, it shared the vision of vocational education, and supplied $26,670 to this end. The Slater Fund, another northern philanthropic group supporting a wider variety of African-American educational projects, supplied an additional $10,875.[49]

By 1937, this total amount had dwindled to less than 24% of its 1930 contributions, a total of $13,479. Of this, $600 came from the GEB, $9,241 from the Jeanes Foundation, $610 from the Rosenwald Fund, and $3,028 from the Slater Fund.[50] By 1940, the *Annual Report* did not list any contributions other than two positions funded by the GEB. Local schools, state institutions, and the state department of education all felt the loss of these dollars in forms such as missing construction funds. This loss also helped account for the aforementioned dramatic decline in African-American teacher salaries at the height of the Great Depression—a condition that, due to local support and state efforts, would be balanced by 1940.

In spite of these financial setbacks, African-American schools continued to grow during the Great Depression. Local communities of African-Americans in South Carolina were used to serious financial setbacks. Since the Civil War, for example, they had endured a system of dual taxation to support both white and African-American schools in their communities. African-Americans rallied what support they could in a variety of forms: financial, building materials, construction and instruction labor, and other forms of moral and community support. These local efforts, combined with the lip service coming from the State Department of Education, encouraged many firsts for African-American education during this period.

In 1929, the first state diplomas were awarded to African-American students from Columbia, Darlington, and Union high schools. By 1940, there were 37 accredited African-American high schools in South Carolina. Additionally, the number of one-teacher African-American schools dwindled from 1,471 to 805 while the number of African-American high schools with three or more teachers increased from 210 to 531 by 1940. The length of term of African-American schools increased from 114 days in 1929 to 147 days in 1940. While average teacher salaries dropped, between 1929 and 1940 the average African-American teacher's salary rose. While still considerably lower than their white counterparts and in spite of descending to a low point in the mid 1930s, African-American salaries increased overall from $316 in 1929 annually to $525 in 1940.[51]

Educational Expansion

Across the state, the public schools benefited from New Deal reform efforts such as the WPA. When President Roosevelt got South Carolina back to work, much of the work was for the benefit of the schools. The WPA expanded educational facilities in South Carolina by making school construction one of its primary goals. A new high school was built in Greenville, for example, as a result of the WPA. In Columbia, the African-American Booker T. Washington school saw the

construction of a new field house for the athletic field and gymnasium thanks to WPA efforts.[52] In its first three years of operation in
state, the agency constructed 228 new schools and made additions or
improvements on 632 others. By July 1943, when the program came to
an end, 2,179 schools were constructed or improved in some way. In
addition to these efforts, the PWA built 87 buildings for public school
and university use in South Carolina.[53]

The WPA assisted with school equipment as well as facilities.
WPA workers built thousands of desks to replace benches, added athletic fields, constructed 5,659 school toilets, landscaped school
grounds, removed fire hazards, improved ventilation by adding or
altering windows, and painted interiors and exteriors. Historian Jack
Hayes comments that thanks to the WPA, the majority of white students in South Carolina attended schools that were "adequate, safe,
and comfortable."[54]

Many of the New Deal construction programs in schools were
specifically designed to make students employable by expanding vocational and commercial training. In this respect, the programs pre-
dated the state's School-to-Work initiative of 1996, but the goals were
the same. In 1938, for example, the PWA constructed the vocational
department addition of Columbia's Olympia High School. This new
wing featured both a textile and an auto repair shop, and had classrooms for shorthand, typing, bookkeeping, commercial law, home
economics, and diversified occupations.[55]

The New South rhetoric did not affect South Carolina's schools.
Either in spite of South Carolina's agricultural problems, or as a
means to improve them, many schools continued to promote agricultural education. The National Youth Administration (NYA) built farm
shops in schools with "regular teachers" of agriculture. These shops
not only trained students in the newest agricultural techniques, but
also "provided work for youth" and "provided facilities for farmers
to make and remodel many of the articles needed on the farm and in
the farm home."[56]

This move to vocationalism was also reflected in the South Carolina High School League's Mental Contest Program. During the Depression, the program added several commercial and vocational contests to what had hitherto been almost exclusively an academic series.
Bookkeeping was added in 1935, as was an entire battery of industrial
contests. Included in these were textile, woodworking, drawing, and
tool craft. However, the commerce contests (typewriting and stenog-

raphy) were abolished from 1932 until 1934 due to problems with their expenses.[57]

The improvements to South Carolina's infrastructure as a result of New Deal programs also had benefit to the state's educational system. Prior to the New Deal programs, the majority of South Carolina lacked electricity and paved roads. School districts did not begin transporting their students until 1916, and most school districts during the 1920s still did not offer public transportation. As a result, the State Department of Education recommended that districts build schools no more than five miles apart, as any greater distance would be too much for students to walk.[58] Following this mentality, many districts operated one, two, or three teacher schools out of geographic necessity.

Through a variety of initiatives, New Deal relief programs built an infrastructure that would make this a trend of the past. During its four months of operation, beginning in November 1933, the Civil Works Administration (CWA) spent almost a third of its budget attempting to give every family access to a paved road. Many other New Deal programs improved roads as well. For example, the SCERA constructed or repaired more than 2,200 miles of road and 116 miles of sidewalks. The WPA added 100 miles of paved roads, 3,476 miles of unpaved roads, 380 new bridges, and 125 improved bridges. The PWA sponsored 179 highway projects, although more would have been completed had not Governor Johnson attacked the state highway department, leading to a two-year court battle.[59]

The expansion of the roads led schools to extend their transportation networks. Money spent on transporting white students went from a low of $642,086 in 1933 to $1,111,709 in 1940, when 1,644 buses transported white students.[60] Unfortunately, the transportation of African-American students was not so extensive. In 1931, the State Agent of Negro Schools noted that "Negro children all walk to school."[61] Money spent on transporting African-American students grew at a rate much greater than that of white students, yet remained insufficient throughout the Depression. In 1933, the state spent $642,086 transporting white students but only $628 on African-American students. By 1940, South Carolina spent $4,361 operating a mere 8 buses for African-American students, averaging approximately one bus per six counties.[62]

Electrification also benefited South Carolina's schools. Without electricity, many regions of the state kept the bulk of their schools, in particular secondary schools, in county seats, towns, and cities. By the Great Depression, the majority of high schools in South Carolina were in cities and towns. However, the Rural Electrification Authority erected power lines to be served by the newly-constructed Santee Cooper and Buzzard Roost hydroelectric plants. The private electric companies, such as Duke Power and South Carolina Electric Company, balked at these efforts but when the Supreme Court upheld the Tennessee Valley Authority, the private companies extended their lines as well. In 1936, for example, these private companies built 1,200 miles of rural power lines. The end result was productive: in 1934, only 2% of South Carolina was electrified; by 1940, 14.5% of the state had electricity.[63]

With these new roads and electrical lines in place, distance and size of town were no longer factors in school maintenance. It can be deduced that since transportation and new facilities were cost effective, many districts in South Carolina were able to consolidate their schools. Districts built multi-room schoolhouses and comprehensive high schools that offered a wealth of academic and vocational coursework. It can also be deduced that transportation and electrification meant schools could exist in outlying reaches of the state that previously had been unable to accommodate more than one-room schoolhouses.

By 1940, the rhetoric of relief gave way to notions of national security raised by the impending idea of United States intervention in World War II. Although the talk had changed, the programs remained the same. In the 1940 *Annual Report*, the state superintendent and his agents described relief agencies serving the schools and the state in terms of "our schools: an indispensable line of defense." Teaching vocational agriculture was now titled "defense education of rural youth under agriculture." These were not the only programs getting renamed in wartime terms; in addition, there were programs in "defense education in home economics," offering home-making training, and "defense training in trades and industrial education," in order to "train persons in occupations essential to national defense."[64]

Conclusion

The "accepted wisdom" regarding education during the Great Depression was that of declining opportunity and loss in funding.[65]

South Carolina proves that this was not the case. Overall, the effects of the New Deal programs in South Carolina's educational system were extensive and far-reaching. Schools continued their transformation during this period into a new system of public education. While the improvements were not equitable for white and African-American students, both made substantive gains in educational opportunities.

Acts of legislation, many in the works since the turn of the century, passed regularly. Relief programs provided the populace with income that translated into local school-supporting taxes. Buildings were expanded, improved, or built new, many of which are still in serviceable operation as public schools at the time of this writing. A school lunch program started serving the needs of South Carolina's students. The growth of infrastructure transformed consolidated schools from an idea into a reality.

Schools during the Great Depression underwent a shift in purpose. Schools began serving a wide spectrum of purposes: curricular programs, such as vocational education; non-curricular programs, such as school lunches; and extracurricular activities, such as competitions, all marked a shift toward a social, messianic purpose in education. While the purposes of schools and programs offered in the schools were expanding, however, funding was not expanding at the same rate. Nationally, the effects of the New Deal programs on education were not as profound. The short-term gains made under these programs did not, in fact, begin a permanent pattern of federal aid for the schools, which would not occur until the litigious times of the 1950s. The most profound effect of the Great Depression was not an economic or concrete improvement; rather, it was the philosophical shift in beliefs of South Carolinians towards education that led the state to a "remarkable renaissance of education."[66] This shift and its concomitant progressive attitudes began the process of ushering South Carolina into what would eventually become a post-*Brown v. Board of Education* world.

Notes

1.   *Sixty-Fourth Annual Report of the State Superintendent of Education of the State of South Carolina* [hereafter *Annual Report*] (Columbia: Joint Committee on Printing, General Assembly of South Carolina, 1932), p. 15.
2.   Walter Edgar, *South Carolina: A History* (Columbia: University of South Carolina Press, 1998), p. 499.
3.   Idem, *South Carolina in the Modern Age* (Columbia: University of South Carolina Press, 1992), p. 48.
4.   Dominic Moreo, *Schools in the Great Depression* (New York: Garland Publishing, 1996), p. 4. See also David B. Tyack, Robert Lowe, and Elizabeth Hansot, *Public Schools in Hard Times: The Great Depression and Recent Years* (Cambridge, Mass.: Harvard University Press, 1984).
5.   For further discussion of the New South, see W. J. Cash, "Of quandary— And the birth of a dream," in *The Mind of the South* (Garden City, NY: Doubleday Anchor Books, 1941); James Cooke, "The New South," in Donald Sheehan, and Harold Syrett, eds., *Essays in American Historiography* (Baton Rouge: Louisiana State University Press, 1960); Paul Gaston, "The 'New South'," in Arthur Link and William Rembert, eds., *Writing Southern History: Essays in Historiography in Honor of Fletcher M. Green* (Baton Rouge: Louisiana State University Press, 1967); John Crowe Ransom, "Reconstructed but Unregenerate," in *I'll Take My Stand: The South and the Agrarian Tradition* (New York: Harper Torchbooks, 1962); C. Vann Woodward, "A Southern Critique for the Gilded Age," in *The Burden of Southern History* (New York: New American Library, 1968).
6.   Jack Irby Hayes, *South Carolina and the New Deal* (Columbia: University of South Carolina Press, 2001), pp. xi, 157.
7.   Edgar, *South Carolina: A History*, p. 449.
8.   Edgar, *South Carolina in the Modern Age*, pp. 55–56.
9.   Tim Hollis, *Dixie before Disney: 100 years of Roadside Fun* (Jackson: University Press of Mississippi, 1999), p. xi.
10.   This exposition proved to be a financial failure due to a lack of local business interest, a boycott from the African-American community, unseasonably cold weather, and competition from the World's Fair in Buffalo, New York. The buildings of the expo, called the "Ivory City," were demolished and sold for scrap to pay off its debts.
11.   Edgar, *South Carolina: A History*, pp. 55–56.
12.   Hollis, *Dixie before Disney*, p. 127.
13.   Edgar, *South Carolina in the Modern Age*.
14.   Hollis, *Dixie before Disney*, p. xi.
15.   Hayes, *South Carolina and the New Deal*, pp. 8–9.
16.   Edgar, *South Carolina: A History*, p. 499.
17.   In this usage, the term "mills" refers to the rate of property taxation. Each county and municipality applies its millage rate to assessed value of property to determine the tax due. The millage rate is equivalent to the tax per $1,000 of assessed value. The millage rate varies among taxing districts; in

this case, Charleston would charge $8 per $1000 value of property. If a home was worth $10,000, the resident would pay $80 in taxes; that same home in Colleton County would pay $300 in taxes.

18. *Annual Report* (1928), pp. 60–67.

19. The 4-Mill Ad Valorem Tax was repealed in 1935, replaced by a statewide sales tax to help finance education.

20. *Annual Report* (1933), p. 17.

21. On school closures, see Hayes, *South Carolina and the New Deal*. State Superintendent Hope refuted this report on school closures in his 1934 report, in which he writes "we have not closed a single school during the period of the depression." *Annual Report* (1934).

22. Regina Werum, "Warehousing the Unemployed? Federal Job Training Programs in the Depression-era South," *American Journal of Education,* Vol. 109, No. 2 (2001), p. 232.

23. Hayes, *South Carolina and the New Deal*, p. 44.

24. In 1931 the People's State Bank of South Carolina failed, triggering a run on other banks across the state. One typical story of the panic occurred when two armed men broke into the closed Monck's Corners branch of the People's State Bank and took the amount of money they had on deposit. The two men buried the money and turned themselves into local law enforcement. The jury refused to convict and the two men became local folk heroes. Slightly different accounts of this story are included in both Edgar's *South Carolina: A History* and Hayes' *South Carolina and the New Deal*.

25. Edgar, *South Carolina: A History*, p. 498.

26. Charles Biebel, "Private Foundations and Public Policy: The Case of Secondary Education during the Great Depression," *History of Education Quarterly*, Vol. 16, No. 1 (1977), p. 382.

27. "State Department of Education and Bank Failure 1933–1940," General Education Board Archives, *Series 1: Appropriations; Subseries 1: The Early Southern Program* (New York: Rockefeller University, 1994), Roll #103, Frame #0855.

28. Ibid.

29. *Annual Reports*, (1930), p. 35; (1940) p. 9.

30. Edgar, *South Carolina: A History*, p. 499.

31. *Annual Reports* (1928), p. 73; (1935), p. 87.

32. Moreo, *Schools in the Great Depression*, p. 8.

33. *Annual Reports* (1928), p. 73; (1935), p. 87.

34. *Annual Report* (1933), p. 17.

35. Moreo, *Schools in the Great Depression*, p. 8.

36. *Annual Report* (1933), p. 17.

37. Henry Perkinson, *The Imperfect Panacea: American Faith in Education 1865–1965* (New York: Random House, 1968), pp. 3–12.

38. A. Mitchell and J. Siren, eds., *Allendale High School Days 1928–1956: An Oral History* (Bamberg, SC: Kilgus Printing Company, Inc., 1993).

39. Mary Ariail and Nancy Smith, *Weaver of Dreams: A History of the Parker District* (Columbia, SC: R.L. Bryan and Co., 1977), p. 47.

40. Ibid.

41.   *The History of Robert Smalls School* (Beaufort, SC: The Robert Smalls Association Printing, 1991), pp. 3–5.

42.   Clinton Harvey, *Some Recollections of the University High School, Columbia SC 1932–1966* (Columbia: University of South Carolina Press, 1992), pp. 5–6.

43.   Ibid.

44.   Edgar, *South Carolina: A History*, p. 506; Hayes, *South Carolina and the New Deal*, p. 188.

45.   *Annual Report* (1937), p. 20.

46.   *Annual Report* (1940), p. 17.

47.   *Annual Report* (1931), p. 3.

48.   Hayes, *South Carolina and the New Deal*, p. 165.

49.   *Annual Report* (1930), p. 121.

50.   *Annual Report* (1937), p. 72.

51.   *Annual Reports* (1929), pp. 14, 47–49; (1940), p. 72.

52.   Nancy Dunbar, "Public Secondary Education in Columbia, SC, 1895–1950," (Ph.D. Dissertation: University of South Carolina College of Education, 1986), p. 58.

53.   Hayes, *South Carolina and the New Deal*, pp. 60, 75.

54.   Ibid.

55.   Dunbar, "Public Secondary Education in Columbia, SC," p. 88.

56.   *Annual Report* (1937), p. 38.

57.   Charles Lockwood, "Organization and Development of the South Carolina High School League," (M.A. Thesis: University of South Carolina College of Education, 1938), p. 51.

58.   *Annual Report* (1937), p. 54.

59.   Hayes, *South Carolina and the New Deal*, pp. 41, 59, 72.

60.   *Annual Reports* (1933), p. 75; (1940), p. 93.

61.   *Annual Report* (1931), p. 69.

62.   *Annual Reports* (1933), p. 75; (1940), p. 93.

63.   Hayes, *South Carolina and the New Deal*, p. 135.

64.   *Annual Report* (1940), pp. 19–45.

65.   For further discussion, see Moreo, *Schools in the Great Depression*; Perkinson, *Imperfect Panacea*; Tyack, Lowe, and Hansot, *Public Schools in Hard Times*.

66.   *Annual Report* (1936), p. 20.

Chapter Seven

The Sugarbag Years: Politics and Education Intersect in New Zealand

Carol Mutch

The Depression was greyness. That's a physical reaction. It's the only way that I can describe the sort of hopelessness that seemed to spread around among people who, in earlier parts of their lives, had been accustomed to security. It was the result of the discovery, a shock really, a discovery that life was not secure any longer.[1]

There were [many] teachers unemployed. Classes were big, expenditure was low, wages were cut, five year olds were kicked out. The total expenditure on education in one year was two and a half million pounds. They're spending more than that now between Monday and Friday of every week.[2]

The above quotes from people's personal experiences, collected by Tony Simpson for his oral history of the Great Depression in New Zealand, illustrate that the effects of the Great Depression were not just confined to Europe and North America but were felt as far afield as New Zealand and impacted on all sectors of society. This era in New Zealand, now known colloquially as the "Sugarbag Years,"[3] provides an interesting snapshot of the intersection of events and personalities that were to have a marked influence on New Zealand's political, social and educational future. Several key factors led to this convergence. Firstly, the Great Depression set the scene for a change of political ideology and ensured that the Labour Party with its vision of a fairer, more just society would form a government. The Labour Government, once in power, set about implementing wide ranging social reforms to achieve this vision. Secondly, because of their childhood experiences, key members of the Labour Government were committed to the importance of education for all in order to achieve this vision. The Labour Party's educational philosophy, especially that of the Prime Minister, Peter Fraser, resonated with liberal educational ideas of the time emanating from the United States and Europe, as exemplified through the work of the New Education Foundation. Finally, Fraser was able to find, in his own Department of Education, a partner in Clarence Beeby, who shared his beliefs and was also in position to transform this vision into a reality.

New Zealand's move to establish an identity separate from its colonial roots, the economic downturn prior to the Great Depression itself, and the rise of socialism meant the time was ripe for political
change and educational progressivism. Ideas that had been ferment-
ing before and after the First World War found their time had come.
Political activists and radical reformers became members of the first
Labour government, and forward-thinking educationalists became
accepted as mainstream. Economic downturn slowed the passage of
some supportive policies relating to women and children but, in general, social and educational reform movements flourished through the
rise of the Labour Party from 1913 to culminate in the development of
the Welfare State from 1935.

This chapter positions the Great Depression in New Zealand in its
historical context before moving to consider the impact that the economic slump was to have on society and the changes it foreshad-
owed. Particular emphasis is given to key individuals who rose to
prominence during this time (Michael Joseph Savage and Fraser in
politics, and Beeby in education) and whose influence was felt for the
next fifty years until the economic downturn of the 1970s and educational reforms of the 1980s largely cast aside New Zealand's liberal-
progressive tradition.

While the Great Depression was a time of deprivation and hardship, it also provided a chance for New Zealanders to re-evaluate
their developing identity especially as expressed through politics,
education and the arts. The opportunity was taken to re-evaluate traditional ties to the "Homeland" of the more recent settlers, to look
more globally at political and educational ideas and to re-define these
for a New Zealand context. This paradox is summed up by Simpson
in this way: "The Depression is part of the folklore of my childhood, a
grey and ill-defined monster, an unspeakable disaster, and yet a major triumphant chord."[4] This chapter examines some of these para-
doxes in an attempt to explain why such a bleak time produced such
radical change.

New Zealand's Colonial History

Elsewhere the author has described New Zealand's educational history as being characterized by polarized ideological tensions.[5] These
tensions are grouped chronologically as three overlapping eras: in-

digenous versus colonial (pre-European contact–1900); traditional conservative versus liberal progressive (1900–1970s); and new right versus liberal left (1970s to the present). The 1800s saw the indigenous people, the Maori, in ascendancy but by the beginning of the 1900s they were politically, economically and educationally marginalized with the colonial presence fully in control. The First World War and the beginnings of economic destabilization in the 1920s saw conservative dominance decline and more liberal progressive ideas strengthen up to the onset of the Second World War. The 1950s and 1960s saw a slow return to conservatism with further economic downturn in the 1970s leading a new right (both neo-liberal and neo-conservative) response to economic and educational issues.

Originally settled by Polynesian travellers *circa* 800 BCE, New Zealand remained relatively isolated until the 1800s, when sealers, whalers, soldiers, missionaries, settlers and later, gold prospectors, from Europe (mainly Great Britain) changed the social landscape. The Maori established a political system based around tribal lands, and an economic system dependent on hunting, gathering, growing crops and inter-tribal trade. The arrival of the European, or Pakeha as they were called, changed the political and economic foundations of society. In 1840, the Treaty of Waitangi was signed between representatives of the British Crown and some Maori tribes. It gave the British the right of sovereignty and the right to settle in New Zealand. In return, the Maori were to keep authority over their land and affairs and to gain the rights of British citizens. A period commenced which has been described as one of "treaty optimism."[6]

The optimism was short-lived. By the 1860s, the Maori were fighting British soldiers in the Land Wars. By the end of the century, the Maori were politically and economically marginalized, having been reduced to only four percent of the population.[7] As D. Green explains, "By 1900 Maori had lost most of their land through military conquest and a sale process carried out with varying degrees of unfairness."[8] Between 1847 and 1877, the colonizers went on to institute systems of government and education based on British models. After fierce debate, the 1877 Education Act was passed which laid the foundation for the education system as it is today. It made primary schooling free, compulsory and secular. The school syllabus was drawn up by the Department of Education's first Inspector General of Schools, Reverend W. J. Habens, whose prescriptions were described by another school inspector of the times as being "more ambitious in aim than any in the British Empire."[9] By 1891, four-fifths of the country's five- to fifteen-year-olds were receiving a primary education.[10] Education for Maori was covered by the 1847 Native Schools Act, which a politician of the times claimed, sought "to bring an uninitiated but intelligent and high spirited people into line with our civilization."[11]

With the arrival of more British settlers, many of whom claimed a parcel of land in a sparsely populated country with a temperate climate, agriculture became the mainstay of the country's economy. The advent of refrigerated shipping, in 1882, led to Great Britain becoming the key market for New Zealand's meat, wool and dairy produce. In the period between 1875 and the middle of the next century, eighty percent of New Zealand's exports went to Great Britain and at least half of New Zealand's imports came from there.[12]

The Land Wars and the slump of wool and gold prices led to an economic crisis in the late 1870s. The government of the time borrowed twenty million pounds over the period of a decade and left the country dependent on export income to pay off overseas debts.[13] By the 1890s, a steady rise in export receipts allowed Richard Seddon's new Liberal Government to expand public works, extend the rural economy and embark on social reform. The Liberal Party has been described as holding "the New World belief that the state's role was to assist the 'ordinary working man' and his family onto the land."[14] Other key social and political changes carried out in this period of increasing prosperity were the granting of the vote to women (1893), setting up a mechanism for peacefully settling industrial disputes (1894) and the introduction of old-age pensions (1898).

As a new century was ushered in, the tone of the country was again positive and optimistic. But, as E. Olssen points out, a transformation in society was about to occur as New Zealanders came to terms with their developing identity:

> New Zealand was moving along the continuum from pre-industrial to industrial, from pre-modern to modern; a new society was emerging, characterized by towns and cities, bureaucracy, specialization, and organization. The social structure became more complex, the division more intricate, the distinction between urban and rural more obvious.[15]

A tension can be seen between these social and economic developments and the place of education. Olssen considers that the changes lead to a demand for improved educational standards and opportunities to procure settled employment and social mobility. However, as society became more developed and the need for broader educational access more apparent, disparities became more obvious. As M. Bassett and M. King claim: "Relativities were shifting; some groups of people were doing better than others. Small farming was in the ascendancy as rising export prices lifted rural incomes. Wage workers were restless."[16] These tensions were to be further exacerbated as the first decades of the new century were caught up in different sorts of turmoil—first world war and then world-wide economic depression.

Industrial Unrest and World War One

In 1900, New Zealand's political status was that of a self-governing colony of Great Britain. It had responsibility for running its own affairs (except for foreign policy), and this autonomy was to be later recognized in 1907, when New Zealand became a dominion. At that time, it was seen as "one of the world's most democratic countries."[17] The Liberals were halfway through two decades of uninterrupted power, but emerging economic developments were to de-stabilise their political support.

Farmers, who were originally helped on to the land with cheap government loans and long-term leases, began to prosper. The supporting infrastructure of state-run railways, roads and shipping added to their financial success. Farmers were now able to free-hold their land, and this status raised them from the working classes to the employing classes. Meanwhile, urban workers began to see their wages fall and felt they were unable to benefit from the country's increasing prosperity. This discontent was fuelled by union militants from Great Britain and Australia.

By 1912, a new party, the Reform Party, was in government. William Massey, its leader, was determined to crush increasing union militancy, as evident in his government's handling of the 1912 Waihi goldmine dispute and the 1913 Wellington waterfront lockout. Union militants and left-wing political activists, dubbed the "Red Feds," joined forces to create a Federation of Labour and later, in 1916, the Labour Party. Factors that prevented ideological confrontation turning to class war or revolution, as in other settings, were first, that class differences were less acute in New Zealand than elsewhere;[18] second, that the emerging leaders on the left sought to promote their solutions through more subtle political means;[19] and third, New Zealand's involvement in World War I.

Because of the historical and political ties to Great Britain, New Zealand contributed soldiers to the Allied Forces. Although there was a strong movement opposed to compulsory military conscription introduced in 1916, one tenth of New Zealand's population of one million served in World War I and one in six of those was killed.[20] Such carnage was one early factor leading to New Zealand's changing view of its relationship with Britain and the development of its own identity and view of its place in the world.

War slowed, but did not remove, domestic divisions. While New Zealand enjoyed guaranteed markets in Great Britain for its produce, and farmers profited from this, in urban settings the cost of living rose and the value of wages decreased. Returning servicemen were given loans to set them up on the land and this in turn fuelled the rise in land prices. But as Green states, "still tied firmly to Britain's imperial apron-strings, New Zealand's economy was buffeted by volatile world commodity prices."[21] In 1921 and 1922, export prices fell sharply and the government needed to step in to prevent the economic crisis from worsening. Before outlining how the post-war economic decline was to foreshadow later economic crises, it is timely to place educational developments alongside those that occurred in the political and economic spheres.

Education in the Early Part of the Century

The 1877 Education Act had set in place the framework for both the content and organization of compulsory primary schooling. C. Bailey describes how Habens' successor as Inspector General of Schools, George Hogben, found education in New Zealand on his appointment in 1899: "a system of non-relating parts: a primary system indubitably democratic, a secondary system indubitably not; a barely viable technical system...a teacher-training system largely beyond departmental control, and to cap it all, a lack of means of evaluating the work of the schools."[22]

Along with the liberal reforms occurring in the political and social spheres, Hogben and Seddon began a series of educational reforms that were to foreshadow those following the Great Depression. They expanded the system to include free secondary education from 1903, upgraded teacher training, created a special education division, and modernized the curriculum. Hogben was, however, unable to achieve his ultimate vision of a fully unified education system as his successors, William Anderson in 1914, and later T. B. Strong, faced war, post-war rehabilitation and eventually the Great Depression.

Bailey describes Strong's time as one "characterized by educational economising, and, avowedly in the interests of economy, a strengthening of central authority."[23] In spite of, or maybe because of tighter central control, some significant developments did still proceed. The writing of a new school syllabus (1929) was long overdue and welcomed, but the amalgamation of schools in various districts for economic rather than educational reasons was not. A forward-thinking review, the Atmore-Bodkin Report in 1930, that proposed restructuring the administration of the education system was another attempt to streamline the system by smoothing transitions between levels of schooling and broadening the opportunities for secondary education. Two measures suggested to meet these goals were the introduction of intermediate schools (to provide a transition between primary and secondary schooling) and raising the school leaving age to fifteen. A further suggested measure to improve teacher quality was to place teacher training within the university system rather than in stand-alone colleges. Although all these recommendations eventually came to pass in one way or another, it took until the end of the century for the right moment in time for each of them to be achieved. The most immediate cause for lack of progress at this time was the economic retrenchment put in place to cope with the effects of the Great Depression and subsequently, New Zealand's involvement in World War II.

The Sugarbag Years

Although the Wall Street crash in 1929, is generally portrayed as the pivotal event leading to the Great Depression, New Zealand commentators have observed that the signs were obvious in the years prior to this, and often state 1926 as the start of this economic down-turn.[24] One anonymous contributor to Simpson's oral history of the Great Depression in New Zealand recalled this wide-spread perception of the origins of the crisis:

> People think the Depression started about 1929. Well it didn't. It was differ-
> ent from America where you could point to the Wall Street crash and say:
> That's when it began. It started years before that.[25]

Another contributor described how the political effects of the impending crisis were felt even earlier in the 1920s:

> But as far as New Zealand was concerned, the Wall Street crash only accen-
> tuated the problem in New Zealand. It began in 1927 and in fact I think it
> was the fundamental thing that put the government out in 1928...[26]

The Reverend Scrimgeour, a popular radio commentator and humanitarian during the Great Depression, later described how international events exacerbated problems already apparent within New
Zealand:

> A lot of people believe that the Depression was caused by the collapse of
> Wall Street. It was a creeping affair. It came with a terrible gradualness. It
> simply was a fact that mankind had produced abundantly and nobody had
> paid attention to the fashioning of a distribution system—a social security, if
> you like.[27]

The Great Depression and the political, social and educational
changes that followed were in part shaped by New Zealand's dependence on overseas trade. In the early 1900s, more than ninety percent of New Zealand's export income came from the sale of farm
products, mainly wool, meat, butter and cheese, to other countries.[28]
    Several factors were to affect New Zealand's overseas earning
power. The first was the oversupply of farm products and manufac-
tured goods after the war, which caused prices to fall. As Great Britain bought the bulk of New Zealand's produce, the increase in British
production coupled with the lessened demand for these products was
to severely hit New Zealand. To compound this, during the 1920s
other countries introduced import tariffs to protect their home-grown
products. For a country so dependent on exports this also hit New
Zealand hard.
    At first, New Zealand farmers tried to off-set lower prices by in-
creasing production but this only exacerbated the oversupply. As
summarized by K. Boon, "a great deal of farm produce rotted in
warehouses while people in other countries starved."[29] As the income
and spending power of farmers dropped, so did their demand for
goods and services, which in turn affected other businesses. The effect

of this economic down-turn was to lower trade prices, reduce production and income, and increase unemployment and poverty. Olssen also notes 1926 as the time when economic decline was first visible in towns in New Zealand and claims the Great Depression did not cause but only intensified the already visible "economic dislocation, social distress and political disorder."[30] Simpson states that between 1928 and 1931 export prices fell by 40%. Government revenue fell to half its normal total revenue, which led to cuts in public costs.[31]

As the effects of the Great Depression hit hard in the early 1930s, Peter Fraser, then Deputy Leader of the Opposition warned: "It is as if the farmer were struggling in the water and in danger of drowning. Instead of the government throwing him a lifebelt or sending out a boat to rescue him, it was decided to throw in the worker to drown along with him."[32] At the height of the Great Depression, unemployment accounted for about 40% of all male workers between the ages of sixteen and sixty-five and one in five of all the labour force. Government cost-cutting measures included the following: public works expenditure was cut by 75%; civil service wages were cut by 10%; and old age and war pensions were cut by 30%. Bandages in hospitals were re-used; hospital patients' food was reduced; nurses wages were reduced; and hospital staffing was cut.[33] The Public Works Department sacked all its men and then re-employed them on relief rates to do the same work.[34] An even harsher measure was to require men (single and married) to go into isolated rural work camps to qualify for relief payments. As Simpson states, "It wasn't much of a life, and the worst of it seemed to be that it had no end. A man on relief could only watch his wife and children starve. There was almost nowhere he could turn."[35]

Many of those who experienced the Great Depression were to use it as a touchstone for implementing their vision for a fairer world. Reverend Scrimgeour, interviewed many years later by Simpson, gives some insight into how economic dislocation altered not only people's social situation but also their expectations and hopes:

> If you want to understand those years you have to begin in the middle, in 1932. As distress deepened I was increasingly interested in money reform, wondering how people were going to find their way out of the labyrinth of misery…It's true to say that after 1931 the problem grew and grew. We were overwhelmed with despairing people. They weren't only without the means of a frugal life, they were becoming people without hope…I saw people during the Depression shrink, become overwhelmed with shame as they re-

ceived help. I know all about the shame of poverty. And saw people who shrank become coarse and hard as week after week they came to save their families from hunger.[36]

This is supported by a further quote from a contributor to Simpson's oral history:

> My overwhelming experience had two aspects: tremendous frustration, tre-
> mendous resentment against economic autocracy, old and rat-faced men
> coming out from England and telling us that we'd got to tighten our belts,
> take wage cuts, when we had no more notches to take in. And secondly,
> feeling that the normal things of life, the prospect of marrying, the prospect
> of exploiting your talent, were not there. It was in my mind looking back
> now, an overwhelming experience of passive violence.[37]

The education sector was not immune to the effects of the Great Depression. It was one of the areas to face severe cutbacks. Although schooling was only compulsory from age six, children had, in practice, begun their schooling on their fifth birthday. The fact that this was only custom and not regulation meant that the government could cut costs by excluding five-year olds from schools. Other cost cutting measures were aimed at teachers more directly: married women were prevented from teaching (unless they went as a husband and wife team to geographically isolated areas), teachers' wages were cut, and newly trained teachers were not employed. The results were that class sizes grew (up to 65 pupils per class is one figure cited). One of Simpson's oral history respondents tells of describes how sacked teachers were put on relief work tidying the playgrounds, "It got to such a stage that there were empty rooms and big classes in the rooms that were used in the schools, but outside teachers were picking weeds out of the garden."[38] Historian Keith Sinclair makes the point that it is important to dispel the myth that only the unskilled worker was affected by the Great Depression: "Even some professional men were unemployed. By 1935 1200 teachers were receiving rationed work and being paid relief rates. Many others received no help at all."[39]

Further measures focused on the broader educational infrastructure. Teachers' training colleges were closed and the number of school inspectors and departmental officers was reduced. Resources were also reduced: chalk and paper were rationed, as another of Simpson's oral history respondents comments:

You got nothing. For instance, you had to keep a workbook but you weren't supplied with one…Chalk was rationed. You used to draw your chalk each day from a box. There was no money for repairs, no money for building… They really had nothing, it was really grim.[40]

The same respondent talks of how this led to teachers joining the political unrest:

There was a tremendous radicalism amongst teachers in all directions… There were God's amount of kids about, that wasn't the problem. Oh no, the teachers were radicalized because of the conditions. They were radicalized because they were getting such a bloody raw deal…For teachers in New Zealand to take such a stand at that time was not only unprecedented, it was alarming to many people. But the conditions were bad.[41]

Children's health was to suffer along with their education. Simpson cites surveys that show seven out of ten Auckland school children had physical defects and that children in Canterbury were suffering from malnutrition and lack of clothing.[42] Simpson also cites an appeal by Auckland clergymen to the Government:

Widespread malnutrition in a primary-producing country is nothing short of a national scandal…To expect men, women and children to have to depend permanently upon the supply of cast-off clothing is a prostitution of Christian charity to which we cannot subscribe…Unspeakable suffering is endured by thousands of honest and respectable citizens who should not be placed in this humiliating position.[43]

This humiliation led at times to violence. A meeting in Auckland in 1932 to discuss unemployment led to a clash between police and participants. What became known as the "Queen Street riot" was echoed in other cities as those affected by the Great Depression, including the once compliant teaching force, many of whom were now out of work, expressed their anger and frustration. As the community felt the bite of the Great Depression, the conservative coalition government was removed from power and Michael Joseph Savage and his Labour Party with their promises of a fairer and more just society swept to victory in the 1935 election.

The developments following the Great Depression in education, social welfare and the arts were unprecedented in scale. They were in part a response to the unfairness and deprivation that had just been experienced, but they were also another opportunity to continue the liberalization begun by Seddon and halted by war and economic de-

164   Mutch

pression. Finally, they represented a further break with colonial ties to
Britain as a distinctive New Zealand identity and voice was forged. In
order to understand some of these changes it is important to understand the key figures that brought them about. It will be argued that
they were not only, as they are now commonly viewed in hindsight,
extraordinary men, but also that the time for their ideas was right and
they were able to take advantage of this.

Two Key Figures in New Zealand's Political History

The men in power[44] following the Great Depression, and two in particular, Savage and his deputy, Fraser, were to have a profound effect
on the direction of social and educational reform in New Zealand for
the next thirty years. As historian Edmund Bohan explains:

> Savage had been Labour's leader since 1933 and now seemed to be the man
> to provide the right kind of leadership for the country; Labour's policies
> seemed to be like a moral crusade for justice and fairness. It seemed dis-
> graceful for a government to allow "God's Own Country" to have to rely on
> food handouts or to force professional men such as lawyers, accountants
> and teachers to have to work on relief clearing parks, digging school
> grounds, planting pine forests or building roads.[45]

Historian Barry Gustafson describes Savage as "one of New Zealand's
most beloved Prime Ministers."[46] After emigrating from Australia in
1907, he became immersed in union politics, becoming the first permanent secretary of the New Zealand Labour Party. By 1933, he was
the party's leader and, by 1935, the first Labour Prime Minister.
Gustafson attributes this success to his tireless work through the Depression years: "Savage came to personify a humanitarian approach
to the problems of the Depression, and his sincerity and eloquence
helped lead Labour to victory in the election of 1935."[47] Miles describes him as "the right man at the right time."[48]

After winning power, the government began turning its election
manifesto into reality. Social historian Elizabeth Hanson explains:

> During its first year in power it proceeded to carry through a wide-ranging
> series of reforms in what was perhaps the most productive legislative ses-
> sion in New Zealand's history...Along with the immediate priorities re-
> flected in most of these measures—that of restoring financial and economic

security to the country—work also began in 1936 on the implementation of Labour's social policies.[49]

The Minister of Health and Education in the first Labour Government was Fraser. Strongly influenced in his youth in Scotland by the work of British socialists, Fraser became a vocal union militant. Historian John Cawte Beaglehole describes him as "an incisive and forceful orator, and a tireless organiser [who] led the Labourer's Union in successful strikes."[50] He began his political career in the Social Democratic party before playing an important role in the foundation of the New Zealand Labour Party. In his role as Minister, and later as Prime Minister, he was responsible for much social reform, including the creation of a free national health service, and through his work with Beeby, was responsible for major developments in education. Beaglehole concludes, "although never regarded with the same affection as Savage, Fraser was nevertheless among New Zealand's greatest Prime Ministers."[51] Bassett and King state, "Peter Fraser, was arguably the most able leader New Zealand has had; not the most efficient, not the most charismatic, not the most lovable, but the most able."[52] They go on to explain, "Fraser was a political animal with an insatiable appetite for the business of politics: committee work, strategic thinking, minute-taking, intrigue, debate. He had the kind of energy that, for most of his life, drove him long after his associates had flagged."[53]

Basset and King note that educational initiatives were to take precedence even over restoring the health system.[54] That such a high priority was given to education can be explained by the personal histories of the key members of the new Labour government. Both Savage and Fraser (along with other members of their government) had had little formal schooling themselves yet were widely read and passionate about the value of education. They saw a broad and generous education as the right of every individual as well as the anchor for a socially just society. As they had gained much of their education through worker education schemes, they were strong proponents of what we would now call "lifelong learning" and were determined to improve access for all to adult education and to university.[55] The confluence of influential individuals, along with their histories and personalities, and the mood of the times in response to the Great Depression led to a remarkable period of social, economic and educational reform.

Developments following the Great Depression

Labour took office in 1935 as economic conditions were beginning to improve due mainly to improved prices for exports. They also found considerable financial reserves left behind by the previous government that allowed them to undertake a vast program of public works. Green describes the first Labour Government as "genuinely reformist." He goes on to outline some of their key reforms:

> After enacting progressive industrial legislation (a minimum wage, a standard 40-hour working week, compulsory unionism) it introduced a comprehensive system of social security which provided a safety net "from the cradle to the grave" for those who needed it.[56]

Labour also worked to improve the lot of the Maori. Public Health Officers were employed to upgrade sanitation and housing and Maori people were assisted to access welfare benefits. Urban dwellers were assisted into homes following the substantial state housing program (government-owned rental accommodation), which was also able to employ many skilled labourers out of work following the Depression.

Cuts in wages and conditions of employment were reversed and unemployment fell. The State Advances Corporation helped farmers who had fallen into debt remain on the land and financed private housing in urban areas. Private and state houses were built in the same suburbs in a flourish of egalitarian idealism. The success of the Welfare State and public admiration for the Labour Party leader, Savage, were to ensure the re-election of the Labour Party in 1938.

Many historians have commented on literary and artistic responses to the Depression.[57] Sinclair explains: "Although in comparative terms unemployment was much less in New Zealand than in Australia or Britain (not to mention the United States or Germany), by 1935 it had created a much greater sense of outrage."[58] Simpson describes "the flowering of our literature such as has never been seen before or since."[59] He cites poets and novelists A.R.D. Fairburn, Denis Glover, Alan Curnow and John Mulgan as "people for whom [the Depression] opened up great vistas of social and political action which they had never dreamed possible and now seemed to be in their grasp."[60] Lawrence Jones cites writer Elsie Locke as saying, "the slump itself stimulated an extra liveliness of thought and feeling and human concern,"[61] and another writer, Robin Hyde, as exclaiming, "No New Zealand writer regrets the depression."[62]

A tone of social realism dominated both the literary and visual arts. Writers and artists rejected the influences of the British tradition of evoking "a green and pleasant land" and wrote in a manner that was "markedly anti-romantic" and "earnestly grim."[63] In painting, "Clarity and harshness now dominated the genre."[64] The Great Depression provided both the subject matter and the opportunity for writers and artists to take up a different lifestyle that enabled them to write about these experiences. More importantly, Jones suggests, it challenged the belief in the myth that New Zealand was "God's own country." As artists and writers struggled to forge a distinctive New Zealand voice to express their outrage, they strengthened the rejection of the idea that New Zealand would become a copy of "Great Britain in the South Seas."[65] As K. Sinclair declares: "On this occasion...the literary [and artistic] movement, stimulated by poverty, did not die out when prosperity returned."[66]

Just as the Great Depression provided the backdrop and impetus for developments in literature and the arts, it provided the purpose and starting point for developments in education. An education system would be forged based on trends from overseas but adapted to meet New Zealand ideals. The person charged with the strengthening of progressive education and child-centred pedagogy was Beeby.

Clarence Beeby and Progressive Education in New Zealand

Beeby, like Savage and Fraser, found himself in a time when the beliefs he held dear were able to be brought to fruition due to both national and international responses to the deprivation and injustices of the Depression. It was to be, however, his partnership with Fraser that provided the stimulus for change to occur on the scale that it did.

Three events leading to the progressive education reforms in New Zealand in the 1930s and 1940s are all linked in some way to Beeby: first, his appointment as the first Director of the New Zealand Council for Educational Research; second, the New Education Fellowship Conference of 1937; and third, his appointment to the post of Assistant Director of Education. Beeby was appointed to the directorship of the New Zealand Council for Educational Research (NZCER) in 1934. This newly established body was set up following a similar development in Australia. The fact that it was able to be set up in a time of economic retrenchment was due solely to the funding available from its benefactors, the Carnegie Corporation of New York. Beeby set out his aims for education research in New Zealand as follows: "If the Council did nothing but ask intelligent questions it would have done a job worth doing. A few may even be answered, but intelligent questions, like most living things, breed; and there should be more unanswered questions in five years' time than there are now."[67]

During his four-year term, Beeby sponsored publications on current initiatives in education, educational history and educational research in New Zealand. He fostered the establishment of local research institutes and museum education officers. As his background was in educational psychology, he also promoted the standardization of educational tests for New Zealand conditions. He served on the planning committee for the 1937 New Education Fellowship Conference, a conference that was to bring the latest in progressive educational thought to New Zealand. Beeby's biographer, Nolene Alcorn, notes that his time at NZCER was pivotal to the rest of his career:

> His work there established him as a significant figure in New Zealand education with a network of influential friends and colleagues. He was able to widen his international contacts. He developed and honed skills of communication, analysis, and reporting and learned how to encourage others to work with him to achieve broadly defined goals. He gained an overview of the New Zealand education system as well as a personal acquaintance with many of its key figures and institutions. The election of the first Labour Government at the end of 1935 meant that he was in a key position in Wellington, when a new Minister, whose agenda was radical change to democratise education, was seeking ways to implement his vision.[68]

The New Education Fellowship (NEF) was an organization with its origins in Europe in the aftermath of the horror and outrage of World War I. It advocated schooling that was "liberal, holistic and democratic and valued self-expression, dialogue and creativity."[69] Educator Jane Abbiss describes the NEF as providing "an agency for collaboration between educational innovators and recognition of 'radical' movements in education...It stood at the 'progressive' edge of educational thought but not beyond the boundary of academic and political respectability."[70] As NEF ideas were spread through international conferences, the Australian Council for Educational Research and its New Zealand counterpart, NZCER, sought ways to bring guest speakers to this part of the world. With Fraser as Minister of Education, the New Zealand planning committee was able to gain funding from the Government. The Department of Education, under the Minister's instructions also re-arranged the school holidays to ensure teachers were free to attend.

In 1937, fourteen speakers from Great Britain, the United States, Canada, South Africa, Finland and Austria were heard by over 5,000 educators in person and by even more through radio broadcasts. Week long sessions were held in the four main centres—Auckland, Wellington, Christchurch and Dunedin. The conference captured the interest of educators, politicians (especially Minister of Education Fraser) and the general public. Alcorn elaborates, "Those who were there remembered the feeling of inspiration: the sense that education was of crucial importance, that it was a liberating force, that home and school would work together, that education could and should be an active process."[71]

Several speakers were to have a profound impact on the direction New Zealand education would take. Susan Isaacs was particularly influential in the way teaching would develop in the early childhood and junior primary areas, leading to the introduction of the Playcentre movement in the 1940s, largely through the efforts of Beeby's wife, Beatrice. The work of Harold Rugg, already known to Beeby, opened up wider social and systemic issues that were close to the hearts of teachers after the Great Depression. I. L. Kandel, who spent additional time in New Zealand, was to challenge the narrowness of the secondary curriculum and the stifling nature of the education bureaucracy which struck chords with both Fraser and Beeby whose aim it was to open up the secondary system and make it relevant to all students. The conference was to alter the way Beeby viewed, and was later to implement, ideas on progressive education.[72]

In terms of Beeby's career, however, the most significant meetings took place in private, the culmination of which was Fraser asking Beeby to consider the new position of Assistant Director of Education. In 1938, Beeby took up this position which Alcorn describes as, "a role of national importance, in which he was charged with the oversight of a government-sanctioned revolution in New Zealand education."[73]

Politics and Education Converge

The paths of the two men, Fraser and Beeby, who were to influence educational directions for the next fifty years, converged first at the NEF Conference and later as Minister of Education and Director-

General of Education, respectively. Political historian Brian Easton describes this as an "extraordinarily creative partnership,"[74] while J. Abbiss claims, "This association would facilitate educational reform in the 1930s and establish progressive education as the new orthodoxy."[75] It was through the NEF Conference that Beeby was able to display his skills and broader grasp of educational issues. It was also through the NEF Conference that Fraser was able to view Beeby first hand and to gain opinions of him from others.

As the Minister and Assistant Director began to travel and work together, they came to understand where their ideas about education converged and where they differed. They gained a respect for each other and an appreciation of their similar visions for education (albeit achieved through different routes and with different justifications). As Easton claims: "Education has a key role in nation building in that it may, or may not, transmit to the next generation a national set of values, images, stories, and aspirations—a culture. Undoubtedly Fraser and Beeby had such an objective in mind, and largely succeeded in pursuing it."[76] Since Fraser had entered office, he had retracted many of the measures put in place to deal with the economic crisis of the Great Depression but had also set his eyes on wider reform. In order to make secondary schooling (whether academic or vocational) more accessible to all students he extended the number of intermediate schools, abolished the Proficiency Examination (which limited entry to secondary schooling) and made secondary education free until the age of nineteen.

Following the Great Depression, the general public had become more interested in matters of health and nutrition. Fraser supported the introduction of free milk in schools, claiming it was "one of the most progressive instalments of socialism New Zealand ever had."[77] Rural school children were to benefit from the consolidation of country schools, boarding and transport allowances, the expansion of the Correspondence School, and the development of the Country Library Service. In urban areas, class numbers were reduced and classroom sizes increased, as Fraser believed that the quality of education received by each student would consequently benefit.[78] Many of these measures meant more children in schools, which led to the construction of more buildings and the need to train and employ more teachers. Education at this time had a sense of growth and momentum that was never to be repeated.

Bassett and King make the point that these reforms were not carried out in a dictatorial manner but involved full consultation with education boards and teachers (represented by the teacher union, the New Zealand Educational Institute). Fraser set up consultative committees to the extent that William Renwick, a later Director-General of Education was to claim that they "changed the expectations that teachers and members of the public came to have of Ministers of Education."[79] The militancy of teachers during the Depression was channelled in a positive direction as they were invited to become intimately involved in the progressive education reforms, to the extent that "some of the stridency amongst teachers' unions in later years can be traced back to Fraser's time, and to the expectations that he gave them that commanding the state's resources was their right."[80]

By 1940, Fraser had become Prime Minister following the death of Savage, and Beeby, Director General of Education. Although continuing as a strong force, they are best known for the following statement from 1936, penned by Beeby but based on the sentiments of Fraser. This was to become the cornerstone of educational philosophy for many years to come and one of the most quoted statements regarding education in New Zealand:

> The Government's objective, broadly expressed, is that every person whatever his level of academic ability, whether he be rich or poor, whether he live in town or country, has a right as a citizen, to a free education of the kind for which he is best fitted, and to the fullest extent of his powers. So far is this from being a mere pious platitude that the full acceptance of the principle will involve the reorientation of the education system.[81]

Beeby's task as Director General to continue the reform of education was to coincide with the onset of World War II. Alcorn describes his first five years in the job as, "a time of extraordinary progress, [but] also a time of tremendous strain."[82] While reforms progressed, shortages had to be dealt with. While New Zealand school children had to be accommodated, so too, did evacuees from England and refugees from Europe. The revision of the primary school curriculum, the reform of the inspectorial system, the improvement of teaching resources especially the "School Journals" (educational publications provided free to schools), the establishment of the Visiting Teaching Service (to deal with the "delinquency problem"), and the implementation of the School Psychologist Service were all tasks achieved in those first five years.

To discuss Beeby's work beyond the 1940s is somewhat outside the scope of this chapter, but the legacy of the man who spent twenty years as Director-General (not to mention the years before and after that term) working for the good of education in New Zealand, is as strongly felt today as it was then. Alcorn in her biography of Beeby states, that although at the time "Beebyism" was both a term "of opprobrium and of approbation," Beeby has outlived his critics.[83] He is now seen as the dominant figure in the educational scene from the time following the Great Depression until the 1960s. Alcorn attributes this to "his industry, energy and determination to succeed [and] his driving conviction and sense of purpose."[84]

With over half a century of hindsight, Savage, Fraser and Beeby are still spoken about in reverential terms. Was it the men themselves, or was it something about the nature of the times that reached into the depths of a person's character and created extra-ordinary people in response to extra-ordinary times? The author has argued that the seeds of discontent with the social and political system (and by implication, the education system as the way to access improved conditions) were apparent before the collapse of the economy and the onset of the Great Depression. Savage, Fraser and Beeby were products of their time in that their liberal beliefs were in response to the unfinished business of the Seddon government, the political unrest of the early 1900s, the decimation of young men in the First World War and economic downturn in the 1920s, all precursors to the devastating social effects of the Great Depression. These were certainly extraordinary times. That Savage and Fraser were able to gain and maintain a political mandate to undertake the necessary social and economic reforms and that Fraser was able to set up such a formidable partnership with Beeby to institute the accompanying educational reforms was, however, tribute to them as extra-ordinary people. The convergence of extra-ordinary times and extra-ordinary people led to these extra-ordinary feats of social, political and educational development in New Zealand's history.

Conclusion

As stated at the outset, the Great Depression provides an interesting snapshot of the intersection of events and personalities that were to have a profound effect on the next fifty years of New Zealand's history. The time following the Great Depression saw economic, social and educational development on an unprecedented scale. The key figures of the times, Savage, Fraser and Beeby, live on in the nation's collective memory as somewhat superhuman entities who changed the course of history and helped shape New Zealand's national identity. Let the final words rest with Simpson, whose title, *The Sugarbag Years*, is borrowed for this chapter:

> The Depression, which began as an episode in our history has ended as an element of our national mythology. Myth is more uniform than history. It is a display of the shared semantic systems which enable members of a society to understand each other and the world they inhabit. A fixed point in a changing universe. In New Zealand the depression has become The Depression, a part of the manner in which we justify the way we act communally.[85]

The first edition of Simpson's book, in 1974, was published as the economic downturn of the 1970s was being felt. The second edition was published as a new Labour Government swept to office in New Zealand in 1984 with a public mandate to deal with the new economic crisis. This time the solution was the opposite—to decrease state dependency and make individuals more accountable. Much has been written in the past decade on how this has changed the shape of education. How will educational historians view this time in history, this response to economic crisis, this intersection of people and events, seventy-five years hence?

Notes

1. T. Simpson, *The Sugarbag Years. An oral history of the 1930s Depression in New Zealand* (Auckland: Hodder and Stoughton, 1984) p. 29.
2. Simpson, *Sugarbag Years*, p. 152
3. One of the enduring photographic images of the Great Depression in New Zealand is of men on relief work wearing outer clothing made from sugar sacks. From this photograph the term "the Sugarbag Years" was coined.
4. Simpson, *Sugarbag Years*, p. 18
5. See C. Mutch, "Values Education in New Zealand: Old ideas in new garb," *Children's Social and Economics Education* Vol. 4, No. 1 (2000); idem, "Contesting forces: the political and economic context of curriculum development in New Zealand," *Asia Pacific Education Review* Vol. 2, No. 1 (2001).
6. H. Barr, P. Hunter, and P. Keown, "The common good in the New Zealand social studies curriculum," Paper presented at the Annual Conference of the National Council for Social Studies, (1999).
7. J. Simon, "Historical perspectives on education in New Zealand," in E. Coxon, K. Jenkins, J. Marshall and L. Massey, eds., *The politics of learning and teaching in Aotearoa-New Zealand* (Palmerston North: Dunmore Press, 1994).
8. D. Green, "New Zealand in the 20th century," in *New Zealand official yearbook 2000* (Auckland: Statistics New Zealand, 2000) p. 17.
9. Cited in I. McLaren, "Curriculum making in New Zealand 1877–1962," in D. Ramsay, ed., *Curriculum issues in New Zealand* (Wellington: New Zealand Educational Institute, 1980).
10. Statistics New Zealand, *New Zealand official yearbook '95* (Auckland: Author, 1995).
11. Cited in C. Bailey, "A short survey of national education in New Zealand," *Education* vol. 9 (1977) pp. 2–11.
12. Statistics New Zealand, *New Zealand official yearbook '95.*
13. Ibid.
14. Green, "New Zealand in the 20th century," p. 17.
15. E. Olssen, "Towards a new society," in W. Oliver, ed., *The Oxford history of New Zealand* (Wellington: Oxford University Press, 1981) p. 250.
16. M. Bassett and M. King, *Tomorrow comes the song. A life of Peter Fraser* (Auckland: Penguin, 2000) p. 36.
17. Green, "New Zealand in the 20th century," p. 17.
18. Simon, "Historical perspectives on education in New Zealand."
19. Bassett and King, *Tomorrow comes the song.*
20. Green, "New Zealand in the 20th century."
21. Ibid., p. 18.
22. Bailey, "A short survey of national education in New Zealand," p. 4.
23. Ibid., p. 4.
24. See, for example, Simpson, *Sugarbag Years.*
25. Ibid., p. 26.
26. Ibid., p. 20.

27. C. G. Scrimgeour, J. A. Lee, and T. Simpson, *The Scrim-Lee Papers. C. G. Scrimgeour and John A. Lee remember the crisis years 1930–40* (Wellington: A. H. and A.W. Reed, 1976) p. 19.
28. K. Boon, *The Great Depression* (Wellington: Kotuku Publishing, 1994).
29. Boon, *The Great Depression*, p. 9.
30. Olssen, "Towards a new society," p. 272.
31. Simpson, *Sugarbag Years*.
32. Ibid., p. 13.
33. Ibid.; idem, *A vision betrayed. The decline of democracy in New Zealand* (Auckland: Hodder and Stoughton, 1984).
34. See, for example, Simpson, *Sugarbag Years*; Boon, *The Great Depression*.
35. Simpson, *Sugarbag Years*, p. 15.
36. Scrimgeour, Lee, and Simpson, *Scrim-Lee Papers*, pp. 1, 16.
37. Simpson, *Sugarbag Years*, pp. 28–29.
38. Ibid., p. 154.
39. K. Sinclair, ed., *The Oxford illustrated history of New Zealand* (Auckland: Oxford University Press, 1990) p. 218.
40. Simpson, *Sugarbag Years*, p. 152.
41. Ibid., p. 152.
42. Ibid.
43. Ibid., p. 16.
44. The word "men" is used deliberately. Although women won the vote in 1893, they were not eligible to stand for Parliament until 1919 and the first woman Member of Parliament was not elected until 1933.
45. E. Bohan, *New Zealand. The story so far. A short history.* (Auckland: HarperCollins, 1997) p. 81.
46. Cited in Statistics New Zealand, *New Zealand official yearbook '95*, p. 19.
47. Ibid, p. 19.
48. S. Miles, *50 famous New Zealanders* (Auckland: Burnham House Publishing, 1985) p. 88.
49. E. Hanson, *The politics of social security* (Auckland: Auckland University Press, 1980) p. 41.
50. Cited in Statistics New Zealand, *New Zealand official yearbook 2000* (Auckland: Author, 2000) p. 20.
51. Ibid, p. 20.
52. Bassett and King, *Tomorrow comes the song*, p. 9.
53. Ibid., p. 10.
54. Ibid.
55. See Ibid.; Bohan, *New Zealand*; B. Easton, *The nationbuilders* (Auckland: Auckland University Press, 2001); Sinclair, ed., *Oxford illustrated history of New Zealand*; B. Gustafson, *From the cradle to the grave. A biography of Michael Joseph Savage* (Auckland: Reed Methuen, 1986).
56. Green, "New Zealand in the 20th century," p. 18.
57. For example, Bohan, *New Zealand*; L. Jones, *Picking up the traces: The making of a New Zealand literary culture 1932–1945* (Wellington: Victoria University Press, 2003) p. 297; Simpson, *Sugarbag Years*; Sinclair, ed., *Oxford illustrated history of New Zealand*.

58.   Sinclair, ed., *Oxford illustrated history of New Zealand.*
59.   Simpson, *Sugarbag Years*, p. 16.
60.   Ibid., p. 17.
61.   Jones, *Picking up the traces*, p. 297.
62.   Ibid., p. 297.
63.   Bohan, *New Zealand*, p. 85.
64.   Sinclair, ed., *Oxford illustrated history of New Zealand*, p. 220.
65.   Jones, *Picking up the traces.*
66.   Sinclair, ed., *Oxford illustrated history of New Zealand*, p. 281.
67.   Beeby cited in N. Alcorn, *To the fullest extent of his powers. C. E. Beeby's life in education* (Wellington: Victoria University Press, 1999) p. 62.
68.   Alcorn, *To the fullest extent of his powers*, p. 55.
69.   Ibid., p. 80.
70.   J. Abbiss, "The 'New Education Fellowship' in New Zealand: Its activity and influence in the 1930s and 1940s," *New Zealand Journal of Educational Studies* Vol. 33, No. 1 (1998) p. 81.
71.   Alcorn, *To the fullest extent of his powers*, p. 84.
72.   Abbiss, "The 'New Education Fellowship' in New Zealand."
73.   Alcorn, *To the fullest extent of his powers*, p. 92.
74.   Easton, *The nationbuilders*, p. 66.
75.   Abbiss, "The 'New Education Fellowship' in New Zealand, " p. 83. Both Beeby and Fraser were to benefit from the unpopular directorship of T.B. Strong who saw education through the worst of the Great Depression. Although some of the retrenchment factors were beyond Strong's control and his 1929 syllabus was generally well received, he possessed a strident personality and authoritarian manner.
76.   Easton, *The nationbuilders.*
77.   Cited in Bassett and King, *Tomorrow comes the song*, p. 146.
78.   Ibid.
79.   Cited in Ibid., p. 144.
80.   Ibid., p. 144.
81.   Alcorn, *To the fullest extent of his powers*, p. 99.
82.   Ibid., p. 105.
83.   Ibid., p. 9.
84.   Ibid., p. 370.
85.   Simpson, *Sugarbag Years*, p. 18.

Chapter Eight

One-Room and Country Schools Depicted in Farm Security Administration Photographs

Eugene F. Provenzo, Jr.

From 1935 to 1943, a remarkable experiment in social photography was undertaken by the administration of President Franklin
Delano Roosevelt. Under the supervision of the Farm Security
Administration (FSA), one of the minor agencies of the New Deal, a
photographic survey of rural American life was undertaken. The project was directed by Roy Emerson Stryker, a former Economics instructor at Columbia University. Through his efforts, and those of the
photographers who worked with him, the FSA produced approximately 164,000 black and white images, as well as several thousand
color photographs. Nearly all of these photographs are currently
available online through the Prints and Photography Division of the
Library of Congress, and represent an outstanding photographic record of the Great Depression in the United States.[1]

Dozens of photographers participated in the FSA photographic
project. Many, such as Walker Evans, Dorothea Lange, Russell Lee,
Arthur Rothstein, Ben Shahn, Jack Delano, Marion Post Wolcott,
Gordon Parks, John Vachon, and Carl Mydans, would emerge as the
great American photographers of their generation. Their images for
the FSA became equally famous. For example, Lange's 1936 photograph of a mother and child, commonly known as the "Migrant
Mother," taken in February or March of 1936 in Nipomo, California
is, arguably, the most famous photograph taken during the Great Depression. Other images, such as Evans' 1935 Hale County, Alabama
pictures, and Stryker's dustbowl photographs of Oklahoma and the
Great Plains are comparable icons of the Great Depression and
American social documentary photography.

The FSA photographers were given specific subjects and geo-
graphical regions to document. They were also provided with extensive shooting scripts. Included in the Roy Stryker Collection at the
University of Louisville is "a check outline for photo documentation"
of the small town. The list includes detailed descriptions of subjects

that photographers sent out into the field by the FSA were asked to document, including everything from street traffic to hotels, churches to schools. Under the heading of "Schools," Stryker listed subjects including: "The buildings inside and out," "The Teachers," "The pupils—at work and at play—going to school," "Special schools," and "Consolidated school buses." Several thousand photographs dealing with educational issues were eventually taken by the FSA. They provide unique documentation of the conditions of rural education throughout the United States during the Great Depression.

If a single subject dominates the FSA photographs of schools, it is the one-room school. To a remarkable degree, the FSA photographs provide a comprehensive national survey of the traditional country or one-room schoolhouse, and of its replacement by consolidated school districts. Examples can be found in every region of the country where FSA photographers did their work. Not only are architectural shots of the exterior of schools provided, but also interior photographs of students and teachers working in their classroom. It is the thesis of this chapter that the photographs of one-room and country schools taken by the FSA's photographers document a tradition of rural education that was in significant decline by the beginning of the Depression. While these photographs accurately portray rural conditions of poverty and isolation during the period, they probably are more reflective of conditions found in late nineteenth and early twentieth century American culture.

Typical are the photographs taken by Vachon of various schools in rural Wisconsin in September 1939. In an exterior photograph of a one-room schoolhouse and its playground, identified only as a "Rural School, Wisconsin," we see a single teacher on the porch of the school, surrounded in the foreground by a dozen students varying in age from roughly eight to the early teens (Photograph 1). The wide difference in age among the students attending the school is evident in photographs of its interior in which students, probably six or seven years difference in age, sit together studying in the same classroom. Mixed age groups is a common unifying element in the FSA rural school photographs (Photograph 2).

Many of the photographs suggest a bygone era, when students walked to school and carried their lunches with them in meal pails and buckets. The clothing of the students is simple and homespun. Boys in the Northern and Mid-Western states typically wear coveralls and shirts. Girls dress in simple cotton dresses. Slacks and skirts are almost never seen. In the South and Southwest, student clothing is much the same—although often a bit shabbier and well-worn.

The teachers photographed in their rural schools are almost exclusively women. They seem solitary in their work, usually the only adult evident in these rural school photographs. They are almost always young, giving the impression that being in charge of a rural school was temporary work—not something one pursued as a lifelong career. Often, these teachers are photographed alone in front of their schools, which are typically roughly built and weathered—usually lacking any playground equipment or even a faint attempt at landscaping. In many instances the school buildings seem to have originally had another purpose when they were built, rather than as a place to teach children. Barns, for example, were often adopted for school use. Their small windows and lack of ventilation clearly made them difficult places to teach and learn (Photographs 3 and 4). Running water was a rarity, and outhouses were the norm—typically one for the boys and one for the girls. These images are repeated over and over again in the country school photographs taken for the FSA.

What was the experience of teaching in a one-room schoolhouse like? Probably the most famous literary account of teaching in these schools is John Steinbeck's *East of Eden* (1952), where a country teacher in Salinas County, California is described in these terms:

> Olive Hamilton had not only to teach everything, but to all ages. Very few youths went past the eighth grade in those days, and what with farm duties some of them took fourteen or fifteen years to do it. Olive also had to practice rudimentary medicine, for there were constant accidents. She sewed up knife cuts after a fight in the schoolyard. When a small bare-footed boy was bitten by a rattlesnake, it was her duty to suck his toe to draw the poison out. . . . It was far from an easy job, and it had duties and obligations beyond belief. The teacher had no private life. She was watched jealously for any weakness of character. She could not board with one family for more than one term, for that would cause jealousy—a family gained social ascendency by boarding the teacher. If a marriageable son belonged to the family where she boarded a proposal was automatic; if there was more than one claimant, vicious fights occurred over her hand. The Aguita boys, three of them, nearly clawed each other to death over Olive Hamilton. Teachers rarely lasted very long in country schools. The work was so hard and the proposals so constant that they married within a very short time.[2]

Steinbeck's description matches many of the descriptions in the diaries and letters of country and rural schoolteachers during the second half of the nineteenth and early decades of the twentieth century. In general, teaching in a country or rural school was a demanding and often, an underpaid and underappreciated occupation. Such was almost certainly the case into the Depression (Photographs 5 and 6).

As pointed out by authors such as Andrew Gulliford and Wayne E. Fuller, one-room country schoolhouses were not only important centers for learning, but were also social centers for members of rural communities. It was at these schools that children not only learned to read and write, but that members of the adult community came together "to hold meetings, cast ballots and participate in fund raisers and celebrations."[3] While dating from a half generation before the Depression, the description by Lillian Grace Chadwick Warburton, of Grouse Creek, Utah, of a community dance held in 1918 at a school where she taught in located in Etna, Utah, was probably typical of schools in the 1930s as well:

> They decided they would have a real dance, so we pushed back all the desks and benches against the wall to make as many seats as we could for anybody who came. We erased anything we had on the board such as phonics and wrote: "Come one, come all, come short, come tall, come jump the tracks at Etna Hall." They got an accordion player and he played the polka and the Virginia reels and all the square dances you could think of. Those boards just hopped along with the rest of us. It was really lively. There wasn't room for everybody to get on the floor at once. We had a really good time.[4]

Many of the one-room schools documented in the FSA photographs reflect the social and economic conditions of the communities in which they are located. Black schools in the rural South often show crowded conditions and a lack of equipment, and are in marked contrast to more affluent regions of the country. Schools in the Midwest or near the East Coast, in areas such as Central Pennsylvania, appear to have much greater resources. Black schools in the South typically do not have individual desks for students, but instead rudely constructed benches on which students must uncomfortably sit (Photograph 7). Desks for teachers are never seen. Black schools are often extremely dilapidated—some actually on the edge of collapse (Photograph 8). In the rural Southwest, the physical resources in schools are limited as well, as can be seen in the schools serving Spanish speaking communities in Ojo Sarco, New Mexico and the school at

Tono, near Ranchos de Taos, New Mexico, both photographed by John Collier in January 1943 (Photographs 9 and 10).

These and similar images from the Southwest are different than those taken of black schools in the rural South. In the photograph of the school at Ojo Sarco, for example, it is interesting to see how the Spanish speaking children are posed to emphasize their learning under the supervision of a teacher, while the students in the black school are not supervised. In the New Mexico school the American flag is prominent—literally overlooking the students. In the case of the black school, there is no equivalent of the flag, nor in the other interior photographs of the school from the series. The New Mexico school, while poor, nonetheless has some bought furniture and resources for the students and teacher. While both photographs were posed, there is clearly a very different atmosphere in each school.

The FSA photographs of one-room rural and country schools taken during the Depression document the passing of an important social institution in the United States. Their decline had begun well before the Depression. Much of the reason for their elimination had to do with the loss of rural populations in the United States. In 1900, for example, the rural population represented 60% of the country's total population. By 1910, rural Americans represented only 54% of the population.[5]

This decline in the rural population became an issue of national concern. In 1908, President Theodore Roosevelt appointed a Commission on Country Life to determine why farmers were leaving rural areas to move to cities. Over 100,000 farmers from around the country were surveyed by the commission.[6] Issuing its report in 1909, the Commission concluded that intemperance, poor sanitation, poor roads, poor communication facilities, poor leadership, and limited social life were the major factors cited by the people surveyed as reasons for leaving the country. More than any single factor, poor rural schools were found to be largely responsible for the movement from rural areas to the towns.[7]

The consolidation of small district schools into larger districts became more and more widespread over the course of the next few decades. Despite significant local opposition in many communities, smaller schools, particularly one-room schools, were eliminated as students were transported via wagon and bus to centralized facilities. In Indiana, for example, between 1918 and 1936 the number of one-room schools declined from 67.2% to 39.1%. In Ohio, the number dropped from 72.6% to 39.8% during the same period.[8] By the end of Depression, it was clear that consolidated school systems were becoming the norm. In Iowa, for example, by 1935 only 26.1% of students were attending one-room schools. It was only at the end of the decade that this shift became evident in FSA photographs, as the school bus taking children to consolidated schools appeared as a new image of the modernization of education towards the end of the Depression era.

Conclusion

The FSA photographs created by Roy Stryker and his staff are an important record of a now vanished element of rural American life—the one-room or country school. The hundreds of photographs of one-room and country schools that were included as part of the FSA photographic project provide a record of not only the condition of education in rural America's poorest schools during the Depression, but also provide visual evidence of the increasing consolidation of rural schools into the modern American school system that was fully realized in the decades following the Second World War. As such, they represent an invaluable documentary source of the history of education and American culture.

In interpreting the FSA photographs of country and one-room schools, it is important to keep in mind that they were taken for the purpose of promoting the New Deal and the recovery from the Depression. While they carefully document many of the conditions found in poor rural schools across the United States during the 1930s, they may in fact more accurately reflect the final vestiges of an important tradition in American education that had begun its decline earlier in the century. In this context, their use as a means of interpreting education during the Depression may be of greatest value in providing evidence of a rural tradition that was rapidly being eclipsed as a result of demographic shifts in rural populations, and the consolidation and modernization of rural schools in the United States.

Photograph 1. Rural school, Wisconsin. John Vachon, photographer, 1939. All images in this chapter are courtesy of the Library of Congress.

Photograph 2. Rural school, Wisconsin. John Vachon, 1939.

Photograph 3. Ozark schoolteacher, Arkansas. Ben Shahn, 1935.

Photograph 4. Ozark school building, Arkansas. Ben Shahn, 1935.

Photograph 5. One-room schoolhouse. Grundy County, Iowa. Arthur Rothstein 1939.

Photograph 6. Education in rural school, early grades. Williams County, North Dakota. Russell Lee, photographer, October 1937.

Photograph 7. One-teacher Negro school in Veazy, Greene County, Georgia. Jack Delano, 1941.

Photograph 8. Front of old Negro school house. Greene County, Georgia. Marion Post Wolcott, 1939.

Photograph 9. Ojo Sarco, New Mexico. One-room school with eight grades and two teachers in an isolated Spanish-American community, John Collier, 1943.

Photograph 10. Tono, near Ranchos de Taos, New Mexico. School. John Collier, 1943.

Notes

1. "America from the Great Depression to World War II: Photographs from the FSA-OWI, 1935–1943," at the Library of Congress, Prints and Photography Division website: http://memory.loc.gov/ammem/fsowhome.html.

2. Quoted by A. Gulliford, *America's Country Schools* (Niwot: University Press of Colorado, 1996) p. 67. See also Wayne E. Fuller, *The Old Country School: The Story of Rural Education in the Middle West* (Chicago: University of Chicago Press, 1982).

3. Gulliford, *America's Country Schools*, p. 35.

4. Quoted in Ibid, p. 82.

5. Fuller, *Old Country School*, p. 219.

6. Ibid, p. 220.

7. Ibid.

8. Ibid, p. 244.

Chapter Nine

The Pedagogy of Work and Thrift: Economic Intentionality as Turkish Educational Priority

Barak A. Salmoni

Though the Republic of Turkey was particularly hard-hit by the Depression, it was not the country's first economic crisis. After emerging in 1922–1923 as a sovereign nation-state in the aftermath of a decade of the Balkan Wars, World War I, and the War of Independence, Turkey faced continual economic hardship as it sought to make up for the extreme human losses and decline in agricultural and crafts production of the preceding years. Economic concerns predominated in the press, gave rise to national-level meetings, and figured into Turkish positions in international negotiations. After registering modest success through state expansion of industrial infrastructure and mildly protectionist cultivation of a domestic entrepreneurial bourgeoisie, Turkish economic planners confronted the shock waves of the Depression from the early 1930s. Agricultural prices declined by over 60%, and the country faced a severe foreign exchange crisis. As external terms of trade turned negative, domestic terms of trade also moved against agriculturalists, the majority of the country's population. The state's response crystallized from the early 1930s as statism (*devletçilik*). Along with a much more pronounced protectionism and control of foreign trade, the state committed itself to being the chief producer and investor in Turkey's urban economy, and undertook to be the main engine of the country's industrialization, through state-owned enterprises and support for private sector manufacturers. Enshrined in Turkey's constitution from the mid-1930s, statism became a central component of the official approach to society and economy.[1]

If the Depression thus worked more to strengthen rather than elicit official and societal attention to economics, this was doubly the case in the realm of education. Late Ottoman educators from the 1910s had emphasized the need for economically attuned pedagogy able to assist national development. smail Hakkı Baltacıo lu, one of Republican Turkey's most prolific and long-serving pedagogues, insisted during World War I that the desideratum of contemporary nations' education was "to raise children as [economic] producers." The

Western world to which Turkey aspired had transformed into "a civilization of economics," in which successful states embraced a production and manufacturing-oriented pedagogy.[2] Though criticized by older teachers,[3] Baltacıolu's incipient economic nationalism captured emergent trends, as it mirrored a growing official economic intentionality during the Young Turk years (1908–1919), and found support among other younger pedagogues. The latter called for a more manufacturing-commerce-agricultural orientation in curriculum, to prepare youth to survive in the "contemporary era's civilization."[4]

A few years later, the new Turkish state's leaders officially espoused the education-economics-national survival linkage. Even while the Turkish War of Independence was raging nearby, Mustafa Kemal (Atatürk; president from 1923–38) and Education Minister H.S. Tanrıöver spoke to teachers at the Ankara Education Congress (July 1921) about the "contribution to the national economy" expected of them. Thus inspired, the 1923 First Turkish Economic Congress in zmir, attended by 1100 delegates representing economic enterprises from all over Anatolia, focused on the need for economic independence to match political independence, and considered schooling as "the basic element of the national economy." Such phrasing was incorporated into the emerging ruling Republican People's Party platform in the same year.

Even before the Depression then, the conceptualization of economics as an issue of central *national* significance prompted sustained consideration of the school's role in fostering particular economic attitudes and aptitudes. For some teachers, the kind of economy necessary for Turkey was integral to formulating the educational effort's goal. Because the Turkish curriculum had already been shaped by a pedagogical economic intentionality by the late 1920s, the onset of the Depression mostly served to reinvigorate processes underway. This chapter first surveys Turkish educators' attitudes and curricular approaches to national economy in the pre-1929 years, after which it examines evolving approaches in the 1930s and 1940s. Ultimately, the Turkish educational record illustrates three main themes. First, local schooling processes prefigured the global impact. Second, global events strengthened local educational agendas. Third, economic intentionality as a nationalist educational priority acted synergistically with official views regarding statism, paths of economic development, and the proper socio-political order of a modernizing state presenting itself as fully integrated into Western civilization.

Prelude: 1920–1929

Reflecting broader trends in Turkish nationalist thinking, educators addressing the economy usually assumed Ottoman negligence, profligacy, and dependence on other countries, as well as the latters' frequent penetration of Turkey with the help of foreign (non-Muslim) residents. In this view, Ottoman leaders had misconstrued the state as unrelated to economics. Furthermore, those economic organs within Ottoman society that could have aided competitive industrialization—the guilds—had been eliminated in the post–1830 era of modernization (the *Tanzimat*), with no formation to replace them. According to the early Republican educational official Kâzım Nami (Duru), this was "a great mistake... of the Tanzimat," as it cut off the path to indigenous private enterprise and left the field open to foreign states and "European capitalists' protégés" within Turkey.[5] This policy had direct ramifications for the new Turkish Republic, especially as foreign states' intentions had remained sinister. While they had learned that it was impossible to conquer Turkey militarily, "great and economically powerful states...will try to enslave us easily through economics."[6]

For education to be truly complete, it thus needed to produce new citizens who considered economics within the realm of their specifically national responsibilities. Indeed, the experienced late Ottoman and Republican educational official Zeki Mesud, a member of the high-level Instruction and Education Commission, dismissed any conception of nationalist education omitting economics:

> According to my way of thinking, "national education" is more encompassing. General, vocational, and patriotic education are all included in this. Today the Turkish nation needs the skilled workers and small industrialists to save us from slavery to the large industry of Europe.

Economics was thus "included in the concept of national education"[7] not as a matter of choice, rather it was a law of modern existence: "society—especially in those countries where large industry controls economic life—wants the individual before anything else to be directed toward vocational specialty." If curricula allowed students sufficient individual freedom while ensuring preparation for economic roles, it would provide a "harmony between general and vocational instruction."[8] As a Republican educational official in the mid 1920s, Baltacıo lu naturally shared these sentiments. For him, economically-minded pedagogy was integral to the nation's political nature. To be a sincerely democratic country, Turkey needed to value vocational, labor-oriented education equally with theoretical or professional education: "this country has at the least six million farmers and laborers. Is there an education for the others [professional] and not for these?"[9] In a fully democratic education sufficiently concerned with economic needs, schools created "an independent economic unit" resisting international encroachment.[10]

Curriculum writers rose to the challenge in the mid 1920s, when the Republic's first two series of official syllabi emerged. The primary schooling level (ilkokul) clearly reflected priorities of educators examined above—many of whom worked on the curriculum itself. In history classes, youth learned that while Ottoman sultans had ignored the economy in a stupor of financial excess, European nations experiencing the scientific and industrial revolutions had revealed the irrefutable fact of modern life that economic vitality preconditioned national strength. Only with the advent of the Turkish Republic had leaders devoted attention to narrowing society's socio-economic imbalances, and only the new state had begun to take the economy in hand.[11]

Civics class was an even more potent arena to teach emerging citizens that economic mindedness equaled political duty. In 1924, when Education Minister İsmail Safa (Özler) declared labor training to be essential to the international struggle for civilization,[12] national curricula advised teachers to emphasize the centrality to young citizens' duties of "observing the pact of national economy" emerging from the First Turkish Economic Congress as integral.[13] In particular, syllabi focused students' attention on the importance of frugality (tasarruf), as well as joint, cooperative work for common economic goals. Such a "work activism" would lessen unemployment and prove to the world that "the Turkish nation is quite capable [of] work done successfully in little time with proper management."[14] Putting the matter in moral terms, text writers assured students that "hardworking people are honorable."[15]

Yet, unlike the Ottoman era, individuals would not be forced to fend for themselves in the struggle for economic survival. Now, the state itself protected the local economy and created favorable conditions for private enterprise. Rather than destabilizing intrusion, students learned that the state's economic "intervention is in the name of the public interest," to protect urbanites against socio-economic evils such as "expensiveness of life, profiteering, and a housing crisis" (*mesken buhranı*).[16] In the rural milieu, the central government acted as a positive, protective force against "usurers, cheating middlemen, and monopolists" (*faizcılar, madrabazlar, mühtekirler*—perhaps a reference to non-Muslims), through an agricultural bank and legal safeguards. In 1927 in particular, teachers portrayed a uniquely Turkish approach to the economy, which balanced government action with private enterprise and support of small entrepreneurship. Turkey was thus "a land of work and family" (*aile ve i   yurdu*), and "a democratic state relying on the basis of proprietorship [*mülkiyet*] and families." Lest this appear to favor middle and upper-middle classes (the minority of Turks in the 1920s), students were repeatedly informed that rather than socio-economically stratified groups, Turkey possessed a functional division of labor (*i   bölümü*), through which all Turks cooperated for common economic advance.[17]

Already by the mid-1920s, economic intentionality had become an integral if not dominating component of Turkish educational thought and curricularizing. Pedagogues espoused schools' involvement in the production of modern economic agents, linking this task with education's nationalist role. Further, curriculum communicated quite effectively the Turkish economic policy of government involvement and protection along with facilitation of private sector initiatives. Just as important, while rejecting class-consciousness, curricularists affirmed a scientifically rational division of labor. Finally, by referring to ideas such as nationalism, government attention to the people, and collective economic action for the good of all, both pedagogical discourse as well as curriculum ensured that students absorbed economic messages in the terms and ethos of the larger symbols and priorities of the Kemalist revolution in Turkey.

Depression Era Schooling: Frugality and Work

The onset of the Great Depression caused a contraction of world trade. As demand for agricultural products decreased, countries such as Turkey which occupied an economically dependent position experienced a significant decrease in the revenue earned from foreign trade, which in turn prevented the accumulation of capital needed to purchase industrial equipment and invest in further economic development.[18] In these difficult conditions, the Turkish government in-

creased its involvement in the economy. Along with catalyzing government economic measures such as statism, central direction, and
the development of Soviet-inspired five-year plans, the Depression
energized educational approaches. Indeed, the 1930s left-wing Kemalist state-aligned Kadro movement, which perceived state-led industrialization as a *sine qua non* for preserving political independence,
suggests the invigorated economics-educational linkage, as some key
writers worked as teachers.[19] From these years, educational thinkers
manifested a faith that it was a task specifically of the schools to educate towards national economy, with teachers leading the way. As
one senior educator proclaimed, "frugality and the wise use of finances (*tasarruf*) is a matter for education. This task falls to us."[20]

Some pedagogues feared the schools had quite a ways to go in
this respect. Looking back on national education during the first decade of the Republic, the experienced educator Osman Nuri was
highly critical of what he perceived as a total lack of attention to a socially useful, production-oriented education. Since Turkey faced great
difficulty in transforming educational policies into action due to rapid
turn-over at the top of the Education Ministry, Nuri claimed, albeit
with some exaggeration, that students graduating from Turkish
schools encountered nothing about how to be an effective producer as
opposed to mere consumer. Such a deficient education churned out
diploma-bearing youth who found no work. All then tried to obtain
government positions, with only the lucky finding salvation in the
"parachute of officialdom." This was part of his overall critique of
Turkish education: "our schools sufficiently aid neither our country's
economic and productive life, nor its scientific arena, nor the uplift of
the people's civilizational level." All rungs of schooling thus required
curricula and field trips focusing on the national economic activities
of regions surrounding schools. These tangible experiences would
"awaken in the student the desire to play a large role in the development of these economic formations of the country."[21]

Specific classroom activities could aid in this venture. One element of this was handicrafts. Part of a life-centered educational approach inspired by "Progressive Education" and recent Western visitors who recommended schooling measures to assist individuals'
economic development,[22] handicrafts were also meant to inculcate the
value of seeing to one's own material needs. One teacher and textbook author portrayed handicrafts skills as a trait of "people exposed
to the developments of the world... a civilized man."[23] Furthermore,

this kind of labor as a youth would prepare the emerging citizen for a vocation in later life. Of course, close teacher supervision as well as continual testing and grading could also direct students to proper educational slots for future economically productive activity. The teacher and school—and through them, the state—could thus determine the distribution of students into different labor sectors, realizing the Republic's scientific goal of functional division of labor rather than socio-economic class formation.[24] In the same fashion, a female teacher affirmed that in an era of global Depression, "the pedagogue's duty is to show every citizen that economic responsibility is entrusted to him, and to invite him with this feeling of responsibility to a particular [economic] duty."[25]

Given concerns from the early 1920s, a proper economic education would also have to emphasize frugality (*tasarruf*). In 1930, Halil Fikret Kanat, an influential professor of pedagogy at the prestigious Gazi Pedagogy Institute in Ankara, exhorted young teachers to encourage students to live modestly and wear simple clothing to school. As well, students needed to conserve material goods and save money in change-boxes (*kumbara*). In the same vein, Kanat instructed teachers to portray the importance of purchasing only local goods produced in Turkey (*yerli mal*) as a national duty on par with paying taxes or serving in the army. And, as may be expected, "in order to awaken in children a spirit appropriate to the habit of frugality, it is necessary to make them love and do work." Focus on frugality (*tasarruf*) and work would "totally break the connection with the old" generation's complete profligacy and extravagance, and thus free Turkish society from the evil Ottoman legacy. The love of work would engender modesty: "a person who is of modest spirit works to be economical and modest in public life and in his own manner of living." Finally, "frugality's national value…is to fully possess our material independence."[26]

Teaching Citizens to Be Producers

Kanat and his colleagues' programmatic discourse paralleled curricular dynamics crystallizing at all levels of schooling. On the one hand, from the late 1920s into the 1930s, more attention was devoted to establishing specialized vocational-technical schools, as was the case in other Middle Eastern countries.[27] On the other hand, there were even more important processes underway in Turkey's general national educational track. From 1929, *ilkokul* third-graders began learning Turkish in the new Latinized script. At the same time, reading classes taught them how to act as properly economics-minded Turks. In one reading segment, a father admonished his child not to ridicule physical laborers: "Rather than saying 'dirty' about workers [*i çiler*]," *ilkokul* youth learned that "one must say 'how beautiful'" it was to actually labor with one's hands in a productive capacity, altering nature to serve the larger Turkish social collective. Later passages in the same text taught grammar and vocabulary while also detailing the activities of street cleaners, miners, and carpenters, exhorting young citizens "let's all go to work a little [*i ba ına biraz imdi*]...he who works sees to all matters."[28] By contrast, drunkards and those remaining idle in cafes undermined national life and the sense of community spirit. Finally, *ilkokul* third-graders also learned about the need to save national and personal wealth. Passages informed them that by putting spare change into the change-boxes [*kumbara*] every week, even children became integral contributors to their families' economic advance. Just as in their civics class they would later read that the nation was a collection of families, at the younger age they learned that their *kumbara*-savings were actually national economy investments.[29]

Fourth-grade civics, or "homeland knowledge" (*yurt bilgisi*), itself reinforced notions encountered in reading by exploring general principles to motivate daily behavior in and out of school. Most notably, basic texts presented *economic* traits to be valued in a young country fighting the effects of the Depression in a fashion synergistically linking up with general *socio-political* and *ethical* qualities desired of Turks. Thus, sandwiched in among chapters dealing with national feeling, republic, freedom, equality, and anti-fanaticist good will, the student came upon the concept of social help (*içtimai yardım*), followed a few pages later by sequential chapters on the division of labor, social bonds, and the importance of work and a profession. State-commissioned authors informed readers that "social help is a mandatory matter [or work] for the making of a civilized nation and strong state...For this reason, the people love workers."[30]

Having primed students' minds, the text moved on to work itself. Mixing in proverb and proverb-like maxims, texts taught students that "to live, to be a real person [*adam*], and to defend our homeland, one must work. He who works gains,...the person who does not work gets no taste from life...Work is a duty." Indeed, there was neither beauty nor merit to anything obtained without burdensome effort.

Just as "for now our vocation is being a student," everyone was obli-
gated—and had the privilege—of pursuing productive work later in
life according to one's interests and capabilities. And since "working
exalts a person ethically [*ahlakça*]," every job—from working as a por-
ter to engineering—was "worthy of respect. No vocation [*meslek*]
should be seen as vulgar or lowly."[31]

This discursive technique helped the student to grasp the lesson
by starting with the near and tangible—the school experience—and
extending the logic to later life. At the same time, it established the
key ideological linkage between variegated economic activity and national uplift. Just as important, by affirming the equality of all occupations, whether manual or professional, the civics curriculum prepared
students for the notion of a functional division of labor [*i bölümü*].
On the face of it, the idea that different people undertook unique
tasks to which they were uniquely suited, and thus formed an economic whole fulfilling all society's needs, was relatively basic. Yet,
discussing this notion in primary school actually tapped into a key
principle of official Republican nationalism, known as populism
(*halkçılık*). Part of the ruling party's platform and later included in the
Constitution, populism entailed both the government's equal valuation of all citizens as members of the Turkish collective, and the societal rejection of status differences based on wealth, profession, lineage,
etc. So by saying, "everyone performs their own particular work, but
also needs the work of others," texts could claim that "the division of
labor so ties people together that even if they wanted to separate, they
could not." Indeed, "Such is work divided among is, but it also binds
us to each other so strongly that we will never be broken apart."[32] A
civics curriculum focusing on work and economy thus also taught political convictions. At the same time, curriculum implied that Turkey
was immune to class stratification that was a negative by-product of
ailing Western capitalism, thus obviating the need to turn to more
dangerous approaches such as communism or labor unionization.

Building on these language and civics classes, the fifth-grade curriculum on global/Turkish history attempted to prove the veracity of
such assertions by enfolding implicit lessons about economy within a
larger meta-narrative of Turks in world history. Turkish pre-Islamic
antiquity thus emerged as an era of tremendous political accom-
plishment, mirrored by innovations in animal husbandry, agriculture,
commercial transportation, regional trade, and urban architecture.[33]
Though the "Arab onslaught" wrecked the economic bases of earlier

Turkish grandeur, youth in the 1930s could see that they possessed productive potentials. Indeed, a key characteristic of the earlier (and more Turkish) Ottoman centuries involved industrial vitality: "leatherworking, saddling, and textile working all progressed greatly. All the weapons the army used over time were made at home."[34] Likewise, the famed Sultans Selim and Suleyman (1512–1520 and 1520–1566) displayed a shrewd sense of early modern economic intentionality through plans to build a canal at Suez. Yet, profligate and inattentive successors allowed such plans to go to waste, while granting foreign countries inequitably favorable trading agreements (the Capitulations), thus facilitating a gradual process whereby Turkey's self-sufficiency [*yerli mal*] was undermined by foreign products.

Students then learned that this waste occurred at a time when national economies became the central motor of the modern world. Dynamic individual producers and merchants combined with alert governments in Europe to create global commercial empires with political benefits in the form of colonies: "because of commerce and industry, a wealthy class emerged. In short, even though Europe's territory was the smallest, it became the richest and most powerful" politically.[35] Perspicacious students would then see that economics, on the personal and state level, was integral to political power and national survival. Indeed, later "Ottoman rulers' and administrators' maladroitness and lack of comprehension of their era's essence and needs" as demonstrated through the Capitulations, loans from Europe, and disregard for economic infrastructure, led directly to the weakness, dependence on others, and final demise that preceded the Kemalist revolution.[36]

Ottoman disregard contrasted starkly with Republican care for the nation's economic uplift. In passages illustrated by pictures of factories, bridges, rail-lines, and grain silos built by the state—in addition to pictures of Turkish president Mustafa Kemal operating a tractor and Prime Minister İnönü inaugurating a train line—youngsters learned that the Republic had abolished Ottoman-era Capitulations, permitting an industrial effervescence befitting Turkish nature:

> National industry made tremendous advances. The demand for local commodities increased. Our workers began to find many new jobs…Among Turkish harbors, carrying of freight and passengers only by boats carrying Turkish flags was secured.[37]

According to this curriculum, class stratification, unionization, labor disruptions, and miring of economic decisions in domestic politics—all ills of European society since the nineteenth century that had contributed to the Depression—were avoided in Turkey by a caring government devoted to statist economic policies and a populism entailing functional division of labor but not class formation. Ultimately, after language class had introduced *ideas* that civics class then explicated as general *principles* and history proved as *truths*, classes such as art, drawing, and handicrafts could inoculate youth with *behavioral inclinations*, by "accustoming youth to work continuously for the sake of a particular goal, giving them an appreciation for work, and bringing about in them a habit of work."[38]

Turkish education from the 1920s through the 1940s involved much attrition from primary to middle school and then middle to secondary school. This problem did not inhibit curricularists from reinforcing economic messages with socio-political ramifications on these levels. Along with history classes continuing to demonstrate industrialization and economic intentionality as *the* motors of modern history and successful (European) nation states—the analogues to which students encountered in the Turkish Republic's own actions— civics classes examined in even more detail the significance of work and the division of labor. Seminal texts setting the mold for curricular production throughout the 1930s and 1940s emphasized the nationalist duty of every young citizen to find productive employment, just as the requirements of paying taxes, purchasing local goods, and supporting local industries were cast as characterizing the Turkish essence, and as equal to military service in civic merit. In even more concrete terms than primary school, however, *ortaokul* curricula delegitimized socio-economic approaches other than the statist division of labor. While the latter guaranteed Republican democracy, organizing on class lines through "syndicalism" or "bolshevism...weakened and undermined national unity, order, and strength" through "all sorts of fantastical promises and demagogical [*avamfrip*] declarations to delude public opinion."[39]

This concern continued onto the secondary level (*lise*), particularly in sociology courses. An ideological capstone for those completing all rungs of the pre-collegiate Turkish educational system, sociology covered elements of history, civics, and a secular assessment of religion. Notably, its final unit dealt with economics quite comprehensively. Curricular guidelines highlighted as a prime socio-economic danger "the harm of syndicates being used in some countries as a means of class struggle" (*sınıf mücadelesi vasıtası*). Rather, *lise* students saw that "from the perspective of the division of labor for individual and societal life," Turkey must be "a society divided up for all types of working people" serving social solidarity (*tesanüt*), as opposed to a land of class stratification.

Coordinating this division of labor was a state-led economy, under whose guidance industry had expanded greatly, partly because of "the value in nationalizing [*ulusla tırma*] means of heavy transport." As well, state monopolies assisted citizens to undertake the moral obligation (*ahlakî mükelliflik*) of investing their income "as national money." Still, secondary-school sociology reminded citizens about to enter the working world that personal property was indeed a public right (*kamusal hak*), yet was to be kept in line with statism, as personal ownership's "limit will be the existence and interest of the state."[40] Resonating well with Depression-era economic policies, curriculum worked to legitimate potentially unpopular regime measures.[41]

Learning by Doing

From the Turkish Republican perspective, a significant shortcoming of Ottoman education was that teaching methods relied excessively on books and lectures. So, in addition to written curricula, Republican educators implemented several hands-on learning opportunities for youth, particularly in the years after 1929. National economy was an ideal curricular category for such methods, and the primary school was a central arena for covering innovative messages encouraging economic productivity while cultivating broader socio-political traits. Before students even encountered discrete classes such as history or civics, the *ilkokul* program called for the first three years to be devoted to "life knowledge" (*hayat bilgisi*). Based on local understandings of Euro-American approaches, *hayat bilgisi* linked topics such as civics, history, language, physical education and even math and science into a connected pedagogy (*toplu tedris*) whose very purpose was to inculcate inclinations towards doing for and by oneself—essentially the prerequisites for life as an economic producer (*mustahsil*). Thus, for example, the beginning of an academic year served as a perfect opportunity for students to clean the classroom and decorate it themselves, through which they gained mathematics skills in measuring, handicrafts capabilities in cutting with scissors, and a socialization towards cooperativeness and social solidarity through group projects.[42]

Such hands-on activities also communicated concepts of building and cleanliness as moral values. Indeed, the "advice for Turkish children" sections of *hayat bilgisi* texts taught youth the rule that "in order to be useful you must not stop [working] even for a moment,... Do not [even] wipe the sweat from your brow...to live is to work... you must not at all remain behind other nations." Working while intellectually and physically toiling was here introduced to the youngest Turkish students as a central nationalist contribution. For reinforcement, homework assignments required youth to survey their neighborhoods and urban quarters for the most prominent workshops and financial offices, in addition to the municipal government offices responsible for economic infrastructure—thus demonstrating the state itself to be the greatest benefactor of private enterprises serving national economy.[43]

Through pedagogical techniques shown here, communicating cognitive and academic skills facilitated inculcation of economic-mindedness enveloped in Republican patriotism. Field trips around urban quarters drove such messages home. Touring bridges, harbors, and docks demonstrated Republican attention to economic infrastructure, while teachers were instructed to make explicit contrasts to Ottoman negligence. Likewise, new banks founded by the state or with state support were to be noted, again in contrast to regime disinterest and foreign financial control in the Ottoman era. During field trips through urban areas teachers also warned students of the dangers of lacking work-mindedness in their own personal lives. While counseling *hayat bilgisi* teachers on this negative reinforcement, one 1931 guide by an experienced educator summarized the convictions young Turks were to espouse regarding personal economic conduct in a national context during the Depression years. The willfully unemployed—*i sizler*, as opposed to the needy (*muhtaçlar*)—spent "all hours of the day sitting with their hands open to passers-by, requesting help," even though a glance at their bodies and limbs showed "they are all physically sound people." So, even though a student might be inclined to help the indigent, teachers needed to make youth understand that "when you see that they are able to work, and that if they worked they could earn money, the feeling of compassion within you is erased."[44]

Such criticism was even more warranted regarding students' truant peers. Playing roughly in the streets, these "lazybones children" would loiter in mosque courtyards, obtaining money through "others' pity by hypocritically and falsely portraying themselves as needy." Undermining efforts of diligent students, such children "are people bringing disgrace upon both themselves and others, as well as to society." More broadly, while "the unemployed do not repay their obligation to their county or society... and are harmful people," Turkish youngsters must remember that "Turkey is a land of work" (*i yurdu*).[45] The message for students was clear: they must continue in school, treating it as an occupation serving the nation, after which they would work productively, facilitating personal survival and that of the country as a whole. Remembering images of school-skipping adolescents lurking near mosques, students would know that laziness was in fact the falsehood of religious escapism—the evil Ottoman alter ego of the secular nationalist Republic.

Celebrating Economy, Learning Thrifty Production

For a new state attempting to create a complete and indigenous economic society, implicit value-communication to young students through individual assignments, field trips, and other curricular innovations required explicit value communication through actions at specific, regularized times throughout one's primary school years. A key example of active learning tied to the larger realities of Turkey's economic needs and national calendar emerges from "National Economy and Domestic Commodities Week," celebrated in *ilkokul* and other schooling levels. Also dubbed "Thrift and Domestic Goods Week" and instituted in 1929—perhaps not coincidentally the same time as the Depression began in the US—it was celebrated nationwide, becoming an integral component of *hayat bilgisi*. The holiday began with radio broadcasts by the Education Minister and Chair of the National Thrift Committee, allowing students to learn how "civilization was established through thrift" as they gathered for school assemblies. The following day students in Ankara, Istanbul, and other large cities would make pilgrimage through streets decorated with banners celebrating Republican economic accomplishments, to exhibits put up by the National Commission for Economy and Growth.[46] Along the way, young students sang songs about use of local commodities. Portions of them bear quoting, as they demonstrate the equation of thrift and use of Turkish goods with patriotism and national defense—ideas that gained in importance during World War II:

> Buy local [national] goods/ money must remain in the homeland/ one must eat local goods/ money must stay at home. If we acquire foreign goods/ if we [thus] allow [our] money to be stolen/ it will become a cannon to destroy us, if we take foreign goods. We must buy local goods/ money must stay at home/ it will become [our] cannon, rifle, aircraft and remain [here]/ it will destroy the enemies.[47]

Thus primed, students wandered among photographs of state-financed factories, train-lines, and commercial vessels, as well as examples of local textiles, agricultural goods, and produce. These images then provided the material for later class sessions. Thus, teachers in conversation class would motivate student responses through questions such as:

> What kind of person is called extravagant? Who is frugal? Does a spend-thrift harm only himself? What are the dangers of a profligate person [*müsrif*] to his family, nation, and homeland? What is the significance of using a *kumbara*?

After comparing samples of foreign- and locally-made cloth, students could then speak of "the strength and beauty of local goods," while also contemplating "the disasters brought upon us by the mentality of considering European goods superior." Practicing Turkish pronunciation and oral expression, youngsters would turn to memorizing lines for a play about thrift and national economy.[48] Likewise, composition and grammar focused on writing about the Turkish proverbs "a lake is filled drop by drop" and "a white coin is for a dark day." Math class taught students to save change by having them calculate how much money they would have in a week, month, and year after putting a fixed amount of small change in their *kumbaras*. Later, students in handicrafts would trace maps of Turkey showing new rail lines and ports, while constructing signs, placards, and banners exhorting citizens to save money by using only locally produced goods.[49]

These decorations featured prominently in campus ceremonies, where younger students listened to speeches by older schoolmates about Turkey's natural resources, Ottoman economic failure and financial wastefulness as contrasted to the modern Republic's accomplishments, and the requirements of every citizen to be thrifty and work oriented. Indeed, learning activities for older *ilkokul* and *ortaokul* students were quite similar to those of "life knowledge," involving visits to local exhibits, participation in school celebrations and plays, study of Turkey's economic infrastructure in geography and nature classes, as well as essays on the tremendous importance of Turkish economic autarky. Students from different grades would also cooperate on the week's centerpiece: their own national economy exhibits. Taking after the 1930s practice of erecting displays celebrating Turkey's president and prime minister, these "national goods corners" (*yerli mal kö esi*) featured products of the week's efforts in all grades: maps of Turkey indicating factories, rail lines, and ports; change-boxes in which passing students were encouraged to drop coins; a selection of regionally produced textiles, vegetables, and fruits; and pictures of government officials visiting or inaugurating strategic economic enterprises.[50] Ultimately, by working together on the *yerli mal kö esi*, students acted out lessons learned at all levels of Turkish schooling about cooperative solidarity for common goals, while physically laboring to concretely affirm an economic nationalism celebrating regime leaders. These same ideas were then reinforced in school magazines as well as periodicals intended for students to read in their free time—in essence, permitting the school-as-state-agent to reach beyond the campus and continue its national economic pedagogical mission.[51]

Conclusion

This chapter has concentrated on educators' attitudes, written curriculum, school activities, and educational reinforcement through school celebration. Given limitations of space, it has focused solely on the state-run general educational sector for mass schooling. It has not dealt with vocational and technical schooling—of ever-greater importance in the Depression years—just as it has not examined rural schooling initiatives such as the Village Institutes, a major goal of which was to produce literate citizens able to contribute to the national economy through scientific agriculture and rural industry.[52] Likewise, when discussing didactic techniques beyond curriculum, relative concentration on the primary level of schooling—which touched the greatest number of Turkish students—should not obscure the fact that *ortaokul* and *lise* also deployed specific practices to teach nationalist economic solidarism throughout the 1930s and 1940s. At these levels, cooperativism in particular inculcated frugality, work-mindedness, and the pooling of efforts for national economic production, by bringing youth together to produce a newspaper or a small commodity. During these years teachers also used school cooperatives to cultivate social responsibility and mutual help by encouraging adolescents to look after financially less fortunate classmates. While *tasarruf* was central to the cooperatives' lesson, curricular planners who asserted that "the cooperative ideal should not be forced into a narrow merchant's formula" (*bazirgan formülü*) also emphasized that all economics-focused school activities should elicit broader social and political habits befitting modern Turks.[53]

This chapter has thus illuminated several key dynamics in the interaction between the Depression and Turkish national schooling. First, the global economic crisis from 1929 did not awaken Turkish educators to the need for economic intentionality in schooling. Rather, these events further strengthened initiatives suggested even in the 1910s and curricularly implemented from the 1920s—partially due to a particular reading of Euro-American pedagogical advances, and partially in response to advice from Western educational experts. Global economic dynamics thus acted synergistically with local pedagogical tendencies already underway. Second, the increasing frequency of curricular synergy—both across topics in one level of schooling and over sequential rungs in the educational ladder—as well as the implementation of *hayat bilgisi* and the conscious linkages among national calendars, school celebrations, and didactic goals indicate the tremendous commitment to pedagogical innovation elicited by economic developmental needs.

Most significantly, though Turkey joined other Middle Eastern countries whose educators found economics a prominent venue for pedagogic activity,[54] this case appears quite unique in the degree to which Depression era education for economics was so firmly welded to the over-arching nationalist project of creating a new citizen collective. Thus, beyond teaching emerging citizens to think about life in economic terms and their own responsibilities as producers, a major and determining thrust of the curricular message comprised linking such elements into the overall mission of communicating proper socio-political Turkish nationalism. Discussing economic intentionality as a rule of civilizational modernity served to highlight the new Turkish Republic's membership of the modern, scientific (European) world, just as it worked to condemn the Ottoman political order the Republican regime had replaced.

Likewise, teaching *ilkokul* students about state-built economic infrastructure, and reinforcing such knowledge in middle school by discussion of government ministries concerned with finances, transportation, and trade served to galvanize both a love of the regime and a Kemalist state-focused nationalism, in a sense the political counterpart to economic statism. Just as important, examination of the Turkish primordial past for evidence of agricultural and commercial achievement supported the nationalist claim that in essence the Turkish people were equal to Europeans in productive capabilities, even having surpassed them in earlier eras. Finally, emphasis on mutual solidarity, collective efforts for economic ends, and a functional division of labor rejecting class stratification, syndicalism, and communism sought to elicit in youth a commitment to those very traits deemed required of Turks under the rubric of populism, enshrined along with statism and nationalism in the Republic's constitution.

To conclude, a glimpse of Depression-era Turkish educators' surveys of foreign pedagogical initiatives demonstrates the extent to which teaching socio-economics became central to inculcating socio-political norms valued by the Republic. Reporting on the *Social Frontier* movement in the United States, one Turkish pedagogue detected "a healthy anti-individualist current of education powerfully working to express itself in America." Just like Turkey, "American society too is passing through a stage of deep revolutions," where great educators such as John Dewey realized that "*laissez faire* and individualism were not principles meeting the needs of today." Just like in Turkey, their cause was one of "national wealth's collective control, societal planning of production and consumption, establishing societal benefit instead of personal gain, and undoing class differences born of wealth." Ultimately, the American approach amounted to "societalness [*cemiyetçilik*] and collectivism."[55] Reflecting on the integration of work, frugality, and social solidarity into the curriculum for the sake of Turkey's nationalism, populism, and statism, Turkish authors could claim that their educational efforts would firmly establish the Republic as a modern, scientific state paralleling Western advances.

Notes

1. For a general survey of Turkey's economy in this era, see Roger Owen and evket Pamuk, *Middle East Economies in the Twentieth Century* (Cambridge: Harvard University Press, 1999) pp. 10–29. For statism in particular, see Korkut Boratov, "Kemalist Economic Policies and Etatism," in A. Kazancıl and E. Özbudun, eds., *Atatürk: Founder of a Modern State* (London: C. Hurst, 1981).

2. smail Hakkı, "Asrımızın Terbiye Gayeleri," *Muallim* Vol. 1, No. 1 (July 15, 1332) p. 10.

3. See Satı (al-Husri) "Terbiye ve Millet," *Muallim* Vol. 1, No. 4 (1332) p. 103.

4. See M. Cevdet, "Mekatib-i ptidaiye Ahlak ve Malumat-i Vataniye Dersleri Programı Etrafında," *Tedrisat Mecmuası* Vol. 4, No. 25 (1913) p. 285; Fazıl Ahmet, *Terbiyeye Dair* (stanbul: Tanin, 1326 [1910/11]) p. 47.

5. Kâzım Nami, "Bize Nasıl bir Mektep Sistemi Lazım?" *Muallimler Mecmuası* Vol. 9, No. 26–27 (February March 1932) p. 189.

6. Kâzım Nami, " ktisat Harbinde Bizim Vazifemiz," *Muallimler Mecmuası* Vol. 7, No. 2 (February 15, 1930) p. 21.

7. Zeki Mesud, "Millî Terbiye," *Muallim Birli i* Vol. 2, No. 14 (August 1926) pp. 597, 599. This piece was originally read as a lecture in the stanbul Teachers Union's 1926 congress.

8. Zeki Mesud, "Yeni Terbiyede Gaye," *Muallimler Birli i* Vol. 2, No. 16 (October 1926) pp. 691–692.

9. smail Hakkı Baltacıo lu, "Meslekî ve ktisadî bir Tedrisat Temeli" (June 15, 1926) in *Terbiye* (stanbul: Sühület, 1932) p. 65.

10. Mesud, "Millî Terbiye," p. 599.

11. *lk Mekteplerin Müfredât Programı* (stanbul: Devlet Matbaası, 1927) pp. 73–74.

12. See Yahya Akyüz, "Atatürk ve 1921 E itim Kongresi," in *Cumhuriyet Döneminde E itim* (Ankara: Millî E itim Bakanlı ı, 1982) p. 98; Howard Wilson and lhan Ba göz, *Educational Problems in Turkey* (Bloomington: Indiana University, 1968) pp. 56–57; smail Hakkı Tonguç, *lkö retim Kavramı* (stanbul: Remzi Kitabevi, 1946) p. 217.

13. *lk Mektepler Müfredât Programı* (stanbul: Matbaa-yı Amiriye, 1340) p. 36.

14. *lk Mekteplerin Müfredât Programı*, p. 91.

15. Refik Ahmet, *lkmekteplere Yurtbilgisi,4. Sınıf* (stanbul: Sühulet Kütüphanesi– kdam Matbaası, 1928) p. 36.

16. *lk Mektepler Müfredât Programı*, p. 35.

17. *lk Mekteplerin Müfredât Programı*, pp. 83–86.

18. Dietmar Rothermund, *The Global Impact of the Great Depression, 1929–1939* (London: Routledge, 1996) pp. 74–81.

19. For more on Kadro, see Mustafa Türke , "The Ideology of The Kadro Movement: A Patriotic Leftist Movement in Turkey," *Middle Eastern Studies* Vol. 34, No. 4 (October 1998) pp. 93–119; idem., *Kadro Hareketi: Ulusçu Sol bir Akım* (Ankara: mge Kitabevi, 1999); Temuçin Faik Ertan, *Kadrocular ve*

208 Salmoni

Kadro Hareketi:Görü ler, Yorumlar, De erlendirmeler (Ankara: T.C. Kültür Bakanlı ı, 1994). Key Kadro affiliates involved in education include .S. Aydemir, .H. Tökin, and B.A. Belge.

20. Kâzım Nami, " ktisat Harbinde Bizim Vazifemiz," p. 22.
21. Osman Nuri (Çermen), *Maarifimizin Mihveri Ne Olmalıdır* (stanbul: Kurtulu Basımevi, 1933) pp. 2, 16, 18.
22. For Western visitors, including John Dewey (1924), Georg Kersensteiner's protégé Kuhne (1926), Omar Buyse (1927), and the Walter Kemerrer group (1933), see lhan Ba göz and Howard Wilson, *Educational Problems in Turkey*, pp. 63–73.
23. M. Baha Arıkan, "Okulda Hayat Adamı Nasıl Yeti ir?" *Ö retmenler Gazetesi* Vol. 14 (April 5, 1936) p. 3.
24. See Sadrettin Celal, "Testler ve Muallim," *Muallimler Mecmuası* Vol. 7, No. 4 (March 15, 1930).
25. Celile Enis, " ktisadî Zihniyet Terbiyesi," p. 174.
26. Halil Fikret Kanat, "Tasarruf Terbiyesi," *Terbiye* Vol. 5, No. 25 (May 1930) pp. 44, 50.
27. For contemporary views of these efforts, see Süleyman Kazmaz, "Türkiye'de Teknik Yöneli ler," *Ülkü* Vol. 3, No. 27 (November 1942) pp. 12–17; H. Fikret Kanat, *Milliyet deal ve Topyekûn Milli Terbiye* (Ankara: Çankaya Matbaası, 1942) pp. 217–223.
28. Ahmet Cevat, *Cumhuriyet Çocu una Türkçe Kıraatı* (stanbul: Ebuzziya Matbaası, 1929) pp. 30, 78.
29. Ibid., pp. 57–59, 132–135.
30. Türk Cumhuriyeti Maarif Vekaleti, *lkmektep Kitaplar: 4. Sınıf Yurtbilgisi* (stanbul: Devlet Matbaası, 1937) p. 43.
31. Ibid., pp. 52, 54.
32. Ibid., p. 49.
33. Türk Tarih Kurulu, *lkokul Kitapları: Tarih 5. Sınıf* (stanbul: Devlet Matbaası, 1938) p. 35; also see Emin Ali, *Türk Çocuklarına Tarih Dersleri*, 3rd ed. (stanbul: Burhan Cahit ve urekası Matbaası, 1928) pp. 141–145.
34. Türk Tarih Kurulu, *lkokul Kitapları: Tarih 5. Sınıf*, p. 135.
35. Ibid., p. 75.
36. *lkokul Programı* (stanbul: Devlet Matbaas, 1936) p. 78.
37. Türk Tarih Kurulu, *lkokul Kitapları: Tarih 5. Sınıf*, p. 196.
38. *lk Mekteplerin Müfredât Programı* (1927) p. 109.
39. Afet nan, *Vatanda çin Medeni Bilgiler* (stanbul: Maarif Matbaası, 1931) p. 23; Recep, *Vatanda çin Medeni Bilgiler II. Kitap* (stanbul: Devlet Matbaası, 1931) pp. 73–77.
40. *Lise Programı: Erkek ve Kız Liseleri Haftalik Ders Cetveli, 1938* (stanbul: Devlet Basımevi, 1938) pp. 17–18, 23.
41. For a modern educational sociologist's theoretical view on this matter, see R. Dale, "Education and the Capitalist State: Contributions and Contradictions" in idem, et al., eds., *Education and the State: Schooling and the National Interest* Vol. 1 (Sussex: Falmer and Open University Press, 1981).

42.   For an in-depth study of *hayat bilgisi*, see my "Turkish Knowledge for a Modern Life: Innovative Pedagogy and Nationalist Substance in Primary Schooling, 1927–1950," *Turkish Studies Journal* Vol. 4, No. 3 (2003).

43.   For one example of such "advices"—ubiquitous in *hayat bilgisi* texts—see Ramazan G. Arkin, *Uçüncü Sınıf Kitabı: lkbahar-Yaz* (stanbul: Türkiye Yayınevi, 1945) p. 4.

44.   M. Zekeriye, *Muallimlere Mahsus Hayat Bilgisi Rehberi* Pt. 3 (stanbul: Kanaat Kitaphanesi, 1931) pp. 3, 4.

45.   Ibid., pp. 4, 5.

46.   Hıfzırrahman Ra it Öymen, "Milli Ekonomi ve Yerlimal Haftası," lkö retim Vol. 2, No. 30 (December 1939) p. 178.

47.   See *Birinci Sınıf Dergisi* Vol. 4, No. 4 (April 1942) pp. 5, 10, 11.

48.   Salim Siret, *Uçüncü Sınıf Ö retmeninin Kitabı* (stanbul: Güven Basımevi, 1940) pp. 282–284.

49.   Nimet Temizer, "Ekonomi Haftası Münasebetiyle IV.ncü Sınıfta Be Ders," lkö retim Vol. 2, No. 30 (December 1939) p. 181.

50.   "Sınıf ve Okul Kö eleri Nasıl Yapılır," lkö retim Vol. 2, No. 38, (January 1941) p. 310.

51.   For just a few examples intended for middle schoolers and *lise* students, see "Türk Anası, Kızı, O lu Durmadan Çalı ıyor," *Ortaokul* Vol. 6 (May 1941) p. 5; A Fuat, "Zengin Olmak Yolu," *Mektep* Vol. 1 (January 1932) p. 11; idem., "Pogram ve Tasarruf," *Mektep* Vol. 1 (June 1932) p. 267.

52.   For a literary reflection of these efforts, see Frank A. Stone, *The Rub of Cultures in Modern Turkey: Literary Views of Education* (Bloomington: Indiana University Press, 1973) pp. 133–40.

53.   Ali Haydar et al., "Mektepte Kooperatif," *Muallimler Mecmuası* Vol. 21–22 (October 1931) p. 17.

54.   For other cases in the Middle East, see in this volume Amy J. Johnson, "Encouraging Education, Increasing Income: The al-Manayil Village School and Rural Education in Egypt." Also see Misako Ikeda, "Sociopolitical Debates in Late Parliamentary Egypt, 1945–1952," (PhD Diss., Harvard University, 1998) pp. 161–240; Rudi Mathee, "Transforming Dangerous Nomads into Useful Artisans, Technicians, Agriculturalists: Education in the Reza Shah Period," in Stephanie Cronin, ed *Riza Shah and the Making of Modern Iran* (London: Routledge, 2003) pp. 123–45.

55.   Muzaffer erif, "Roosevelt Amerikasında Terbiyede Fertçili in Yıkılı ı," *Ülkü* (September 1937) pp. 43–48.

Chapter Ten

"Shall the Youngest Suffer Most?" U.S. Kindergartens in the Depression

Kristen D. Nawrotzki

In November 1929, the Division of Statistics for the United States Bureau of Education published an ill-timed report entitled "Encouraging Signs of Kindergarten Expansion."[1] The report noted impressive gains of 30% in urban kindergarten attendance and a 12% increase in the number of cities having kindergartens over the course of the 1920s.[2] That autumn, US public school kindergartens enrolled more four- and five-year-old children in more cities and towns than ever before and the increase in kindergarten was nearly double the contemporaneous increase in elementary school attendance. Kindergarten advocates were convinced that the kindergarten had been wholly accepted as part of American public schools, that it had, in a word, arrived.[3]

They were wrong. After 1929, amidst a climate of significant financial retrenchment in public school districts across the nation, kindergarten expansion was all but cut off and extant kindergarten programs faced elimination. In the three years after 1929, the National Education Association reported a 12.2% decrease in the number of kindergarten classes among cities reporting. In this same period, kindergarten enrollments in the reporting cities decreased more than 20%.[4] After the initial shock, kindergarten advocates and organizations on the national, state, and local levels campaigned for the maintenance of kindergarten programs and to encourage what little kindergarten expansion localities could muster. Both the widespread kindergarten cutbacks and the extensive mobilization of pro-kindergarten activism during this period of national crisis make this an important moment in history for understanding the development of public kindergartens, long-standing public attitudes toward early education, and the impact of the Depression on the US public schools more broadly.

By 1929, educators and the public had accepted kindergartens as a positive addition to public schooling but did not regard them as a necessity. As a result, kindergartens' status within the schools was insecure and their relatively recent entry into public education made them especially vulnerable, an easy target.[5] In many places, kinder-garten classes might simply have fallen victim as "last hired, first fired." Moreover, kindergartens were expensive, requiring specially trained teachers, low pupil/teacher ratios and a wide range of equip-ment and materials. Most important of all, the overall idea of taking young children out of the home and away from their mothers was a hard sell. It was difficult for the public to understand what it was that kindergartens were supposed to achieve, given that they normally did not teach measurable three-Rs skills.[6]

In response to the budget crises of the Depression years, local school districts adopted numerous responses, all of which were det-rimental to the kindergartens. Although educators, child develop-ment specialists and psychologists squarely backed kindergartens, public school systems—especially in smaller cities and towns—still eliminated kindergartens in part or entirely in the early 1930s.[7] Kin-dergarten closure was not the only (nor even the first) option school districts chose when they needed to cut costs. At the first sign of budgetary retrenchment, school districts increased the number of pu-pils per kindergarten teacher and made sure all kindergarten teachers taught two sessions per day.[8] Cities making cuts also raised minimum school entrance age in order to shrink the pool of kindergarten-eligible children.[9] In the early 1930s, per pupil expenditures in kin-dergartens shrank 20%, from an average of $51.00 to an average of $39.95; when calculated in real dollars, however, the decrease be-comes an increase of eight dollars.[10] Whether expenditures remained the same or not, keeping kindergartens open often meant firing some teachers and their supervisors and lowering the salaries of those who remained.[11]

In some places, the kindergarten was the only part of the budget which a school board had the legal authority to cut, since other as-pects of the curriculum were protected by statute.[12] Articles in *Child-hood Education*, the journal of the Association for Childhood Educa-tion (ACE, previously the International Kindergarten Union, or IKU) in the early 1930s listed other reasons for kindergarten cuts, including "taxpayers' protests against kindergarten on former scale" and "a be-lief on the part of the school board that the kindergarten is less essen-tial than other phases of school work."[13] Where kindergartens were maintained, it was often because of "a belief on the part of the school board that the kindergarten is too important a service to be curtailed" as well as due to parental demand.[14] Public opinion, informed by kindergarten advocacy campaigns, thus played an important role in school boards' decisions to cut, preserve, or expand kindergarten provision.

Even before these cuts, at the peak of 1920s kindergarten expansion, six out of seven young children in the US lacked access to kindergarten education.[15] Most of these children were in rural areas, especially the rural South, marking a clear gap between what educational psychologists said was best for children and what local school authorities in different US regions were willing to accept, approve, and fund.[16] By the end of the 1920s, public kindergartens in the South, even as pilot projects, were still limited to a handful of cities, including New Orleans, Louisville, and Atlanta. The low priority assigned to kindergartens in the South in general made them seem even less necessary for African-American children.[17]

Kindergartens in the Depression were weakened because the strategy which kindergarten advocates used to help expand kindergarten provision in times of apparent economic plenty (presenting the kindergarten as different from the early grades) did not lend itself to the defense of kindergartens in the face of economic retrenchment. The ultimate survival of US public kindergartens was due to the multi-faceted national campaigns mounted by kindergarten advocates who both identified young children's need for education and prescribed public fulfillment of this need in the form of kindergartens.

Prior to the onset of economic depression, the professional kindergarten organizations in the US, led by the Department of Interior's Bureau of Education, the IKU, and the National Kindergarten Association (NKA), had focused first and foremost on expanding public school kindergarten provision nationwide. The efforts of these organizations, in conjunction with teachers' colleges, formed the core of the American kindergarten movement through the 1930s. Working separately and in concert, these groups and institutions defined, promoted and defended the interests of young children and of early childhood education (ECE) professionals under the banner of the kindergarten.

How did kindergarten proponents market their particular type of education and their institution as valuable and as value-for-money to extraordinarily frugal Depression-era school board members and taxpayers? How did they create, fill and defend a niche for the kindergarten in the market for state-sector education despite the rapidly changing social and economic climates in the 1930s? What happened to kindergartens during the Depression to change them from well-loved to expendable? What does this transition reveal about the relationship between pedagogy and markets in the context of the Depression and more generally? This history of the kindergarten in crisis suggests answers to these questions. The forms and functions of US public schools are shaped at all times by a dynamic network of state and local school policies and parent, teacher, and other expert opinion about the best methods of teaching and caring for young children. Leaders of the organized movement for kindergarten education in the US had long been aware of the importance of all of these factors, and the exigencies of the Depression years brought them and their relationship to each other into relief. The trials of the Depression years disrupted extant patterns of kindergarten expansion and required marked changes in local and national strategy and discourse in order to defend the kindergarten's values and to demonstrate its value-for-money.

NKA and IKU leaders hoped to boost public school kindergarten provision by refashioning the kindergarten as a central link in the Nursery-Kindergarten-Primary (N-K-P) foundation of American education. Kindergarten leaders did this by cooperating with (and sometimes by co-opting) the work of nursery schools and the primary grades of the public school. In the 1920s, their emphasis on the kindergarten's flexibility helped fuel the rapid expansion of kindergarten programs and enrollments. Before 1929, advocates presented the kindergarten as an early education program that could respond flexibly to the diverse needs of individual communities and their schools, supporting the pedagogy of the primary school without duplicating it. In the 1930s, however, this flexibility became a liability. The nebulous nature of this relationship vis-à-vis the primary grades made kindergartens appear to be dispensable. It also undermined kindergarten advocates' common cause with nursery and primary school proponents, making the task of helping young children and families in the Depression more difficult.

The Kindergarten and the Primary School

Prior to the onset of the Depression in 1929, progress in the movement for universal public kindergarten education had been achieved through legal advocacy, campaigns for public funding, and demands for kindergartens' administrative independence within the public schools. In some states, the use of state or county funds for the education of children younger than compulsory school age (which itself varied from state to state) was not specifically allowed; in other states it was proscribed by law. As a result, the IKU, the NKA and the Kindergarten Department of the US Bureau of Education had long lobbied states for kindergarten legislation.[18] They had also worked to integrate the work of kindergartens further with that of the primary school and tried in vain to show how the kindergarten's goals related to those of the public schools in general. Once the full effects of the Depression became evident, the lack of clarity on this topic led many educators to believe that the kindergarten could be axed without affecting schooling in the primary grades.

The kindergarten's connections to both nursery schools for younger children and the primary grades for older children were both tenuous and shifting, making it difficult to build alliances for the expansion and protection of public early childhood education programs.[19] From the late nineteenth century, the kindergarten movement's leaders positioned the kindergarten as a discrete and autonomous program. Proponents of the kindergarten continued to assert the superiority of child-centered, non-academic kindergartens in opposition to the rigid, teacher-centered pedagogy still often seen in primary grades.[20] Despite these efforts by proponents, many administrators, taxpayers, and parents remained unconvinced of the purpose and value of the kindergartens.

These long-standing conflicts culminated in the 1920s in the combination of kindergarten and primary teacher training, pedagogy, and curricula. Kindergarten-primary connections were built through programs of the IKU in conjunction with the US Bureau of Education, the National Education Association (NEA), state and local teachers' associations, training and normal schools, and individual school districts and schools.[21] By mid-decade, approximately 130 teacher-training institutions (80% of the total) which formerly gave separate kindergarten and primary courses now offered combined kindergarten-primary training.[22] In public schools, the newly-established connections between kindergarten and primary grades were visible in the informal organization of some primary classrooms and in the efforts of kindergarten teachers to anticipate first grade lessons; 72% of city school systems with kindergartens placed kindergartens and primary grades under joint supervision.[23] Even so, there was a lot of variation in what kindergarten-primary meant in practice, whether it was to be a kindergarten-first grade affair, or whether it should include the second and third grades as well. By the same token, it was difficult for teachers and school administrators to identify the pedagogical and curricular implications of each of these forms of education.[24]

Attempts to standardize combined kindergarten-first grade curricula and teacher-training gained a great deal of attention among educators, but they did not lead to professional consensus.[25] Furthermore, as earnest as these attempts at kindergarten-primary unification were, they could not overcome the systematization of mass schooling which limited the extension of activity-based and child-centered pedagogy in primary school classrooms.[26] In the biggest school districts, this included the introduction of age-grade standards which matched children's ages to their school years, eliminating individual advancement. Likewise, school testing procedures encouraged the categorization and division of pupils according to norms and shaped classroom instruction accordingly. Moreover, increasing layers of bureaucracy at the school and district level combined with teacher conservatism to make activity-based, child-centered pedagogy rare in classroom practice.[27] Even well-intentioned efforts at kindergarten-primary unification could not overcome these trends.

The Kindergarten and Laboratory Nursery Schools

Alongside the already tenuous relationship between the kindergarten and the primary school came the laboratory nursery school. From the 1920s through the 1930s, the growth of laboratory nursery schools challenged kindergarten teachers and movement leaders to redefine their programs and their profession according to the terms of the new science of child development. Institutions called nursery schools started to appear in the United States in 1919, appearing under the auspices of university-based preschool laboratories in which the psychological, cognitive, and physiological development of young children could be measured and studied by experts, many of whom had close ties to the kindergarten movement.[28] With the exception of the Ruggles Street Nursery School in Boston, these were not social welfare institutions. Rather, they were intended to support the education and training of (white, middle-class) mothers and kindergarten and nursery school teachers.[29] In their early years, laboratory nursery schools distanced themselves from the development of early childhood pedagogy or curricula.[30]

As with the American kindergarten in its early days, the nursery school idea soon grew to include many different types of pre-school education, all under the name "nursery school." These were mostly private institutions, many founded by trained kindergarten teachers, others founded by teachers, social workers or parents, both trained and untrained.[31] Their foci were as various as their sources of support and their clientele: some were intended (like traditional day nurseries) to relieve parents of child care, while others were attached to social settlements, day hospitals, or public health centers.[32] In the 1920s, the number of entities calling themselves "nursery schools" doubled every two years, reaching 262 in 1930.[33]

With the formation and growth of nursery school advocacy organizations, the leaders of kindergarten organizations such as the ACE encouraged kindergarten teachers to critically examine their own procedures. While many aspects of the nursery schools were similar to the kindergarten, in their day-to-day practices both kindergartens and nursery schools varied so much that it was difficult to say how similar they were. The ACE itself had a hard time differentiating the kindergarten from the nursery school, even while it sought to maintain kindergarten teachers' special status as teachers and early childhood experts. To the question, "How does a nursery school differ from a kindergarten?" an ACE pamphlet diplomatically responded: "Essentially it does not differ at all...Any differences that exist are within the children themselves, due to their abilities, their past experience, and the nature of the guidance given them."[34]

Another commonality between the kindergarten and the nursery school was the reliance on child study and the science of child development. The kindergarten movement embraced these as means by which to advance kindergarten education, while the American nursery school more or less owed its existence to these new fields of study. Some of the greatest names in these fields, including George D. Stoddard, Director of the pioneering Iowa Child Welfare Research Station, had come out in unqualified support of both nursery schools and public kindergartens.[35]

Although kindergarten advocates were pleased with the attention given to young children by the nursery schools, the growth of nursery schooling put the once-certain future of the kindergarten into question. As Patty Smith Hill warned fellow kindergarten advocates in 1929, prior to the onset of the Depression:

> The kindergarten was the first school to work with and for parents...We were pioneers in this field, but we are in danger of losing our birth right as it is passing over into the hands of those who are preparing themselves more scientifically in child psychology and "parent psychology."[36]

One way kindergarten proponents sought to maintain this "birth right" was to continue reaching across institutional boundaries. During the 1925/26 school year, the Kindergarten Section of the US Bureau of Education fell in line with the "modern tendency toward unification in education and to provide guiding and helpful material through research" and became the Nursery-Kindergarten-Primary (N-K-P) Section with a focus on the education of children from ages two to eight.[37] Similar measures were undertaken by local and state teachers' groups as well as national organizations such as the NEA and the IKU; the NEA's Kindergarten Department became a Kindergarten-Primary Department in 1926.[38] In 1929, the IKU's membership voted to change its name to the more encompassing Association for Childhood Education.

However, despite all these changes, real integration between nursery, kindergarten, primary professionals and pedagogy was not achieved in the 1920s. Within most teacher training institutions and even within the all-encompassing ACE, the nursery, kindergarten, and primary sections maintained their separate identities. On a single university campus, research on children under age five took place outside of schools of education, in home economics or psychology departments, while schools of education remained focused on elementary education with peripheral interest in kindergarten education.[39] What is more, the propinquity of public kindergartens and primary grades within school buildings did not lessen their pedagogical differences, nor could the similarities between nursery school and kindergarten pedagogies overcome their physical separation.

All of these changes within the professional community in the 1910s and 1920s played out against the backdrop of the kindergarten's existence as an expensive and seemingly peripheral part of public schools. Although the social benefits of kindergarten programs had long been celebrated by urban school administrators, questions began to arise about whether attendance at kindergarten actually helped children's academic progress in the primary grades. Well before the crisis years of the Great Depression, urban school districts were in dire financial straits caused by burgeoning primary and high school enrollments. Forced to choose between kindergartens and the even more expensive high schools, school boards like those in Washington, D.C. favored the latter with higher budgets supporting greater enrollments.[40] Indeed, some of the school districts that had had public kindergartens in the nineteenth century—Columbus, Ohio, for example—discontinued them in a round of financial cuts in response to the financial crises of the 1890s. Both the district's kindergartens and its schools' telephones were deemed non-essential at the time and both were eliminated.[41] Both were eventually reinstated, as one era's extravagance became another's necessity.

In response to critics' calls for proof of kindergarten's value-for-money, kindergarten proponents in the late 1910s and early 1920s began demanding more "scientific" kindergarten teacher training and started calling for systematic surveys to determine the effect of kindergarten attendance on children's progress through the primary grades. Teachers, training school students and instructors, and independent research institutes devised and carried out surveys of kindergarten education.[42] By the mid-1920s, kindergarten proponents such as Nina Vandewalker pointed to the studies, claiming that "kindergarten attendance reduces retardation and failure, and thereby saves money to the school."[43]

Many of these surveys, including those conducted by the US Bureau of Education's Kindergarten Department, claimed that kindergarten children later performed better than others in reading and writing even though the kindergarten (by definition) offered no lessons in the three Rs.[44] However, some kindergartens did in fact include lessons in reading, writing, and simple arithmetic in preparation for the first grade.[45] Kindergarten teachers claimed this was the unfortunate result of misguided pressure from parents, primary grades teachers, and school administrators who wanted to see concrete and recognizable three Rs results.[46] Kindergarten experts attempted to counteract these tendencies, but the problem, an old one, persisted.[47]

As kindergartens were attached to more and more public schools in the 1920s, there developed a professional tug-of-war between teachers and administrators who represented the non-academic or "developmental" kindergarten interests and those who gave priority to the academic goals and didactic methods of the primary school.[48]

While N-K-P efforts seem to have increased communication and understanding between teachers and other professionals operating at the three levels, they did not completely heal the rifts between them which resulted from their different professional histories, identities, and pedagogical cultures.

The ACE sought collaboration between the nursery school, kindergarten, and primary grades but insisted that the kindergarten was the most important part. A leader and leading critic of the kindergarten and nursery school movements, Patty Smith Hill urged her colleagues in 1929 to take stock of their work:

> [D]oes the kindergarten really hold a strategic position in American education?...If so, what evidences can we offer to make good our claim?...We...can double and quadruple our contributions if we secure the sympathetic and intelligent cooperation of school administrators, taxpayers and parents.[49]

Amid the tribulations of the 1930s, the clear formulation of the kindergarten's importance would help garner the kinds of "sympathetic and intelligent cooperation" required to keep kindergartens open. Kindergarten leaders believed there was room for both the kindergarten and the nursery school in helping to meet the needs of young children, but it became difficult to convince the federal government and the public of the need to support both. For its part, in response to the Depression, the federal government would fund health- and welfare-based nursery schools and not the development-oriented, school-based kindergartens, which were put on the defensive.

In Defense of Kindergartens

After decades of rising enrollments and other "encouraging signs," US public school kindergartens were in need of defense after 1929. As can be seen in Table 10.1, the Depression disrupted a long-term increase in US public kindergarten enrollments. The 50% increase in enrollments between 1920 and 1930 was followed by a total decrease of 20% to the end of the 1930s. To the extent that enrollments serve as a proxy for the provision of kindergarten spaces, we can see that Depression-era cuts in kindergarten provision meant that at least twenty percent fewer children (that is, 150,000 fewer children) could attend kindergarten by 1940. What is more, 694 cities reporting to the National Education Association in 1934 reported cuts of 21.2% in kindergarten enrollments.[50]

Table 10.1: Enrollment in US Public Kindergartens:[51]

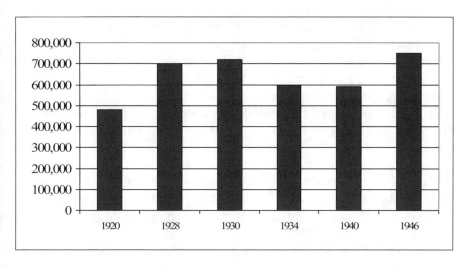

The ACE, NKA, and Bureau of Education responded to the post-1929 "crisis in kindergarten education" with a multi-faceted and aggressive strategy against kindergarten closure.[52] First, their national publications and reports stressed the social value of public kindergartens in times of national crisis. They asserted, among other things, that the moral and character education offered by the kindergarten was especially needed in times of economic uncertainty and disruption of family relationships.[53] They also insisted, contrary to reports in newspapers and elsewhere, that the national trend showed localities maintaining rather than discontinuing kindergartens.[54] At a time when it seemed nearly every segment of society was suffering, kindergarten advocates asked: "Shall the youngest suffer most?"[55] William F. Russell, Dean of Teachers College, wrote in *The New York Times* in 1933: "Good roads can be postponed; bridge construction can be delayed; canals and waterways can be put to one side; but children cannot wait...This is their only chance, and we must help them to make the most of it, in times of depression as well as in prosperity."[56] George Stoddard boiled it all down to one question: "[A]re we saving money or are we saving children?"[57] For kindergarten proponents, the lack or closure of kindergartens constituted the worst sort of false economy, costing the nation's children above all.

Secondly, they continued and fortified their ongoing efforts at federal, state and local levels of government to insist on the expansion of public kindergartens (or, failing public funds, philanthropic and cooperative kindergartens) and of kindergarten legislation. Where public school kindergartens simply could not be introduced or sustained, the NKA encouraged parents' and women's clubs to operate kindergartens. For example, Mrs. Ethel M. Hughes (Kindergarten Chairman, Pitcher Pre-School Association; NKA Field Secretary for Missouri; and wife of the State Superintendent of Public Instruction for Missouri) wrote to the NKA about her fundraising in the form of ice cream socials including string music and a free picture show, featuring films donated by Paramount studios. Like their predecessors who worked to expand free kindergartens in the late nineteenth century, kindergarten advocates in the 1930s raised money via bake sales and sewing, home talent entertainments, quilt raffles, and annual subscriptions.[58] From 1931 to 1934, despite closures and cutbacks in many places, the NKA's guidance led to the founding of 350 new public kindergartens in the USA, including a "fine" one in Woodside, Maryland.[59]

A third strategy of kindergarten movement leaders involved repeated appeals to the federal government. ACE, the Bureau of Education, and other organizations supported the NKA's work toward federal kindergarten legislation. The most notable example of this was the failed Copeland-Bloom Bill of 1937, which attempted to guarantee federal funds for kindergartens as a crime-prevention measure. This measure, like others, died as a result of the federal government's insistence that education, even early education, was outside its mandate and should remain a matter for the individual states.[60] These organizations undertook a policy of "careful education" to acquaint policymakers with the kindergarten's child-centered philosophy and social and educational value, insisting, among other things, that the kindergarten would prevent crime.[61]

Finally, with the notable exception of the NKA, kindergarten advocates supported the expansion of publicly funded nursery schools for children under kindergarten age—even in areas where kindergartens did not exist. The NKA's refusal to do so was based on the belief that the vital home-school link was compromised without the kindergarten, and the benefits of nursery schooling would diminish if a child had no access to kindergarten (and thus stayed home or played in the streets) in the year or two between the end of nursery schooling (age 4) and the primary grades (age 6).

The only way kindergarten leaders saw out of this dilemma was to speak the language of value-for-money and measurable results while simultaneously defending their Froebelian heritage and modern child-development expertise. Kindergarten propaganda included the full spectrum of claims running from kindergartens' literal value-for-money to the question of "what price would we pay if we should dispense with the kindergarten?"[62] Dr. Joy Elmer Morgan, editor of the *Journal of the National Education Association*, exhorted in 1932:

> The kindergarten is the best part of the school. It lays foundations; it establishes basic habits; it makes the transition from home life to classroom activity. *It probably yields a larger return for every dollar spent than any other unit of the school.* Are you, as a teacher, helping parents and citizens to understand that in the choice between the dollar and the child, it is not good economy to abolish the kindergarten?[63]

And in the ACE's own journal, kindergarten teachers were told that they "must learn to speak to parents and taxpayers, to boards of education and to city commissionors (sic) in terms of economics as well as of education. They must show that kindergarten training is an economy in the educational life of the child and that it gives full value for the money expended."[64] The work of the ACE, NKA, NEA, and Bureau of Education in the 1930s went far to help teachers in this capacity, with notable victories.[65]

In the trying times of the 1930s, the NKA led other groups in a major push for pro-kindergarten legislation. A 1933 report from Mary Dabney Davis showed the extreme variation in mostly hard-won state-level legislation: 40 states and Washington, D.C. had laws permitting or requiring establishment of kindergartens. Only four states lacked specific legal sanction either to organize kindergartens or to educate children below age six in public schools. In three of these states, kindergartens were maintained in one or more places anyway.[66]

In 26 states, any district could open a kindergarten (with some requiring minimum enrollment or other specifications); in 15 states, only large cities could open kindergartens. In 29 of the states having permissive or mandatory laws for kindergarten establishment, the entrance ages were three, four, or four and a half years.[67] Kindergarten entrance requirements were usually based solely on chronological age, but sometimes they used a mental test or tests of physical or social characteristics. All of these restrictions were ways of winnowing the numbers of eligible children down to match the number of available spaces. Kindergarten funding came from some combination of local taxes and/or special funds from locality or state and/or general school funds.[68]

States with mandatory-on-petition laws had a higher percentage of 4- and 5-year-olds in kindergarten. However, the extremely high percentage of (urban) children in kindergarten in Michigan (where the law was permissive) and in cities in Nebraska (where there was no kindergarten law) showed that "community conviction of the value of education and local initiative" were the key elements in the expansion of public kindergarten enrollment.[69] In the 1920s, community conviction about the value of kindergartens had been cemented by the local efforts of the National Congress of Parents and Teachers, American Association of University Women, General Federation of Women's Clubs, American Legion, Federation of Labor, Rotary, Kiwanis, and others who were mobilized by NKA field secretaries.[70] In the crisis years of the 1930s, it was much more difficult to maintain local support for kindergartens in places where their provision was not guaranteed by law.

As part of its support of local initiatives, the ACE planned a nationwide Kindergarten Centennial celebration for 1937 including a reintroduction to the kindergarten's Froebelian roots.[71] As one of the centennial committee members explained:

> In short, one of our main objectives throughout this year should be to "sell our goods" to the public—to parents of young children, to teachers of higher grades, to superintendents of schools, and to the taxpayers and "townfathers" who all too often economize at our end of the educational ladder![72]

Although the committee felt that "[a] satisfied parent is our best advertiser," others warned against trying to impress parents and taxpayers by having children do "projects—masterpieces of teacher-pupil coercion—carried on for the sake of 'something to show visitors'."[73] These efforts to define the value of kindergartens in the 1930s were successful in protecting a majority of public kindergartens at a time when they were under attack. While many districts did discontinue kindergartens in the 1930s, most districts decided to maintain their kindergartens.[74] A few districts managed to open new ones. The price kindergartens paid for this success on the local level is that they failed even during the national economic and social crisis to garner the federal government support they had long sought.[75]

The Kindergarten and the Emergency Nursery School

At the same time that public kindergartens were threatened by financial cutbacks and other challenges, the federal government announced its own nationwide early childhood education initiative. Instead of supporting or expanding extant public kindergartens for four- and five-year-old children (for which the NKA continued to lobby), the government initiated a new program for even younger children: emergency nursery schools. Begun in 1933 under the Federal Emergency Relief Administration (FERA) and continued after 1935 under the Works Progress Administration (WPA), the emergency nursery schools were intended to alleviate "the physical and mental handicaps being imposed" upon "young children of preschool age in the homes of needy and unemployed parents" as a result of the economic crisis.[76] A main goal of the program was to provide work relief wages for unemployed teachers and other workers. Expansion of kindergarten education (which required highly-trained kindergarten teachers) would not have achieved this goal on such a large scale. The federal government would not interfere with public kindergartens since they were part of the schools and thus the sole province of the several states, but its emergency nursery school programs and their specific administration fell under the jurisdiction of public school superintendents and local relief administrators.

The National Advisory Committee on Emergency Nursery Schools (NAC), a voluntary standards body designed to make recommendations to FERA, included representatives from the ACE.[77] While fearing the challenges of such a large-scale government-regulated enterprise, these early childhood education leaders were excited to have the opportunity to bring pilot and demonstration programs to communities nationwide. They also hoped that these programs, by definition temporary, would be taken on permanently after emergency conditions subsided.

Because they were supervised and controlled by local public school systems, emergency nursery schools varied in their emphases. Some were "units for preschool children within elementary schools," while others functioned primarily as "laboratories for courses in the care and education of preschool children in high schools, normal schools and colleges" in line with the US model of nursery schooling more generally. Still other WPA emergency nursery schools were initiated as "units in urban and rural areas of need such as mining, factory and mill districts" and Native American reservations.[78] Emergency nursery schools were differentiated, administratively at least, from kindergartens; nursery schools were to be for a younger and particularly poverty-stricken clientele, children eligible for relief who were between the age of two and the local minimum age for school admission.[79] Where there were no kindergartens, kindergarten-aged children would be admitted, but for nursery school, not kindergarten education. The WPA refused to bail out public school kindergartens hurt by economic strictures. As a relief agency (and a temporary one at that), it did not want to get involved in the business of education.[80]

In 1932, there had been 13 nursery schools under public-school control; by the spring of 1934, the emergency nursery schools program had raised the number to over 1,500 schools, enrolling nearly 40,000 children aged two to six and employing approximately 3,000 teachers and 1,000 nutritional, health, or other mostly unskilled staff members.[81] At the height of their nine-year run, the WPA nursery schools comprised nearly 3,000 local programs enrolling half a million children, mostly for a full six-hour school day. Even as their own livelihoods were threatened, kindergarten advocates and educators used their expertise to ensure that nursery schools gave the best possible care despite high teacher-pupil ratios, inadequately trained staff, and the lack of appropriate space and equipment which dogged the programs.[82] NKA field secretaries alone helped 97 localities benefit from Federal Emergency Nursery Funds by helping them to submit suitable proposals to the government.[83]

As the New Deal government began to shift its weight with the easing of the Depression in the late 1930s, the WPA nursery schools program was transformed. After 1935, the programs were funded by the states rather than the federal government. The word "emergency" was dropped from the program's title in 1937. Then, in 1942, as defense-related industrial growth ended the need for unemployment relief projects, the programs came under an altogether new (and non-education-related) heading: WPA Child Protection Program.[84] With the dissolution of the WPA in December of 1942, the liquidation of WPA nursery schools was set for early 1943.

Although psychologists and other experts insisted that young children's need for education and care continued during and after the Second World War and post-war period, federal government support for nursery schools was terminated. The government thus marked the end of the national economic crisis and its interest in staying out of education and the related and more controversial field of child care. Although NAC members and early childhood education leaders nationwide had hoped that the WPA nursery schools would be taken on by local public schools, this did not happen. Most likely this failure was due to a combination of quality and cost issues paired with the newly acquired stigma of nursery schooling as an emergency poverty-track institution.[85] Some of them were transferred to other projects financed partly by federal grants to the states under the Community Facilities (Lanham Act) 1940 and its amendments. Most others were disbanded, having failed to find other local or private sources of funds in an atmosphere in which at-home mothers were preferable, from a policy standpoint, to waged working mothers in need of institutional child-care.[86] More than two decades—a generation—would pass before concerted federal government interest in this age group would return to the national stage in the form of Head Start programs in the 1960s.

Alongside their work in supporting the federal government's emergency nursery schools in the 1930s, US kindergarten organizations attempted to reinvigorate their earlier campaigns to expand kindergarten provision nationwide. The ACE and NKA were struggling to keep kindergartens on the educational agenda as the nation shifted from Depression-mode to wartime defense mode.[87] While the short term impact of the Great Depression on kindergarten provision was significant, the long term trend of increase in provision resumed with economic recovery. The number of children in the US aged three to five in 1940 was approximately 6 million, of whom nearly 650,000 were enrolled in some kind of school, be it nursery, kindergarten, or first grade.[88] The ACE, NANE, and the US Bureau of Education continued their efforts to expand provision to the other 5,350,000 children in the 1940s. They also continued efforts to reinforce earlier moves toward N-K-P unification.[89]

Trying to boost the morale of kindergarten proponents and to build hope for future kindergarten expansion, the ACE advertised the results of a survey of cities and towns in 12 states in 1940. The results were encouraging enough: superintendents reported the maintenance or increase of kindergarten budgets, and there was a two percent increase in the number of cities or towns having kindergartens on the previous year. These results were, however, based on a biased sample of kindergarten-friendly states.[90]

Conclusion

According to its authors, the ACE's 1940 survey "prove[d] that kindergarten [was] definitely spreading to smaller communities" and described a kindergarten movement with "a virility and strength not always apparent to those who may be dismayed and disheartened by set-backs in their own communities."[91] Here they distinguished between the short-term fiscal impact of the Depression and the long-term psychological, political and organizational struggles with which the kindergarten movement was engaged. On careful examination, it is apparent that various factors, philosophical and pecuniary, local as well as national, led kindergartens to be either axed or else spared from elimination due to Depression-era budgetary cutbacks. After all, kindergartens were (and are) expensive programs and Americans have had a long history of ambivalence toward public early childhood education. School boards were (and are) fickle, for one reason or another backtracking or reneging on programs they had wholeheartedly endorsed in previous years.

As with other educational programs, Depression-era school administrators wanted proof that the kindergarten was effective in aiding young children's socio-emotional development and that it did so cost-effectively, proof that was especially hard to come by in a non-academic program. Cost-effectiveness seemed self-evident, but how could one quantify increases in a child's self-confidence or in the depth of a child's creative expression? In the absence of quantifiable, testable data, kindergarten advocates employed a discourse of quantification and measurement to explain both kindergarten values and kindergartens' value-for-money to a discerning public of school board-members and taxpayers. Later advocates of publicly funded early childhood education in the USA, including those promoting Head Start programs from the 1960s through to the present, would also be forced to present quantifiable, testable data as well as qualitative, affective "proof" of their programs' values and value-for-money.

In the 1920s, the US kindergarten movement achieved significant success in expanding the meager provision of kindergarten education nationwide. Over the course of that decade, public kindergarten enrollments had increased 52%, to include nearly three-quarters of a million children by 1930. Kindergarten advocates got the name and idea of the kindergarten on the minds and on the agendas of parents and school boards alike. One of the great strengths of the US kindergarten movement and its constituent organizations was their ability to adapt to shifts in social and pedagogical trends in order to meet the needs of diverse communities.

Another strength of the movement lay in its earlier position of administrative connection with and curricular independence from the primary school. This upheld a vision of the kindergarten as the pedagogically and philosophically superior half of the kindergarten-primary pairing. However, some of the reasons school boards gave for cutting kindergarten programs in the 1930s showed that the kindergarten's tradition of autonomy had left it vulnerable to attack as an "extra" or "frill." This, in turn, hampered kindergarten teachers' efforts to define their programs as a fundamental part of public education. Teachers' inability to resolve lingering ambiguities about the kindergarten's role in American public education, especially *vis-à-vis* the primary schools, meant that the kindergarten would never be immune from challenge, even at times when early childhood education services were perceived as essential to national well-being. It also meant that the kindergarten could be shaped and reshaped according to pedagogical trends and social and political demands. In this ambiguity and flexibility, in the partnership with and tenuous relationship to the primary school and the nursery school, lay the roots of the kindergarten's Depression-era precariousness as well as the seeds of its future expansion.

Kindergarten advocates looked to federal, state, and local governments during this crisis at the same time that the federal government was determined to leave costly educational matters to the states and pre-school care to temporary emergency programs. Nonetheless, kindergarten teachers managed to defend their status as professionals with early childhood expertise while re-packaging the work of kindergartens and helping young children through emergency nursery schools. Rather than competing with the short-lived emergency nursery schools, kindergarten advocates tried to guide them in children's best interests, to provide children with stable and healthy educational environments to counteract the upheaval experienced in their homes and in the society at large. Despite changing social and economic climates, kindergarten leaders devised discursive and other strategies for filling and defending a flexible niche in the market for state-sector education. In defending their own programs against cuts, kindergarten advocates brought the needs of young children into the national spotlight at a time when the nation as a whole was suffering. The result was that, although public kindergarten provision decreased, hundreds of thousands of American pre-school children were served by a patchwork of federal and local care and education programs.

Notes

1. Frank M. Phillips, "Encouraging Signs of Kindergarten Expansion," *Childhood Education* Vol. 14, No. 3 (1929) pp. 122–123. In the archival and print sources used for this study, this agency is referred to, variously, as the Office of Education (OoE) and the Bureau of Education (BoE) under the US Department of the Interior (DoI). I have tried to remain true to the usage of the sources, at the risk of appearing inconsistent.

2. Ibid.

3. D. E. W., "The Challenge to the Kindergarten," *Childhood Education* Vol. 14, no. 1 (1938) p. 4; Worth McClure, "Kindergarten 'Gifts' and the Next Hundred Years," *Childhood Education* Vol. 14, no. 5 (1938) pp. 197–199.

4. Timon Covert, Emery M. Foster, and Lester B. Herlihy, *City Schools and the Economic Situation* Circular No. 124, (Washington, D.C.: US Department of the Interior, Office of Education, 1933); William G. Carr, "The Status of the Kindergarten (Part I)," *Childhood Education* Vol. 10, No. 6 (1934) pp. 283–285, 332.

5. Peter Becker Jr., *Friederich Froebel Started Something* (Washington, D.C.: Association for Childhood Education International, 1940).

6. Evelyn Weber, *The Kindergarten: Its Encounter with Educational Thought in America* (New York: Teachers College Press, 1969) p. 195.

7. William G. Carr, "The Status of the Kindergarten. Part III. Extent of Curtailment and Future Outlook," *Childhood Education* Vol. 10, no. 8 (1934) pp. 425–427.

8. Carr, "The Status of the Kindergarten (Part I)," p. 284.

9. William G. Carr, "The Status of the Kindergarten (Part II)," *Childhood Education* Vol. 10, No. 7 (1934) p. 376; Mary Dabney Davis, *Kindergartens in Public Schools*, Circular No. 88 (US Dept. of Interior, Office of Education, Washington, D.C.: USGPO, 1933) p. 10.

10. Carr, "The Status of the Kindergarten (Part II)," The amounts correspond to $552.35 (average 1929 per-pupil kindergarten expenditure) and $560.51 (average 1934 per-pupil kindergarten expenditure).

11. Ibid., p. 374.

12. National Kindergarten Association (NKA) *Annual Report*, (1930) pp. 1–2, NKA Papers, Special Collections, Milbank Memorial Library, Teachers College, Columbia University.

13. Carr, "The Status of the Kindergarten (Part III)," p. 427; Elizabeth Webster, "Making Kindergarten Values Known," *Childhood Education* Vol. 11, No. 2 (1934) pp. 64–67.

14. Carr, "The Status of the Kindergarten (Part III)," p. 427.

15. Bess Goodykoontz, Mary Dabney Davis, Mina M. Langvick, *Biennial Survey of Education in the United States, chapter II, Elementary Education* (Washington: DoI, OoE, 1931).

16. The few consolidated rural all-day kindergartens offered mid-day meals, naps and weekly showers as a health service for children who came, according to *Childhood Education*, "from small farms where not only bathrooms are

few but water often not easily accessible." Grace W. Mink, "An All Day Kindergarten in a Rural Consolidated School," *Childhood Education* Vol. 13, No. 7 (1937) p. 264; Mary Dabney Davis, *Nursery-Kindergarten-Primary Education 1924–1926* (Washington, D.C.: DoI, OoE, 1927) p. 35. A 1927 survey by the ACE found that "approximately one-fifth of the children four and five years of age in the Eastern, Great Lakes, and Western States are enrolled in kindergartens; one-tenth in the Great Plains States, and one-fortieth in the Southern States." Lucy Gage, "The South's Interest in Primary Education," *Childhood Education* Vol. 6, No. 1 (1929) p. 16.

17.   Ibid., p. 16.

18.   "Kindergarten Education 1917," ACEI Papers, Historical Manuscripts and Archives Department, University of Maryland College Park Libraries, College Park, Maryland. Eighteen states had in-progress lobbying efforts for kindergarten in 1919 state legislatures. "Kindergarten Education 1918," ACEI Papers. There were several different types of kindergarten legislation, namely enabling/permissive, mandatory-on-petition, and others. Enabling legislation merely permitted the use of public funds for kindergartens without making any provision for the institution of kindergartens. Mandatory-on-petition obligates a school board to provide kindergartens when a specified number of citizens (usually 25 parents) register a demand for them. Mary Dabney Davis, *State Legislation Relating to Kindergartens in Effect 1931*, pamphlet No. 30 (Washington, D.C.: DoI, BoE, 1932).

19.   Kristen Dombkowski, "Will the real kindergarten please stand up?: defining and redefining the twentieth-century US kindergarten," *History of Education* Vol. 30, No. 6 (2001) pp. 527–545.

20.   Larry Cuban, *How Teachers Taught: Constancy and Change in American Classrooms, 1880–1990* (New York: Teachers College Press, 1993).

21.   Alice Temple, "The Kindergarten in America—Modern Period," *Childhood Education* Vol. 13, No. 8 (1937) pp. 358–363, 387; *Proceedings of the twenty-sixth Annual meeting of the International Kindergarten Union Baltimore, MD May 19–23, 1919*, 93, ACEI Papers.

22.   Nina C. Vandewalker, "The Outlook for Kindergarten Education," *Childhood Education* Vol. 1, No. 2 (1924) p. 62; Davis, *Nursery-Kindergarten-Primary Education*, pp. 31–38.

23.   Davis, *Nursery-Kindergarten-Primary Education*, p. 41.

24.   Mabel E. Simpson, "The Kindergarten-Primary Unit. Coordination through a unified curriculum," *Childhood Education* Vol. 6, No. 3 (1929) p. 111.

25.   Examples include Patty Smith Hill, et al., *A Conduct Curriculum for the Kindergarten and First Grade* (New York: Scribner's, 1923); Subcommittee of the Bureau of Education, Committee of the IKU, *A Kindergarten-First Grade Curriculum*, Bureau of Education Bulletin No. 15 (Washington, D.C.; 1922); Alice Temple and Samuel C. Parker, *Unified Kindergarten and First Grade Teaching* (Boston: Ginn & Co., 1925); Helen M. Reynolds, *Course of Study in Terms of Children's Activities for Kindergarten and Primary Grades* (Seattle: [n.p.] 1925); Julia S. Bothwell, *Course of Study for Kindergartens* (Cincinnati: [undated] 1920s); Luella A. Palmer, *A Syllabus for Kindergarten and Kindergarten Extension Classes* (New York: [undated] 1920s); Simpson, "The Kindergarten-

Primary Unit," pp. 110–115.

26. Nina Vandewalker, "The History of Kindergarten Influence on Elementary Education, The Kindergarten and Its Relation to Elementary Education," *Sixth Yearbook of the National Society for the Study of Education*, Part II (Bloomington, Ill., 1907) pp. 115–138.

27. Cuban, *How Teachers Taught*; Weber, *The Kindergarten*.

28. Early US nursery schools included the Bureau of Educational Experiments nursery school (1919) in New York, the Merrill-Palmer Nursery School (1921) in Detroit, Ruggles Street Nursery School (1922) in Boston.

29. Some city school systems offered laboratory nursery schools to train high school students in home-economics, or else as a link with its kindergarten-primary department. "City School Systems, Kindergarten Education, Pre-school Education, 1927. Drawn from Annual Report of the Commissioner of Education to the Secretary of the Interior for Fiscal Year Ended June 30, 1927," ACEI Papers.

30. Shirley A. Kessler and Beth Blue Swadener, eds. *Reconceptualizing the Early Childhood Curriculum: Beginning the Dialogue* (New York: Teachers College, 1992) p. 13.

31. Temple, "The Kindergarten in America—Modern Period," p. 363.

32. Elizabeth Rose, *A Mother's Job: The History of Day Care, 1890–1960* (New York: Oxford University Press, 1999).

33. Bess Goodykoontz, Mary Dabney Davis, Mina M. Langvick, *Biennial Survey of Education in the United States, chapter II, Elementary Education* (Washington: US DoI, OoE, 1931) p. 6. Two public school systems reported having nursery schools. Elizabeth Neterer and Lovisa C. Wagoner, *What Is a Nursery School?* (Washington, D.C.: ACEI, 1940) p. 5.

34. Ibid., p. 3.

35. George D. Stoddard, "Research Findings in Relation to Kindergarten Training as a Factor in School Life," ACEI Extended Report (undated, possibly 1930) #705418/760209 G:16, NKA Papers; idem, "The Kindergarten and the Nursery School," *NEA Journal*, Vol. 21 (December 1932) pp. 279–281; idem, "Surviving Educational Myths," *Childhood Education* Vol. 10, No. 4 (1934) p. 173.

36. Patty Smith Hill, "The Strategic Position of the Kindergarten in American Education," *Childhood Education* Vol. 6, No. 4 (1929) p. 152.

37. Annual Report of the Commissioner of Education to the Secretary of the Interior, June 30, 1926, cited in ACE, *The Kindergarten Centennial 1837–1937, A Brief Historical Outline of Early Childhood Education* (Washington, D.C.: ACE, 1937) p. 7.

38. Edgar B. Wesley, *NEA, The first hundred years: The building of the teaching profession* (New York: Harper & Row, 1957) pp. 162–164.

39. Kessler and Swadener, eds. *Reconceptualizing the Early Childhood Curriculum*, p. 13.

40. "School Days at Hand," *The Washington Post*, September 10, 1901, p. 9; "Public School Facilities," *The New York Times*, September 12, 1897, p. 10; "Huge Sum is Needed in Schools," *Los Angeles Times*, June 23, 1923, II, p. 1.

41. Robert Melvin Tank, "Young Children, Families, and Society in America

234 Nawrotzki

since the 1820s: The evolution of health, education, and child care programs for preschool children" (Ph.D. thesis, University of Michigan, 1980); Michael Steven Shapiro, *Child's Garden: the kindergarten movement from Froebel to Dewey* (University Park: Pennsylvania State University Press, 1983); Columbus (Ohio) Public Schools, *Notable Milestones in the History of the Columbus Public Schools* [PDF] (accessed 29 March 2004); available from http://www.columbus.k12.oh.us/.

42. W. D. Commins and Theodore Shank, "Kindergarten Training and Grade Achievement," *Education* Vol. 48 (March 1928) pp. 410–415; W. J. Peters, "The Progress of Kindergarten Pupils in the Elementary Grades," *Journal of Educational Research*, Vol. 7 (1923) pp. 117–126; Colleen M. Smith, "A Study to Determine the Effectiveness of Kindergarten Training," *Elementary School Journal*, Vol. 28 (December 1927) pp. 286–289; Ruth G. Strickland, "The Contribution of the Kindergarten," *NEA Journal*, Vol. 20 (March 1931) pp. 77–78; Stoddard, "Kindergarten and the Nursery School," pp. 279–281; idem, "Research Findings in Relation to Kindergarten Training."

43. Vandewalker, "Outlook for Kindergarten Education," pp. 61–62.

44. Edward William Goetch, *The Kindergarten as a Factor in Elementary School Achievement and Progress* (Iowa City; 1926); Mary Dabney Davis, *General Practice in Kindergarten Education in the United States* (Washington, D.C.: NEA, 1925) Chapter 2; H. A. Greene, "The Kindergarten and Later School Achievement," in Josephine Maclatchy, ed., *Studies of Childhood* (Washington: IKU, 1930) pp. 21–38; Gertrude Hildreth, quoted in Hill, "The Strategic Position of the Kindergarten," p. 149.

45. Gage, "The South's Interest in Primary Education," p. 16.

46. Stoddard, "Surviving Educational Myths," p. 173; Patty Smith Hill, "The Function of the Kindergarten," *Young Children* Vol. 42, No. 5 (1987) p. 15.

47. Subcommittee on Curriculum of the BoE Committee of the IKU, DoI, OoE, *The Kindergarten Curriculum*, Bulletin 19 (Washington, D.C.: USGPO, 1919).

48. Dombkowski, "Will the real kindergarten please stand up?"

49. Hill, "The Strategic Position of the Kindergarten,"p. 147.

50. Carr, "The Status of the Kindergarten (Part I)," pp. 283–285, 332.

51. National Kindergarten Association Archives, "Children Enrolled in Kindergarten in U.S.; Figures from Bulletins 'Statistics of State School Systems'," FL/MG16=NKA; #750418/760209, NKA Papers.

52. Olga Adams, "The Present Crisis in Kindergarten Education," *Childhood Education* Vol. 10, No. 8 (1934) p. 423.

53. R. Stewart MacDougall, "The Kindergarten Pays," *Childhood Education* Vol. 11, No. 1 (1934) pp. 29–34; Webster, "Making Kindergarten Values Known."

54. Matilda Remy, "The Closing of Kindergartens," *Childhood Education* Vol. 9, No. 9 (1933) pp. 479, 489.

55. Patty Smith Hill, "Shall the Youngest Suffer Most?" *Childhood Education* Vol. 8, No. 10 (1931) p. 500.

56. William F. Russell, "Federal Aid Issue Rises," *New York Times*, February 26, 1933, p. 6.

57. George D. Stoddard, "Emergency Nursery Schools on Trial," *Childhood Education* Vol. 11, No. 6 (1935) p. 260.

58. National Kindergarten Association *Annual Report*, 1931, 3–5, NKA Papers.

59. Triennial report of National Kindergarten Association to National Council of Women of the United States June 4, 1934, NKA Papers. Woodside Elementary School (Woodside, Maryland) opened a new kindergarten (including a building addition) in January 1935. "The kindergarten, said to be one of the finest in the States, is of the newest and most approved type." "Silver Tea to Open New Kindergarten," *The Washington Post*, January 9, 1935, p. 6.

60. S. 1355, 75th Congress, 1st session, National Kindergarten Association, Annual Report 1937 (Given at Annual Meeting, January 21, 1938) p. 11, NKA Papers. NKA, "Regarding the Kindergarten Bills: S.2510 and H.R. 6474," #750418/760209, NKA Papers.

61. Annual Report National Kindergarten Association, 1937 (Given at Annual Meeting, January 21, 1938) p. 9; Annual Report National Kindergarten Association, 1941 (Given at Annual Meeting, January 29, 1942) pp. 2–11, NKA Papers.

62. Nila Banton Smith, "What Price Kindergartens?" *Childhood Education* Vol. 10, No. 9 (1934) p. 467.

63. Emphasis in the original. Patty Smith Hill, ed., *The Practical Value of Early Childhood Education: Objectives and Results of Nursery School, Kindergarten and First Grade Education* (Washington, D.C.: ACEI, 1934).

64. Webster, "Making Kindergarten Values Known," p. 67.

65. Remy, "The Closing of Kindergartens."

66. Davis, *A Primer of Information about Kindergarten Education*, p. 2.

67. Mary Dabney Davis, *Some Phases of Nursery-Kindergarten-Primary Education, 1926–1928* Bulletin No. 29 (Washington, D.C.: DoI, OoE, 1929) p. 15.

68. Davis, "Reconstructing Legislation," p. 13.

69. Ibid., p. 12.

70. Ibid., p. 14.

71. ACE, *The Kindergarten Centennial 1837–1937. A Brief Historical Outline of Early Childhood Education* (Washington, D.C: ACE, 1937).

72. Mary C. Shute, "The Kindergarten Centennial—Why and How," *Childhood Education* Vol. 12, No. 3 (1936) p. 169.

73. Ibid.; D.E.W., "The Challenge to the Kindergarten," *Childhood Education* Vol. 15, No. 1 (1938) p. 4.

74. Remy, "The Closing of Kindergartens."

75. Kristen Nawrotzki, Anna Mills Smith, and Maris Vinovskis, "Social Science Research and Early Education," in Hamilton Cravens, ed., *The Social Sciences Go to Washington: The Politics of Knowledge in the Postmodern Age* (Piscataway, NJ: Rutgers University Press, 2003).

76. Harry L. Hopkins, "Announcement of Emergency Nursery Schools," *Childhood Education* Vol. 10, No. 3 (1933) p. 155.

77. National Advisory Committee on Emergency Nursery Schools, *Emergency Nursery Schools During the First Year 1933–1934*, 1, ACEI Papers; V. Celia Lascarides and Blythe F. Hinitz, *History of Early Childhood Education* (London: Falmer Press, 2000) pp. 385–386.

78. Mary Dabney Davis, "Emergency Nursery Schools," *Childhood Education* Vol. 10, No. 4 (1934) p. 201.

79. National Advisory Committee on Emergency Nursery Schools, *Emergency Nursery Schools during the Second Year, 1934–35*, 21–23. Record Group 4, Box 6, ACEI Papers.

80. Davis, "Emergency Nursery Schools," p. 202.

81. Mary Dabney Davis, "Emergency Nursery Schools," *Childhood Education* Vol. 10, No. 8 (1934) p. 430; Ward W. Keesecker and Mary Dabney Davis, *Legislation Concerning Early Childhood Education* Pamphlet No. 62 (Washington: DoI, OoE, 1935) p. 2.

82. Barbara Beatty, *Preschool Education in America: The culture of young children from the colonial era to the present* (New Haven: Yale University Press, 1995) pp. 179–183.

83. "National Kindergarten Association Definite Achievements to January, 1935," NKA Papers.

84. Lascarides and Hinitz, *History of Early Childhood Education*, pp. 383–384.

85. Beatty, *Preschool Education*, p. 185; Tank, "Young Children," pp. 352–360.

86. Katharine F. Lenroot, "The Children's Bureau Program for the Care of Children of Working Mothers," *Childhood Education* Vol. 19, No. 7 (1943) p. 324.

87. Becker, *Friederich Froebel Started Something*.

88. John K. Norton, "The Place of Nursery Schools in Public Education," *Childhood Education* Vol. 21, No. 5 (1945) p. 215.

89. Winifred E. Bain, "Bridging the Gaps Between Kindergarten and First Grade," *Childhood Education* Vol. 18, No. 1 (1941) pp. 29–34; Lucy Wheelock, "From the Kindergarten to the Primary School," *Childhood Education* Vol. 18, No. 9 (1942) pp. 414–416; Dorothy Koehring, "Kindergarten Contributions to Present-day Elementary Education," *Childhood Education* Vol. 18, No. 9 (1941) pp. 398–403.

90. Becker, *Friederich Froebel Started Something*.

91. Ibid.

Chapter Eleven

Progressive Schools for a Democratic Society: Reforming Education in Rio de Janeiro

Alberto Gawryszewski and
Michael L. Conniff

When the young educational reformer Anísio Teixeira assumed the position of Director of Education in Rio de Janeiro in 1931, it seemed that he would be able to institute major changes in that city's schools, long neglected by the elite. Having studied with John Dewey and other intellectuals at Columbia University, Teixeira had extremely ambitious ideas of about how education could literally change society for the better. Nobody could have predicted that a brief four years later Teixeira would be hounded out of his job and the city by political enemies and forced to take up life as a virtual fugitive in his native state of Bahia.

This study attempts to understand the evolution of public education in Rio de Janeiro between 1929 and 1935, the years that Brazil was most subject to the economic, social, and political disruption of the Great Depression. The country had enjoyed a generation of prosperity, based on the export of tropical products like coffee, rubber, cocoa, and sugar, but the crash of 1929 brought that to a shuddering halt. Political stability, based on full employment and fraudulent elections, also suffered, as the lead-up to the 1930 presidential election became a battleground. The contest, fought over by the incumbents and outsiders who first claimed to be reformers and then called themselves revolutionaries, ended up being settled by armed forces in ten states and the Federal District of Rio de Janeiro. The outsiders won, neutralized the federal army, and installed Getúlio Vargas as provisional president of a revolutionary government in November 1930.

As federal capital, largest city, and showcase of Brazilian civilization, Rio de Janeiro had always been given special treatment in federal budgets. The city had been completely remodeled in the early 1900s and again in the early 1920s. Social and medical services for the upper middle class approached levels available in Europe and North America. Rio's public education, however, had traditionally been given a low priority, since children of well-to-do families went to private schools, typically run by the Catholic Church.

Rio's public schools were extremely selective and academic. Previous administrations had not invested in expanding public schools, much less in changing their book-based teaching methods, in which the teacher was the center of the educational process and determined what students should learn. The Department of Education did little to supervise actual classroom teaching, and the Normal School did not discuss philosophy or methods. In the late 1920s, an educational reform movement had arisen to improve public education in the capital, but the economic crash and political crisis put these reforms on hold.[1]

Vargas appointed a physician, Pedro Ernesto Baptista, to serve as mayor of Rio in 1931 and to carry out a number of social and educational reforms in the capital. Pedro Ernesto, as he came to be known publicly, took a leadership position in the revolutionary movement and became a national figure whose words and deeds excited a broad range of citizens, in Rio and throughout the country.

Pedro Ernesto appointed a bright young lawyer, Anísio Teixeira, as Director of Education. This study looks at how Teixeira influenced educational thought and deeply altered the school system. The first part looks at the onset of the Great Depression in Brazil and in particular Rio de Janeiro. The second part examines Teixeira's writings, especially as they were shaped by his work with Dewey and other U.S. philosophers. The third part examines Teixeira's accomplishments, both as achievements and processes put into motion during his administration. And the last part probes the differences between Teixeira's work, with its emphasis on citizenship and educational expansion, and the opposition of the Catholic Church and other social conservatives, who eventually forced his resignation.

In the end, we argue, Teixeira's progressive reforms were defeated by conservative elements in society, especially the Church, and by traditional bureaucrats within the school system, who resisted any change in their work. The Depression exacerbated the opposition to Teixeira while making it harder to actually implement his reforms.

The Great Depression in Rio de Janeiro

During the 1930 election campaign and subsequent political revolt, Brazil's gross national product plunged about 30%, due to shrinking capital, collapsing domestic demand, and declining prices on world commodity markets. In 1932, for example, Brazil's export prices stood at only 43% of the 1928 levels. Getúlio Vargas, who had run for president on an opposition ticket, was soon thrust into the leadership of a conspiracy to overthrow the incumbent government and install a revolutionary regime. The pressures for change came from three major sources. The first and mildest emerged from the 1920s reformist movements. These movements were led by middle and upper middle class professionals who sought to modernize society by reforming its economy, society, culture, and institutions. They sought higher levels of literacy, public health, safety, sobriety, national security, and economic justice. With regard to education, the most active reform group had been the Pioneers, which emerged from the Brazilian Education Association (ABE).

Most of these reform-minded citizens, especially in major cities, probably supported Getúlio Vargas for president. Yet another force that would deeply affect education was the Catholic Revitalization movement, led by well-to-do youth associated with the Church. This group was based in the Centro Dom Vital, headed by writer/intellectual Alceu de Amoroso Lima. It would push for greater Church influence in public life and a return of religious instruction to the public schools.[2]

Additional pressure for changes came from politicians who were fed up with the politics of the previous generation and wished to create a more competitive and open system of governance. They staffed out the Liberal Alliance party that conducted Vargas's campaign in 1929 and 1930. Many of them also saw the need to forge new institutions that could meet the challenges presented by modern, industrial society. Yet some, like Francisco Campos from Minas Gerais, who would become Vargas's first Minister of Education in 1931, held deeply conservative views of what directions Brazil should take during the crisis years of the 1930s.

The third and most radical impetus for reform was the Tenente Movement, composed of hundreds of military cadets and officers who had participated in revolts in the 1920s and had coalesced into the core of Vargas's military organization. They were joined by a small number of civilians who had given them clandestine support. Once they took over, the Tenentes purged the armed services of high officers and took over key positions in the military, states, and central government. The Tenentes came from diverse political backgrounds, and their influence after 1930 was quite heterogeneous and autocratic. Only later, under the guidance of President Vargas and mayor Pedro Ernesto, would a more coherent policy thrust, known as Tenentismo, become visible. Better education was one of their central goals. As noted below, Rio physician Pedro Ernesto served as president of the Tenente club for several years.[3]

Thus the Vargas regime took office in the midst of a crisis of historic proportions: the Depression and attendant fiscal crisis, the violent overthrow of the republic that had ruled for forty years, an overhaul of major branches of government, and multiple demands for social, political, economic, and institutional reform. This situation produced an urgency that had not been seen in the previous three decades.

Vargas responded by forming two new ministries, those of education and labor. These had been promised in his election campaign in 1929, and constituencies in his new government pressed him to follow through. As it turned out, Vargas could only create the skeletons of these ministries, for he did not have the authority or the funding to make them effective across the nation. Thus, the two ministries primarily operated in the capital city for a number of years.

In late 1931 Vargas appointed Tenente leader Pedro Ernesto as mayor of Rio and urged him to create a program and a party that could convert the revolutionary zeal of his colleagues into a political movement that would steer the country back to constitutional politics. The federal government made emergency resources available to Pedro Ernesto, from foreign loans contracted before 1930.[4] The mayor quickly brought order to the capital and then undertook social reforms that caught the attention of the entire nation. He went on to become the first true populist in Brazil's history. His program, which became a campaign slogan for the 1933 and 1934 elections, was simply "schools and hospitals." By the end of his administration in 1936, he had overseen construction starts on 28 new schools and six new hospitals, nearly doubling the capacity of the city to provide educational and medical services to the population. In a period when the economy still reeled from the Depression, this was an enormous achievement.

Pedro Ernesto had begun his career in politics in 1924, when he supported Tenente rebels in São Paulo by providing arms and supplies, and also by hiding and treating wounded rebels in his Rio surgical clinic. He came to be known as the "mother of the Tenentes."

With the victory of the revolution of 1930, which was led militarily by the Tenentes, Pedro Ernesto won appointment as mayor of Rio de Janeiro. He billed his approach as one of honesty, justice, and work, qualities that would address the aspirations of his supporters and offer relief from the Depression. Unlike earlier municipal leaders who had relied too heavily on borrowing and bonds, Pedro Ernesto tried to balance his budgets because of the exigencies of the Depression. All of the public works, including school construction, were paid out of current revenues.[5] His administration emphasized education and health, because he gave priority to public investment in these programs, especially in neighborhoods poorly served by the city.

In 1932 a counterrevolution broke out in São Paulo, where the state leaders demanded a return to the ancien regime, in which São Paulo led the nation. Although this revolt failed, Vargas did in fact move the country back to a constitutional democracy by holding elections for a constitutional assembly in 1933. He promulgated a constitution and held elections for Congress the following year. As a compromise, Vargas was chosen by the Assembly to serve the first four-year term under the new charter.

One of Pedro Ernesto's most important, and later controversial, appointments was a Director of Education who was also committed to rebuilding the curriculum, services, and even philosophy of the school system, Anísio Teixeira. Simultaneously, though, President Vargas appointed a conservative Catholic to head the new Ministry of Education, Francisco Campos. The latter had served in the state administration of Minas Gerais, whose governor recommended Campos because of his ties to the Church and especially to Cardinal Sebastião Leme. These elements were important for legitimizing the new regime. Over time a powerful group of religious education advocates formed around Campos and Cardinal Leme.

Therefore, in the highly contentious and financially difficult climate of the Depression, two opposing forces and philosophies attacked the glaring need for educational reforms from different perspectives, one from the left and one from the right.

The Educational Thought of Anísio Teixeira

Anísio Teixeira, born in the state of Bahia in 1900, belonged to an influential political family. When the family's ally won gubernatorial

elections in 1924, the governor elect invited Texieira to become director of public education during his four-year term. Teixeira accepted,
but because he had studied law in college and had little experience in
education, he went on an extended tour of the state's schools to assess
their quality. What he found was chaotic: demand that far exceeded
classroom space available, low retention and promotion rates, poorly
prepared teachers, etc. Because of the huge challenges he faced during this time, upon leaving office he sought out more knowledge
about education elsewhere so that he could improve schools in his
own country.[6]

Anísio Teixeira went to the United States two times before he took
over the position of Director of Education for the Federal District of
Rio de Janeiro. The first time was in 1927, when he traveled to study
teaching methods in U.S. institutions. He enrolled in Columbia University's Teachers College, under the guidance of Heloisa Brainerd.
The following year he returned to Columbia with a scholarship from
the Macy Student Fund International Institute. During these visits, he
became acquainted with leading U.S. philosophers and educators,
through their books and lectures. Among these were Dewey, his
teacher and source of his personal philosophy, and William Heard
Kilpatrick, who helped him develop his educational theories.[7] In particular, Teixeira was deeply influenced by three of Kilpatrick's lectures that were later published in Brazil under the title, "Education
for a Civilization in Transformation," that laid out the author's ideas
of about U.S. democracy and the evolution of capitalist society.[8]
Teixeira thus served as a conduit through which the ideas of Dewey,
Kilpatrick, and others, traveled from the United States to Brazil during the 1930s.

Teixeira also discovered quantitative research methods, which
would allow school administrators to analyze, measure, and evaluate
student outcomes as well as teaching approaches. He hoped these
methodologies would allow individualized treatment of students and
overall guidance of instruction. IQ tests, for example, provided individual scores for students while allowing for a broader assessment of
teaching methods. These statistical methods were among the most
powerful tools he acquired in the United States and then employed to
implement his reforms in Brazil.

Despite such advanced discussions in academic circles, Teixeira
discovered through his experiences and Rugg's *The Child Centered
School*, published in 1928, that the majority of U.S. schools continued

to operate by traditional teaching methods with little influence from the new pedagogy.[9] As part of his self-education, then, Teixeira visited six U.S. states, to observe schools first hand. Exploring the United States, especially the East Coast, where social mobility and democracy were realities, where diverse cultures could coexist, and where science, technology, and mechanization were everyday facts, Teixeira was forced to ask what role education played in this kaleidoscopic society. American progressive educators helped him to answer these questions, because they placed the school at the center of these modernizing processes, as in this statement by Kilpatrick:

> The material progress of civilization threatens to exceed our social and moral capacity to understand problems that arise...We must, therefore, develop a new point of view and create an educational system to accommodate such changes, one that takes into consideration the fact of accelerating change. If we do not, civilization itself is in jeopardy.[10]

Thus, Teixeira absorbed from these philosophers and his own observations the notion that the western world had undergone tremendous changes in the first three decades of the twentieth century—such as the maturation of science, industrialization, and the preeminence of democracy as a political system. Moreover, these processes were still underway.

Science introduced new ways to see the world, through the lens of scientific experimentation, allowing citizens to understand the world and determine facts in an objective fashion, free from dogma and prejudice. In this view, everything was susceptible to analysis. The old social and moral order, thought to be eternal until then, could be subjected to the scientist's scrutiny. Industrialism formed yet another facet of modern life, born of the application of science to everyday life. Industrialism worked to integrate the world, making knowledge interdependent, so that information became universal. Finally, democratization of society, in which every person counted and whose ideas and personality were respected, would improve governance immensely.[11] Unquestionably these revelations about the western world contrasted sharply with the reality of Brazil. By embracing these views and the reforms they implied, Teixeira necessarily become an agent of transformation upon his return to Brazil.

Of course, Brazil had also undergone social and economic transformations in the first three decades of the century. Industrial production rose, giving rise to working class and urban expansion, both propitious for social conflict. The government of the First Republic (1889–1930), meanwhile, was not known for improving the lives of the poor. On the contrary, it defended the interests of capitalists by suppressing unions and keeping wages low. The urban shantytowns, called *favelas*, had in fact made their debut in these years because little housing existed for these new factory workers. Teixeira, therefore, saw his country growing economically but without the kind of income distribution, social mobility, and liberal democracy observed in the United States.

Teixeira formulated the outlines of a new educational strategy for Brazil in relation to this emerging vision of the modern world. It would prepare a new man for a new world, because without adapting man would be at a disadvantage. As Kilpatrick had stated, the "old" educational approaches no longer satisfied the needs of the western democracies. The traditional school, failing to take into account the changes that were underway, still envisioned forms of education confined to the classroom and to book learning. It assumed that students would graduate into a known world familiar to their parents, whom they would eventually replace. The traditional approach assumed a static world where the social, moral, and religious elements coalesced into one. In that way knowledge was passed on by teachers and memorized by students, who were expected to accept it without any criticism.

Teixeira's progressive school was virtually the opposite side of the coin. By "progressive" he meant a school that was always changing and re-inventing itself to remain relevant to society's needs. It would be based on real life experience that led students to acquire new habits of thinking and acting. In this school, the student, at the center of the learning process, would have an active role alongside the teacher in creating the curriculum and constituent elements of the learning process.[12]

Teixeira took the concept of "experience" from Dewey, who construed it as the relationship between entities in nature. To the extent that experience occurs, it takes the form of contacts among entities, especially humans, and results in an exchange of influences, an adaptation to the world, and changes in the relationships. Life, then, is made up of a series of experiences. In Dewey's conception, educational experience is one involving intelligence, in which thinking occurs, where one perceives new relationships and continuities. Experience is life, and at the same time learning.[13] In this context, since the progressive school is based on life, one lives in it, it is not where one prepares to live. Teixeira used Dewey, then, to define the concept of education as "a process of reconstruction and reorganization of experience, by means of which we perceive our senses more sharply, and thereby we become better able to manage future experiences."[14]

For Dewey education was not a mechanism for correcting and adjusting the individual to societal structures, but rather a factor in changing structures through the action of the individual. Education and society are two fundamental processes in life which influence each other. Teixieira concluded that society and education do not exist separately—rather they are processes that co-exist.

Teixeira held that a relationship combining friendship and mutual understanding should prevail between teacher and student, because that is the axis of all learning. The curriculum and its component parts needed to develop together, based on students' life experiences, and not on a simple listing of subjects. Therefore, instructional design would evolve democratically by agreement between teacher and student—although the teacher would have the prerogative of posing problems—and learning tasks would be developed by all. Research would take place in the library, on sports fields, in school administration, and elsewhere. The scientific method would be used to produce knowledge for social fulfillment, that is, the ultimate objective of education. Schooling would necessarily be enjoyable, stimulating, and fulfilling, as it created new knowledge and behavior.

For Teixeira, the new school should give priority to eliminating negative elements in society, because it should not perpetuate social defects. In a progressive society, the school plays an important part in achieving improvements. Democracy is in a state of permanent development. In the case of Brazil, the new school should become a great home, where societal conflicts, prejudices, and religious differences would not fit, so that a spirit of equality and communion would prevail.[15]

Of course, Brazilian society was very far from the ideal one Teixeira imagined. It was shaped by profound structural differences, concentrated wealth, and disdain for manual vs. non-manual labor, the overwhelming influence of the Catholic Church, electoral fraud, and other patterns of social and political inequity. Teixeira planned to use his new educational approaches to bring about social change, an extremely ambitious goal. His new society would be democratic, tolerant of different opinions, and encouraging of social mobility.

The changes Teixeira envisioned for his new schools could not be implemented quickly. In 1934 he wrote, "The means we propose to solve educational problems in Rio de Janeiro is through experimentation and gradual solutions, keeping in mind the primacy of local conditions."[16] In reality, he sought structural changes in society more than simply changes in educational practice. Therefore, they should be implemented in stages: first, experimental schools that could be expanded to the extent that teachers could be trained for them; second, introduction by one hour a day of the new school in traditional settings. The transformation would then focus on training teachers in the new approaches. They would be encouraged to experiment with methods adapted to the environment. In consultation with parents they would explore changes in the missions of their schools. Relationships between students and teachers ought to be reviewed and adjusted. Teachers should be given a larger role in the design of curriculum. Had Teixeira known how difficult progressive education had been to implement in the United States, he might have been less sanguine about its chances in Brazil

A Proposal for School Reform

The 1929 crisis stabbed deeply into Brazil's traditional economy, disrupting the balance of payments, forcing currency devaluation, and inducing mild inflation. These effects channeled what domestic capital existed out of the coffee sector into industry, which until then had not been producing at full capacity. Manufacturing growth, in turn, forced workers to switch jobs and employers to find new markets for their goods. The government, for its part, adopted a policy of import substitution, which further favored the growth of manufacturing. Teixeira's reforms should be understood in this light, because employers needed workers with new skills who were able to learn more complex production processes.

Yet the democratic interaction of citizens that industrial employment required simply did not exist in Brazil. Teixeira, Pedro Ernesto, and other progressive leaders in the Vargas administration believed that they should move society toward real democracy. Again, in this way Teixeira's progressive school was an inherent part of a much larger, more ambitious social program. Schools should induce democracy and social mobility: "The greatest social problem we face is achieving real democracy...one which gives each person a place in society that fits his or her natural talents, regardless of any social or economic restrictions."[17]

When Pedro Ernesto took over the Rio government, he invited Teixeira to serve as Director of the Department of Education in the Federal District. This appointment reflected a political alliance based on similar philosophical positions and a shared view of how schools could move the country in the democratic directions they believed appropriate. So their close collaboration went beyond simply providing services to the electorate in exchange for votes—they sought to create a new citizenry as the children they educated left the progressive school and took up their adult lives.

The Rio school system was in terrible shape when Pedro Ernesto and Teixeira took office. Schools did not attempt to educate all of the city's children—they enrolled only a fraction and graduated even less. The data, while inexact, make it clear what was happening in 1932: school age children numbered about 120,000, but only 85,000 actually attended. This meant that at least 35,000 children received no formal schooling. Many students were held back each year. Students' lack of progress through the grades was also evident from enrollment figures: the number of students dropped from 40,000 in first grade, to 19,260 in second, 13,500 in third, 7,600 in fourth, and 4,150 in fifth grade.[18] This meant that nearly half of all students were in the first grade. It also meant that many students failed to pass, creating mixed age groups in each grade. The high proportion of students repeating grades was evident in the statistics compiled in 1936, presented in Table 11.1.

Table 11.1: Percentage of Students Repeating, by Grade Level:[19]

Grade	1st time	2nd time	3rd time	4th time	5th time	6th time
First	47%	40%	11%	2%	0.1%	0.02%
Second	70%	27%	3%	0.3%	0.04%	
Third	74%	23%	2%	1%	0.09%	
Fourth	83%	16%	1%	0.04%		
Fifth	94%	6%	0.1%			

Teachers who had spent years in this deficient school system had become blind to its limitations and did not recognize the need to change it. As we will see, they as much as conservative elements in society would present obstacles to the new administration's efforts to improve education.

Teixeira inherited, therefore, a dysfunctional educational system. He launched a full-scale reform program based on his concept of the progressive school. Teixeira's administration of the Department of Education between 1931 and 1935 sought not only to transform the existing schools but also to broaden them to include kindergarten and post-secondary levels. In order to pay for this expansion, the city created an educational fund, but it was never fully financed. Rather, the majority of the funds came from taxes collected from gambling casinos. Rio de Janeiro continued to attract tourists despite the Depression, and Pedro Ernesto took steps to increase the tourist trade by investing in infrastructure. By 1933 the mayor could boast of much new business and public revenue from tourism, even affirming that it helped the city overcome the crisis of the Depression.[20] The mayor committed most of the new revenue to the Department of Education, so that it enjoyed a privileged position in city budgets despite the hard times.

Teixeira's reforms targeted a number of deficient areas in Rio's schools: teacher training and renewal; extension courses and in-service training; conversion of the Normal School into the Educational Institute and expansion of its role and capacity; developing coherent steps for teachers' rank, status, and salary; experimental schools; libraries; new buildings and rehabilitation of existing ones, according to new school needs; and more space for students. These reforms are detailed in the paragraphs that follow.

Several months after assuming the position of Director of Education in October 1931, Teixeira signaled his reformist intention by restructuring the Department of Education. He set up the following divisions: enrollment and attendance; grade level and promotion; teaching disciplines; buildings and furniture; social work (before and after school programs); health and hygiene; physical education, recreation, and games; music and chorale; secondary and professional teaching; administration and public relations; personnel and archives; accounting; and the Central Educational Library. These reforms indicate the central importance attached to developing the primary grades. Teixeira considered schools essential for maintaining a viable social order, that is, each person occupying a position in society according to his or her abilities and aptitudes. This required schools to go beyond simply reading, writing and arithmetic, to help form character, intelligence, and critical thinking.[21]

Teixeira employed administrative and scientific methods to solve the dismal attrition problem. He established the Grade Promotion and Classification Service, which attempted to establish objective criteria for classifying students by grade level and reorganizing the classes to assure the highest success rates. As noted above, the previous system made little distinction among students by ability or age, so that they experienced high grade repetition. Because classifying students could not be done in isolation, but rather in the context of restructuring the whole Department, Teixeira tried to develop simple criteria along two scales: children's mental age and IQ, and their real age and academic achievement. Classes in each grade level would be split into two achievement levels, A and B for advanced and normal. These would then be subdivided into three subgroups, X, Y, and Z, for slow, normal, and advanced. Students in these different groups would progress at different paces. For example, a student in the Z subgroup could take four years to complete the 5-year primary grades, in the Y subgroup five years (normal), and in the X subgroup, six years. Teixeira had seen such grouping done in the United States.

According to Nunes, writing many years later, the results of the IQ tests were not wholly reliable and could not be used rigorously.[22] Isaías Alves, who was head of the Testing Division and close advisor to Teixeira, had been to the United States in 1930 to report on the results of their testing in Brazil: "...we have discussed testing here and do not have good evidence of its efficacy in our culture. In the United States few even question test results, because of the abundant instruments available, unlike our situation in Brazil."[23] So both Alves and Nunes cited Kilpatrick in preferring not to use scientific testing, while Teixeira wished to use it along with other measures.

Simultaneous with this reclassification of students, Teixeira set out to change and reorganize the early grades. He divided the first five years into a primary phase of three years and an intermediate phase of two years. This would allow differentiation of goals and processes. The primary phase would concentrate on reading, writing, and arithmetic, while the intermediate phase would stress application of these skills to enrich the intellectual development of the students.[24]

Until the early 1930s little attention was given to enrollment and attendance, matters that were left to individual teachers. Many children worked part time, at home or in the streets, e.g., as shoeshine boys or vendors. In rural zones they had to gather firewood or tend agricultural fields. These social factors, added to the hardships of the Depression, caused many families to keep their children out of school for longer periods of time. School authorities tended to accommodate these families by allowing students to come and go as they wished. This irregular attendance, of course, created difficulties for the teachers, who could not easily monitor the pace and content of the curriculum for individual students. Teixeira, believing in the centrality of the student in the learning process, tried to improve this situation, so that teachers and supervisors could track students' progress individually, through their enrollment, attendance, and transfer files. This would help combat the major ills of truancy, grade repetition, and family difficulties. He also set for the first time definite dates for enrollment, to help solve fluctuations in class size.[25]

While attrition and grade repetition had been the leading problems in primary education, high schools suffered from disarticulation with the earlier grades. High schools had been the responsibility of the federal government, but Teixeira saw the need to have them integrated into the municipal school system so they could articulate with the lower grades. The lack of public high schools created disarticulation among the levels and types of schools available in Rio—primary and vocational at the municipal level, secondary at the state level, and university at the federal level. This lack of articulation made it difficult for students to proceed up the grades. Teixeira also hoped to break the tracking of poor students into vocational studies and well-to-do students into academic high schools and beyond. Pedro Ernesto, who enjoyed a close relationship with President Vargas at the time, approved transferring high schools to municipal control and managed to overcome turf and political obstacles to accomplishing this, especially on the part of the Minister of Education, Francisco Campos.[26]

Teixeira's innovative high school curriculum was based on the need to train persons in technical fields, while at the same time helping students to develop a sense of identity and to understand the world around them. The new study plans were considerably more complicated than traditional high schools in Brazil. Vocational tracks for commercial, industrial, and domestic services would be available alongside the regular academic courses, instead of putting them in separate schools. This would integrate studies rather than split them between "thought" and "action." This was a crucial part of Teixeira's overall reform, to break the dual and elitist character of the previous educational system, which had become fragmented by class. As Pedro Ernesto stated:

> Today's technical high schools, that replaced the old vocational schools, represent our attempt to implement the latest principles of secondary education and reinforce the democratic nature of our society. These new schools employ our most powerful tools so far to keep schools from perpetuating the inequalities that exist in society; instead, they are voluntary and purposeful instruments for putting so-called academic and manual training on the same level of dignity and social value.[27]

As suggested, the vocational secondary education incorporated both technical and academic studies, providing for both continuity and cohesion in the curriculum. A course would begin with a common content in the first year and then branch out into various specializations in the second. Between 1931 and 1934, the number of students in these high schools rose from 2,300 to over 5,000.[28]

The implementation of educational reform required new teachers trained especially for its mission, and these teachers did not exist. In truth, not even the traditional elementary teachers were ready to follow the path-breaking directions Teixeira charted for them. Concerned about this, he issued decree 3810 on March 19, 1932, to convert the Normal School into the Education Institute. The Institute offered classes at all levels: kindergarten, primary, and secondary, as well as teacher training. Thus, a student could spend sixteen years in the Institute: three in kindergarten, five in primary, six in secondary, and two in teacher training.

It became necessary to differentiate two training tracks according to the background and training of the teachers, as well as the level of physical and psychological development of their students. The first program worked with teachers in primary grades and the second with teachers in secondary grades. In addition, teachers also needed preparation in specialty fields, like music, drawing, industrial arts, and home economics, which had been introduced previously and which fit nicely in the progressive school.

According to Teixeira, the teacher training program was eminently a professional school, designed to prepare future teachers in the fields they would be responsible for in the classroom. The kindergarten, primary, and secondary classrooms, therefore, would allow for experimentation and practice by trainees. Beyond the technical training, teachers would gain scientific and cultural knowledge that would give them a global and up-to-date vision of education—that is, integrate the several pedagogical fields (psychology, sociology, philosophy, and history of education) with the actual disciplines they would teach (e.g. history, math, science).[29]

Also in the area of teacher education, Teixeira's major innovations were creating the Teachers College at the university level and a special high school. This latter was divided into two parts: a basic five-year program that covered the course of study of the Pedro II College (an elite federal secondary school) plus hygiene, childhood health, and manual arts; and a complementary one-year program covering literature, English or German, psychology, educational statistics, history of philosophy, sociology, design, and physical education. The complementary program was mandatory for persons wishing to go on for a teaching credential. Thus, the high school served as preparatory for the Teachers College, in addition to readying students for any other university-level career. In reality, candidates for the Teachers College had to study at the high school operated in the Education Institute, since it guaranteed that the student would get the highest quality training possible.[30]

The Education Institute operated in a building inaugurated in 1928, designed especially to house the Normal School. Teixeira expanded the plant to accommodate classrooms for particular disciplines, as well as special displays on hygiene and health. He also installed a conference room, an auditorium, a medical and dental clinic, and an up-to-date library that included maps and audiovisual equipment. The Institute inaugurated one of Rio's first radio stations (Educational Radio), that broadcast lectures, radio classes, and exercise programs on teaching and professional development for teachers. In 1934 the station received nearly eleven thousand papers submitted by radio students.[31]

In sum, the Education Institute became a beacon that disseminated modern pedagogy, created in-service and continuing education courses that covered many disciplines. It also offered courses for professional advancement, like administration, counseling, and supervision. In 1934 about a thousand teachers took part in these courses, which became a major criterion for promotion and raises.[32]

The Central Educational Library also played an important role in Teixeira's overall program. Its goals were to improve the professional and general knowledge of teachers, broaden the habits of reading among the citizenry (especially for children, in their own building), promote good school libraries, and intensify learning through images and films. In 1934 the Library began to offer extension courses for teachers and employees of the Education Department. The response was so large they could not accept all applicants. These courses generally dealt with foreign languages, statistics, and the socioeconomic evolution of Brazil. The Library purchased books and journals from the United States, England, France, Italy, Spain, and Germany, making the foreign language courses all the more necessary. The Library also bought and distributed books and other publications for individual schools and cultural institutions (Brazilian and foreign). It sent out 6,600 books in 1932; 24,000 in 1933; and 63,600 in 1934, an increase of over a thousand percent. A significant portion of these books was targeted to elementary school readers.

In order to promote a spirit of knowledge and research, Teixeira designed an Institute for Educational Research (IPE), which came into existence in September 1933. It was charged with investigating and disseminating information about student performance and teaching methods. One key area was curriculum and after-school activities, including lesson plans and the use of radios in the classroom. Another was measurements in general, including assessment, mental hygiene, and anthropometrics as a way to evaluate student types.[33]

Five experimental or practice schools were attached to the IPE, where teachers could try out the progressive pedagogy. They could discover the best practices for Rio students. According to Teixeira: "For two years we have been experimenting with new teaching methods, and thereby familiarizing teachers with how to vary their approaches and gradually improve students' learning. Thanks to the experimental schools, teaching methods are evolving slowly and surely." Mexico School, for example, which opened in 1935, adopted a system of self-government whereby students assumed responsibility for certain jobs and their completion. This illustrated the notion that schools should help form future citizens. Another school, Amaro Cavalcanti, also tried this approach, but it was heavily criticized by teachers who did not understand the pedagogical purpose of sharing authority with students. Teachers and journalists married to traditional systems of education did not easily relinquish their hierarchical vision of society.[34]

The IPE specialists working on extracurricular activities developed six teaching guides, covering language, mathematics, children's games, social sciences, music, and science, which made up a total of eight volumes. In 1934 more than thirty independent publications had been issued by the Department of Education. These were divided into five series: monographs, plans and research, programs (including teaching guides), translations, and dissemination. These and many other publications helped the IPE justify its existence. For example, a publication on languages exhausted its first print run of 3,000 in Rio and elicited requests for copies from several other states.[35] Because of the IPE, gradually the idea of professional development and in-service training came to be accepted as a path to advancement. The long-term significance of these teaching guides became evident when they were republished in the 1960s by the Brazilian Ministry of Education.

New teachers and methods were deployed, yet the buildings were old and inadequate for learning, unhealthy, and too cramped for the innovative educational approaches Teixeira proposed. His ambitious plans clashed with Depression economic realities. New buildings alone would be extremely expensive. Even though the mayor, Pedro Ernesto, was willing to favor education, he still needed powerful justifications for any new capital outlays. In order to muster a convincing case, Teixeira's accountants turned to statistical analysis.[36]

The division charged with schools and equipment studied student enrollment and attendance, school locations, and physical conditions of the buildings. Regarding the latter, the report concluded that of 79 buildings in 1932, only 12 were adequate, needing only small repairs and painting. Thirty-two needed significant improvements and expansion. And the remaining 35 should not even be used as schools. In terms of classrooms, this meant that of 739 rooms, only 309 (42%) were useable, keeping in mind that the minimum size of the classrooms was 40 square meters. As for the other school buildings that were rented from private owners, they had virtually no pedagogical or health qualities to recommend them. Often the owners were politicians or friends of politicians who used their influence to "sell" the rentals to the city. Given this, the buildings and equipment division proposed a minimum new construction plan, which resulted in the construction of twenty-six new schools: eleven with room for 1,000 students; two mini-schools for 240 students; ten platoon style schools for 1,000–2,000 students; one special school for 560 students; one addition for 1,000 students; and a school-park. Altogether, these new schools accommodated 26,500 more students, or 323 classes. The new buildings, moreover, had special rooms, auditoriums, libraries, gymnasiums, and other facilities. In other words, they were appropriate for the educational reforms instituted by Anísio Teixeira.

In order to determine where new schools should be located, school planners carried out a study of student demand. Historically, poor districts—working class neighborhoods, the shantytown *favelas,* and tenement districts—were poorly served by all public agencies. This pattern existed for schools as well, so the greatest need for schools was in poor zones. Under Pedro Ernesto, however, the city government—including the Department of Education—did its best to reach out to poor constituents. This was partly the promise of the revolutionaries of 1930 and partly an electoral strategy, because the Vargas regime sought to win public support by providing new services to the poorest sectors of society. In this sense, Rio was a model for later urban politics throughout the country.

Even with the populist tenor of Pedro Ernesto's administration, the locations of the new school buildings surprised observers: they were mostly sited in poor zones, densely populated and with low per capita income. In order to find spaces for a few, architects even located some schools in public plazas. Without question, this radical new strategy made education more accessible to the poorest sectors of society.

These processes—finding locations for new buildings with minimum conditions and comfort for students, changing the hours in some cases by creating a third period or diminishing the hours of existing periods, expanding the available school facilities—made it possible to increase the carrying load of the system. While the 1931 primary school enrollment had been 84,000, within several years the capacity shot up to 124,000 and enrollments to 107,000. The same increases occurred in kindergarten, high school, night school, adult education, and the University of the Federal District (UDF).

The University of the Federal District was a pet project of the Pedro Ernesto administration. It crowned the Teixeira/Pedro Ernesto vision of creating a continuous system of education that could change the character of Brazilian society. Their aim was not simply to increase the system capacity, it was to overhaul its production standards. The UDF would be the capstone experience for students who moved up through the Rio de Janeiro school system. The UDF would train future intellectuals in an entirely secular and scientific learning environment. Teixeira cited the United States as a model, where a large number of universities, some centuries old, helped build and sustain the nation and provide its cultural underpinnings. Universities supplied curriculum and guidance for high schools, which in turn helped improve primary schools. Brazil, in contrast, had few universities, and these suffered from shortcomings: "Our country awards degrees that are largely honorary, our schools offer narrow curricula of limited relevance, and we favor cultural preparation over practical careers. In our country an education is merely a way to obtain a degree so its holder can get a job." Teixeira intended to break that tradition and create new citizens. "The university should maintain an atmosphere of learning and knowledge, and should train citizens to serve society and produce knowledge. We should seek living knowledge, not dead facts...We should understand the human condition, which is constantly changing."[37]

The UDF was composed of five colleges: philosophy and letters, science, economics and law, arts, and teacher education. These in turn offered a total of 27 degrees, some interdisciplinary. The founders of the UDF recruited some of the best minds in the country, as well as professors from Europe and the United States. The Catholic Church criticized the UDF fervently, as did the conservative politicians, because of the intellectual freedom UDF enjoyed and its teaching staff, whose ideas were said to be contrary to those underpinning Brazilian culture. Little by little, in fact, conservatives and Catholics increasingly condemned the entire Teixeira/Pedro Ernesto overhaul of the educational system. The growing opposition movement will be discussed in more detail below.

The Department of Education gave incentives for teachers who participated in professional development and in-service training. They were used in conjunction with other measures of productivity, such as publications, adoption of new teaching methods, and regular attendance. High performance ratings led to promotions in grade and salary raises. And in more general fashion, Teixeira attempted to raise the overall pay levels for teachers and supervisors and to establish coherent promotion tracks.[38]

Finally, Teixeira set up twenty-one new adult night courses for citizens at large. He offered a long list of subjects: Portuguese, French, English, math, accounting, typing, stenography, science, design, mechanics, electricity, geography, history, technology, sericulture, hat-making, sewing, knitting, flowers, and lace-making. When these classes began in 1934, the enrollment of 1,400 far exceeded expectations. Classes were offered in various parts of the city, especially in poor districts.

It would be impossible to describe the entire gamut of reforms Teixeira introduced during his four years as Director of Education. By way of summary, Teixeira brought a rich store of educational philosophies, information, and observations from the United States, which he attempted to apply in 1930s Rio de Janeiro. Until that time reformers had only tinkered at the edges of the possible for the city's schools. Teixeira sought to change the very essence of learning, create a progressive school environment, and expand public education in terms of number of school-age children and length of coverage, from kindergarten to university. Despite the economic crisis caused by the Depression, he was able to use tax revenues coming from a relatively new source, international tourism. These ambitious undertakings were unfortunately cut short by the premature end of Teixeira's appointment and shortly afterward by that of the mayor himself.

Education as a Political Problem

During the 1920s and into the 1930s, liberalism in the western world was under attack, and Brazil was not immune to this development. In 1930 Brazil underwent a major turnaround in politics. The movement called the Revolution of 1930 was supported by the middle class (loosely represented by the Tenente Movement), the industrial bourgeoisie (favoring more tariff protection for its factories), and the working class (seeking to keep up with inflation and gain benefits like retirement and disability). The Revolution overthrew President Washington Luis and ushered in the regime of Getúlio Vargas.

These rapid and confused events, plus a seeming breakdown in the world order, led to a sharp polarization of Brazilian politics in the mid-1930s. A fascist movement formed on the right, with considerable support from business sectors, while a communist movement arose to challenge it and perhaps seize power in a coup. Vargas and his closest advisors drifted to the right in an attempt to stem disorder and to preserve themselves in power.[39]

In this increasingly contentious situation, Pedro Ernesto attempted to maintain a middle ground between the extremes. Resisting Vargas's growing conservatism, Pedro Ernesto continued to carry out reforms and protect civil liberties in the capital. Soon he was seen as a rival to Vargas, and by 1935 he became Brazil's first populist leader. He appealed to citizens from all walks of life and social strata while defending democratic freedoms. Increasingly he came under fire from conservatives, who pushed Vargas to order his arrest. In mid-1937, in fact, Vargas shut down the government and decreed a fascist-inspired regime called the Estado Novo.

The growing antagonism between the left and right could not fail to target Teixeira's educational program. As early as 1932 he and his followers had signed a manifesto calling for, among other things, educational reform and secular instruction. Teixeira went further, defending a monopoly on elementary education by public schools.[40]

Yet in a country where the majority was Catholic and where the Church operated most schools, Teixeira's position in favor of secular education could not fail to evoke a strong reaction. In precisely those years the Church organized a campaign to strengthen its political hand through the creation of the Catholic Electoral Leagues, endorsement of favored candidates in elections, and restructuring the Catholic Workers' Leagues. Many Catholic educators resigned from the Brazilian Education Association (ABE), in which Teixeira and other leaders had been actively promoting the progressive school agenda of decentralized secular education. Instead, they joined its rival, the Brazilian Catholic Education Confederation, which promoted religious instruction in public schools and advocated more hierarchical and disciplined culture in schools than that favored by the ABE. The clash between the two approaches could not be reconciled and would end up destroying Teixeira's program in Rio.[41]

According to Hermes Lima, who was a personal friend of Teixeira, a journalist, and a law professor at the UDF, for four years Pedro Ernesto stood up to intense pressure from priests and Catholic leaders, even in his own political party, regarding the school reforms and the UDF. But the time approached when he would no longer be able to survive politically and also defend Teixeira from such criticism. The pressures became so powerful, especially after the communist coup attempt in November 1935, that Pedro Ernesto was forced to ask for Teixeira's resignation. He complied, but his letter of resignation affirmed that the role of Director of Education was to carry out reforms in the schools, in a way that would promote democracy, and not to partake in violent movements of the sort that opposed the progressive school.[42]

Pedro Ernesto was obliged to appoint the jurist Francisco Campos as the new Director of Education. Because the mayor only served for five more months, the new secretary could not carry out any major innovations. Rather, the appointment was an attempt by the mayor to save his own embattled career. Campos's speech on taking office was eminently political: he spoke of the subversive movements that had occurred and of the need to suppress radical doctrines. He clearly criticized the ideas that underlay the reform movement of Anísio Teixeira. Moreover, he praised the educational system of Nazi Germany and Fascist Italy, that is, systems that served the purposes of conservative governments. This contrasted sharply with Teixeira's vision of education serving the interests of the individual and democratic society as well. Teixeira assumed the two were compatible, but his opponent did not. The two also split over the propriety of religious instruction in the schools, which Campos supported. The powerful forces of conservatism that swept Anísio Teixeira out of the Department of Education in December 1935 were the same as those that overthrew Pedro Ernesto four months later.

Teixeira, hounded and threatened by his political enemies in Rio, left for his native state of Bahia shortly after resigning. Even there, however, he did not feel safe, so he took refuge in his family's rural plantation in the backlands. For several years he lived as a fugitive in his own land. After World War II and the overthrow of Vargas, Teixeira's career revived and he became a leader in progressive educational circles. Perhaps the highlight of his work was serving as founding president of the University of Brasília, in the nation's new capital, in the early 1960s.

Conclusion

Pedro Ernesto, who called himself a humanist and admirer of Franklin Roosevelt and the New Deal, believed in the possibility of building democracy in Brazil. Anísio Teixeira, who was trained in Jesuit schools, discovered the progressive school movement in the United States. Through the influence of Dewey and Kirkpatrick, his greatest teachers, he developed personal and educational philosophies in which the school is regarded as an institution in constant change, even as an agency of social change itself, and in which science provides students with understanding and motivation, helping find roads for life's travel.

With the full support of Pedro Ernesto, given the budgetary restraints of the time, Teixeira made a reality of his pedagogical vision, expanding the network of schools and the ways the public could learn (radio, cinema, libraries, adult education). Because he had strong backing from Pedro Ernesto, he was also able to build twenty-six new schools to the highest educational standards of the day, thereby augmenting the capacity of the system.

This educational experiment took place during a time of great turbulence in Brazilian history, when conflicts between the left and right destroyed much of the moderate middle ground in politics. Neither Pedro Ernesto nor Anísio Teixeira was a leftist, yet their positions favoring academic freedom in the schools, social reform, democratization, and social mobility led Catholics and conservatives to brand them as leftists. In this context, neither could continue with his political and educational programs. Conservative forces overwhelmed them both.

The progressive pedagogy that Teixeira designed in the 1930s did not die, however, for after World War II he was called back to service in his native state of Bahia, in the national government, and even briefly in UNESCO. Teixeira enjoyed great prestige for his pioneering work in educational reform, and he was joined by a cadre of new thinkers in the 1950s and 1960s. Foremost among these were Paulo Freire, also from the Northeast of the country, and Darcy Ribeiro, with whom Teixeira founded the University of Brasília. Even though this group again fell from favor after the military coup of 1964, it had an enormous influence among educators throughout the western world. Thus the creative forces unleashed in Brazil during the economic and political crisis of the 1930s continue to inform modern debates about the relationship between schools and society.

Notes

1. Ana Luiza Bustamante Smolka and Maria Cristina Menezes, eds., *Anísio Teixeira, 1900/2000: Provocações em educação*, (Bragança Paulista: USF, 2000).
2. Michael L. Conniff, *Urban Politics in Brazil: The Rise of Populism, 1925–1945*, (Pittsburgh: University of Pittsburgh Press, 1981) pp. 54–55, 112–13.
3. Idem, "The Tenentes in Power," *Journal of Latin American Studies*, Vol. 10 (1978) pp. 61–82.
4. Jeronymo Cerqueira, "Relatório apresentado pelo Diretor de Fazenda," *O Partido Autonomista*, (Rio de Janeiro: Imprensa Oficial, 1935) p. 76.
5. Pedro Ernesto, "Relatório apresentado ao Exmo. Sr. Chefe do Governo Provisório Sr. Dr. Getúlio Vargas," in *O Partido Autonomista* (Rio de Janeiro: Imprensa Oficial, 1935) p. 8; Cerqueira, "Relatório apresentado pelo Diretor de Fazenda," p. 80.
6. Clarice Nunes, *Anísio Teixeira: a poesia da ação* (Bragança Paulista: USF, 2000); Jaime Abreu, "Anísio Teixeira e a educação na Bahia," *Anísio Teixeira. Pensamento e ação* (Rio de Janeiro: Civilização Brasileira, 1960) pp. 1–68.
7. Anísio S. Teixeira, "A pedagogia de Dewey," *Dewey* (São Paulo: Abril Cultural, 1980).
8. William Heard Kilpatrick, *Educação para uma civilização em mudança* (Rio de Janeiro: Cia. Melhoramentos Biblioteca de Educação, 1933).
9. Nunes, *Anísio Teixeira*, p. 193.
10. Kilpatrick, *Educação para uma civilização em mudança*, p. 53.
11. Anísio S. Teixeira, *Educação progressiva*, 2nd ed. (Rio de Janeiro: Cia. Editora Nacional, 1934) pp. 27, 34–36.
12. Vera Lúcia Marques Leite, "Da crítica à escola única à defesa da escola comum. Anísio Teixeira, 1924/35," (Masters Thesis, Catholic University of Rio de Janeiro, 1990).
13. Teixeira, "A pedagogia de Dewey," p. 116.
14. Ibid, p. 119.
15. Anísio S. Teixeira, *Educação para a democracia* (Rio de Janeiro: José Olímpio, 1936) p. 280.
16. Idem, "O sistema escolar do distrito Federal," *A Escola Primária*, No. 12 (March 1934) p. 220.
17. Teixeira, *Educação para a democracia*, p. 276.
18. Ibid, p. 146.
19. Ibid, p. 146.
20. Lourival Fontes, "Turismo," *O Partido Autonomista*, (Rio de Janeiro: Imprensa Oficial, 1935) p. 187; Ernesto, "Relatório apresentado ao Exmo," pp. 8–9.
21. Anísio S. Teixeira, *Educação progressiva*, 2nd ed. (Rio de Janeiro: Cia. Editora Nacional, 1934); idem, *Educação para a democracia*.
22. Nunes, *Anísio Teixeira*, pp. 265–266.
23. Isaías Alves, *Os testes e a reorganização escolar*, (Rio de Janeiro: Francisco Alves, 2nd ed., 1934) pp. 10–11.
24. Teixeira, *Educação para a democracia*, p. 191.

25. Juracy Silveira, "Alguns aspectos da reforma Anísio Teixeira no Rio de Janeiro," in *Anísio Teixeira. Pensamento e ação*, (Rio de Janeiro: Civilização Brasileira, 1960) p. 199.

26. Anísio S. Teixeira, "Exposição de motivos," *Boletim de Educação Pública*, (January June 1932) p. 101; idem, *Educação para a democracia*, p. 105.

27. Pedro Ernesto, "Discurso na abertura do VII Congresso Nacional de Educação," *A Escola Primária*, No. 3 (June 1935) p. 51.

28. Nunes, *Anísio Teixeira*, p. 303.

29. Anísio S. Teixeira, "Administração e desenvolvimento–Escola Pública," *Boletim de Educação Pública*, (July/December 1934) p. 170.

30. Ibid, p. 172.

31. Edgard Roquette Pinto, "Rádio Educação Popular," *Boletim da Casa do Estudante do Brasil*, (1935).

32. Anísio S. Teixeira, "A reconstrução Educacional do Rio de Janeiro," *A Escola Primária*, No. 7, (October 1934) p. 135; Paschoal Leme, (n.d.) *Memórias*, (Unpublished manuscript).

33. Teixeira, *Educação para a democracia*, pp. 165–166.

34. Teixeira *Educação progressiva*, p. 136; Juraci Silveira, Interview with Alberto Gawryszewski, Rio de Janeiro, March 28, 1985; Nunes, *Anísio Teixeira*, pp. 296–299.

35. Alberto Gawryszewski, "Administração Pedro Ernesto: Rio de Janeiro (DF) 1931–1936," (M.A. Thesis, Universidade Federal Fluminense, 1988) p. 118.

36. Ernesto, "Relatório apresentado ao Exmo," p. 12.

37. Teixeira, *Educação para a democracia*, pp. 124, 127.

38. Gawryszewski, "Administração Pedro Ernesto," p. 116.

39. Conniff, *Urban Politics in Brazil*.

40. Teixeira, "O sistema escolar do distrito Federal," p. 223.

41. Maria Cecília Sanchez Teixeira, *Discurso pedagógico e ideologia: o imaginário de Paulo Freire e de Anísio Teixeira*, (Rio de Janeiro: Quartet, 2000).

42. Hermes Lima, *Anísio Teixeira, Estadista da Educação*, (Rio de Janeiro: Civilização Brasileira, 1978) p. 137; Gawryszewski, "Administração Pedro Ernesto," p. 41.

Chapter Twelve

"A Magnificent Adventure": Negotiating and Structuring Curricular Change in Virginia

David Hicks and Stephanie Van Hover

Our teachers have never been challenged in this way before, and we have reason to believe that a large proportion of them will respond. I look upon the Curriculum Revision Program as a magnificent adventure, which takes teachers far beyond the uninspiring cycle of memorizing textbooks on the part of pupils and lesson hearing and testing on the part of the teacher.[1]

In October 1931, the newly appointed State Superintendent for Instruction, Dr. Sidney B. Hall, initiated a comprehensive statewide curriculum revision program designed to improve instruction in the Commonwealth of Virginia. The Superintendent's official announcement enthusiastically advocated the importance of frontier thinking, careful planning, critical study and experimentation, enhanced supervision, and statewide teacher participation in order to create and implement a curriculum designed to meet the needs of modern times:

> The development of plans for a complete statewide curriculum revision program in the elementary and high schools of the State marks a new era in the history of public education in Virginia...The fact that every teacher in the State will face the challenge of finding more positive justification for much that is now being done in the classroom is perhaps the crux of the program. *This program as tentatively set up provides opportunity for 100% teacher participation.*[2]

The Virginia Curriculum Revision Program (Virginia Program) garnered national attention from curriculum specialists for both its design and implementation.[3] Conceptualized and designed by Hall and curriculum advisors Hollis Caswell and Doak Campbell from Peabody College and Paul Hanna from Teachers College,[4] the Virginia Program moved away from locally organized, discipline-oriented curriculum toward a State-wide Core Curriculum that focused on a sequence of specific student based centers of interest and merged them with major functions of social life with the social studies used as the frame of reference.

This chapter seeks to illuminate the dominant values and networks of influence that led the predominantly rural state of Virginia
to attempt to redefine the nature of schooling and, in doing so, to represent itself as a leader in the "magnificent adventure" that was curriculum development during the Great Depression. This involves examining the extent to which the Depression served as a catalyst
through which the educational philosophies and agendas of educational leaders and curriculum specialists were implemented and
brought to fruition within the curriculum laboratory that Virginia became between 1931 and 1934. The reported successful implementation
of the Virginia Program had more to do with the processes by which a
network of influential educational leaders and curriculum designers
conceptualized and managed the structure of curriculum reform
while skillfully employing the rhetoric of teacher involvement and
cooperation, than the ongoing and thorough participation of Virginia
teachers during a period of economic and social crisis.

The Impact of Depression on Education

The collapse of the Stock market in 1929 brought immediate financial
ruin to thousands and highlighted the weaknesses of the nation's
economic system, as outlined in this summary:

> [F]rom 1929 to 1933 the gross national product dropped from $103.1 billion
> to $55.6; personal income fell from $85.9 billion to $47.0; and estimated un-
> employment (no one really knows how many were out of work) soared from
> 3.2 percent of the civilian labor force to 24.9. From 1929 to 1932 the Dow
> Jones average of sixty-five stocks nose dived from $125.43 to $26.82, while
> the profits of corporations after taxes fell from $8.6 billion to minus $2.7 bil-
> lion. Income produced in agriculture declined by over one-half, manufactur-
> ing by almost two thirds, and construction by almost four-fifths.[5]

Though Virginia was predominantly a rural state and therefore did
not see the concentrated effects of industrial dislocation, the drought
of 1930 and ongoing depression heightened concerns regarding the
increasing numbers of the State's rural poor, or what sociologist W. E
Garnett called the "marginal population." His research indicated that:

> One of the most important, as well as most complex, problems now con-
> fronting rural Virginia is the fact that around a half million white people
> may be considered marginal from the standpoint of ability, income, and liv-

ing standards. Here is literally "the forgotten man"...the term *marginal* population refers to those who are so near the margin economically and culturally that they are on a bare subsistence plane of living...The whole cultural level of the State is lowered by the presence of the large marginal population, white and black.[6]

While the ranks of the unemployed continued to grow across the nation, the Depression was, according to one historical account, "slow to affect the political economy of the public school in many parts of the nation, particularly in urban systems and prosperous states, where most of the professional elite worked."[7] Within two years, however, the impact was felt in Virginia's schools. In 1931, Hugh Sulfridge, the president of the Virginia Educational Association, noted that "because of the financial depression which has been deepened by the effects of the drought, school boards in many sections of the State are facing serious financial problems."[8] Sulfridge went on to note that while the situation was serious, there were signs that many communities were trying to maintain educational services:

> In the midst of this crisis, some recent efforts to save the schools are encouraging. Up in Stuart's Draft, a few weeks ago it was reported that a reduction of taxes would be urged, the Community League composed of farmers and dairy men who have suffered most from the drought,...passed by a rising vote a resolution "that if a tax reduction could mean a lowering of the standard of our schools in any way we are strongly opposed to such reduction"...over in Mecklenburg County, it appears the teachers have decided to make a financial sacrifice for the same purpose...The situation is serious enough but every effort should be made to prevent a backward step...Any failure now to maintain these standards may mean a loss of all that has been gained in the way of more efficient schools...it is a question of what effect the lowering of the present high standards will have upon the lives of thousands of school children.[9]

As the Depression continued, school districts began to turn to the State Department of Education for support. In October 1931, the Wythe County School Board adopted a resolution, which stated, in "view of the present depression, as affecting the farmer, his land values, and his personal property," the state should cover the cost of instruction so that all children could have an equal share of the benefits of attending public schools.[10] Similarly in February 1933, the Montgomery county school district board instructed Supt. Shelbourne to report to Hall that the school lacked the means to raise sufficient funds to run the county schools for more than seven months.[11]

Hall acknowledged the impact of the economic crisis on Virginia's schools. In his 1931–1932 annual report, Hall noted that maintaining an unimpaired service to the children of the state was becoming difficult, especially since state funds were cut by 15% and local funds were reduced through delinquent taxes and curtailed budgets. Hall contended that the Depression threatened the progress made toward the education required for democratic citizenry:

> Because of the economic breakdown, our schools today are being crushed, as it were, between two very strong opposing forces—increased responsibilities on the one hand and decreased resources on the other. Unemployment and the depression conditions which exist generally are causing more and more children to enter school. However, on the other hand a serious situation which we have to face is the insistent demand on the part of some individuals to reduce and economize...It would never do for the people of Virginia to insist upon the development of a school program such as we have today and then in a pinch of time to attack the very institution which they have forced, from time to time, to be developed for the boys and girls of the State...What progress has been made, has been made against bitter opposition of class interests over a long period of time. Every step of progress has been contested by ignorance and selfishness. Educational advance has been very slow—almost unbelievably slow and difficult. Today all that has been won stands in peril. Public education is our first and our last line of national defense. If we have to economize to the extent of breaking down the basic foundations of Virginia's democracy, then we have no-one to blame but those who are responsible for it.[12]

In a letter to district superintendents, Hall made a similar argument:

> It should be recognized that education is the basis of all social and economic progress of our country...The present situation affords an opportunity to make a close study of educational organization, administration and curriculum of offerings for the purposes of securing the maximum possible in compactness and efficiency.[13]

In his previous position as State Supervisor for Secondary Education in Virginia, Hall was well acquainted with the administrative reforms undertaken at the state level during the 1920's. The danger of having to roll back the educational gains previously made within the Virginia school system during the 1920's served as a rallying call for carefully planned and fiscally efficient curriculum reform for both Sulfridge and Hall.

Prior to the onset of the Depression, Hall's predecessor, Superintendent Hart, suggested that the administrative foundations had been laid and it was now necessary to begin to implement instructional reforms designed to meet the needs of the children of the state.[14] Hart's call to improve instruction mirrored the recommendation within Michael O'Shea's 1928 *Survey of Public Education in Virginia.* O'Shea argued that "to keep abreast of other states that are going forward in material prosperity so that it may provide for its citizens the advantages and comforts that are enjoyed by the citizens of other States" the State Department of Education would need to take the lead in reforming the patterned genre of instructional practices that the survey staff had observed in Virginia schools:

> It is still generally true that the educational work of the State is not designed to train boys and girls for an understanding of and efficiency in the real situations of daily life. Virginia education has emphasized *verbalism* and *symbolism* rather than *realism.* In the choice of subjects of instruction and in methods of teaching, the guiding principle has been and still is, to some extent, to store the mind with knowledge without reference to the application of this knowledge to the betterment of the material and social conditions in the State.

Successful modification of the entire educational system, the survey concluded, would only occur with the development of an awareness and "determination to deal with education as a State function."[15]

Three years later, as the new State Superintendent, Hall laid out an agenda for necessary statewide curricula reform as previously advocated by his colleagues Hart and O'Shea:

> In assuming the responsible duties of the office of State Superintendent of Public Instruction in Virginia...I wish to pledge to you, all my energies and ability to the problem of securing for our school children a progressive and constructive program for the further development of public education in the State. It is pretty generally considered by the best educational thought in America that public education is primarily a State function and it follows that the State will be more interested in equalizing educational opportunity, controlling the standards of teacher certificates, and directing and supervising the instruction going on in every classroom.

Among the "tangible objectives for the future," Hall specifically mentioned maintaining "the most economical organization for the operation of the schools of the State without any loss of efficiency," revision of the elementary and high school courses of study "in keeping with modern trends in curriculum construction," an eight, or preferably nine, month school year, and an "acceptable and adequate library" in every school.[16]

Within one month of Hall announcing the plan to carry out state-wide curriculum revision, Sulfridge notified VEA members that the theme of the 1931 convention would be curriculum revision:

> Under the leadership of our new superintendent, Dr. Sidney B. Hall, a complete revision of both high school and elementary school curriculum has been initiated. In view of this fact, we have chosen to make "curriculum revision" the theme of this convention...Our whole educational effort is face to face with a serious situation. Now, as never before, education in every field should be completely awakened to the necessity of organization and cooperation, otherwise much ground already gained in the way of educational progress may be lost.[17]

Sulfridge went on to affirm his support for curriculum revision and the need for teacher participation, cooperation, and action within the revision process during his opening remarks at the Convention:

> Thirteen thousand teachers, properly organized and active in behalf of the children and the schools, can insure a continuation of our educational progress in Virginia in spite of the depression. Though hard enough, the financial situation in Virginia is not as hopeless as it might be...Schools are an economic necessity.[18]

As the VEA conference wrapped up, the die had been cast. In the face of economic crisis, Virginia was to undertake steps in redefining the curriculum. Hall's goals for curriculum revision, however, were not developed in isolation. Hall's previous work as a State Supervisor under Superintendent Hart, his work with O'Shea's survey of Virginia public education, and the presence of such progressive educators and curriculum specialists as Hollis Caswell of Peabody College and Herbert Bruner of Teachers College, Columbia University as keynote speakers on curriculum revision at the VEA conference only begin to illuminate the networks of influence and support that would lead to conceptualizing Virginia as a state-wide curricular laboratory.

Ideological Influences and Networks of Support

Hall's arguments regarding the need for shoring up educational institutions and embarking upon cooperative curricular reform designed to prepare children for life in the modern world reveal an intellectual and ideological kinship with a growing group of progressive educators who, in the 1930s, were networked through time and space via their affiliations to such organizations as the Progressive Educational Association (PEA), the National Education Association (NEA), and the Society for Curriculum Specialists. The presence of Bruner and Caswell at the VEA convention reflects the influence of Teachers College as the intellectual crossroads through which many influential progressive educators would pass. Both Bruner and Caswell, alongside the likes of Harold Rugg, William Heard Kilpatrick, Isaac Kandell, William Bagley, George Counts, John Dewey, Paul Hanna, L. Thomas Hopkins, John Childs, and Jesse Newlon, formed part of the "one big unhappy family" at Teachers College who engaged in extensive intellectual arguments over the purpose of education.[19]

As the Depression continued, the emergence of a growing number of progressive educators who argued that schools should serve as levers of social and cultural reconstruction added a new level of complexity to the concept of progressive education. According to Hanna, ongoing debate and discussion, alongside Counts' challenge to the PEA to rethink the purpose of education, split "those who fraternize in this movement of progressive education" into two distinct camps. Hanna labeled the first camp "the progressive school of *romanticism*," who would recognize:

> [t]he major maladjustments in our age, but they would not organize the curriculum to deal directly with negative aspects of our environment. Children, they say, must be protected from the destructive influences of poverty, squalor, corruption, meanness and fear...So this group would organize the curriculum primarily around those experiences which serve to insulate and isolate children from all of that environment which is unpleasant.[20]

Members of the second camp, according to Hanna:

> believe that our children cannot escape from the world of reality into a world of romance fantasy...How can the children or the adults of a family on relief...be fit from the standpoint of bodily health and vigor, mental security, or emotional stability to partake in the culturally creative enterprises which we stress so much in the progressive school of romanticism...This second group of educators believe that the major task of progressive education is to assist in these years of transition in reshaping and modifying those institutions which prevent the full utilization of the benefits which the application of intelligence has given us...the curriculum must be re-made to de-

velop a clear understanding of the present dilemma...the major emphasis, it
seems to me, must be an analysis of life today and the designing of a new
social order which guarantees the basic structure in which the good life will
be possible for all. If this movement in progressive education to attain a
good life could be characterized by a phrase, we should probably call it the
movement for "cultural reconstruction."[21]

Both Bruner and Caswell brought to the VEA conference a developing
ideological agenda that broadly aligned them with social and cultural
reconstructionists as they discussed the nature and purpose of schooling and curriculum. As Caswell later acknowledged:

Social ills, economic depression and political impotence have directed attention to the nature of the obligation of the school to society... It is my belief
that the American school has three large responsibilities. They may be stated
as follows: (1) The school should discover and define the ideals of American
democratic society; (2) it should provide for the continuous redefinition and
reinterpretation for social ideals in the light of economic, political and social
change; and (3) it should make possible their greatest contributions to the
realization of social ideals.[22]

Caswell, a graduate of Teachers College, Columbia, had been a colleague of Hall's at Peabody College. Both men were part of this growing network of progressive educators who recognized the opportunities for educational reform in the face of economic Depression. It is
within this context that Hall recruited Caswell and Campbell from
Peabody College to serve as the Curriculum Advisor and Special
Consultant in Secondary Education, respectively. Hanna, Caswell's
former classmate and a faculty member at Teachers College, was chosen as the Social Studies Curriculum Advisor for the Virginia Program of Instruction. Hall's out-of-state advisors were all young men,
just beginning their careers, who recognized the importance of a
"more fundamental consideration of the major problems in the political, economic, social, moral and aesthetic fields and their implications
for curriculum building."[23] They were also practical and functional
curriculum makers, who were ready, willing, and able to build on
their own previous curriculum work as well as the work of their colleagues and mentors at Teachers College in their efforts in Virginia.

Hall and his advisors envisioned a program for curriculum revision that would progress through three years of phases or steps:

The first year will be utilized as a period for education and orientation. During this period, the purposes, values, and procedures of the curriculum program will be studied and discussed by all classroom teachers, superintendents, and supervisors throughout the state. The second year will be devoted to curriculum production. The third year will be used as a period of trial when the materials, the subject matter, and the activities embodied in the new courses of study will be tested in a sampling of school centers for the purposes of making intelligent and necessary revision before the courses are distributed for general use.[24]

This plan for curriculum revision required the cooperation and participation of every public school teacher. As Caswell noted:

[I]t seems that if we wish to modify the curriculum of Virginia Schools we must get the teachers in these schools to guide boys and girls in new and enriched experiences…it is desirable for all the teachers in the State of Virginia to engage in curriculum revision. Only in that way will the curriculum of the schools in the State be truly revised.[25]

Caswell stressed that the new revision program was not intended to support the development of a unified course of study but to help support teachers to develop courses of study designed to meet the needs of children within their own communities:

[I]t is not the objective of the State curriculum program to bring all local units to a dead level of conformity and force them to start at the same point but rather it is the purpose to encourage them to continue work that has already been started…the State Department of Education is now going to endeavor through the State curriculum program to make such work possible throughout the State at a minimum cost in both time and money.[26]

To this end, Hall immediately reorganized the State Department of Education, and instructed the newly installed Director for the Division of Instruction, Dr. D. W. Peters, to "carry through a state-wide curriculum revision program, believing such a program to be the most effective type of supervisory service through which teachers may receive in service training, improved teaching materials and professional stimulation."[27] Working with Peters and his curriculum advisors, Hall recruited a network of educators from across the state to form the key committees charged with conceptualizing, organizing, and overseeing the curriculum revision. The Aims Committee was chaired by Fred M. Alexander, principal of Newport News High School; the Principals' Committee was chaired by E. E. Windes from

the University of Virginia; the Definitions Committee was chaired by
W. J. Gifford from Harrisonburg State Teachers College; and the Production Committee was chaired by Hugh L. Sulfridge, the VEA
President.[28] Each of these four committees "enjoyed the guidance or
counseling of Dr. Hollis Caswell, the General Curriculum Advisor
from George Peabody College, and of two other distinguished educators, Dr. Paul Hanna of Columbia University, and Dr. Doak S. Campbell of George Peabody College."[29]

In addition, Hall met with the Presidents and Deans of Education
of the State Colleges to organize support mechanisms to foster the
Curriculum Revision process. The result was an agreement to develop
curriculum revision centers at Farmville State Teachers College, the
College of William and Mary, Harrisonburg State Teachers College,
the University of Virginia, Fredericksburg State Teachers College,
Radford State Teachers College, Virginia Polytechnic Institute, and
Virginia State College for Negroes. Each center was designed to
stimulate teacher participation by organizing evening and Saturday
classes and summer school courses directly focused on Curriculum
Revision. Curriculum consultants across the range of disciplines at
both the elementary and secondary level were also picked from these
colleges. The high degree of overlap between members of the committees, curriculum center chairs and curriculum consultants, created a
select and tightly woven network of like-minded educators within
and across Virginia, who, under the guidance of Hall and his associates, would chart the course for reform.[30]

Managing the Structure of Reform

Building upon the administrative changes within the Division of Instruction, the impetus of the 1931 VEA convention, the publicity for
curriculum revision within the *Virginia Journal of Education*, and several meetings across the state detailing the initial phases for the reform, a series of three State Department bulletins were produced to
specifically outline and manage the structure of the initial three year
period of revision. In January 1932, the *Study Course for Virginia State
Curriculum Program* was sent to all schools. In March, the State Department issued the *Organization for Virginia State Curriculum Program*
and in the following July, the *Procedures for Virginia State Curriculum*

Program were issued. The bulletins set the trajectory for curriculum revision as envisioned by their authors: Caswell, Hall, and Peters.

In the foreword of the *Study Course,* Hall detailed the importance of reforming Virginia's curriculum to keep pace with the "discoveries in the field of education during the last twenty years…Improved instruction is of first concern to every true teacher."[31] Mirroring Newlon's contention that for teachers to successfully contribute to the development of curriculum revision, "every teacher in America must become a student of the fundamental problems of American life and in education,"[32] the bulletin stressed the importance of beginning the process of curriculum revision with a foundational period of "education and orientation" for the teachers in the state:

> Since prolonged disagreement on such issues would jeopardize the development of a program it is necessary to depend largely on group discussion and decision to develop a working basis for action. Intelligent group action depends to a large extent on a clear understanding by all concerned of the several issues involved and the terminology employed. This study course has been prepared to aid the teachers of Virginia in achieving these two ends preparatory to engaging in the production phase of the State Curriculum program.[33]

Seven topics were listed to facilitate "intelligent group action":

> 1) What is the Curriculum? 2) Developments Which Have Resulted in a Need for Curriculum Revision; 3) What is the Place of Subject Matter in Education? 4) Determining Educational Objectives; 5) Organizing Instruction; 6) Selecting Subject Matter; and 7) Measuring the Outcomes of Education.

Following a brief introductory discussion to each topic, leading questions were provided along with a list of references. The minimal reference list for the seven topics totaled eleven texts. The chosen texts clearly reveal that the objective of the study course was to create a controlled and uniform understanding of the nature and purpose of curriculum revision that was based upon the ideas of such Teachers College faculty as Dewey, Kilpatrick, Hopkins, Bode, and Rugg. To facilitate the direction of the course of study, Hall appointed county and city advisors to help form study groups and serve as supports at teachers' meeting and local planning conferences. It was suggested that study groups within schools should meet on a weekly or bi-weekly basis and that each group should select presiding officers.

With the study program underway, Hall and his advisors sought to develop a strong cadence with which to move forward with the process of curriculum revision. By March 1932, the *Organization for Virginia State Curriculum Program* was distributed to schools to lay the foundation for the production phase of the curriculum revision program that would run through 1934. The bulletin reiterated that "it is the hope of the State Department of Education that all divisions will find it possible to have their own curriculum programs so well under way that the work of the State Department will be that of assisting them through the conduct of special researchers, of providing expert guidance and counsel, and of making available to all divisions illustrations of unusually good curriculum work done by other divisions."[34]

The State Department requested school superintendents to provide the names of the division and group chairmen and report the number of teachers within the study groups. This request served two purposes: on the one hand, it provided the State Department with data to determine the level, if not the quality, of teacher participation and subsequently advertise progress in Virginia with regard to curriculum revision. On the other hand, such a request, during a period where many superintendents were turning to the State Department for support to maintain some level of service, carried with it an implicit expectation that all school districts would participate in the process of curriculum revision. The data detailing the level of teacher participation was reported within the *Procedures for Virginia State Curriculum Program*. Published in November 1932, the bulletin reported that more than 10,000 teachers in 86 of the 112 school divisions took part in the study course. Within 61 divisions, the bulletin reported that teacher participation in discussion groups ranged from 60% to 100%. In a further 25 divisions, study groups "were less completely organized and a smaller percent of teachers participated. However, in these divisions hundreds of teachers participated seriously in the program through study and regular meetings with discussion groups."[35] These figures, Hall argued, represented "the wide opportunity for participation in the first step of this program has been seized by the teachers of Virginia in a most gratifying way. The eager interest evidenced throughout the state speaks for the results achieved."[36]

Beyond reporting the level of teacher involvement, the *Procedures for Virginia State Curriculum Program* outlined the theoretical principles, aims and direction of the production phase of the Virginia Curriculum Program.[37] The 160-page document identified "six guiding principles for the program" and a list of 62 "aims of education." It is through the principles and aims that it is possible to see the efforts made by Caswell and the committee leaders to be responsive to the context of the period. The six principles were:

> 1) The school is an agency of society for its perpetuation and recreation; 2) Growth processes in individuals and in society are resultants of continuing interaction between individuals and society; 3) Individuals differ in interests and abilities, attitudes, appreciations and understandings, habits and skills and in capacity to learn; 4) Growth is continuous; 5) All learning comes from experience; 6) An individual tends to avoid experiences which annoy, and to seek experiences which satisfy.[38]

The aims stressed the importance of stability, community, harmony, and the ability of man to use scientific advancements to work towards solving social problems. The school was described as a major creative institution whose major responsibility was to: "1. Discover and define the ideals of a democratic society. 2. Provide for the continuous re-definition and re-interpretation of the social ideals in light of economic, political and social changes."[39] Reflecting the impact of the Depression, the aims noted the importance of the role capitalism played in enhancing the material wealth of the nation, but also stressed the need to examine the shortcomings of capitalism, including the uneven distribution of wealth, waste, and economic slumps.

Teachers on the local division committees were asked to study the aims and to identify what "things children can do that will result in learning of the type indicated by your aims."[40] They were then to begin developing specific unit plans and outlines that fulfilled the committee's aims of education.[41] Caswell argued that these aims, once employed by teachers will "take on a meaning sufficiently clear to provide a real guide for instruction."[42] Faculty at State Teachers Colleges curriculum centers were expected to support teachers. As J. P. Wynne of Farmville State Teachers College noted:

> It seems that we are now entering upon a new stage in curriculum work...Since the College is part and parcel of the state system of education, the efforts of the faculty will now be guided by the demands of the more inclusive program.[43]

Throughout this period the leaders in the curriculum revision program continued to encourage participation from teachers. Both

Caswell and Campbell, among others, attended a conference in January of 1933 at Radford where they met with "about 50 teachers and supervisors for South West Virginia."[44] State advisors took advantage of opportunities to meet with teachers to support the production phase. For example, in November 1932, Hanna attended the social science section at the VEA, while Dr. Helen Foss Weeks met with the science section at the same meeting. At the meeting, Hanna stressed that the new program would seek the "utilization of the hundreds of opportunities in daily school experiences to teach lessons in social behavior." He emphasized that the new curriculum should seek to teach a vision of America "as it might be." In order to carry out this form of "effective teaching," he added, the key was for teachers to be "re-educated" so that they could see the social conditions and needs in society.[45] Weeks, a faculty member from the College of William and Mary and curriculum consultant for the Production Committees in Science for Secondary Schools, "emphasized the ideas that the science curriculum in the high school should be an integrated plan and not a 'little college' course."[46] Once the teachers had a clear understanding of the rationale for curriculum change, it was hoped that teachers would be ready, willing and able to develop units of study during the production phase of the program.

Rhetoric versus Reality in Curriculum Revision

Local school board minutes and a steady flow of articles detailing the development of units within the *Virginia Journal of Education* highlight the opportunities that were created to encourage teachers to participate in the production phase of the Virginia Program. The Montgomery County Board of Education in October 1932 approved the appropriation of $100.00 for the extension curriculum course offered to high school teachers by the University of Virginia.[47] Henrico County reported that all its 117 elementary teachers had been looking forward to the day when the revised course of study would be passed down. It was reported that they had invested a great deal of time in participating in the process of change, "the teachers worked for real 'conviction,'...having been carefully directed in their participation in the three year program leading up to the initiation of the Revised Courses of Study."[48] Saylor suggests that "teachers played a prominent part in most state committees, and since much of the actual preparation of materials was done by local committees on which teachers undoubt-edly predominated, the participation by teachers in production work was evidently extensive."[49] As teachers worked on creating units based on the observed interests of children and activities that grew out of children's interests, Caswell drafted a memorandum suggest-ing that "an adequate curriculum design should give attention to con-tent as well as social functions and children's interests" and hoped that the Reviewing committee "would give the teacher a content framework against which to check the child's progressive organiza-tion of his concepts in the direction of mastery of the fields of organ-ized knowledge."[50]

Caswell invited Hanna to assist in the process of designing the ac-tual core curriculum to be based upon "the vague criteria of subject matter, child interest and social meaning (which could then be ap-plied) to the daily task of instruction."[51] According to Seguel, Caswell assigned Hanna to develop guidelines for "centers of interest" while Caswell worked on the "social functions and the relevance of subject matter."[52] Hanna's own recollections, however, indicate that he felt he assumed the greater level of responsibility for the work leading to the scope and sequence chart upon which the core curriculum would be based.[53] Hanna hoped that the units based upon student interest de-veloped by teacher, "would give us what (we had) assumed: namely, that there were inborn interests of children which would show us what kind of a social studies curriculum we should have."[54] Once the units were submitted, Hanna and Caswell intended to place a range of units under several unifying topics within specific grade levels that represented the age-specific natural interests of school children.[55] This was a familiar process for Hanna, who had previously co-edited a col-lection of child centered teaching units centered on aviation entitled the *Wonder of Flight*, based on work at Teachers College's Lincoln School. Hanna observed that "if the pupil interest theory of curricu-lum development were correct, then this procedure should give us some evidence that such natural instincts did in fact exist in young-sters and from such evidence we could provide instructional guides for teachers and learning materials for pupils."[56]

Hanna was disappointed, however, with the nature and quality of the final teacher-made products, as he could discern no pattern for why a particular unit would be taught at a certain grade level.[57] Hanna noted, "I had sold myself and my two colleagues on the concept that this experimentation would give us the structure as to how we could build the social studies curriculum. I went home to Columbia pretty much defeated and spent the summer trying to figure out what in the hell I would do."[58] Caswell also acknowledged a sense of frustration with the submitted products:

> As a result of entrusting the writing of courses of study to any and all teachers we have produced numerous relatively worthless pieces of work-courses of study characterized by faulty organization, poor writing, and glaring inconsistencies in philosophy. Teachers must be helped to realize that basic and extended study is necessary and that the writing of a course of study is not to be hurriedly undertaken.[59]

Similarly Peters noted "that most teachers are impatient with theory and that it is difficult to lead them to appreciate the necessity of building a sound background or groundwork through study. Nearly all want to rush at once into the task of production."[60]

Because the submitted units failed to provide a pattern of interest from which he could design a socially oriented curriculum, Hanna sought out another source for what would become the scope and sequence of the Virginia Curriculum. Using two Presidential commission reports on *Recent Economic Trends* and *Recent Social Trends*, Hanna took the report's 23 chapter headings as the basis for the vertical axis that represented the scope of content for the curriculum and termed them "Basic Human Activities." The horizontal axis was based upon grade level, which in turn was tied to centers of students' interest.[61]

Hanna's colleagues at the Virginia Department of Education argued that his chart was much too complicated, and he would have to simplify the scope of the integrated content.[62] Utilizing a design previously developed by the Herbartian Charles McMurry, Hanna worked with Caswell to reconceptualize his sequence; this resulted in a chart revolving around basic human activities. McMurry's "cultural epochs" approach initiated a pattern of teaching that began with the study of the family and community, followed by the state and region, then the nation, and finally the western world.[63] Hanna and Caswell's developing sequence (beginning at grade one) mirrored the same pattern as McMurry's, but their reasoning was not founded upon stages of child development. Rather, Hanna and Caswell based their design on their understanding of children's experiences, whereby "human relations range all the way from the personal relation of 'me' and my family, my school, my community, to the general relation of the exchange of culture between races and nations."[64] The grid design provided the scope and sequence of the curriculum. Vertical items under the heading "Major Functions of Social Life" provided the scope, or the actual content matter. The horizontal items under the headings of "Centers of Interest" formed the sequence.[65]

The curriculum developers envisioned that these experiences would lay a foundation for students as they moved through each grade and each subsequent center of interest within their elementary school careers. Students would develop "an understanding of the ways in which man has adjusted himself to nature, the degree of his control over natural forces, and the social institutions which he has established, all approached primarily through the pupil's interest in his home, his community and his state." Developing such under-standings would prepare secondary students for broader, contempo-rary and socially responsive level of study through engaging in activi-ties that "will enable them to become conscious of and understand the underlying causes of the tensions, conflicts, and contradictions in modern life resulting from mechanization. They should develop also an appreciation of the necessity for and methods of improving human relations and individual and social well being."[66]

The design and nature of the scope and sequence reflected the ideological agenda of Hall and his curriculum consultants. The result, Hanna contended, was a core curriculum designed to promote de-mocratic values that lent itself to an analysis of life today and "the de-signing of a new social order which guarantees the basic structure in which the good life will be possible for all."[67] While undoubtedly op-portunities were created to facilitate teacher participation in the proc-ess of curriculum revision, it is clear that in spite of promised oppor-tunities for and ongoing rhetoric of teacher participation, the actual trajectory and form of core curriculum were ultimately negotiated and articulated through the work of Hall, Caswell, and Hanna at the Department of Education.

Encouraging Compliance and Minimizing Dissenting Voices

The careful management of the revision process continued during the trial run of the curriculum. Fifty-two school divisions, with approxi-mately 300 elementary teachers and 250 high school teachers, made up the trial run. While this was one-half of the school divisions within the state, the actual numbers of participating teachers was by comparison very small. Participation in the trial was "limited to divisions which had elementary supervision and within this group to those in which supervisors and teachers had been active in the production phase."[68] As a result successful reporting was likely to be guaranteed. Following the successful trial run, the new program was issued to schools. The printed form came in two separate volumes: *The Tentative Course of Study for Virginia Elementary Schools, Grades I-VII* (560 pages) and *The Tentative Course of Study for the Core Curriculum of Virginia Secondary Schools, VIII* (300 pages). Conferences at both the College of William and Mary in June 1934 and the University of Virginia in August 1934 were organized to introduce the new program to superintendents, principals, supervisors and teachers. These conferences were followed by another series of conferences to support the curriculum program held around the state in November 1934.

In harmony with the overall tenor and rhetoric of participation and cooperation, the introduction to the new course of study noted that the work "represents the results of a three year program of work on the part of Virginia Teachers."[69] Yet Hanna offered this philosophy of planned social change:

> If you really want to affect institutions and individuals, you have to work with the framework. You have to support the establishment and work to change that attitudes and understandings...That is, it is the evolutionary concept, not the revolutionary concept.[70]

The introduction to the new course of study stated "this program should not be imposed on the teachers...in brief, this program as it affects various procedures should be evolutionary rather than revolutionary in nature."[71] Reaffirming the voluntary basis for planned change, Hall informed Division Superintendents that:

> the introduction and the installation of the curriculum program will be optional for those divisions maintaining effective supervision. It will be permissive in those divisions only which maintain supervision. It now appears that it would be quite unwise for those divisions without the services of supervision to attempt general installations of the new curriculum program.[72]

At the same time, however, Hall carefully and skillfully publicized and managed the process of curriculum revision through strategies that subtly sought both to "induce compliance with the plan" with regard to schools' participation and utilization of the new course of study, and to minimize the possibility of dissenting voices amongst teachers and administrators.[73]

Within many elementary schools the concept of integrated units and child centered learning was well established. The structure of the new scope and sequence chart simply served to refine and develop what was already going on in many classrooms, not just in Virginia but also in the nation's elementary classrooms. In order to provide a consistent level of state-approved supervision to facilitate school district participation in the curriculum revision at the elementary level, Hall initiated a statewide program of direct curriculum supervision. Under the new program the state paid two-thirds of the salary of elementary supervisors in county divisions in order to provide supervision and guidance at a minimal cost for schools. Supervisors were hired by the school district and were responsible to the district. However, a considerable amount of power with regard to the hiring, and work of the local elementary supervisors lay with the State Department since supervisors "must be selected from a list of eligible candidates compiled by the State Department and their appointment to a specific position must be approved by the officials in the Department."[74]

Furthermore, the State Department required administrators to apply to receive the new course of study. Acceptance to participate in the new program was dependent upon the school division providing evidence of competent teachers, adequate libraries and supervision. For school boards and school superintendents, struggling to keep their schools functioning in the face of the Depression, representing themselves as involved in a statewide plan to improve instruction was, if nothing else, a politically astute move. Seguel notes that as a result "all but a few applied, and about a dozen were denied."[75] Representing the program as innovative, flexible, evolutionary and lacking compulsion further served to minimize dissenting voices within the schools. There is little evidence to indicate that any individual or organized groups of teachers found any public avenue to critically evaluate the revision program. Given the precarious conditions of employment for teachers during the Depression, there was little reason why any teacher would offer up a public critique of the Virginia Program, for as H. M. Henry notes:

the sweating of the teaching profession is the worst effect of the depression on education in Virginia...the hand of every teacher is competitively against

the hand of every other teacher before the cold blooded school superintendents, or school boards, who are inclined to take advantage of the situation
to balance their budgets. We are discounting professional pride and love of
teaching when the teachers are doing their work with the wolf at the door or
placing them in competition with those who teach merely to bridge over a
period of unemployment and will drop out of the schoolroom as soon as
some other place becomes available.[76]

The *Virginia Journal of Education* also did not offer dissenting views of
the new curriculum by teachers, or administrators, as exemplified in
the editorial comments of VEA President John Martin in 1935:

The most conservative among us must admit that the officials and teachers
of Virginia have accomplished a task of supreme importance in devising the
Revised Course of Study. As administrators and teachers we cannot ignore
the contribution to education that has commanded the enthusiastic approval
and even acclaim of leading educators in every section of the country. Because we wish to give the children of Virginia the preparation that is needed
to meet the various problems of modern life, we must join together in trying
out these plans and suggestions as outlined in this remarkable guidebook.[77]

Oppleman notes that "exhortation and instruction about the revision
program in professional journals continued to be part of the tactics of
the State Department and cooperating colleges... it should not be forgotten that every issue of the *Journal [Virginia Journal of Education]* was
used to report and comment on the phases of the Revised Program."[78]
The *Virginia Journal of Education* provided administrators with the
chance to be seen as advocates of modern change and progress during
a period of economic dislocation. For example, D. E. McQuilken, Roanoke County Superintendent, stressed that the new curriculum was
an important advance for "the alert and industrious teacher as a
guide in giving her children the higher type of training for meeting
and solving the problems of this present age."[79] A. L. Bennet, the Superintendent for Albermarle County, praised the concept of the Virginia Program for moving away from the days when college professors handed down the new curriculum or local superintendents
borrowed another city's curriculum and cut the best bits out to use for
themselves.[80] Articles by teachers, such as Francis Sisson of Shawsville
High School, similarly served to evidence teacher cooperation and
participation: "For only in action is there progress... The preparation
for classes and the conducting of classes in this fashion is hard work,
but it is the most interesting and fascinating work in the world."[81] In

addition, "despite the difficulties in objectively rating a movement based upon improving social processes," a number of surveys developed and collected by principals, superintendents and the State Supervisors for secondary and elementary education provided VEA members with data demonstrating the successful implementation of the Virginia Program.[82]

Promoting the ideals and nature of the program went beyond the audience of the school community. In 1935, Hall and his colleagues developed a series of radio programs providing a rationale and explanation for the Curriculum Revision process.[83] Similarly at the Christiansburg Rotary Club Meeting, Radford City School superintendent W. K. Barnett explained, "It is no longer feasible to teach only the three R's. Each pupil must be recognized as an individual and he must be taught how best to adapt himself."[84] Hall, Caswell and Hanna among others recognized the importance of advertising and promoting their work at a time when the Depression had created an opening to reconceptualize the purpose of education. Their writings in state and national publications placed them at the forefront of the curriculum revision field. Caswell had a ready pen and quickly produced articles relating to his work in terms of exploring the school's responsibility in society, the case against subject based curriculum, and approaches to curriculum development.[85] As a result he found himself in demand as an advisor on other statewide curriculum revisions modeled on Virginia's. Similarly, Hanna recognized the importance and excitement of promoting and sharing curriculum work during this period. In 1934, he urged members of the Society for Curriculum Study "to report more promptly and with less modesty, the various curriculum projects in which they are engaged."[86]

Emerging Concerns and Criticism

Below the surface of the steady diet of program promotion, however, a growing chorus of concern and criticism developed from the ranks of college professors who questioned the move from traditional discipline specific teaching toward a core curriculum that they claimed "ignored fundamentals in Education."[87] R. E. Blackwell, President of Randolph Macon College, "voiced a fear that the present methods of teaching elementary schools might lead to the development of a white collar proletariat which could neither be qualified for higher education nor a trade. The new curriculum has certainly left everyone who is past the age of thirty somewhat confused as to just what it was trying to accomplish."[88] Dean John William of Virginia Polytechnic Institute argued that "no boy could expect to survive at VPI without English and Mathematics."[89] In a subsequent critique, Williams continued to express concerns regarding the new Virginia Program, and he specifically questioned the validity of reports praising the implementation of the curriculum as well as the nature of the curriculum itself:

> The Virginia Curriculum Program, which was initiated in 1931 attracted considerable attention...by the end of the session of 1935–36 reports, many of them quite favorable, began to come in, and were published in the daily papers and in the Journals of Education. At this juncture it occurred to me that it might be well to check our records to see from a college standpoint what, if any, justification could be found for such favorable reports. I discovered no such justification. In fact, my findings were distinctly to the contrary...Apparently the only requirement for advancement in some of the schools is a fairly regular attendance and a willingness on the part of the pupil to do his best. Standard curricula have gone with the wind...The leaders themselves must, and will, sooner or later shoulder their part of the responsibility. The great and persistent confusion that followed the World War provided a glorious opportunity for this group. Almost completely neglecting the fundamentals, they have apparently banked their reputation on "methods," "horizontal and vertical integration," and the like. As someone has remarked, their program is producing a set of teachers splendidly equipped with the means to transmit knowledge, but with no more knowledge to transmit.[90]

Questions and concerns regarding the implementation of the core curriculum continued to grow during the latter half of the decade. Problems with the lack of a consistent scheduling of curriculum revision courses at the State Colleges of Education "even at the height of the revision movement," and issues with annual teacher turnover limited the potential for consistent teacher cooperation and participation. Oppleman notes that especially at the high school level the reality was that the evolutionary clause allowed teachers to avoid participation in the curriculum revision process:

> Only one or two teachers in an average school engaged in core experiments, while the rest of the faculty proceeded with traditional instruction...The system of using just those teachers who volunteered for core assignments may have assured enthusiastic instruction in the offerings which were set up, but it contributed to spotty coverage. Frequently there would develop a pattern

of core work in widely separated grades merely because only two teachers had volunteered.[91]

The minimal implementation of the Virginia program within the high schools was highlighted in a 1942 report initiated by Virginia State Chamber of Commerce: "in the high school, however the program encountered obstacles, held back by the inertia of tradition and lack of supervisory service. It cannot therefore be said that our high school curriculum has been modified to meet the needs of all high school pupils."[92] One year later, Hall's successor, Dabney S. Lancaster, also raised questions regarding the impact of the Virginia Program:

> [the Virginia Program] was misunderstood by many teachers who, in their efforts to adopt what was being advocated, cut loose from the old moorings and were adrift. They did not adhere always to the high standards of individual attainment and at times superficial work resulted. Naturally this caused public criticism.[93]

Despite such criticism and the limited participation at the high school level in the second half of the 1930's, Hall remained committed to his agenda of curriculum revision throughout his tenure. Upon his retirement in 1941, he identified a number of initiatives, including the reorganization of the state department of education, the revision of the curriculum for public school, the reorganization of the curricula for preparing teachers, and the development of an elementary and high school supervision program, which he claimed had dramatically improved the state's educational system during a period when Depression and drought threatened to curtail even minimum standards throughout the state.[94]

Manufacturing and Negotiating Curricular Change

The opportunity to embark upon a statewide curriculum revision in Virginia indeed proved to be a magnificent adventure through an uncharted landscape for Hall and his colleagues. Kliebard describes the history of curriculum in the twentieth century as a struggle among competing definitions of the essential purposes of schools, and he uses the metaphor of currents in a stream to describe the co-existing, yet competing perspectives. Within different eras, in response to political, economic, and social contexts, one current emerges to dominate, while the others run, submerged and around the dominant current. When the context changes, society redefines its condition, in turn a new definition of the fundamental purpose of schools develops and a different current emerges as dominant.[95] Prior to the implementation of the Virginia Program, progressive educational leaders networked through the PEA and the Society for Curriculum Study had only begun to shift from debating the nature and purpose of curriculum to actually engaging in curriculum revision to meet the needs of the present. The Depression provided a powerful catalyst for social and cultural reconstructionist ideologies to surface as one of the dominant discourses regarding the nature and purpose of schooling and curriculum.

This fact was not lost on frontier thinkers who had long begun to re-envision and discuss the nature of schooling. As the director of the PEA noted, "the depression made it impossible to remain mute and we spoke out...It was a good time to be alive and it was good that some educators were heard...Give me the 30's."[96] In Virginia, the recognition of the need to improve instruction clearly had its antecedents in the work of Superintendent Hart and the recommendations of O'Shea's survey in the 1920's. However, it was the onset of the Depression, alongside the effects of the drought, that provided the impetus and confidence to move beyond debating the nature of education toward experimenting with new curriculum structures and organizations in Virginia. Hall and his advisors brought an emerging social and cultural reconstructionist agenda informed by the philosophy for planned social change, a bold and pragmatic enthusiasm to engage in a program of curriculum revision, and a willingness to be entrepreneurial and self promoting.

The state's teachers were represented as the center of the curriculum revision process, and the advisors at every turn made efforts to credit them with that. It is clear that opportunities were created for teacher participation, education, and cooperation. As a result the Virginia Program came to represent a model for statewide curriculum revision that was influenced by the leading educational ideologies of the period, dependent upon the participation of teachers, and responsive to the context of the time. However, the actual quality of teacher participation in terms of the development of progressive units of study and their ability to implement the Virginia program is open to question. As early as 1933, in discussions with colleagues in the Society for Curriculum Study, Caswell expressed concerns regarding the

ability of teachers to fully participate in the process of curriculum revision, especially since administrators "put a premium on the teacher
who has been a good follower rather than upon the teacher who does
creative and critical thinking."[97]

In anticipation of such stumbling blocks to curriculum revision,
Hall skillfully managed the curriculum revision process through a select network of committees, advisors, and supervisors who were responsible for its design and implementation, while simultaneously
utilizing the rhetoric of teacher participation and cooperation. Hall
and his advisors systematically identified opportunities to advocate
for, report on, and negotiate the process of curriculum revision
through public statements, meeting with the public, conferences with
administrators and teachers, and bulletins and articles in professional
journals and the press. The development and structure of the Virginia
program, as a result, had more to do with how Hall and his colleagues conceptualized, managed and promoted the Virginia program than with the quality of teacher participation. While the Depression for many fostered uncertainty, fear, and trepidation, for frontier
educational thinkers such as Hall and his associates, the Depression
created opportunities to play in the emerging field of curriculum design.

Notes

1.   J. L. Blair Buck, "The Use of Revised Curriculum Materials in the High Schools of Virginia," *Secondary Education in Virginia No. 2*, (University of Virginia Record Extension Series, August 1937) p. 72.

2.   Sidney B. Hall, "State Department of Education Official Announcements," *Virginia Journal of Education* Vol. 25 (October 1931) p. 75.

3.   See J. L. Blair Buck, *Development of Public Schools In Virginia 1607–1952* (Richmond: State Board of Education, 1952); Mary Louise Seguel, *The Curriculum Field. Its Formative Years* (NY: Teachers College Press, Columbia University, 1966); Lynn M. Burlbaw, "More Than 10,000 Teachers: Hollis Caswell and the Virginia Curriculum Revision Program," *Journal of Curriculum and Supervision* Vol. 6 (Spring, 1991) pp. 233–254.

4.   Educational historians typically link Caswell and Hall to the design and development of the Virginia Program. Doak Campbell is also often identified as working with his colleague Caswell at Peabody to support the design and development of the Virginia Program. However it is important to acknowledge the role of other curriculum consultants such as Paul Hanna from Teachers College in the design and conceptualization of the Virginia Program.

5.   David Tyack, Robert Lowe, and Elisabeth Hansot, *Public Schools in Hard Times: The Great Depression and Recent Years* (Cambridge, Mass: Harvard University Press, 1984). p. 6

6.   W. E. Garnett, "What Will Virginia Do About It?" *Virginia Journal of Education* Vol. 28 (April 1935) pp. 282–284.

7.   Tyack, Lowe, and Hansot, *Public Schools in Hard Times*, p. 20.

8.   Hugh L. Sulfridge, "Backing the Schools," *Virginia Journal of Education* Vol. 24 (March 1931) p. 302.

9.   Ibid.

10.   Wythe County School Board, "Wythe County School Board Minutes," (Wytheville: Wythe Public Schools, November 1931) p. 285.

11.   Montgomery County School Board, "Montgomery County School Board Minutes," (Christiansburg: Montgomery County Schools, February 1933) p. 63.

12.   Sidney B. Hall, "Economies in Education," *Virginia Journal of Education* Vol. 26 (December 1932) pp. 127–130.

13.   Sidney B. Hall, "State Department of Education: Official Announcements," *Virginia Journal of Education* Vol. 28 (April 1932) p. 314.

14.   Virginia State Board of Education, *Annual Report of the Superintendent of Public Instruction, 1929–30* (Richmond: Division of Purchase and Printing, 1930) pp. 15–17.

15.   Michael V. O'Shea, *Public Education in Virginia: Report to the Educational Commission of Virginia of a Survey of the Public Education System of the State.* (Richmond: State Department of Education, 1928) p. 11.

16.   Sidney B. Hall, "Department of High School Principals," *Virginia Journal of Education* Vol. 24 (February 1931) p. 253.

17. Hugh L. Sulfridge, "President Sulfridge Calls Attention to Important Convention Items of Business," *Virginia Journal of Education* Vol. 25 (November 1931) p. 103.

18. Hugh L. Sulfridge, "Annual Address at Richmond, November 27, 1931," *Virginia Journal of Education* Vol. 25 (December 1931) pp. 137–138.

19. L. Cremin, D. Shannon, and M. Townsend. *A History of Teachers College Columbia* (New York: Columbia University Press, 1954) p. 245.

20. Paul R. Hanna, "Romance or Reality: A Curriculum Problem," *Progressive Education* Vol. 12 (May 1935) p. 318.

21. Ibid., pp. 320–322.

22. Hollis L. Caswell, "What Is the School's Responsibility to Society?" *The Nation's Schools* Vol. 12 (September 1933) pp. 33–34.

23. Paul R. Hanna, "New Fundamental Courses in the Curriculum Offered at Teachers College, Columbia University," *Society for Curriculum Study News Bulletin* Vol. 3 (December 7, 1932) pp. 2–3.

24. "News Notes," *Society for Curriculum Specialists, News Bulletin* Vol. 3 (January 8, 1932) p. 13.

25. Hollis L. Caswell, "Curriculum Revision in Rural Schools," *Virginia Journal of Education* Vol. 25 (April 1932) p. 301.

26. Ibid., pp. 302–303.

27. Virginia State Board of Education, *Annual Report of the Superintendent of Public Schools*, 1932–33 (Richmond: Division of Purchase and Printing, 1933) p. 16.

28. Virginia State Board of Education, *Procedures for Virginia State Curriculum* (Richmond: Division of Purchase and Printing, 1932) p. 8.

29. Blair Buck, *Development of Public Schools*, p. 305.

30. Virginia State Board of Education, *Procedures for Virginia State Curriculum*, pp. 8–10.

31. Virginia State Board of Education, *Study Course for Virginia Curriculum Program* (Richmond: Division of Purchase and Printing, 1932) p. 3.

32. Jesse H. Newlon, "The Administration of the Curriculum in a Modern School System," *Society for Curriculum Study, News Bulletin* Vol. 4 (May 29, 1933) p. 3.

33. Virginia State Board of Education, *Study Course for Virginia Curriculum Program* pp. 4–5.

34. Virginia State Board of Education, *Organization for Virginia State Curriculum* (Richmond: Division of Purchase and Printing, 1932) p. 7.

35. Virginia State Board of Education, *Procedures for Virginia State Curriculum* p. 6.

36. Ibid., p. 6.

37. Hollis L. Caswell, "Curriculum Laboratory at Peabody College," *Society for Curriculum Study, News Bulletin* Vol. 4 (April 1, 1933) pp. 11–12.

38. Virginia State Board of Education, *Procedures for Virginia State Curriculum.*

39. Ibid., p. 12.

40. Ibid., p. 24

41. Virginia State Board of Education, *Organization for Virginia State Curriculum* pp. 22–24.

42.   Ibid., p. 16.

43.   J. P. Wynne, "Curriculum Making at State Teachers College, Farmville, Virginia," *Curriculum Study* Vol. 6 (October 1, 1935) p. 15.

44.   State Teacher College, *Radford University: Records of the Board of Visitors 1910–1948*, p. 59.

45.   Virginia Raine, "Social Science Section VEA," *Virginia Journal of Education* Vol. 26 (January 1933) p.184.

46.   George H. Moody, "Science Teachers Section VEA," *Virginia Journal of Education*, Vol. 26 (January 1933) p. 184.

47.   Montgomery County School Board, "County School Board of Montgomery County," (Christiansburg: October 8, 1932) p. 57.

48.   Eliza Kelly Stickley, "Henrico County and the Revised Courses of Study," *Virginia Journal of Education* Vol 29 (October 1935) p. 20.

49.   J. Galen Saylor, *Factors Associated with Participation in Cooperative Programs of Curriculum Development* (New York: Teachers College, Columbia University) p. 59

50.   Seguel, *Curriculum Field,* p. 153

51.   Ibid., p. 152.

52.   Ibid., p. 153.

53.   See Jared R. Stallones, *Paul Robert Hanna: A Life of Expanding Horizons* (Stanford: Hoover Institution, 2002).

54.   Martin Gill, "Paul R. Hanna: The Evolution of an Elementary Social Studies Textbook Series" (Ph.D. diss., Northwestern University, 1974) p. 47.

55.   Paul R. Hanna. Interview by Martin Gill, transcript, 5 September, 1973, p. 5. Hanna Collection Stanford University, quoted in Stallones, *Paul Robert Hanna*, p. 54.

56.   Ibid.

57.   Ibid.

58.   Gill, "Paul R. Hanna: The Evolution of an Elementary Social Studies Textbook Series," p. 48.

59.   Quoted in Harold C. Hand, "Discussion of Installation Phases of Curriculum Programs: Proceedings of the Annual Meeting of the Society for Curriculum Study," *Curriculum Journal* Vol. 6 (March 29, 1935) p. 23.

60.   Ibid.

61.   Ibid., p. 55

62.   Ibid., p. 56

63.   Ibid., p. 56. See also Leo W. LeRiche. "The Expanding Environments Sequence in Elementary Social Studies: The Origins," *Theory and Research in Social Education* Vol. 15 (Summer 1987) pp. 137–154.

64.   P. Hanna, "Social Studies in the New Virginia Curriculum," *Progressive Education* Vol. 12 (May 1934) p. 129.

65.   Virginia State Board of Education, *Tentative Course of Study for Virginia Elementary Schools* (Richmond: State Board of Education, 1934) pp. 20–21.

66.   Ibid., p. 24

67.   Hanna, "Romance or Reality," p. 322.

68.   Saylor, *Factors Associated with Participation*, p. 64

69.   Virginia State Board of Education, *Tentative Course of Study*, p. ix.

70.   Paul R. Hanna, "Readings in the Methods of Social Change," Hanna Collection, Stanford University, 1932 p. 109, cited in Stallones, *Paul Robert Hanna*, p. 48

71.   Virginia State Board of Education, *Tentative Course of Study*, p. xii.

72.   Sidney B. Hall, Mimeographed circular letter to division Superintendents, March 22, 1934, quoted in Saylor, *Factors Associated with Participation*, p. 67.

73.   Dan L. Oppleman, "Development of the Revised Curriculum Program in Virginia Secondary Schools" (Ed.D. Thesis, George Peabody College for Teachers, 1955) p. 47.

74.   Saylor, *Factors Associated with Participation*, p. 69.

75.   Seguel, *Curriculum Field*, p. 155.

76.   H. M. Henry, "The Effects of the Depression on Education in Virginia," *Virginia Journal of Education* Vol. 27 (September 1933) pp. 16, 20. See also W. Herman Bell, "Picking Out and Kicking Out the Teacher," *Virginia Journal of Education* Vol. 27 (September 1933) pp. 11–12.

77.   John Martin, "Editorial Comment: Presidents' Message," *Virginia Journal of Education* Vol. 28 (February 1935) p. 195.

78.   Oppleman, "Development of the Revised Curriculum Program," pp. 68, 71.

79.   D. E. McQuilken, "Interpreting the Revised Curriculum," *Virginia Journal of Education* Vol. 28 (April 1935) p. 286.

80.   A. L. Bennet, "Curriculum Trends in the Elementary School," *Virginia Journal of Education* Vol. 25 (February 1932) p. 229.

81.   Francis Sisson, "How to Make the Principles of the Revised Curriculum Function," *The Virginia Journal of Education* Vol. 38 (June 1938) pp. 374, 377. See Marvin N. Suter "Integration and the Teacher," *Virginia Journal of Education* Vol. 30 (January 1937) pp. 186–187.

82.   Oppleman, "Development of the Revised Curriculum Program," p. 72. See also H. Ruth Henderson, "Progress of the Revised Curriculum Program in Virginia School For Elementary Schools," *Virginia Journal of Education* Vol. 30 (October 1936) pp. 21–22; J. L. Blair Buck, "Progress of the Revised Curriculum Program in Virginia School for the High Schools," *Virginia Journal of Education* Vol. 30 (October 1936) pp. 22, 36; H. R. Elmore, "An Instructional Improvement Program," *Virginia Journal of Education* Vol. 30 (February 1937) pp. 210–211; C. Jenkins Carlton, "The Effects of the Revised Curriculum Program on Pupil Growth," *Virginia Journal of Education* Vol. 32 (May 1939) pp. 357–358.

83.   Sidney B. Hall, "Trends in Public Education in Virginia," *Virginia and Her Public Schools: A Series of Radio Broadcasts* (Richmond: Division of Purchase and Printing, 1935) p. 7.

84.   "Barnett Outlines Teaching Changes," *Montgomery County News Messenger* (April 24, 1935).

85.   See Hollis L. Caswell, "Practical Application of Mechanistic and Organismic Psychologies to Curriculum Making," *Journal of Educational Research*. Vol. 28 (September 1934) pp. 21–24; idem, "The Case Against the Subjects," *Peabody Journal of Education* Vol. 4 (January 1938) pp. 178–185; idem and Doak S. Campbell, *Curriculum Development* (New York: American Book Co., 1935).

86.   Paul R. Hanna, "News Notes," *Society for Curriculum Study, News Bulletin* Vol. 5 no. 1 (January 12, 1934) p. 16.

87.   Quoted in "Fundamentals in Teaching" *Montgomery News Messenger* (December 9, 1936).

88.   Ibid.

89.   Ibid.

90.   John E. Williams, "Trends in Education in Virginia" (Speech to the Science Club March 1, 1938) pp. 1, 5–6. Papers of John E. Williams, Papers on Education, 1930–40, No. 12, Virginia Tech Special Collections, Blacksburg, Va.

91.   Oppleman, "Development of the Revised Curriculum Program," pp. 261–262.

92.   Committee on Education of the Virginia State Chamber of Commerce, *Opportunities for the Improvement of High School Education in Virginia*, (Richmond: Virginia State Chamber of Commerce, 1942) p. 11.

93.   Dabney S. Lancaster, "Address to the Virginia Education Association," *Virginia Journal of Education* Vol. 36 (January, 1943) p. 186.

94.   *Roanoke Times* (September 2, 1942).

95.   Herbert M. Kliebard, *The Struggle for the American Curriculum, 1893–1958* (Boston: Routledge & Kegan Paul, 1986).

96.   Frederick L. Redefer, "On Progressive Education: Two Reviews," *The Teachers College Record* Vol. 71, No. 1 (September 1969) pp. 151–152.

97.   "Report on the 1933 Meeting of the Society for Curriculum Study at Minneapolis, Minnesota," *Society for Curriculum Study, News Bulletin* Vol 4. (April 1, 1933) p. 6. See also Doak S. Campbell, "Possibilities and Limitations of Teachers' Contribution," *Curriculum Journal* Vol. 7 (April 1936) pp. 26–27; Sidney B. Hall, "News Notes," *Curriculum Journal* Vol. 7 (January 1936) p. 2.

Chapter Thirteen

Encouraging Education, Increasing Income: The al-Manayil Village and Rural Education in Egypt

Amy J. Johnson

B y the beginning of the Depression, Egypt had been independent for less than a decade. Its political system was characterized by a three-way struggle between the new monarchy, the populist-nationalist Wafd Party, and the British, who retained considerable interest in and control of Egypt's internal and external affairs. Economically, the country was heavily dependent on agriculture, and Egypt was a major supplier of raw cotton to the international market.

The Depression had serious socio-economic consequences for the nation, as cotton prices declined, prices of foodstuffs rose, and purchasing power fell. Although its economy was based on agriculture, and although an estimated two-thirds of the nation's population were *fellahin* (peasants), the vast majority of Egypt's productive agricultural land was owned by a numerically small rural aristocracy. By the early 1930s, there began to be a growing awareness of the problems of the *fellahin* problems ascribed not to the inequitable distribution of land, but instead, neatly summed up in the phrase "poverty, ignorance, and disease." Many early reformers viewed these problems as ones that could be addressed without fundamental changes to Egypt's political, social, or economic systems.

In the Egyptian countryside, the domestic and international political and economic conditions surrounding the Great Depression played a major role in bringing Egyptian rural poverty to light and in generating support for various types of rural reform plans. The Depression helped accelerate the change in thinking about rural issues as simply lamentable circumstances that could be dealt with through charitable efforts to focusing on "poverty, ignorance, and disease" as crucial national problems, the solutions for which were essential not only for the *fellahin*'s quality of life, but for the economic, political, and social recovery and progress of the nation as a whole.

This chapter explores three interrelated issues concerning education and the Great Depression in Egypt. First, it discusses the effect of the Great Depression on a predominantly agricultural country heavily dependent on commodity exports to the industrial world. Next, it analyzes the ways in which the Great Depression helped focus attention on the Egyptian countryside, including how it served to highlight the weaknesses of the country's educational system in preparing the nation to respond to such crises. Finally, it contends that the Great Depression spurred a broad-ranging debate over socio-economic problems in Egypt and served as a catalyst for the drawing up of numerous types of reform plans. One of these plans, this chapter argues, centered on the formation of a new type of village school designed to make education attractive to rural families and to teach rural children various means of earning extra income. The al-Manayil village school not only brought significant benefits to the citizens of al-Manayil, but it also served as a blueprint for rural education throughout the country, assisted in supplementing the incomes of rural families, and is today remembered as the origin of all social and educational programs in the village.

Egypt in the 1930s

In 1882, Britain invaded Egypt, with the goals of putting down a nationalist revolt led by Ahmed Urabi, protecting the legitimate ruler, the Khedive Tewfiq, protecting British access to the Suez Canal, and, perhaps most importantly, ensuring Egypt repay its debts to its European creditors. Until the declaration of a formal protectorate over Egypt at the beginning of World War I, British authority in Egypt was technically advisory in nature; in reality, Britain controlled substantial portions of the Egyptian government. In 1922, following the war and the Egyptian revolution of 1919, Britain gave Egypt independence. Yet, this independence was limited, as Britain stipulated four "reservations" that amounted to a substantial infringement on Egypt's sovereignty.[1]

Nevertheless, independence allowed for more Egyptian control of the government of Egypt. A monarchy was established, political parties became active, and a constitution was issued in 1923. Although Britain continued to be one of the three most influential forces in Egyptian politics in the pre-1952 period, along with the nationalist Wafd party and the palace, independence and the new constitution brought changes to the Egyptian political scene. The various political parties strove to make useful alliances with the palace and/or the British authorities; for their part, the king and the British administrators also played the game. The result was a political system that was characterized by frequent changes in prime ministers and their cabinets, and consequently, a lack of stability in governmental policy. By 1930, despite a growing awareness of the need for social and economic reform, political affairs were becoming more and more anti-liberal. That year, as Ismai`l Sidqi and his People's (*Shaab*) party took power, a new constitution had been written that gave the government the means to effectively repress all dissent. Opposition continued to grow to the Sidqi government, resulting in its dismissal by the king in 1933. Following the dismissal, further governments were also appointed and dismissed; the 1923 constitution was reinstated in 1936 when the Wafd Party returned to power.[2]

At the same time that successive governments were being appointed and dismissed with alarming rapidity during the 1930s, the world economic crisis, later to become known as the Great Depression, was beginning. By this time, Egypt was actively involved in the world economy, primarily as a supplier of raw cotton and other agricultural goods to the international market, upon which the Egyptian economy was dependent. The collapse of cotton prices at the beginning of the Depression resulted in "falling land prices, higher real tax rates and increased indebtedness for those forced into renewed borrowing to meet existing obligations, such as mortgages."[3] The consequences of the Depression were worsened after the devaluation of the British pound in 1931, which resulted in a significant drop in purchasing power throughout the British Empire.[4]

With the decline in agricultural exports that resulted from the Depression came an increased interest in industrial projects, both to offset losses in agriculture and because industry was seen as essential to the economy of a modern nation. At the same time, there began a debate as to whether any new taxes should be levied primarily on the emerging industrial sector or on the landowning elite, a struggle won, at least temporarily, by the powerful landowners.[5] The onset of the Depression also fueled an upsurge of both political and economic nationalism, including demands for a boycott of British imports.[6]

The fact that the "independent" government was prevented by Britain from setting its own tariffs until 1930 and from levying any new taxes on the foreign community until 1937 also limited the ability of the government to formulate its economic policy.[7] Nevertheless, the government did attempt to protect Egyptian agriculture after 1930 by erecting high tariff barriers to imported flour and cereals, resulting in higher food prices, a burden which fell largely on the shoulders of the poor. The government also reduced tax rates for landowners, founded an agricultural credit bank, and took steps to lower interest rates and allow longer terms for repayment of loans.[8] Taken together, these policies had the effect of allowing the agricultural sector on the whole to weather the Depression better than initially expected, but for the majority of the *fellahin*, the Depression simply meant sinking further into poverty.[9]

The Depression, the drop in agricultural prices, debates over taxation, and the increase in nationalist sentiment all combined to bring more attention to the countryside and to the living conditions of its inhabitants. At a time when the government was enacting policies to ameliorate the effects of the economic crises on the rural aristocracy, nothing was being done to ameliorate their effects on the *fellahin*, with the result that the *fellahin* were becoming more impoverished, making no gains in education, and continuing to fall prey to disease. The plight of the *fellahin* in interwar Egypt was described in stark terms by Don Peretz:

> Egypt's peasants were among the world's most poverty-stricken, with an annual per capita income of $55 to $65. They lived in disease, filth, and on the verge of starvation…Possessions were limited to some reed floor mats, a few simple cooking utensils, and a garment or two per person. Food was cooked over dung fires whose smoke irritated the eyes, usually already infected with trachoma. Most of the rural population was infected by the liver fluke, bilharzia, whose parasites weakened its victims, making them easy prey to dysentery, malaria, and tuberculosis. Most peasants were old at forty, and nearly 80 percent of those of military draft age had to be rejected for service. Disease was spread by the use of filthy Nile water for drinking and washing. Unskilled workers earned the equivalent of about five cents for a twelve-hour day; and real income had actually declined since World War I. This was indicated by the decline in total consumption of tobacco, coffee, meat, textiles, and cereals, despite a 25% increase in population.[10]

Because of these conditions, the issue of rural poverty and rural reform became a popular topic of concern and debate during the 1930s. When international economic conditions caused agricultural prices to fall, both poor peasants and wealthy landowners felt the loss of revenue. The crisis helped direct attention to the countryside, as did the conclusion of the 1936 Anglo-Egyptian Treaty. Although not a nationalist's dream, the treaty was broadly welcomed as a distinct improvement over the 1922 treaty, and as a result of its conclusion, attention began to be focused inward rather than on the foreign enemy.

Books dealing with the conditions of rural life and containing recommendations for reform began to appear in Cairo, and more interest developed in the sciences that would permit a thorough study of rural problems.[11] Agricultural economics became an increasingly popular field of study, and statistics on rural areas began to be kept. Population studies were made and data on land holdings, land rents, and crops were collected with increasing frequency.[12] The centrality of agriculture to the Egyptian economy, the recognition of rural problems, and the fact that the majority of the country's population still lived in these areas combined to make rural reform a key political issue.

However, although rural reform was a key political issue, rural inhabitants were rarely participants. Those debating how to address rural problems were almost exclusively urbanites, although many had rural family backgrounds or other rural ties.[13] As one scholar commented, "For all parties, and above all for the Wafd, the peasantry formed a basis and provided a stake that could not be ignored. It was discussed and studied, its fate was said to be bound up with that of the whole country." Beginning in the late 1930s, political speeches referred to the king as an "honorary *fellah*," and politicians were quick to identify themselves and their parties with the rural population and to praise the *fellahin* as the true backbone of Egypt.[14]

Reforming Egyptian Education

Just as rural reform was becoming a hot topic in the 1930s, educational reform was also becoming an important issue. And just as it was urbanites debating rural issues without the input of the *fellahin*, the debates and policies in the realm of education were controlled by urbanites and large landowners. Here too, the *fellahin* were not included as active participants. While the politicians, many of whom were themselves large landowners, made speeches claiming "We are all *fellahin*," according to an authoritative historical account, "they were also quick to demonstrate the distance which separated them from the peasants when it mattered, for example by conducting a spirited campaign against any increase in expenditure on education for those living in rural areas."[15] One manifestation of this separation was the development of a two-track education system.

During the period of the British occupation, education had been curtailed and fees had been charged, in accordance with the belief of the British administrators (notably Lord Cromer and educational adviser Douglas Dunlop) that Britain's main priority was to ensure repayment of the debt, which meant reducing government expenditures.[16] Cromer also held that education would be valued only if paid for, that education was best left in private hands and was not the responsibility of the government, and that, based on his experience in India, education beyond basic literacy would encourage a generation of nationalist malcontents who would endanger British authority.[17]

Cromer's changes to the state educational system included the elimination of free education, the consolidation and elimination of some higher educational institutions, and significantly reduced enrollments. The predictable result was a rapid decrease in the number of students being educated, as the state system began requiring fees at all levels. Not only did this result in a decrease in literacy, but it also meant an end to education as a means of upward mobility for the poorer classes, thus, in effect, freezing the social structure of Egypt.[18] Those state schools that continued in operation were designed, in essence, to churn out docile lower-level bureaucrats for the Anglo-Egyptian administration. At the same time, the traditional Qur'anic schools (*kuttabs*), with which Britain did not interfere, as they were a part of the religious structure, could continue to provide religious instruction and basic literacy to the rest of society as needed.

With independence came changes in educational policy, yet British control left a legacy of a divided educational system, with one type of education for the elite (fee-based, state schools) and another type for the masses (*kuttab* schools). The 1923 Egyptian constitution provided for free and compulsory education; the aim of such an education, it was later determined, was to educate the masses only to the point of basic literacy, much the same function the *kuttab* schools were to serve during the British period.[19] This free and compulsory elementary education track, begun in 1925, was a terminal education track that offered children schooling for six years. Classes met for half days only as a means of involving the largest possible number of students and as a means of enticing rural families to send their children to school—the children could still work in the fields part of the day.[20] In contrast to this system stood the primary education track, a separate track that was to focus on academic instruction in preparation for admission to secondary and higher education. This track remained fee-based and as such, remained a preserve of the wealthier classes.[21]

Despite the reforms made to the education system after independence, there was widespread recognition that the new system was not successful. Problems included a lack of properly trained teachers, mounting dissatisfaction with the bifurcation of the system, inadequate educational facilities, over-centralization, and high rates of absenteeism, particularly in rural areas where parents were not convinced of the utility of formal instruction for their children.[22] Among other problems, ideas of status and respectability also hampered the educational system; both teachers and students strongly preferred the primary track, as it was the gateway to further education, prestige, and white-collar employment.[23] Politicians responded to this preference, giving the bulk of the education budget, the suitable facilities, and the qualified teachers not to the elementary system, which was designed to educate the majority of the population, but to the primary system, effectively reserved for the elite.[24]

In the economic context of the Great Depression, with no real opportunities for increasing their own income, with an inequitable system of land ownership that served to keep them in poverty, and with much governmental talk about, but little governmental action designed to improve their living conditions, the *fellahin*'s primary hope for improving their standard of living was education. Yet, this option too was effectively removed from their grasp. The two-track system and the allocation of resources to the elite, fee-based, primary track meant that the hopes of many rural families for a better future for their children were being systematically dashed. In the absence of any type of rural education that afforded children either the opportunity to learn skills that could be used to increase family income or the opportunity to learn academic subjects that might prepare them for careers outside of agriculture, many rural families simply chose to keep their children at home.[25]

The al-Manayil Village School

A pilot project of rural reform in the village of al-Manayil, which originated in 1936 as a response to the Depression and other chronic conditions, began processes that would, within the next decade, transform the Egyptian educational system. That year, the Egyptian Association for Social Studies (EASS), a private, voluntary organization in Cairo, began an experimental program of village reform designed to address all the problems of the villages and of the *fellahin* who lived there, problems encapsulated in the popular catch phrase "poverty, ignorance, and disease." Not only was the resulting program of Rural Social Centers revolutionary in its approach to rural reform in that it emphasized integrated, comprehensive development, but it was also revolutionary because it involved villagers as the primary agents of social change in the villages, something unusual for this time, despite the increasing attention being paid to rural issues.

The EASS chose two very different villages, ones they deemed representative of the two kinds of villages to be found in the Egyptian countryside, as the sites of the first two Rural Social Centers. While both were located near Cairo, al-Manayil was a small, traditional village, isolated, in the words of the EASS, from almost all "modern progress," while Shatanuf was a larger village and had more connections to economic and social activities in the region.[26]

Edwin Muller, an American researcher who visited al-Manayil prior to the beginning of the pilot project and again ten years later, described the village as he saw it on his first visit:

> Manayil was perhaps a little worse than the average village, but not much. The streets were rutted and piled with filth. Three stagnant ponds were literally open cesspools. No school. Not even a mosque; the tumble-down old mosque had been condemned. Nearly 90 percent of the villagers were afflicted with Egypt's peculiar curse, bilharzia, worms which live as parasites in the human body, weakening the victim and stupefying him. More than 50 percent of the villagers had hookworm and malaria. Illiteracy was 83 percent. General misery, 100 percent.[27]

Mohammed Shalaby, one of the first staffers of the RSC in al-Manayil, described in his 1950 memoirs what he saw in the village when he arrived to begin work in 1937:

> Houses are damp, dark, ill ventilated and badly constructed of sundried bricks or stones, with roofs covered or made of cotton stalks, floors are of packed clay; doors are roughly made and windows are too small and rarely have glass...The streets were filthy, narrow and irregular passage ways and usually dusty and full of mud. In the surrounding area there were three dirty ponds, an active focus of disease and source of malaria. Piped water was almost unknown...Drinking water was often taken from the small irrigation ditch running from the Nile through the various villages. It was also

used for washing and even for bathing of men and children. Internal sanitation and arrangements for sewage disposal were equally rare, baths were non-existent...The village had no school although children, by law, were obliged to go to school. The nearest school was more than a mile away from the village...The old mosques were used for prayers. Their washing rooms were unhealthy and were closed for several months of the year by order of the public health inspector. Few children received medical care since there were no local services and it was not easy to reach the free crowded hospital (about ten miles from the village) or afford the services of a private physician. Diets are monotonous, high in starch, low in protein and fats and lacking in milk, meat, fruits, or even vegetables. Diarrhea and other illnesses were frequent among the children owing to the lack of sanitation. All these factors mean a low standard of living which undermines resistance and makes the fellaheen an easy mark for disease. In brief, the whole village was completely neglected.[28]

It is important to note that both descriptions of the village call particular attention to the absence of a village school. This highlights one of the problems with the provision of free, compulsory elementary education—the fact that the available schools were often not conveniently located for rural children, something that undermined rural families' motivation to send their children to school, particularly in the absence of seeing any tangible benefit from the type of education the elementary track provided.

In addition, both observers emphasize in their accounts the interconnected nature of the problems of the village, encapsulated in the "poverty, ignorance, and disease" rhetoric of the period. The writings seem also to suggest that further education could alleviate many of the other problems the writers witnessed, an opinion common to urban, educated writers of the era. While this may or may not have been the common view of the rural population as a whole, the residents of al-Manayil viewed the lack of a village school to be one of the primary problems in their village, as the remainder of this section will demonstrate.

There were two central ideas guiding the EASS's pilot project. One was to get the people to participate actively in every aspect of reform. The other was to ensure that the reform was integrated—that it would address medical, economic, educational, social, agricultural, health, and cultural issues in the village at the same time. Thus, the pilot project in each village began with the selection of two staff members—a male social-agricultural specialist whose primary duties centered on the men of the village and on helping improve agricul-

ture and income levels, and a female health visitor, whose duties centered on raising the level of village health through her work with
women and children. Their first step was to make a thorough survey
of the village. However, after that, their roles were limited. They were
to establish relationships with the residents but they were not to suggest reforms actively. Instead, they were to wait for villagers to talk to
them about what they deemed problematic about their villages and
then work with the residents to address those problems. This approach to rural reform was revolutionary at the time. The debates on
"poverty, ignorance, and disease" commonplace in Egypt in the
interwar period were ones from which the rural population was
largely excluded; they were likewise not afforded a voice in the discussions about educational reform in the period. This project gave the
fellahin a forum in which to express their own views, to identify their
own priorities, and to develop their own reforms.

By 1942, six years after the pilot began, the results attributed to
the project included the following: bilharzia rates had been reduced;
literacy rates and school attendance rates were up; community baths
and a clean water supply had been established; and almost all women
now delivered their children in the maternity clinic, under the supervision of the health visitor. Yet for the EASS, these benefits were already clear in 1939, only two years into the pilot project. Thus, when
the Ministry of Social Affairs was founded in 1939 and Ahmed Hussein, the EASS board member who had been in charge of the al-
Manayil project was appointed the first director of the new ministry's
Fellah Department, he used the Manayil model as the basis for a nationwide program of Rural Social Centers (RSCs), designed to serve
as the centerpiece of the government's rural reform efforts. By 1951,
there were 141 rural social centers in existence, all of which demonstrated considerable success rates in the provision of agricultural,
economic, social, educational, cultural, and health services, as they
were able to increase economic prosperity, decrease infant mortality,
and improve levels of health and education in the areas in which they
were located.[29]

These successes are explained by the methodology of the RSC
program; the foundation of the al-Manayil village school provides an
excellent example of how the program worked in the villages. The
demand for the school came from the villagers themselves, and the
RSC and EASS staff worked to facilitate the realization of the villagers' educational priorities. Yet the foundation of the village school is

also significant in several other ways: the school was the origin of a new rural educational curriculum designed in response to the educational and economic needs of rural Egypt in the 1930s, it became the model for a new type of village school throughout Egypt beginning in 1943 and was included in all future RSCs, and with the RSCs, the al-Manayil village school was named a model project by the United Nations. How did this single, rural school in an impoverished village become a model for national policy and international development?

The Manayil school was the fruit of the methodology of the RSCs, and it came about in the following manner. Shalaby, the center's social-agricultural specialist, had obtained a radio and welcomed village men to his home to listen to it in the evenings. He began tuning in to the broadcasts of the Qur'an from Cairo, and eventually a few men began to wander near the house. The first man Shalaby was able to establish a friendly relationship with was Hassan Abou en-Nasr, a seventy-year-old villager who began listening to the radio with Shalaby and who in time brought his seven sons and six sons-in-law to Shalaby's home. After this, more and more of the village men began to listen with them, and a sort of "Men's Club" was born.[30]

One such evening, the men began a discussion of the government's compulsory schooling program. The nearest school was located in another village more than a mile away, and truancy was commonplace. That day, the evening conversation followed the visit of a truant officer to the village and the levying of fines equivalent to a three days' wages on the parents of truant children. Shalaby asked the men why al-Manayil did not have its own school and asked whether the village men did not think the government might build one there. The discussion then continued into broader issues such as the justice of compulsory education laws and the real value of education for the children and their families.[31]

The process involved here was unusual in that the villagers themselves were the ones who defined the problem upon which the discussion centered. For them, the major issue for their families was income; if education (alleviating "ignorance") would help improve family income (and thus alleviate "poverty"), then it would be beneficial. However, in the absence of easy access to education of a type designed to meet these goals, formal education did not seem essential to the villagers.

Following this conversation, the men of the village, without Shalaby's knowledge or direction, drew up a half-page petition to the government complete with three pages of thumbprints as signatures requesting that the government build a school in the village of al-Manayil. The writing of this petition indicates that the villagers believed that the government might be responsive to the demands of the villagers for access to education, and the request for the government to fund a local school suggests that the villagers would be responsive to the requirements of the government's compulsory education law. Shalaby sent the petition to Hussein and his colleagues on the EASS committee in Cairo; the committee then brought up the issue with the governor of the province, a man who had been interested in the reform project from the beginning. The petition was successful and the government agreed to build and maintain the school, provided the villagers would locate and clear an appropriate site.[32]

Initially, the problem of finding a site was puzzling. All the productive land owned by the village was used for agriculture, and the rest was taken up by houses and roads. At Shalaby's suggestion, the villagers chose a stagnant pond, filled it in with refuse and earth obtained by leveling the village streets and thereby created a site for the new school. The result of the conversation following the truant officer's visit, therefore, was not only the building of a village school but also the removal of a significant source of disease (the stagnant pond) and an improvement in village infrastructure and hygiene (leveling the streets and removing the refuse from them).[33]

While the villagers were in the process of filling in the pond, however, the project suffered a setback, this time at the hands of the provincial government. Although the men began filling in the pond in their spare time, the requirements of farming and the weakness brought on by the diseases endemic to the community combined to make progress extremely slow. The governor of the province, impatient with what he perceived as the laziness of the villagers and anxious to have this new project succeed, sent ten policemen to al-Manayil, who dealt with the situation by assembling the men and forcing them to fill up the pond that day using "anything that came to hand, including the cotton and corn stalks that were stored on the flat roofs for fuel."[34] While this action did succeed in filling in the pond, it also nearly destroyed the villagers' confidence and trust in Shalaby, who then had to spend weeks trying to gain back their goodwill and get the project back on track.

In the end, however, the school was built and Shalaby was able to re-establish good relations with the villagers. The presence of a school in al-Manayil increased school attendance dramatically, but the benefits did not end there. Due to the problems with education in the countryside already discussed, plans for a new sort of rural school had been in the works since 1926, but they had not been realized. The EASS in conjunction with the Modern Education League in Cairo established a school board for al-Manayil consisting of representatives of their two groups and representatives of the Qalyubiyyah Provincial Council. The aims of the board were to continue to teach the standard elementary school curriculum (described by Shalaby as "the 4 R's — reading, 'riting, 'rithmetic, and religion")[35] as well as to broaden the scope of education to include practical subjects. This new curriculum fit the goals of the government in enforcing the compulsory elementary education laws, but it was also designed to fit the priorities of the villagers, one of whose main objections to the compulsory schooling laws had been that the schools taught nothing of practical value for rural life.[36] The inclusion of practical subjects in the curriculum served two purposes: first, they gave the students a tangible way to improve their agricultural and rural industrial skills and hence add to family income, and second, offering instruction in practical subjects was the hook used to draw rural children into schools where they would also receive academic instruction.

According to these new ideas, more subjects, such as sewing, poultry raising, modern agriculture, weaving, and furniture making were added to the standard school curriculum. Students spent half their day inside the schoolhouse learning "the 4 R's" and the other half in the workshop learning practical lessons for rural life. While the village girls used the classroom, the boys, as Shalaby explained, "worked in the fields and workshops, planting crops, vegetables, etc., starting a garden or dairy farming, breeding animals, bees, making furniture (from grasses and split palm branches) and weaving cotton and rugs." While the boys received academic instruction, the girls "took silk culture (there being silk worm food in the village's mulberry trees), [learned] fruits and vegetable preserving, sewing and poultry [raising]."[37] The school also became a center for adult education, and Shalaby successfully persuaded the villagers of the benefits of literacy.[38] The EASS reports on the project, the reports of Shalaby, the documentation provided by Hussein, and the assessments of independent researchers like Muller all indicate that the new school model was successful in improving rural education in al-Manayil.[39]

Conclusion

In Egypt, the Great Depression served as the catalyst for intensified debates on subjects as varied as the country's role in the world economy, the equity of the landowning system, the state of public health, the nature of charitable and development activities, the structure of the national education system, and how best to alleviate "poverty, ignorance, and disease." The debates surrounding poverty often encompassed education, and the economic crises of the period stimulated interest both in new development models and in new models of rural education. In the village of al-Manayil in the late 1930s these larger debates, previously engaged in primarily by the educated, urban elite, found expression not through governmental directives or intellectualized discourse but through the voices of the villagers themselves. The RSC program gave the residents of al-Manayil a vehicle through which to express their own frustration with the country's economic and educational woes—and a means of developing their own solutions. The success of their efforts and the innovative approaches designed appear to stand in stark contrast to events occurring in other countries in the Depression era, when western European and US rural schools remained largely impoverished and neglected and when there was not a coordinated effort in most other postcolonial nations to substantively expand or change rural education.

Whether the al-Manayil experiment is truly unique worldwide is a question worth exploring further; it was, however, unique in the development of Egyptian education. The formulation of the new village school at al-Manayil provided the village with the means to meet the compulsory education laws (a school in the village itself), a curriculum designed to meet the practical needs of the children and their families (by including agricultural and rural industrial education), and a center for adult education. It provided Egypt with a model of education that would be acceptable in rural areas, a means of decreasing absenteeism, a means of attracting adults to literacy classes, and a center for instruction in rural industries that would allow the *fellahin* to earn extra income. As a practical, local response to the economic and educational crises of the late 1930s, the al-Manayil village school was a success; as the al-Manayil model was incorporated into rural schools throughout Egypt beginning in 1943, policymakers sought to bring the benefits of the program to the rest of the rural population.[40]

The al-Manayil model was not a panacea for the economic and educational problems of the countryside or the nation, however. The school did not address underlying educational problems such as the bifurcation of the educational system or the use of the educational system to maintain the socio-economic system;[41] it was not until 1948 that an agreement was reached to merge the primary and elementary school tracks. It did not address fundamental economic problems such as the system of land ownership or the country's macroeconomic woes; even the most successful rural initiatives could not alter land distribution, remedy the dependence of the country on agricultural exports, or change Egypt's place in the world economy. The British re-occupation of Egypt during World War II and the 1952 Egyptian revolution significantly affected the government's economic and educational policies and priorities.

But in the 1940s, the school marked a major change in Egyptian educational policy, and its foundation significantly altered the course of rural education. In addition, the al-Manayil school was a successful, small-scale effort to bring some tangible benefits to the *fellahin*. It was the result of both the new approach to social reform encompassed within the Rural Social Centers project and the result of an activist citizenry within the village itself. In addition to the positive results achieved in this village alone, the project is also important in another way: while debates about socio-economic reform and development were commonplace in pre-revolutionary Egypt, the Rural Social Centers project and the new village school that stemmed from it were rare examples of concrete and successful cooperation between citizens, the non-governmental sector, and the government.

More fundamentally, the school, in following the participatory methodology of the Rural Social Centers program, set the stage for continued reform efforts carried out by the villagers themselves. Although the school was founded almost seventy years ago, today's residents still recall the school, the social center, and its staff, and credit it with being the origin of virtually all social and educational services in their village. In 2000, the author conducted survey research in al-Manayil, focusing on citizens' views of rural development in their villages. While the focus of the surveys was not the school itself, respondents' comments on the RSC, on its methodology, and on the manner in which the village came to have its own school were illuminating. This survey research indicates that citizens have carried on the tradition of self-help that resulted in their school being founded almost seventy years ago. Citizens today are not only aware of the history of their village, their school, and the Rural Social Centers project, but they overwhelmingly attribute the expansion of educational and social services in their village to their own efforts to lobby for services, found institutions, and successfully forge partnerships with relevant agents.

Surveys showed that citizens of al-Manayil remembered specific educational services offered through the new village school of the RSC. The services recalled by the respondents indicate the breadth of activities of the school—and its effectiveness in fulfilling the educational and economic goals of the new curriculum. The school provided services designed to combat all aspects of the triumvirate of rural problems: to fight "poverty," the school offered instruction in carpet making, apiaries and honey production, poultry raising and egg production, handicrafts such as tricot, crochet, and needlework, and agricultural classes. It attempted to alleviate "ignorance" by providing services such as foundation of the school itself, adult education classes, educational films, library services, and literacy campaigns. The school also provided services to fight "disease," such as cooking lessons and hygiene instruction. Perhaps even more importantly, citizens of al-Manayil attribute the expansion of services to the RSC in their village and to the methodology it used to successfully implement its first project, the new village school.

Citizens who remarked on the project said things like, "[It] is the reason the village has street lights, schools, and all the services the village has now. It was the foundation. Its success bred more success and people got used to helping provide services."[42] Another remarked, "[It] was important as a means of showing people the way to progress. It was the beginning of everything in the village."[43] A third commented that, "The RSC served the village. The village would not have what it has now if it were not for the RSC. It began the tradition of self-help in the village, and we have continued that with our schools."[44] Another respondent said, "Even after the RSC was gone, it influenced us. We made our own preparatory and secondary schools here."[45] Finally, one resident observed that, "In our village, people rely on cooperation. Since the RSC [and the village school], we got together and did projects for ourselves. There are no projects here that started with the government—all of them began with the people themselves."[46]

The Great Depression played a crucial role in transforming rural poverty from an issue dealt with by small-scale charitable groups to an issue of vital importance to the nation around which heated debates centered. The strategies advocated in these debates for addressing rural problems and affecting rural development differed widely. In all such debates, though, the interconnected nature of "poverty, ignorance and disease" was recognized. Which of the triumvirate should be addressed first and who should be the primary agent of change was another facet of the debates. The solution devised by the EASS and embodied the Rural Social Centers program answered these questions by emphasizing integrated rural reform with the *fellahin* as the primary agents of change. In al-Manayil, the *fellahin* stressed the importance of education by making the foundation of a new type of village school one of their first projects. The al-Manayil village school of the Depression era is important not only as an educational innovation or as a means of improving village income through agricultural, rural industrial, and handicrafts instruction, but as a real attempt to improve the overall standard of living in the village and as the project that set the standard for later reforms, in terms of both success and methodology.

Notes

1. Those four reservations were: protection of imperial communications, defense against foreign aggression, protection of foreign interests and minorities, and control of the Sudan. Arthur Goldschmidt, *A Concise History of the Middle East*, sixth edition (Boulder: Westview Press, 1999) p. 220.

2. Amy J. Johnson, *Reconstructing Rural Egypt: Ahmed Hussein and the History of Egyptian Development* (Syracuse: Syracuse University Press, 2004) pp. 29–30.

3. Roger Owen and Sevket Pamuk, *A History of Middle East Economies in the Twentieth Century* (Cambridge: Harvard University Press, 1999) p. 38.

4. By 1931, about sixty percent of the world's business was done in British pounds. Although the 1931 devaluation of the pound by 23% brought some positive results to the British economy, it resulted in a concomitant loss of purchasing power in Egypt (as well as other British colonies and possessions) where the Egyptian pound was linked to the British pound.

5. Owen and Pamuk, *History of Middle East Economies*, p. 37.

6. See Roger Owen, "The Ideology of Economic Nationalism in its Egyptian Context, 1919–1939," in Marwan R. Buheiry, ed., *Intellectual Life in the Arab East, 1890–1939* (Beirut: American University of Beirut, 1981).

7. Owen and Pamuk, *History of Middle East Economies*, pp. 35–36.

8. Ibid., p. 39.

9. Ibid.

10. Don Peretz, *The Middle East Today* (New York: Praeger, 1988) p. 225.

11. Misako Ikeda, "Sociopolitical Debates in Late Parliamentary Egypt," (Ph.D thesis, Harvard University, 1998) argues that there was a substantial increase in the number of books published on the subject in this period.

12. See Jacques Berque, *Imperialism and Revolution* (New York: Praeger, 1972) chapter 7, "Emergent Groups and Latent Classes," for a detailed discussion.

13. See Ikeda, "Sociopolitical Debates in Late Parliamentary Egypt."

14. Berque, *Imperialism and Revolution*, pp. 485, 489–490.

15. Owen and Pamuk, *History of Middle East Economies*, p. 46.

16. Sir Evelyn Baring (Lord Cromer after 1891) was British Agent and Consul General in Egypt from 1882–1907; he was the primary political power in the country. Douglas Dunlop was in charge of educational policy in Egypt until after World War I.

17. Donald Malcolm Reid, *Cairo University and the Making of Modern Egypt* (Cairo: The American University in Cairo Press, 1991) pp. 18–19. Reid quotes Cromer expressing the view that free education would "turn out from the schools a number of young men who would probably be far happier and far more useful citizens if, instead of endeavouring to rise in the social scale—which usually means looking forward to obtaining a Government-clerkship—they had remained in the ranks of the society in which they were born, and had devoted themselves to some useful and honourable trade or handicraft." For more on Cromer and his views, see Roger Owen, *Lord Cromer: Victorian Imperialist, Edwardian Proconsul* (Oxford: Oxford University Press, 2004).

18. Joseph Szyliowicz, *Education and Modernization in the Middle East* (Ithaca: Cornell University Press, 1973) pp. 122–123.

19. For a detailed discussion, see El Sayed Gamal Zaki, "The Possible Role of Adult Education in Developing the Egyptian Rural Communities," (PhD thesis, University of Indiana, 1958) pp. 95–123.

20. Although this system was not ideal, as one author argues, it did result in the entrance of an additional one million children into the education system within twenty years, and it was the first step in introducing widespread education in Egypt. See Ibrahim E. Metaweh, "Improvement of Rural Teacher Education in Egypt," (PhD thesis, University of Minnesota, 1954) p. 71. The *kuttab* schools continued to function with added curriculum and provided another educational option to those excluded from the primary school track. For some families, *kuttabs* were more attractive than elementary schools—elementary schools taught children topics deemed useless to the farmer, but at least the *kuttabs* taught religion. See Zaki, "The Possible Role of Adult Education," p. 82.

21. Students entering primary school were required to already have achieved basic literacy and to have a basic knowledge of arithmetic, while those entering elementary school were not expected to have those skills. In theory, children from the elementary track could test into the primary track, hence gaining access to the higher education system, but in practice this happened only rarely. See Szyliowicz, *Education and Modernization in the Middle East,* pp. 179–196; Barak A. Salmoni, "Pedagogies of Patriotism: Teaching Socio-Political Community in Twentieth-Century Turkish and Egyptian Education," (PhD Thesis, Harvard University, 2002) pp. 47–60. In 1943, primary school fees were abolished, yet primary school remained a separate, higher-status track; this quickly led to overcrowding in the primary schools, an important factor in the decision to merge the elementary and primary tracks in 1948. Secondary school fees were abolished in 1950. For a detailed discussion, see Roderic Matthews and Matta Akrawi, *Education in the Arab Countries of the Near East* (Washington: American Council on Education, 1949). An additional problem for rural students was that even if they gained access to the primary track, "Primary and secondary schools had virtually no courses useful to a young man who wanted to return to his village," a problem that dated back to the reorganization of the system under British control. Robert Tignor, *Modernization and British Colonial Rule in Egypt, 1882–1914* (Princeton: Princeton University Press, 1966) p. 347.

22. Attempts to address these problems prior to World War II included reorganization of secondary education, curriculum revision, increased funding for education, attempts at decentralization of the educational system to allow more local control, and the development of an inspectorate to regulate teaching quality. See Szyliowicz, *Education and Modernization in the Middle East.*

23. This continues to be an issue today, as students expect education to lead to prestigious, white-collar jobs; manual labor is considered inappropriate for the educated. See Stephanie Krapp, "The Educational and Vocational Train-

ing System in Egypt" *International Journal of Sociology* Vol. 29, No. 1, (Spring 1999) pp. 66–96.

24.   Szyliowicz cites the following as evidence of this trend: "In the 1942–1943 school year, for example, about 57 per cent of all teachers were assigned to elementary schools enrolling 80 per cent of all students; in the modern [primary and higher] schools 43 per cent of the teachers taught 20 per cent of the students." Szyliowicz, *Education and Modernization in the Middle East*, pp. 186–187. An earlier report cites budget figures from 1945–46 to "show that elementary education, which is intended to be available to all children, received 39.4% of the budgetary provisions, while secondary education (in Egypt available to the somewhat privileged classes) received 48.4%, virtually half. In 1944–45 more than a million children attended elementary schools, but only about 328,000 attended other types of schools. Thus, about 24% of the Egyptian school children were receiving approximately 50% of the educational expenditure," Matthews and Akrawi, *Education in the Arab Countries of the Near East* p. 17.

25.   This was a continuation of a problem Muhammad Abduh had identified in the British period, when families would request exemption from educational fees in the hopes that their children could benefit from education as a means to improving their standard of living. See Reid, *Cairo University and the Making of Modern Egypt*, p. 19.

26.   There is little information remaining on the pilot project in Shatanuf. The al-Manayil project seems to have been the focus of the EASS, and much more documentation on it remains.

27.   Edwin Muller, "New Ideas in Old Egypt," *Rotarian* (July 1946) p. 44.

28.   Mohammed Shalaby, *Rural Reconstruction in Egypt* (Cairo: Egyptian Association for Social Studies, 1950) p. 2.

29.   See Johnson, *Reconstructing Rural Egypt*, for a detailed discussion of the Rural Social Centers program.

30.   Shalaby, *Rural Reconstruction in Egypt*, pp. 22–23.

31.   Ibid, p. 23; Muller, "New Ideas in Old Egypt," pp. 44–46.

32.   Shalaby, *Rural Reconstruction in Egypt*, p. 24; Muller, "New Ideas in Old Egypt," pp. 44–46.

33.   Shalaby, *Rural Reconstruction in Egypt*, p. 24.

34.   Ibid., p. 25; Muller, "New Ideas in Old Egypt," pp. 45.

35.   Shalaby, *Rural Reconstruction in Egypt*, pp. 26–28.

36.   Ibid, p. 23; Muller, "New Ideas in Old Egypt," pp. 44–46. One could critique the board's, and, more broadly, the government's approach to rural education here on the grounds that it essentially coincided with the views Cromer expressed—that children should be taught skills appropriate to their particular station in life, rather than being taught material that would create the desire for social and economic advancement that might threaten the established socio-economic and political order. Had the school in al-Manayil been operating in a vacuum, this objection would carry some weight. However, it operated in conjunction with the RSC, which was attempting through its methodology to empower the *fellahin* politically (as well as economically and socially) in a manner that would accustom them to exercising their

rights and challenging established norms. See Johnson, *Reconstructing Rural Egypt,* chapter 3, for a more detailed discussion of the political roles of the RSCs. In addition, it must be remembered that the new village school also taught practical subjects in addition to, not instead of, academic ones.

37.   Shalaby, *Rural Reconstruction in Egypt,* pp. 26–28.
38.   Al-jam`iya al-misriya lil-dirasat al-ijtima`iya, *Al-jam`iya al-misriya lil-dirasat al-ijtima`iyah: mahdiha-hadaruha-mustaqbaluha, 1938–1994* (Al-Qahirah: Al-jamiyyah al-misriyyah lil-dirasat al-ijtima'iyyah, 1994) p. 36. For a discussion of the specific benefits of the school program in al-Manayil, see Johnson, *Reconstructing Rural Egypt.*
39.   See Johnson, *Reconstructing Rural Egypt,* chapters 2–3 for a detailed discussion of the RSC project and the success at al-Manayil and other centers.
40.   From 1943–1945, 78 rural elementary schools based on the al-Manayil model were established. See Matthews and Akrawi, *Education in the Arab Countries of the Near East,* p. 24. World War II interrupted this process, and the 1952 revolution brought significant changes to the educational system, but by 1954, there were 410 rural elementary schools in operation, and many scholars were urging continued expansion. See Metaweh, "Improvement of Rural Teacher Education in Egypt," p. 73.
41.   It should be noted, however, that the RSC program itself, of which the al-Manayil school was a part, was designed to get villagers accustomed to political activism. Within this program, it was the villagers who controlled the centers and their projects and petitioned the government for assistance where needed. Thus, in a sense, the RSCs worked against the maintenance of the socio-economic order that the overall educational system worked to uphold. For full details on the RSCs attempts to accustom the *fellahin* to political participation, see Johnson, *Reconstructing Rural Egypt.*
42.   Al-Manayil survey #9.
43.   Al-Manayil survey #10.
44.   Al-Manayil survey #20.
45.   Al-Manayil survey #21.
46.   Ibid.

Afterword
Lessons from a Global History
E. Thomas Ewing and David Hicks

In June 1938, President Franklin Delano Roosevelt told an audience of educators that the "only real capital of a nation is its natural resources and human beings," and "the teachers of America are the ultimate guardians of the human capital of America, the assets which must be made to pay social dividends if democracy is to survive." Asserting that the New Deal programs implemented in the previous six years had invested substantial federal funds in education, particularly in the poorest communities of the nation, Roosevelt situated his approach to governing at the intersection of economic crisis and educational responsibilities:

> For many years I, like you, have been a pedagogue, striving to inculcate in the youth of America a greater knowledge of and interest in the problems which, with such force, strike the whole world in the face today...No nation can meet this changing world unless its people, individually and collectively, grow in ability to understand and handle the new knowledge as applied to increasingly intricate human relationships...We have believed wholeheartedly in investing the money of all the people on the education of the people... No government can create the human touch and self-sacrifice which the individual teacher gives to the process of education. But what Government can do is to provide financial support and to protect from interference the freedom to learn.[1]

For Roosevelt, as for many of the educators discussed in this collection, the Depression created both challenges and opportunities that illustrated the new role for government in the modern world. Recognizing the balance between supporting schools and interfering in education, the President articulated a vision of collaboration between teachers and the state that offered a more promising future for the young generation that was, in Roosevelt's words, the key to survival as "a strong nation, a successful nation, and a progressive nation."[2]

Roosevelt's commitment to education offers an effective point at which to conclude this collection by considering his appeal to recognize, understand, and remember the relationship between education and the Depression. Just as Roosevelt sought to explain to the National Education Association his vision of the relationship between economics, education, and government, these chapters have explored the ways that pedagogues, policy-makers, teachers, and the public experienced these relationships in their own lives during the 1930s. Four main themes emerge from these studies: the global extent and character of the crisis, the impact of economics on education, the opportunities that emerged for innovation, and the importance of individual and collective responses to a crisis situation. After reviewing the explication of these themes in these case studies, we conclude with some thoughts on the relationship between the Great Depression and the contemporary world.

First, the global extent and character of the crisis is illustrated by comparisons of the impact of the Depression around the world as well as across the United States. The Great Depression is an important example of twentieth century globalization, as economic patterns that emerged in particular contexts shaped similar processes in other contexts in a recurring dynamic. In this collection, the chapters on Egypt and Turkey demonstrate how the economic crisis affected developing nations dependent on world markets, while chapters on New Zealand and Germany demonstrate how the crisis in developed nations was shaped by both global patterns and national policies. Within the United States, local studies of South Carolina, Virginia, Cleveland, Chicago, and New York City illustrate both the consistent patterns and the specific conditions that emerged from the intersection of national, regional, and local conditions. As these chapters illustrate, the Great Depression was historically significant because of the way that economic conditions, such as rising unemployment, bank failures, and decreasing trade, produced social effects, such as community dislocation, decreasing living standards, and loss of confidence, which in turn shaped political responses, such as loss of trust in economic institutions, growing support for political extremes, and demands for public solutions. The Great Depression thus needs to be understood through this integration of national and international perspectives that illustrate the connections between levels of experience and the complex shaping of collective and individual responses.

The second lesson to be learned from these chapters is that the Great Depression exerted a powerful impact on public education at the elementary and secondary level. Throughout the regions and countries examined in this collection, the economic crisis resulted in cuts in public expenditures, which meant decreased funding for schools. As public institutions, schools thus suffered from their dependence on governments which in turn were dependent on both economic conditions and the attitudes of the public. In this collection

of case-studies, the impact of the Depression on education can be seen
in the reductions of state funding for schools in South Carolina and
Virginia, the loss of resources for public schools in New Zealand and
Cleveland, the threats to new educational programs such as kindergartens in the United States, the undermining of teachers' professional standing in Germany and Chicago, and the challenges to initial
gains in educational expansion in Turkey and Egypt. Reading these
chapters together, moreover, demonstrates how so many of these
problems were replicated in other contexts as well, thus lending support to the idea that the Depression exerted a consistently negative
impact on public education in ways that disrupted and delayed the
long-term twentieth century trajectory of expanding public education
in the world.

Yet the third lesson is somewhat contradictory to the previous
point, for these chapters also demonstrate how the Depression created opportunities for educational innovation and transformation.
While the economic crisis exerted a direct impact on educational institutions, it also inspired educators to seek new approaches to improving, expanding, and valuing public schools. Frederick Redefer's re-
flections on his work at the Progressive Education Association
illuminate the contradictory and complex effects of the Depression
within the field of education:

> I was struck by our naiveté about what we could achieve...We were whis-
> tling in the dark, but whistling dispels some of the personal darkness...Of
> course details of what should be done were missing. Of course we fre-
> quently used the well-turned phrase in place of next steps. So did the politi-
> cians, so did Roosevelt. We had to say what we had to say whether the
> teachers of the nation heard our call or not.[3]

Many educators looked at the Depression as an opportunity to prove
their ideas and institutions could not only survive the immediate
conditions of the crisis, but would in fact emerge stronger and more
influential than in the past. Schools always have some element of the
future embedded in them, because of the youth of their constituents,
but in the Depression the schools were assigned even greater significance as the public institutions that could most effectively preserve,
enhance, and project that hope into the future. These chapters provide
numerous examples of these innovations: the transformative promise
of al-Manayil village school in Egypt, the experiments with progressive schools in Rio de Janeiro, the efforts to integrate Cleveland's pub-

lic schools, the synthetic model of the Virginia Curriculum Revision program, the system of rationally planned education attributed to the Soviets, the vision of professional autonomy cherished by American and German teachers, and the narrative of civilizational progress drawn on the walls of Evander Childs High School in New York City. These images and ideals were significant not only in the context of the Depression, but as legacies of an earlier era when crisis conditions provoked experimentation, alternatives, and opportunities.

The final lesson to be derived from this collection, and which is implicit in the list of innovative educators cited above, is the importance of understanding the history of the Great Depression in terms of individual and collective experiences. The Depression was a clear example of the power of economic structures to determine the conditions of human life, as the Wall Street Crash in October 1929 seemed to set in motion a chain of economic effects that reached across the United States and the rest of the world in ways that must have seen inexplicable to the individuals who lost their jobs and their savings, were unable to buy food or pay for housing, and suffered the associated personal and psychological effects. Even those observers who recognized more long-term economic processes thought in terms of broader structures such as agricultural over-production, unequal income distribution, currency devaluation, and accumulation of public debt. These views have tended to prevail in histories of the Great Depression, particularly when studied internationally and globally, where the "social effects" are yielded at best a secondary place in the historical narrative and analysis.[4]

Yet this collection restores this balance by focusing on the ways that circumstances created spaces in which people, often acting in a collective manner, responded in ways that made their own history. Peter Fraser, Clarence Beeby, Mary Brown Martin, George Counts, Mohammad Shalaby, Anisio Teixeira, Sidney Hall, Hollis Caswell, John Fewkes, and James Michael Newell were some of the individuals who transformed the way educators and the public thought about the relationship between education and the Depression. More collectively, the teachers in Chicago and Brandenburg an der Havel, the photographers and artists working for New Deal agencies, the rural educators in Egypt and South Carolina, the forward thinking pedagogues in the United States and Turkey, and boys and girls in schools around the world constructed their own definitions of what education meant in the Great Depression. They made these histories in circumstances that they had not chosen, yet it was their actions and intentions, their beliefs and ideals, and their frustrations and aspirations that shaped the experience of going to school in the Depression.

These histories have acquired new meaning in the three-quarters of a century since the Great Depression. As Wayne Urban and Jennings Waggoner contend, "every history represents an attempt to 'make sense' of the past from the perspective of the present. And for every historian, the way one experiences the present affects to some degree the way one comprehends the past."[5] The 1930s have been reinterpreted differently with each passing generational and contextual shift, and once again historians and educators are in a position to bring new perspectives to the study of the past by drawing on contemporary currents and contexts.[6] The first decade of the twenty-first century, like the 1930s, appears to many in the world as a time of uncertainty, as complex global processes shape national, regional, and local conditions that demand innovative individual and collective responses. Under the influence of neo-liberal ideologies asserting the primacy of private enterprise and free markets, the "lessons learned" from the Great Depression about the value of government intervention in times of economic crisis have seemingly been repudiated in the United States and much of the world. Yet a different lesson can also be learned from these chapters, which is the potential for historical circumstances to yield unexpected results—sometimes destructive and regressive, but often constructive and progressive. No one reading of the past is guaranteed, as suggested by Keith Jenkins: "change the gaze, shift the perspective and new readings appear."[7] In this era of global war, transnational economies, systemic inequality, and widespread deprivation, education is a sphere in which the possibilities of the future remain open to debate, exploration, and transformation. As schools deal with dramatic changes in economics, demography, and ideology, the shared historical experience of the Depression promises to become more relevant in the future.

Towards the end of his speech in June 1938, Roosevelt shifted the focus from economic constraints on education to more explicitly political forms of interference:

> I have spoken of the twin interlocking assets of national and human resources and of the need of developing them hand in hand. But with this goes the equally important and equally difficult problem of keeping education intellectually free. For freedom to learn is the first necessity of guaranteeing that man himself shall be self-reliant enough to be free. Such things

did not need as much emphasis a generation ago; but when the clock of civilization can be turned back by burning libraries, by exiling scientists, artists, musicians, writers and teachers, by dispersing universities, and by censoring news and literature and art, an added burden is placed upon those countries where the torch of free thought and free learning still burns bright... There may be times when men and women in the turmoil of change lose touch with the civilized gains of centuries of education: but the gains of education are never really lost. Books may be burned and cities sacked, but truth, like the yearning for freedom, lives in the hearts of humble men and women. The ultimate victory of tomorrow is with democracy, and through democracy with education, for no people in all the world can be kept eternally ignorant or eternally enslaved.[8]

While Roosevelt's condemnation of book burning, censorship, exile, and the sack of cities referred specifically to the perceived threats of German Nazism and Japanese militarism, the underlying themes of how education can be undermined, constrained, and violated by extreme political forces remains significant through to the present. The early twenty-first century has seen renewed interest in the relationship between economic conditions, educational processes, and radical political ideologies.[9] In this context, a rhetorical commitment to freedom must be accompanied by a greater understanding of how, in specific contexts where these forces have intersected, individuals have made decisions and taken actions that have shaped their lives and the futures of subsequent generations. By providing a series of such case studies, we hope that this volume will contribute to a broader dialogue about the lessons that can be learned from the study of educational history in a global context.

Notes

1. Franklin Delano Roosevelt, "'If the Fires of Freedom and Civil Liberties Burn Low in Other Lands, They Must be Made Brighter in Our Own.' Address Before the National Education Association, New York City, June 20, 1938," in *The Public Papers and Addresses of Franklin D. Roosevelt* Vol. 7 (New York: The Macmillan Company, 1941) pp. 414–418.

2. Roosevelt's policies on education and relations with educators were not always consistent with the impassioned rhetoric of his speeches. The National Education Association was also a frequent critic of the President. See, for example, Willard E. Givens, "New Deal a Raw Deal for Public Schools," *Journal of the National Education Association* Vol. 24 (January December 1935) p. 198. For Roosevelt's policies on education, see David Tyack, Robert Lowe, and Elizabeth Hansot, *Public Schools in Hard Times. The Great Depression and Recent Years* (Cambridge: Harvard University Press, 1984).

3. Frederick L. Redefer, "On Progressive Education: Two Reviews," *The Teachers College Record* Vol. 71, No. 1 (September 1969) p. 151.

4. See, for example, Dietmar Rothermund, *The Global Impact of the Great Depression, 1929–1939* (London: Routledge, 1996); Patricia Clavin, *The Great Depression in Europe, 1929*–1939 (New York: St. Martin's Press, 2000).

5. Wayne Urban and Jennings Wagoner, Jr., *American Education: A History* (New York: McGraw-Hill, 1996) p. xx.

6. For interpretations of the Great Depression in light of late twentieth century globalization, see Robert Tignor, Jeremy Adelman, Stephen Aron, Stephen Kotkin, Suzanne Marchand, Gyan Prakash, and Michael Tsin, *Worlds Together, Worlds Apart. A History of the Modern World from the Mongol Empire to the Present* (New York: Norton, 2002) pp. 346–383; Robbie Robertson, *The Three Waves of Globalization. A History of a Developing Global Consciousness* (London: Zed Books, 2003) pp. 151–168; Joseph E. Stiglitz, *Globalization and Its* Discontents (New York: W. W. Norton, 2002) p. 55; Niall Ferguson, *Colossus. The Rise and Fall of the American Empire* (New York: Penguin Books, 2004) pp. 291–292; David Reynolds, "American Globalism: Mass, Motion, and the Multiplier Effect," in A. G. Hopkins, ed., *Globalization in World History* (New York: W. W. Norton, 2002) pp. 244–263.

7. Keith Jenkins, *Re-thinking History* (London: Routledge, 1991) pp. 13–14.

8. Roosevelt, "'If the Fires of Freedom'," p. 418.

9. For critical evaluations of such claims, see Alan B. Krueger and Jitka Maleckova, "Education, Poverty, and Terrorism: Is There a Causal Connection?" *The Journal of Economic Perspectives* Vol. 17, No. 4 (2003) pp. 119–146; idem, "Does Poverty Cause Terrorism? The Economics and the Education of Suicide Bombers," *The New Republic* June 24, 2002 p. 27; Scott Atran, "Who Wants to Be a Martyr?" *The New York Times* May 5, 2003 p. 23.

Contributors

Michele Cohen received her Ph.D. from the Department of Art History at the City University of New York Graduate Center (2002), and is the Program Director for the Public Art for Public Schools program in New York City.

Michael Conniff earned his Ph.D. in Modern Latin American History from Stanford University (1976), directs the Global Studies program at San José State University, has published on Brazil and Panama, and co-authored *A History of Modern Latin America* (2005).

E. Thomas Ewing received his Ph.D. in Modern Russian History from the University of Michigan (1994), is an Associate Professor in the Department of History at Virginia Tech, and is the author of *The Teachers of Stalinism* (2002) and editor of *Revolution and Pedagogy* (2005).

Alberto Gawryszewski has a Doctorate degree in Economic History from S. Paulo University (1996), is an Associate Professor at the History Department at State University of Londrina, and is the author of *Panela Vazia* (2002) and *Levanta a Poeira* (2005).

David Hicks received his Ph.D. in Curriculum and Instruction (History and Social Science education) in 1999 from Virginia Tech. He is an Associate Professor in the Virginia Tech School of Education, and has published extensively on teaching the social studies.

Edward Janak earned his M.Ed. and Ph.D. from the University of South Carolina, and is a "Temporary Visiting" Academic Professional Lecturer at the University of Wyoming.

Amy J. Johnson received her Ph.D. in History and Middle Eastern Studies from Harvard University in 1998, was an Associate Professor of History at Berry College, and was the author of *Reconstructing Rural Egypt, Ahmed Hussein and the History of Egyptian Development* (2004). Dr. Johnson died unexpectedly in December of 2004.

Charles Lansing received his Ph.D. in Modern German History from Yale University (2004), is an Assistant Professor in the Department of History at the University of Connecticut, and is currently finishing a book on teachers under the Nazi and Communist dictatorships.

John F. Lyons received his Ph.D. from the University of Illinois at Chicago (2001), is an Associate Professor in History at Joliet Junior College, and is the author of *Teachers and Reform* (2006, forthcoming).

Carol Mutch earned her doctorate on curriculum development in the social studies from Griffith University (2004), is Director of Academic Developments and Research at the Christchurch College of Education, and is the author of *Doing Educational Research* (2005).

Kristen D. Nawrotzki received her Ph.D. in US and Comparative History at the University of Michigan (2005), is a Postdoctoral Researcher at Froebel College, Roehampton University, London, and has published on the history of early childhood education.

Eugene F. Provenzo, Jr. is a Professor of Education at the University of Miami, is the author of *Critical Literacy: What Every American Ought to Know* (2005), and is the co-author, with Michael Carlbach, of *Farm Security Administration Photographs of Florida* (1993).

Barak A. Salmoni received his Ph.D. from Harvard University, is Deputy Director of the Center for Advanced Operational Culture Learning for the U.S. Marine Corps and has published articles in *Middle Eastern Review of International Affairs* and *Middle Eastern Studies*.

Stephanie van Hover received her Ph.D. in social studies education from the University of Florida (2001), is an Assistant Professor at the Curry School of Education of the University of Virginia, and is conducting research on teachers, standards and accountability.

Regennia N. Williams received her Ph.D. in Social History and Policy from Case Western Reserve University (2001), is an Assistant Professor in the Department of History at Cleveland State University, and has published on African American history and culture.

HISTORY OF
SCHOOLS &
SCHOOLING

THIS SERIES EXPLORES THE HISTORY OF SCHOOLS AND SCHOOLING in the United States and other countries. Books in this series examine the historical development of schools and educational processes, with special emphasis on issues of educational policy, curriculum and pedagogy, as well as issues relating to race, class, gender, and ethnicity. Special emphasis will be placed on the lessons to be learned from the past for contemporary educational reform and policy. Although the series will publish books related to education in the broadest societal and cultural context, it especially seeks books on the history of specific schools and on the lives of educational leaders and school founders.

For additional information about this series or for the submission of manuscripts, please contact the general editors:

Alan R. Sadovnik   Susan F. Semel
Rutgers University-Newark   The City College of New York, CUNY
Education Dept.   138th Street and Convent Avenue
155 Conklin Hall   NAC 5/208
175 University Avenue   New York, NY 10031
Newark, NJ 07102

To order other books in this series, please contact our Customer Service Department:

800-770-LANG (within the U.S.)
212-647-7706 (outside the U.S.)
212-647-7707 FAX

Or browse online by series at:

www.peterlangusa.com